FRANK DUFF

Frank Duff

A LIFE STORY

FINOLA KENNEDY

Published by Burns & Oates
A Continuum imprint

The Tower Building
11 York Road
London
SE1 7NX

80 Maiden Lane
Suite 704
New York
NY 10038

www.continuumbooks.com

First published 2011

British Library Cataloguing-in-Publication Data
A catalogue record for this book is available from the British Library.

ISBN: 978-1-4411-6747-7

Typeset by Fakenham Prepress Solutions, Fakenham, Norfolk NR21 8NN
Printed and bound in Great Britain

Contents

Acknowledgements

Among those who gave me their time as I worked on this book, Frank Duff's first cousin, Carmel Duff, was uniquely helpful in regard to family history and many other matters. I am grateful to her for permission to quote from Duff's letters. Fr Seán Farragher of Blackrock College placed his work on Duff at my disposal. He was kind and supportive on a number of occasions when I sought his wise counsel. Archbishop (Cardinal) Desmond Connell first welcomed me into the diocesan archives when, some years before I started work on this biography, I was asked by Fr Bede McGregor, OP, Emeritus Professor of Mission Studies at Maynooth and Postulator of the Cause for the Canonization of Frank Duff, to prepare a report on the relationship between Frank Duff and the Archdiocese of Dublin. I wish to thank the Concilium officers of the Legion of Mary, especially Síle ní Chochláin, Declan Lawlor and Legion archivist Anna B. O'Connor. While working in the Legion archives, I often enjoyed the home-made scones of the late Ethna Haughey.

The work of the late Phyllis McGuinness and the small group of helpers whom she assembled soon after Duff's death to sort letters, documents and other personal possessions was vital. Likewise, Dr Michael McGuinness was the source of help and encouragement. Phyllis and Michael were close friends of Duff. Enda Dunleavy, a former president of Concilium, and Marie Dunleavy – also close friends of Duff – provided me with information and anecdotes. Fr Eamonn McCarthy's work in putting Duff's letters and writings into digital form provided an indispensable foundation for this biography.

Former Taoiseach (the Prime Minister and head of government of Ireland) Liam Cosgrave, whose father, President W. T. Cosgrave, opened the way for Duff to meet Pope Pius XI and made premises available to Duff for a hostel for women at Harcourt Street in Dublin, established some critical facts. He also read and commented on a number of chapters.

In the course of writing I learned just how difficult it is to write a biography and was lucky that when I approached writer and biographer John Horgan in relation to the Second Vatican Council, which he had covered as a young journalist, he provided guidance to me. When discussion of publication arose,

John referred me to Jonathan Williams, who ensured that I had a choice of publishers. John Horgan, Jonathan Williams and Robin Baird-Smith, Publishing Director of Continuum, are a triumvirate of enabling men to whom I am grateful. I am also grateful to Rhodri Mogford and Jill Morris of Continuum for their work on the book. Rhodri was especially helpful in regard to the illustrations and Jill did the Index. Special thanks are due to the design team at Continuum for the book's cover. Thanks also to Kim Storry and David Defew at Fakenham Prepress Solutions. Mary Kenny was the first to suggest that Continuum be approached. She was a source of encouragement from start to finish.

Joe Lee, Professor of History and Glucksman Professor of Irish Studies at New York University, helped me when the book was almost complete. He read the manuscript and made some penetrating suggestions, which resulted, for example, in the reshaping of the chapter on the Vatican Council. Diarmaid Ferriter, Professor of Modern History at University College Dublin (UCD), invited me to participate in a programme in the *What If?* series for RTÉ in 2004 and devoted a chapter to Duff in the subsequent book of the same title. Diarmaid also read an early draft of some chapters. The Professor of Modern History at Trinity College Dublin (TCD), Eunan O'Halpin, and his collaborators in the Modern Irish History Seminar series in TCD, Dr Deirdre McMahon of Mary Immaculate College Limerick and Dr Anne Dolan of UCD, invited me to give a seminar on Duff in Trinity in late 2007, which provided an opportunity to present a work in progress. I benefited greatly from the contributions of those present. Deirdre McMahon read and commented helpfully on a number of chapters. Writer and biographer Charles Lysaght read a draft, suggested improvements and spotted some errors.

Margaret MacCurtain, who had done research on the life of Edel Quinn, commented on the early draft of a number of chapters, as did historian Margaret Ó hÓgartaigh, who also tracked an elusive reference. Fr Fergus O'Donoghue, SJ, read the chapter dealing with Duff and the Jesuits, and both he and Damien Burke welcomed me into the Jesuit archives. I would like to thank very specially the distinguished Newman scholar Dom Placid Murray OSB, Glenstal Abbey, who, when I approached him several years ago in relation to the influence of Newman on Duff, was kindness itself and located the sources of many quotations from Newman which Duff had used. I wish to thank Anne Brady, who did the illustrations showing places in Dublin associated with Duff. I also wish to express my thanks to the late Hugh Brady, who explained much in relation to Duff and *Viatores Christi*.

Thanks are also due to Bill Caulfield, Fr Paul Churchill, Dr Mary Cooney, Peter Costello, Seán Cromien, the late Mgr Jerome Curtin, Fr Thomas Davitt, CM, Fr Gerard Deighan, Noelle Dowling (Dublin Diocesan Archives),

Dick Dunne, Lindsey Earner-Byrne, Paddy Fay, Paul Ferguson (Maps Library, Trinity College), Kathleen Frawley, the late John Gavin, Dr Tom Gregg, Joanne Grimes, Mary Guckian, Marie Kilcullen and Mary Prendergast (Institute of Public Administration Library), the late Canon Gerard Healy, Ita and Donal Healy, the late Dr Patrick Hillery, Fiona Hodge, John Holohan, Fr John Hughes, OSA, Soline Humbert, Fr Ignatius (Franciscan Archives), the late Patty Kavanagh, Paula Loughlen, Joe MacDonagh, Tadhg McMahon, Mary McAndrew, Tommy McCabe, Patsy McGarry, Michael McNamara, Edward McParland, the late Louis McRedmond, Fr Seamus Moore, Raymond Mulrooney, Máire ní Cheallaigh, the late Fr Herman Nolan, CP, the late Mgr Michael Nolan, Fr Tom Norris, Ciarán Ó hÓgartaigh, Liam Ó Maolcatha, Eileen O'Reilly, Fr Tim Peacock, Sheila Power (Irish Council for Overseas Students), Tom Quinlan (National Archives), Ellen Rowley, Matt Russell, David Sheehy (formerly Dublin Diocesan Archives), Emeritus Professor Louis Smith, the late Tom Smith, Áine Stack (Jesuit Library, Milltown), the late Sr Coronata Walsh, Gerard Whelan (RDS Library), Dr T. K. Whitaker, Teresa Whitington (Central Catholic Library), Very Reverend Gregory Winterton of the Birmingham Oratory, Peter Williams and Joanna Xiao.

Finally, I thank members of my family for their support. Kieran undertook the task of identifying material in the National Archives relating to Duff's civil service years; he also read an earlier draft. Kieran F., Ruth, Michael, Susan, Lucy and Frank Kennedy and Saran Kennedy Williams form a unique well of talent and kindness from which I have drawn abundantly. Frank's meticulous reading of an earlier draft helped to reignite my efforts when energy was flagging. Lucy's insightful reading of a complete draft was enlightened by her professional editorial experience. She raised many questions, which sent me back to the salt mines and further work. Special thanks are due to my sister Deirdre Humphreys, whose support and encouragement for me in my endeavours extends back the farthest. Together with my late sister, Peggy, who first sparked my interest in Newman many years ago by giving me Fr Stephen Dessain's book on Newman to read, Deirdre has been there to hold my hand in a way that sisters do best.

Totus Tuus

Introduction

Father Herman Nolan was a young priest living at Mount Argus Monastery in Harold's Cross, a suburb of Dublin, when in September 1965 he received a visit from a Ukrainian friend, Fr Michała Matychak. Fr Michała expressed a desire to meet Frank Duff, the founder of the Legion of Mary. On an impulse, Fr Herman set off with his friend for Brunswick Street, on the north side of the city. As they walked up Morning Star Avenue, the cul-de-sac off Brunswick Street where the Legion hostels are situated, Fr Herman recognized Frank Duff approaching. He was carefully picking up littered sweet papers from the avenue and putting them into an old-fashioned wire basket. When the priests introduced themselves, Duff expressed both his pleasure at meeting them and his great interest in Ukraine, mentioning to Fr Matychak that he had met Cardinal Slipyj from his homeland. Then he excused himself, saying that he would love to spend more time with them but that he 'was off to the Vatican Council in the morning and hadn't done a bit of packing'.[1] That encounter gives an indication of the sort of man Frank Duff was – a man interested in his fellow man, concerned about the environment and immersed in the life of the Catholic Church. The encounter drew Father Herman, a member of the Passionist Order and a poet, into a lifelong friendship with Frank Duff.

A few years earlier, the writer of the 'Portrait Gallery' column, then a feature in *The Irish Times*, described Frank Duff as 'the founder of the largest international association that has originated in Ireland, certainly in modern times. Yet he has been, among Irish leaders of his generation, the least publicised.'[2] Duff believed in the influence of the media, describing Telefís Éireann in 1963 as 'the greatest potential force in the country today',[3] but he believed even more in the power of personal contact, of heart speaking to heart. He avoided the cult of celebrity which might have befallen him as the founder of an organization that today has an estimated four million active adult members (aged eighteen years and over) and junior members (under eighteen), together with ten million auxiliary members[4] in close to two hundred countries in almost every diocese of the Catholic Church. To give some examples: in Brazil in 2010 there were over 400,000 active legionaries and in South Korea 300,000. The estimate for Africa is around a million, including 200,000 in Nigeria and 150,000 in the Republic of the Congo. Instead of seeking the limelight, Duff chose to live a life both of prayer and of ceaseless activity far from it. In the Legion of Mary, Duff built an organization that depended on each member playing his or her part, rather than on any individual leader. Describing responsibility as 'the biggest tonic on earth', he warned against thinking that others cannot do things as well as we can ourselves.[5]

The Legion of Mary is described simply in its *Handbook* as an organization of lay Catholics 'at the disposal of the bishop of the diocese and the parish priest for any and every form of social service and Catholic Action which these authorities may deem suitable to legionaries and useful for the welfare of the Church'.[6] Active Legion membership requires attendance at a weekly meeting and the undertaking each week of voluntary work of substance. Auxiliary members say certain prayers daily. The *Handbook*, which Duff wrote, describes the organization and its manner of functioning. It explains that the root of the Legion is the basic Christian duty of serving one's neighbour. Duff valued the definition of a Christian of the French Jesuit Raoul Plus as someone who cares for his or her fellow people.[7] Fr Bede McGregor has suggested that the *Handbook* is Duff's 'spiritual autobiography that gives us a key to understanding everything he stood for'.[8]

From the beginning, the Legion of Mary insisted on the voluntary principle without any paid employees. In a letter to his friend and former civil service colleague John Leydon at Christmas 1973, Duff said, 'We have managed to keep up the primitive idealism to the extent that in all our far-reaching system we have not a single paid employee. This enables us to carry on ambitiously on quite a modest budget.'[9] The headquarters of the Legion, in a relatively poor area of Dublin city, is housed in a modest building adjoining its hostels for the homeless. The organizational structure of the Legion and the theology of the Church on which it is based is set out in the *Handbook*, which has been translated into over one hundred languages and is estimated by the Legion of Mary to have sold over five million copies.

In addition to his singular contribution to the life of the Catholic Church, Duff was one of the small band of civil servants who contributed to building up their country during the critical early years of the Irish state. The thread of Duff's long life, which stretches from 1889 to 1980, is interwoven with the history of modern Ireland, especially through his work as a civil servant at the foundation of the state and through the social history of the Irish people, notably in terms of provision for the marginalized, including his pioneering work for unmarried mothers and their children. Conscious of the significance of history, Duff observed, 'I have always contended that a country which does not know its own history is in the same position as the man who has lost his memory.'[10]

At times, Duff witnessed Irish history in the making. He was present at Portobello Barracks in Dublin when General Michael Collins, the Irish patriot and revolutionary, left on the fateful journey that would end in Collins' death in an ambush. Sometimes he witnessed hidden history, as on one occasion in the residence of the Papal Nuncio in Dublin, where in the spring of 1962 Archbishop Riberi, Apostolic Nuncio to Ireland, hosted a dinner. Riberi, a native of Monte-Carlo in Monaco, was nuncio in Ireland from 1959 to 1962, having served as counsellor at the nunciature in Dublin thirty years earlier from 1930 to 1934, when he got to know Frank Duff well. The dinner was a farewell. Riberi was to leave Ireland for a second time to take up his next posting in Spain, which would commence in May 1962. Among the small number of guests was Frank Duff. Two other guests were W. T. Cosgrave, the first President of the Executive Council of the Irish Free State, and Éamon de Valera, then President of the Republic of Ireland. Duff was seated between de Valera and Cosgrave. Another guest was T. K. Whitaker, at the time Secretary of the Department of Finance, who vividly recalled the occasion.[11]

Duff also witnessed Church history in the making and helped to shape that history. Notwithstanding difficulties in the Archdiocese of Dublin, Duff was a welcome visitor in the Dublin Nunciature and in Rome. This was the case from his meeting with Pope Pius XI in 1931, which was arranged by President Cosgrave, to his final visit to Rome in 1979, the year of his ninetieth birthday, when he was received by Pope John Paul II and had breakfast in the Pope's 'kitchen' in the splendid Torre San Giovanni in the Vatican Gardens. A high note was struck during the Second Vatican Council. Cardinal Suenens, Archbishop of Brussels-Malines, described how Cardinal Heenan, Archbishop of Westminster, held the floor at precisely the moment when Duff took his place. Observing Duff enter, Heenan announced the fact to the assembly. Then the '2,500 bishops rose to give him a warm and moving ovation. It was an unforgettable moment: the thanks of the universal Church to the pioneer of the lay apostolate.'[12] The mobilization of the laity in apostolic effort was recognized at the Second Vatican Council years after Duff had effectively mobilized the laity in practice.

Frank Duff acquired a deep, multi-dimensional knowledge of the Church, drawn from experience, lived day to day. He gained his knowledge from Legion envoys around the world, from the teams of volunteers who went on *Peregrinatio Pro Christo*[13] and through a vast correspondence carried out to the end of his life. Among that correspondence are well in excess of one thousand letters to nunciatures around the world.

A question that awaits an answer is why Frank Duff, who founded what is in effect a home-grown multinational, the Legion of Mary, and who made a unique contribution to the history of the Catholic Church and to the care of the marginalized in his native Dublin, has received relatively little attention from Irish historians? Soon after Duff's death there was a biography by León Ó Broin; ten years ago, in his study of John Charles McQuaid, John Cooney covered aspects of Duff's relationship with McQuaid.[14] In 2010 a number of books were published which refer to Duff, indicating an awakening of interest in him. Maurice Curtis discusses Duff in relation to Catholic Action in Dublin,[15] while Thomas Morrissey, SJ, covers aspects of the relationship of Duff and Archbishop Byrne,[16] and Joe Humphreys looks at some missionary aspects of the Legion of Mary.[17]

Duff's comment that 'the world forgets' is relevant. He observed that history records a necessarily few names, 'and even these are enshrined for reasons which are not always the best – not always even creditable. As the poet has it: "The flowers of fame grow more easily on the battlefield than they do in the gardens of peace."'[18] Duff's neglect by historians may hinge on the fact that he was a layman at a time when the historical role assigned to the laity was 'to pray, to pay and to obey'. The identification of the Roman Catholic Church with the clergy was not alone an Irish phenomenon, but was widespread in the centuries prior to the Second Vatican Council. In the sixteenth century, when Luther attacked the Petrine side of the Church, part of his reform strategy had been to give a role to the laity, including women, based on what he called the 'priesthood of all believers'. He criticized the isolation from the world of the dwellers in monasteries and nunneries, marrying a former nun, Katia von Bora. He encouraged the use of the vernacular by translating the Bible into German. The Roman Catholic Counter Reformation, reflected in the Council of Trent in 1545, affirmed the papacy and introduced important reforms in relation to the education and discipline of the clergy. These reforms were valuable while contributing to a distinctly hierarchical model of the church, rather than one that stressed, as Christ did, the unity of the Vine with the branches, or the unity of all members in the one Body of Christ as expounded by St Paul and the early Fathers of the Church, emphasized by all the Popes since Pius XII and endorsed by the Second Vatican Council.

Historians have not overlooked church figures *per se*. One bishop, John Charles McQuaid, has been studied in all his moods and tenses. Brothers and nuns who in fact started out as lay workers – for example Ignatius Rice and Catherine MacAuley – have been the subject of thorough study. However, historians, analysts and interpreters of Church affairs tended to focus mainly on the clerical dimension. This was the case with the fall of Parnell in 1890 when clerical hostility towards him resulted from Parnell being cited as co-respondent in a divorce case; the interaction of bishops and politics during the struggle for Independence and in the 'Mother and Child' episode in the 1950s when proposals for a free medical scheme for mothers and children up to sixteen years were opposed by bishops and doctors. Dermot Keogh's pioneering work on the relations between Ireland and the Vatican illustrates how Catholic beliefs influenced the behaviour of officials who, in keeping with the spirit of the time, emerge as loyal 'subjects' of Rome.

In John Whyte's work *Church and State in Modern Ireland*, published in 1971, there is never the least suggestion that 'Church' referred to anything other than clergy and hierarchy.[19] The same is true of Tom Inglis's book, *Moral Monopoly*, published nearly twenty years later in 1987, in which Inglis speaks of the Catholic Church 'as a power block that operates mainly in the social and moral spheres of Irish life, but which has a major influence in political and economic life'.[20] Louise Fuller's book *Irish Catholicism Since 1950* provides insight into how closely the church was identified with the clergy and seen as a clerical concern in Ireland. For example, when she says that 'Politicians from the time of independence were very careful not to trespass on what the Church regarded as its own domain,'[21] it is clear that 'politicians', who were overwhelmingly Catholic, are seen as distinct from the 'Church' rather than a part of it. In 1997 Mary Kenny challenged the strictly clerical definition, quoting George Bernard Shaw with approval when he said, 'In Ireland, the people is the Church, and the Church is the people.'[22] In 2007 historian Owen Dudley Edwards described Shaw as 'at least an evangelist for the Christianity of the future'.[23]

It could be argued that Duff has been blotted out of the record on at least two counts. Firstly, he was a marginal man for decades as far as Church authorities in Dublin were concerned, and secondly, many historians viewed the Church predominantly in terms of bishops, priests, nuns and brothers. When lay Catholics are counted in the 'Church', stereotypes are challenged. For example, the contrast between Duff's comment to W. T. Cosgrave in 1932 that 'You actually never refused any request I ever made of you'[24] and Duff's observation to the secretary of the Archbishop ten years later that 'I have never received a personal favour from this diocese'[25] poses a question for historians of church–state relations. In a number of instances it was Cosgrave, statesman and committed Catholic, who displayed his innate independence in giving crucial support to Duff in contradiction of the simple-minded stereotype regarding the rule of the crozier in Independent Ireland. There are possible reasons why such a question has been ignored, which include the traditional emphasis of historians on high politics – 'kings and battles' – although that emphasis has shifted markedly in recent years. There is also the suggestion of Canadian history professor the late Peter Hart who, pointing to a 'revival and intensification' within Catholicism in Ireland in the years surrounding the civil war and mentioning specifically the Legion of Mary, remarks 'historians tend to ignore this, probably because we [historians] are too secular'.[26]

A third reason for Duff's neglect was the lack of availability of archival material. It is only in recent decades that relevant state archives, along with the Dublin Diocesan archives, have become easily accessible – at least to those based in Dublin. For historians, for example Dermot Keogh based in Cork, research in the archives has necessitated endless trips to Dublin. Nor have the Legion of Mary archives generally been accessible because of the confidential and personal nature of much Legion work. Frank Duff and the Legion never placed any priority on publicity, avoiding anything in the nature of a 'publicity department'. León Ó Broin described how, when he was Secretary of the Department of Post and Telegraphs in the 1960s, Duff would not even discuss the idea of RTÉ making programmes about him and his work.[27] Former President of the Legion of Mary *Síle ní* Chochláin, who knew Frank Duff during the last ten years of his life and who spent her own working life in RTÉ, including a number of years as personal assistant to Director General Cathal Goan, said of Duff that 'He was a man who shunned publicity'.[28] When the question of a television interview was raised ten years before his death, he said that he was not as young as he once was and that he needed to concentrate on the burden of work in hand. But publicity is not history. Duff treasured in particular the minutiae of Legion history, giving talks and writing articles on many persons who played significant roles in its life.

A basic rule of the Legion *Handbook* insists 'No Politics in the Legion', so that the Legion never became involved in campaigns on any sort, for example, in relation to the introduction of abortion, divorce or other legal changes.[29] Duff did not believe anything worthwhile was achieved by campaigns of denunciation and condemnation. Writing in 1975, he said 'We have been asking our branches everywhere not to commit themselves as the Legion to anti-contraception campaigns or anti-abortion campaigns.'[30] He said that such campaigns 'always turn into a sort of political movement' where pressure and protest become the currency. Despite this, the Legion has sometimes been falsely accused of mounting protests. A case in point relates to the Yugoslavia–Ireland football match in Dublin in 1955, which resulted in a resounding 4–1 victory for Yugoslavia. Despite a direction to Catholics from the Catholic Archbishop of Dublin not to attend the match, or the fact that, on the advice of the government, President Seán T. Ó Ceallaigh did not attend, or that Radio Éireann declined to broadcast the game, Catholics went in large numbers. The Archbishop's objection to the game was apparently based on the fact that the controversial Croat Cardinal Stepinac had been imprisoned in Yugoslavia. As recently as 1998 the Legion of Mary was accused by a journalist of picketing the match.[31] A contemporary report in the journalist's own newspaper, *The Irish Times*, noted that 'A solitary protest was made outside by a man carrying a Papal flag.' The protester was identified by the *Irish Press* as Mr Gabriel Diskin.[32] Diskin was in fact a journalist then working for the *Irish Press*. At the actual time of the game, Donal Healy was driving Duff to Navan in the company of two other persons. The game was discussed and Healy says that he will never forget Duff's precise comment. He said that the 'ban' (by the Archbishop) simply constituted the 'shutting of another door'. But nothing can guarantee that every individual legionary always complies precisely with Legion rules. No group, from the Catholic Church to political parties to local residents' associations, is immune from an occasional zealot. In the *Handbook*, Duff says that it is inevitable that any organization that has large numbers will find a few persons commonly termed 'cranks'.[33] But he warns that the influence of such persons is not acceptable and is equivalent to the heart 'pumping acid' through the circulation.

Although politicians, including, for example, former Irish cabinet ministers Michael Woods, Martin O'Donoghue and Barry Desmond – the last once described the *Handbook* as the best organizational manual in the world – were each at one stage Legion members, the 'no politics' rule is one that has stood the Legion in good stead, as it has scrupulously avoided engaging in party politics anywhere in the world. In insisting on this rule, Duff may well have been influenced by some unhappy experiences of the Catholic Action movement in Continental Europe, including its politicization in Italy, where it was reined in by the Pope. In the 1937 edition of the *Handbook*, the first to appear with the *imprimatur*[34] of the Dublin Archdiocese, the following quotation from Pius XI appears: 'Catholic Action is above and outside any political party. It does not intend to advance the ideas of a political party.'[35] Duff would also have been acutely aware of conditions in Ireland in the days of the Legion's infancy, when the actions of an anti-Treaty minority led to civil war (1922–23). Specifically with regard to the civil war divisions, Duff claimed of Legion membership, 'When the Legion started we had 50/50 and after the civil war we had 50/50.'[36]

Decades before the Second Vatican Council, not only did Frank Duff emphasize the essential role of the laity, he devised a system whereby lay people could fulfil their baptismal function to spread the Gospel in union with priests, and at the same time priests could fulfil their role of 'building-up' the laity. Duff – who, in the expression of the poet Patrick Kavanagh, had been 'soul-apprenticed' to the bootmaker Joseph Gabbett – did not focus on an intellectual lay élite, nor did he believe that a layperson needed to be 'holy'. Rather, a layperson needed to be 'willing' to play his or her role in the Church. In a striking letter, written in 1949, Duff suggested that the common idea of spiritual books which assert that one had to be holy in order to be used by God for apostolic purposes was false. Pious-seeming as it sounded, it really involved the negation of the whole Christian principle, by asserting that basic Christian duties could be fulfilled only by someone advanced in sanctity. That, he declared, 'is a mischievous error, actually heresy'.[37] Not only did select lay people have a role in the apostolate (that is in the task of bringing others to the knowledge of Christ), but *all* who were willing to do so could play a valuable role, a role that went way beyond any self-centred idea of 'saving one's soul'.

Referring to Ireland, Duff said that religion was being understood and practised only in an individual way without sufficient awareness and commitment to the responsibility each member of the Church bore for his or her fellow members. While Christianity was the chief boast in Ireland at the time, it was a Christianity that was understood and practised only in a partial sense, as an individualistic religion, whereby one beautifies and saves one's own soul. It was not being practised sufficiently as a social religion, concerned with duty in every shape and form towards one's fellow people, individually and corporately. Duff wrote that without 'the practical living of the full Christian duty the theory is fruitless': without it, we get a 'caricature of Christianity'.[38] Decades later, historian Seán Connolly wrote that the picture of religion in Ireland had long been one of 'a private and individualistic piety'.[39]

In 1965 ordinations peaked in Ireland when 447 priests, including priests from religious orders, those destined for overseas missions and approximately 90 diocesan priests, were ordained. Forty-five years later the total number of priests ordained had fallen to eleven. A survey in 2009 showed that, as serving priests die, only one in twenty diocesan priests are being replaced throughout Ireland.[40] The number ordained in 1965 exceeded the places to be filled in parishes so that some priests had to emigrate on a temporary basis to parishes overseas until places could be found for them at home. In 1941 the number of ordinations at the National Seminary in Maynooth peaked at eighty-six. In the 1950s, 'Catholic Ireland' seemed real. Duff, however, saw things differently. He wrote in relation to these very years, 'Religion has become routine. A terrible conservatism exercises relentless sway, and tells the Irish people they must walk by outmoded ways.'[41] In a letter Duff wrote to Fr Aedan McGrath in 1948, he held that where the laity did not fulfil its role, the Church would fail. He insisted that 'an inert laity is only two generations removed from non-practice. Non-practice is only two generations away from non-belief.'[42]

Frank Duff's published writings, foremost of which is the *Handbook* of the Legion of Mary, as well as a number of books and articles, are extensive. His unpublished writings include over 2,000 memos and reflections on a variety of themes. He gave a number of interviews recorded within the Legion of Mary, which provide, in addition to large amounts of factual information about his life and work, insights into an inner life and sources of inspiration. These include a substantial interview on film with the American Mgr Charles Moss, as well as a number of interviews on audiotape. Many of Duff's talks are also on audiotape. The quantity of archival and unpublished material relating to

Duff is of overwhelming dimensions. To give one example: volumes of meticulous minutes exist, dating back to January 1929 in relation to the planning, foundation and operation of the Regina Coeli Hostel for homeless women, in which Duff's role was central. A total of 33,000 of his letters have been collected. Approximately 6,000 letters, more than a fifth of the total, are to priests. His first recorded letter, written in 1919, is to a Sister of Charity and his final letter, written the day before he died, is to a Limerick priest. Fr Michael O'Carroll has suggested that 'Frank Duff's correspondence may be unique in Irish history, in volume and in the international company of those to whom his letters were sent.'[43] Since Duff's death, the letters have been put in digital form by a volunteer team of 350 typists, all Legion members, in various parts of the globe working for a period of three years under the leadership of Cloyne priest, Fr Eamonn McCarthy. McCarthy was well suited to the task, since he had been an engineer and a legionary in London for a number of years before his ordination. A small proportion of Duff's letters were handwritten; for the most part they were typed. From an early stage his letters were dictated to a machine and typed by several volunteers. A large number of wax cylinders and 'Stenorette' tapes were used in the process. A painstaking record of initialled carbon copies was maintained, together with the letters from his correspondents. Bill Caulfield, a legionary and former manager with the Bank of Ireland, completed a huge task in classifying the letters in a most helpful manner.

John Henry Newman in a letter to his sister Anne Mozley observed that 'the true life of a man is in his letters' and that 'Biographers varnish, they assign motives, they conjecture feelings ... but contemporary letters are facts.'[44] Duff's letters yield a wealth of insight about the man. Reading his letters is like eavesdropping on a conversation; he sometimes remarks on the 'pleasure of having this chat'. Archbishop (later Cardinal) Antonio Riberi, writing to Duff from Nanking in 1950, said 'It is always a pleasure to receive any of your letters so full of dynamic optimism nurtured in a genuine Christian spirit.'[45] Duff maintained that optimism to the end. Joacquina Lucas, a university lecturer in Manila who left the university and spent twenty years as a Legion of Mary envoy in several countries, during which time Duff corresponded with her, said that his character emanates from his letters better than from any description. Others agree.[46]

New material in relation to Duff's time in the civil service where he worked from 1908 to 1934 has become available. Lack of access to archive material relating to the Land Commission, which remains in storage, limits what can be said about Duff's work in the Commission between 1908 and 1922, but some important files were identified by Enda Dunleavy, formerly of the Office of Public Works, and made available to me. I also had access to duplicate material Duff himself kept for the period 1922–23 when he worked directly to the Minister for Lands, Agriculture and Fisheries, Patrick Hogan, including a lengthy memorandum he wrote on land purchase, a central issue of the time. An important window was thrown open in January 2007 when Carmel Keane, then Assistant Secretary and Head of the Corporate Services Division in the Department of Finance, gave permission to examine the personal file of Frank Duff, which contained details of his employment in the civil service. Following a request from Keane, two Registry Officials examined files for the sample year of 1929. They identified 228 files in the Finance Division of the Department to which Duff contributed in 1929. One of the officials remarked that Duff 'sure was a hard worker'. While it was noted that Duff worked on almost every file associated with Shannon Electricity Scheme, all but three of 140 files on the Scheme listed for 1929 have been destroyed. Kieran Kennedy, a former official of the Department of Finance, together with Donal Healy, Jim Kenny and Pat Muldoon, followed up with the identification of all the files on which Duff worked in the Department until his retirement in 1934.[47]

In the three decades since his death in 1980, as attested to above, there have been a number of biographies of Frank Duff. The first was written by León Ó Broin and was published in 1982, two years after Duff's death.[48] Ó Broin, a noted historian and biographer, had been a colleague of Duff's in the civil service and described Duff as 'my oldest and dearest friend'.[49] Duff was godfather to Ó Broin's daughter Eithne. A few years later biographies were published by the Austrian legionary Hilde Firtel[50] and by the Irish priest Fr Robert Bradshaw.[51] Both these concentrate on Duff's Legion of Mary work. There have been a number of short memoirs, which include those by Liverpool priest Francis Ripley and Irish Vincentian priest Tom O'Flynn as well as a concise and striking tribute that summarizes the role of Duff in the Church: *Frank Duff: Pioneer of the New Evangelisation* by Léon Joseph Cardinal Suenens.

When Fr Bede McGregor suggested to me some years ago that I might tackle a biography of Duff, I ruled it out firmly on two occasions. I said that I was an economist, not a historian or biographer, and I suggested a number of well-qualified persons who might write one. Then, almost in secret, I began to jot down an outline, exploring what, if anything, I might be able to accomplish. The outline grew into this book, which represents my words, but will certainly not be the last word written on Frank Duff. McGregor expressed the hope that the biography 'would be read by as many people as possible'. Dismissing any 'whiff of hagiographical exaggeration', he said, 'One cannot avoid interpretation of the facts. But the biography should be above all true to the facts.'[52] Truth to the facts has been my guiding principle. But facts do not explain themselves: responsibility both for the choice of facts and testimony to their significance is mine alone. Historical biographer Antonia Fraser stresses the importance of the work necessary to achieve historical truth. But she also says that if 'you don't thrill to your subject' you can hardly expect your reader to do so.

The life of Frank Duff is inseparable from the life of the Legion of Mary. Although this book does not seek to include a history of the Legion of Mary, it must cover the story of the Legion in so far as it is intrinsic to Duff's life, just as it must cover the twenty-six years when he worked as a civil servant. The biography attempts to cover both 'saol agus saothar' – life and work. A specific problem that confronted me in regard to the sequence of the biography was that for a period of around fifteen years, from 1920 until 1934 when Duff left the Department of Finance, he lived a double life. By day he was a civil servant. Outside the office he was immersed in founding hostels for prostitutes and for the homeless and taking responsibility for the fledgling Legion of Mary. The resolution to this problem was to have alternate chapters dealing with his civil service career and his hostel and Legion of Mary work during these years.

Virginia Woolf observed that a painter could penetrate to the character of a person without the necessity of writing three or four hundred pages. And it is no accident that Joyce called his book *A Portrait of the Artist as a Young Man*. If I could paint, I asked myself, how would I paint Frank Duff? Of all the images I retain of him, that which made the deepest impression was of Duff, hand cupped behind one ear, listening, intent in conversation, with a boy named John Mahon who had grown up in the Regina Coeli Hostel, the hostel opened by Duff for homeless women and their children. John had an abnormally large head, the result of hydrocephalus. The occasion was the funeral of Peg MacDonald, a legionary who had worked full-time as a volunteer in the Regina Coeli. In the small front room of the hostel, many persons gathered, some of relative importance in the Legion world. Duff was intensely absorbed with John. It is an image I could not forget and one words do not convey.

Frank Duff was a presence in my life as a child and young woman as he was a friend of my father and mother. My parents asked him to be my godfather, a role he accepted. In the 1960s a Patrician Group, or Legion discussion group, frequently attended by Frank Duff, met in our home in Dublin. Its participants included a number of those who had been on opposite sides in the civil war. Frank Duff never asked me to join the Legion, but I think he was pleased when I first joined a student praesidium in Fribourg in Switzerland. When I was expecting my first child, I resigned from the Legion and did not rejoin until two legionaries knocked on my door and asked me to join a parish praesidium many years later, about a decade after Frank Duff died. I approached the biography with a degree of familiarity with my subject, but as I progressed, the realization grew that I was dealing with no ordinary man, although Duff continually emphasized that the Legion of Mary was for the ordinary person. I did indeed 'thrill to my subject'.

The Fiftieth Eucharistic Congress – that is, a large meeting of members of the Church, priests and people, in honour of the Eucharist, which is at the centre of Catholic belief – will be held in Dublin in June 2012. It is tempting to speculate on what Frank Duff would think about Ireland and the Church in Ireland today. He would recall the Eucharistic Congress held in Dublin in June 1932, which sparked the rapid expansion of the Legion around the world, an expansion driven by the fact that Duff took Christ at His word: he sought to give effect to Christ's global commandment, 'Go out into the whole world and deliver to each one my gospel'(Matthew 28). In addition to the next Eucharistic Congress, there are a number of events and anniversaries which render timely a closer examination of Frank Duff. To coincide with the fiftieth anniversary of the Second Vatican Council, the years 2012–15 have been designated 'years of the Council'. Blackrock College, Duff's *alma mater*, celebrated one hundred and fifty years during the academic year 2009–10. In 2011 the Legion of Mary celebrates its ninetieth birthday. Drawing on the substantial volume of work, both published and unpublished, already done by others, and in light of the volume of new material available to me, it is now possible to take this closer look at Duff's life and work.

Notes to Introduction

1. Author's interview with Nolan, 23 November 2007.
2. Portrait Gallery: Frank Duff, *The Irish Times*, 3 October 1959.
3. Frank Duff, 'Potentialities of Telefís Éireann', *Hibernia*, April 1963.
4. Data supplied by the Legion of Mary.
5. Duff to Firtel, 21 January 1957. All letters written by Duff, unless otherwise stated, are from Legion of Mary archives (LOMA).
6. *Handbook* of the Legion of Mary, 1993 edition, pp. 11–12.
7. ibid., p. 183.
8. Address at Glasnevin cemetery, 11 June 2000, printed in booklet form as *Frank Duff and the Legion of Mary*, undated.
9. Duff to Leydon, 22 December 1973.
10. Duff to Bernard McGuckian, SJ, 22 December 1973.
11. T. K. Whitaker to author, 28 July 2007, and conversation with author, 14 November 2007. Whitaker mentioned the dinner in the course of a radio programme in the 'Judging Dev' series, 16 December 2007. On the occasion of a talk on W. T. Cosgrave by biographer Anthony Jordan, on 26 April 2007, Liam Cosgrave, former Taoiseach and son of W. T. Cosgrave, said to the author that the dinner at the Nunciature was the only occasion that the two men had spoken to each other since the civil war.
12. Léon Joseph Cardinal Suenens, *Frank Duff: Pioneer of the New Evangelisation*. Belgium: FIAT, 2004, p. 79.
13. See Glossary for this and other Latin terms used in the Legion.
14. John Cooney, *John Charles McQuaid: Ruler of Catholic Ireland*. Dublin: O'Brien Press, 1999.
15. Maurice Curtis, *A Challenge to Democracy: Militant Catholicism in Modern Ireland*. Dublin: The History Press of Ireland, 2010.

16. Thomas J. Morrissey, SJ, *Edward J. Byrne 1872–1941: The Forgotten Archbishop of Dublin*. Blackrock: Columba Press, 2010. In fact Byrne died in 1940.
17. Joe Humphreys, *God's Entrepreneurs: How Irish Missionaries Tried to Change the World*. Dublin: New Island, 2010.
18. Frank Duff, talk on Frank Sweeney, tape 34 (a), LOMA.
19. J. H. Whyte, *Church and State in Modern Ireland, 1923–1970*. Dublin: Gill and Macmillan, 1971.
20. Tom Inglis, *Moral Monopoly: The Catholic Church in Modern Irish Society*. Dublin: Gill and Macmillan, 1987, p. 6.
21. Louise Fuller, *Irish Catholicism Since 1950: The Undoing of a Culture*. Dublin: Gill and Macmillan, 2002.
22. Mary Kenny, *Goodbye to Catholic Ireland*. Dublin: Sinclair Stevenson,1997, p. xxiv.
23. Owen Dudley Edwards, 'Shaw and Christianity: Towards 1916' in Felix M. Larkin (ed.), *Librarians, Poets and Scholars*. Dublin: Four Court Press, 2007, p. 119.
24. Duff to Cosgrave, 8 March 1932.
25. Duff to Mangan, 25 March 1943, LOM file, Dublin Diocesan Archives (DDA).
26. Quoted in Gerry McCarthy, 'Rebel Hart', *Sunday Times* Culture Magazine, January 2004.
27. León Ó Broin, *Frank Duff: A Biography*. Dublin: Gill and Macmillan, 1982, p. 77.
28. Supplement to the *Irish Catholic*, 31 October 2002.
29. *Handbook*, p. 28.
30. Duff to Murray, 19 December 1975. He gives a reference to the *Handbook* where this aspect is considered in detail in 'Section 38 paragraph 17'.
31. Tom Humphries, *The Irish Times*, 5 October 1998.
32. *Irish Press*, 20 October 1955.
33. *Handbook*, p. 160.
34. See Glossary.
35. *Handbook of the Legion of Mary*, Dublin 1937, p. 240.
36. Duff said this to Fr Herman Nolan, CP; author's interview with Nolan, 23 November 2007.
37. Duff to Firtel, 19 June 1949.
38. Frank Duff, *True Devotion to the Nation*. Dundalk: Dundalgan Press, 1966, p. 8.
39. S. J. Connolly, '"The Moving Statue and the Turtle Dove": Approaches to the History of Irish Religion', *Irish Economic and Social History*, vol. XXXI (2004), p. 13.
40. Michael Kelly, 'Survey: Only 1 in 20 priests is Replaced', *The Irish Catholic*, 7 May 2009, p. 3.
41. Cited in Ó Broin, *Frank Duff*, p. 58.
42. Duff to McGrath, 13 March 1948.
43. Michael O'Carroll, 'Frank Duff and Priests', *Maria Legionis*, vol. 26, no. 1, 1981, p. 10.
44. Newman to Anne Mozley, 18 May 1863.
45. Riberi to Duff, 5 December 1950.
46. Hilde Firtel, *A Man for Our Time: Frank Duff and the Legion of Mary*. Cork: Mercier Press, 1985, p. 126.
47. For example, using the Register of Finance Files for 1929, Kennedy compiled a list of 620 files on which Duff is recorded as having worked. Of these, 307 have been stamped on the Register as 'destroyed'. The largest number of files was destroyed in relation to the Shannon Scheme (F 35) and Law charges (F115). In the case of the Shannon Scheme, Duff was noted as having worked on almost every file, although only three out of 140 files had survived. In the case of Law Charges, Duff had worked on 221 of the 241 files listed, but 168 of these had been marked on the Register as 'destroyed'.
48. Ó Broin, *Frank Duff*.
49. León Ó Broin, *Just like Yesterday: An Autobiography*. Dublin: Gill and Macmillan, 1986, p. 244.
50. Firtel, *A Man for Our Time*.
51. Robert Bradshaw, *Frank Duff: Founder of the Legion of Mary*. New York: Montfort, 1985.
52. McGregor, e-mail to author, 6 September 2007.

CHAPTER 1

Beginnings

'From my very earliest years my mother would read to us usually one of the fairy books, which were very numerous.'
DUFF TO FR ROBERT BRADSHAW

Frank Duff's roots were in County Meath, a place for which he retained a deep affection throughout his life. When in 1964, aged close to seventy-five and recuperating from a serious illness in the Navan home of his sister and her husband, both medical doctors, he described his morning walks in the Boyne Valley between Stackallen Bridge and Navan Bridge. He spoke of 'the absolutely divine character of the country between the Boyne and the old disused canal. The river itself is majestic with innumerable falls, and the valley is cut away from the outer world by hills and trees … . I do not think I know of a more beautiful walk.'[1] Frank had known Meath since boyhood from visits there to his paternal grandfather, who was land steward to Lord Dunsany, and to his maternal grandfather, Michael Freehill, in Trim.

The country into which Frank Duff was born in 1889 was part of Queen Victoria's United Kingdom of Great Britain and Ireland. He was a Victorian child who came to manhood in Edwardian Dublin. The twin issues of religious belief and land ownership dominated Ireland in the nineteenth century. From the time of the Tudors in the sixteenth century, fertile Irish land had been confiscated and planted by settlers from England and Scotland. In the early eighteenth century the Penal Laws, which debarred Catholics from the franchise, from membership of parliament, from some professions and trades and restricted their acquisition of land, were added to existing legislation which proscribed the practice of the Catholic faith. The laws were not always rigidly enforced and some Catholics and Dissenters managed to hold on to their lands through the cooperation of Protestant neighbours. The nineteenth century brought two remarkable achievements for Irish Catholics: Catholic Emancipation and the partial repossession of the land. Daniel O'Connell played a vital role in winning Catholic Emancipation, while Michael Davitt and Charles Stewart Parnell led the way to obtaining the land. In the late nineteenth century the government of Ireland largely lay in the hands of the Chief Secretary. In 1887 Arthur Balfour, a nephew of the Prime Minister Lord Salisbury, was appointed Chief Secretary by his uncle. He, in turn, was succeeded by his brother Gerald in 1895 and by George Wyndham (1900–05). Steady reform took place under the Balfours and Wyndham. The policy became known as 'killing Home Rule with kindness' after a phrase adopted from a speech made by Gerald Balfour in Leeds in October 1895 when he said that 'they [the government] would be glad enough to kill Home Rule with kindness if they could. ...' Land Acts in 1870 and 1881 modified the power of the landlords. In 1903, towards the end of a lengthy period of Conservative government, tenant ownership was introduced under the Wyndham Land Act.

The Church into which Frank Duff was born was ruled by Pope Leo XIII, who had been elected in 1878. Born in 1810, Pope Leo was the oldest-ever Pope when he died aged ninety-three in 1903. His papacy coincided with the emergence of European socialism and the alienation of many working-class people from the Church. In response, in 1891 he published the encyclical on Capital and Labour, *Rerum Novarum*. In Dublin, the Church was led by Archbishop William Walsh, who became Archbishop in 1885 and remained so for thirty-six years until his death in 1921.

The years following Catholic Emancipation saw a growth in the visible presence of the Catholic Church as a major programme of church-building got underway. As the decades unfolded, the Church began to play an increasingly important role in education and in health. In the middle of the century John Henry Newman was invited by Archbishop (later Cardinal) Cullen to found a Catholic university in Dublin. Newman envisaged a greater role for the laity in both the university and in the Church than did the hierarchy, which led to his eventual resignation as Rector. Following the committal of the university to the care of the Jesuit Order, links were forged with Catholic schools, including those of the Jesuits – Clongowes and Belvedere College – as well as the Catholic University School under the Marist Fathers and Blackrock College and Rockwell in the care of the Holy Ghost Fathers. With the expansion of education and the emergence of a cycle of economic prosperity in the late nineteenth and early twentieth centuries, the Catholic professional class began to expand, but the occupation of the people was still overwhelmingly in agriculture.

The society into which Frank Duff was born was divided on class lines with the landlords at the top and the landless labourers and urban poor at the bottom of the pile. Frank's family enjoyed modest comfort and would have ranked as middle-class. His family had links with both the land and with education. Frank's first cousin Carmel has suggested that the Duff family had a Scottish connection, possibly a Presbyterian one, noting that her father frequently referred to Sunday as the 'Sabbath'.[2]

Frank's paternal grandfather, Francis Michael Duff, married Sarah Byrne in the Church of St Mary, Maynooth, Co. Kildare, in February 1860. Sarah died in

1866, leaving three young sons: John (Jack), who would become the father of Frank Duff, born in 1861, Francis (Frank) and Edward (Ned). Francis married Mary Reynolds in 1917 and they had two daughters, Margaret Mary, who died a few weeks after her birth in 1921, and Carmel Frances, who was born in 1923. Edward married Lucy Parker and they had a son called Frank, known in the family as 'Liverpool Frank' because he was born in that city.

Frank Duff's maternal grandfather, Michael Freehill, who had connections with County Cavan, was born in 1822. In 1851 Freehill married Susan Devey and she bore eleven children, five sons and six daughters, over a period of twenty-five years. The seventh child, Susan Letitia ('Lettie'), would become the mother of Frank Duff. All six of her older siblings had died before her birth. Of the six, four are commemorated on a tombstone their father had erected to their memory at Newtown-Trim cemetery. Following a catalogue of deaths, the arrival of Lettie in 1863 must have brought fresh hope to the family. Two years after Lettie's birth another girl, Eva Mary, was born. She survived until the age of seventeen. Three more sons were born: Eugene, Michael George Henry, known as George, and Albert Walter. Albert did not marry and emigrated to the USA, where he died. Both George and Eugene married Protestants in the Registry Office in Dublin at a time when 'mixed marriages' were viewed less seriously all round, prior to the *Ne Temere* decree in 1907, which introduced the promise by a non-Roman Catholic spouse to bring up the children as Roman Catholics.

Michael Freehill had been educated in a hedge school, one of the many unofficial schools operated by individual headmasters at a time when, before the establishment of the National Board of Education in 1831, the majority of officially recognized schools were under the control of the Kildare Place Society, an evangelical body. Freehill was the first Catholic to be appointed headmaster to a Model School: that in Trim when it opened in 1850. The first district Model School in Ireland had been opened in Newry in 1849. According to the Dominican historian Sister Máire Kealy, OP, 'The Model Schools were a training ground for teachers, using a kind of apprenticeship system; they were seen by the bishops as agents of proselytism.'[3] The fact that Michael Freehill, a Catholic, accepted a job in a school disapproved of by the bishops, although in this case supported by the parish priest, suggests a degree of independence on his part. Both Frank Duff's father and mother, Jack Duff and Lettie Freehill, attended respectively the boys' and girls' section of the Model School.

Lettie was a highly intelligent girl who in May 1881 was awarded a Queen's Prize in science. The prize, a copy of *The Malay Archipelago* by Alfred Russel Wallace, deals with his scientific explorations in Malaysia, Indonesia and Singapore. The book, dedicated to Charles Darwin, is inscribed 'Queen's Prize obtained by Susan L. Freehill in the Examination of Science Schools, May 1881' and is today among Duff's books in his former home. When the civil service opened to women in 1881, Lettie Freehill gained second place in the entrance examination for women clerks and took up a job in the Post Office in London in July 1882.[4]

Michael Freehill possessed a good library by the standards of the time and had a particular interest in scientific subjects. His library would pass to his daughter Lettie, and then to his grandson Frank. The memoirs of Dean Richard Butler, the Church of Ireland Vicar of Trim, indicated that scientific subjects were taught in the Model School. In his later years Butler paid frequent visits to the school,

> listening to the examination of barefooted boys in astronomy and algebra and chemistry and many other things that I know nothing about; and reading to them Scott's Napoleon, and telling stories to them, enjoying present happiness, and I hope helping to make a wiser and happier generation than the one passing away.[5]

According to Conwell's *A Ramble around Trim*:

> On the occasion of one of his [Butler's] daily visits to the Trim Model School in 1857, while the senior boys happened to be under instruction in photography by Mr. Freehill, the Head Master, the Dean was asked to sit for his portrait. Mr. Freehill still retains with affectionate respect the photograph then taken on glass.[6]

A spirit of religious cooperation permeated this Model School, as evidenced in the memoir written following Butler's death in 1862 by his widow, Harriett. Harriett, a daughter of Richard Lovell Edgeworth by his fourth wife, Frances Beaufort, and a half-sister of the writer Maria Edgeworth, refers to Freehill as the 'able and enlightened' master of the Model School and describes the arrangements in the school for the teaching of religion, whereby the Dean would take the Protestant boys and girls and Fr O'Connell would attend to the Catholic children.[7]

When Michael Freehill retired from teaching, he moved to a house at St Patrick's Road in Drumcondra, today a quiet road which links Whitworth Road and the Royal Canal and St Alphonsus Road on the north side of the city of Dublin. At the time the houses were surrounded by a field. The house into which Freehill moved, number 55, is situated close to the Redemptoristine convent where an enclosed order of nuns baked altar breads for use at Masses in Dublin churches. Freehill's brother-in-law James Cahill, also a teacher, lived next door in 53 St Patrick's Road. Cahill had married Mary Devey, a younger sister of Freehill's wife, Susan. Cahill, who taught at the Central Model School in Dublin, kept a journal covering forty years from 1851 to 1892 in which he recorded the move to St Patrick's Road on 8 March 1882.[8]

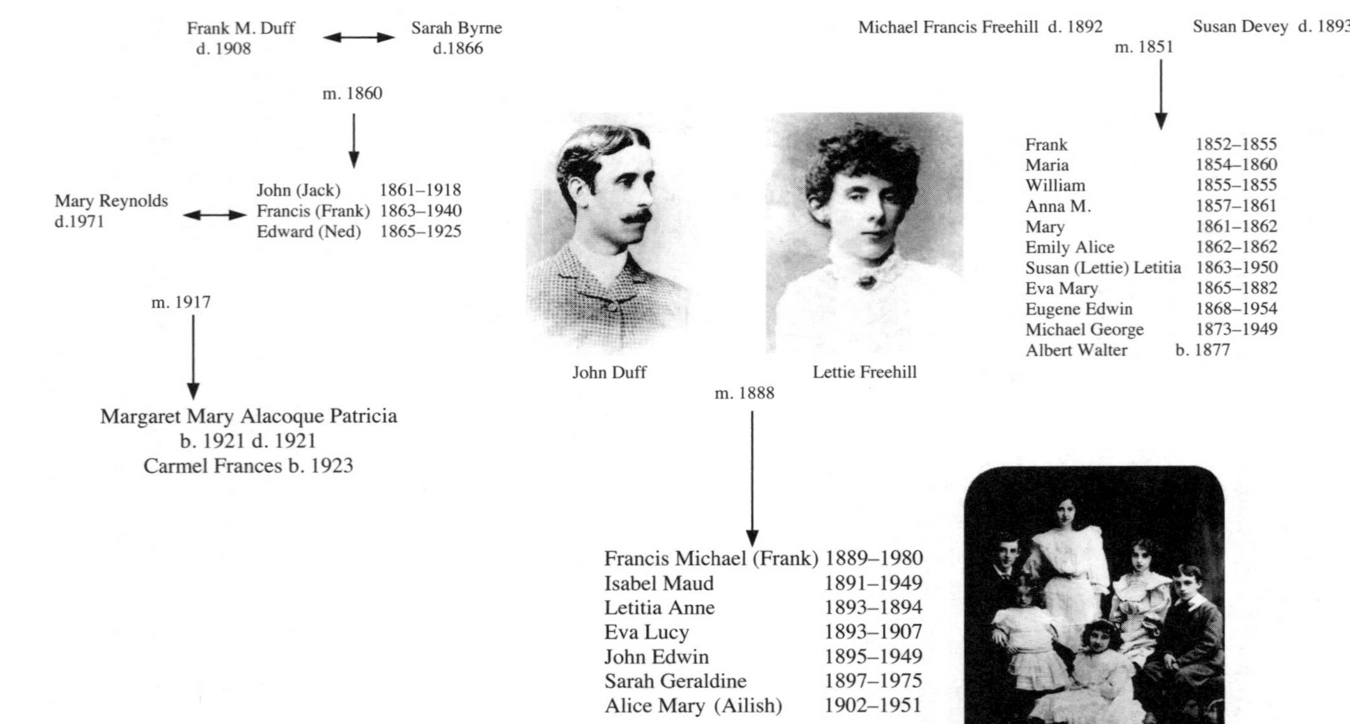
Family Tree of Frank Duff
Frank M. Duff d. 1908
Sarah Byrne d.1866
m. 1860
John (Jack) 1861–1918
Francis (Frank) 1863–1940
Edward (Ned) 1865–1925
Mary Reynolds d.1971
m. 1917
Margaret Mary Alacoque Patricia b. 1921 d. 1921
Carmel Frances b. 1923
Michael Francis Freehill d. 1892
Susan Devey d. 1893
m. 1851
Frank 1852–1855
Maria 1854–1860
William 1855–1855
Anna M. 1857–1861
Mary 1861–1862
Emily Alice 1862–1862
Susan (Lettie) Letitia 1863–1950
Eva Mary 1865–1882
Eugene Edwin 1868–1954
Michael George 1873–1949
Albert Walter b. 1877
John Duff
Lettie Freehill
m. 1888
Francis Michael (Frank) 1889–1980
Isabel Maud 1891–1949
Letitia Anne 1893–1894
Eva Lucy 1893–1907
John Edwin 1895–1949
Sarah Geraldine 1897–1975
Alice Mary (Ailish) 1902–1951

In the 1880s Drumcondra was in the process of development and, according to Cahill's journal, a large number of new houses had been built. The district was 'already supplied with Vartry water' and gas and 'good roads' were on the way. The area was 'well accommodated with two beautiful Chapels, one belonging to the Convent and the other to Clonliffe College'. Drumcondra, however, was not without its problems, which included pollution of the Tolka River, and a number of burglaries and break-ins. Residents in Drumcondra 'complained bitterly of the riotous behaviour of the bands of roughs from the city and elsewhere who meet to do battle with the football and hurling clubs in Clonturk Park on Sundays'.[9] High drama occurred on St Patrick's Road when Samuel Childs, who lived at number 51, next door to the Cahills and two doors up from the Duffs, was charged with the murder of his brother Thomas. The trial of Childs, which resulted in his acquittal, took place on 19–21 October 1899, some months after the Duff family moved to Kingstown (later renamed Dún Laoghaire). The Childs murder case is referred to as 'a gruesome case' in James Joyce's *Ulysses*.[10] By 1901 Childs, the Cahills and the Duffs had respectively vacated Numbers 51, 53 and 55 St Patrick's Road.[11] In 1902 the young James Joyce and his family moved into 7 St Peter's Terrace (now 5 St Peter's Road) in Phibsborough, across the canal from St Patrick's Road in Drumcondra, where they stayed until 1904, the year in which *Ulysses* is set.

Following the opening of jobs to women in the Post Office in Ireland, Lettie Freehill took up work in the Accountant Branch in the Post Office in Dublin in December 1883. She went to live with her parents, Michael and Susan, at 55 St Patrick's Road. Also working in the public service in the Local Government Board was Jack Duff, who was living at 173 Clonliffe Road, a short walk away. Lettie met her future husband when he paid a visit to his former teacher, her father Michael Freehill. Freehill used to give grinds to some of his past pupils in preparation for civil service and other examinations. Lettie is said to have had at least one other admirer before Jack Duff: Tom King, the father of the originator of the cartoon strip 'Curly Wee and Gussie Goose', Marion King.[12]

Lettie Freehill and Jack Duff were married on 5 November 1888 by the Parish Priest, John Byrne, in the Church of St Joseph at Berkeley Street, then a chapel-of-ease to St Michan's.[13] They were aged twenty-five and twenty-seven respectively. The church records indicate that the banns of marriage had been dispensed with by Archdeacon Walsh. The witnesses were the bride's brother Eugene and her first cousin Annie Cahill. It is not clear where the newlyweds lived immediately after their marriage, but on 7 June 1889, when their first child, Francis Michael, was born, just seven months to the day after the wedding, the birth notice in *The Freeman's Journal* on 11 June 1889 read

'Duff – June 7, 1889, at 97 Phibsborough Road, the wife of John Duff, of a son, prematurely.' According to *Thom's Directory*, numbers 92–98 Phibsborough Road were built only in 1889 and the first recorded owner in 1890 is Mr William Millar, so that it is possible that the Duffs rented the premises from him in mid-1889. On one occasion Frank said that, following his parents' marriage, 'They must have had a flat of some kind in Phibsborough.'[14] Number 97 is part of a terrace on Phibsborough Road between Connaught Street and Munster Street.

Frank Duff told friends that he had not been expected to live at the time of his birth. He said that he was baptized in St Joseph's, Berkeley Road.[15] To date, no record of his baptism has been found, although it must have been available at the time of his First Communion and Confirmation because proof of baptism is required for reception of these sacraments. It is possible that Frank was baptized immediately after his birth because of the danger of imminent death.

In 1891 the Duffs moved to 59 St Patrick's Road where a daughter, Isabel Maud, was born the same year.[16] Early the next year Lettie's father died and Lettie, Jack, Frank and Isabel moved into 55 St Patrick's Road, where Lettie's mother, Susan, lived until her own death in January 1893. Later that year Lettie gave birth to twins – Letitia Anne and Eva Lucy. Letitia lived just nine months, while Eva Lucy died aged fourteen in 1907. In 1895 she gave birth to a second son, John Edwin, and two years later in 1897 she gave birth to a daughter, Sarah Geraldine. The last of the Duff children, Alice Mary (Ailish), was born in 1902. Frank was twelve when Ailish was born and he had a special affection for her throughout her life. The responsibilities of the eldest member of a big family devolved on Frank, who would survive all his siblings.

He was very close to both his parents. When he was young, his mother called him 'Old Reliability'. In later years he remarked, 'My mother could not have imagined the extent to which her words sank in and gave my thoughts an inclination. I valued that commendation and tried to live up to it.'[17] Duff spoke of how he received encouragement from his mother and how she waited up for him when he came home late at night, even though 'he was too tired to talk to her'.[18] Devoted to his mother and drawing from his own experience, he wrote to a young man a few years before he died, 'As you go through life you will find there is no love like the love of a mother for her child.'[19]

In 1892 new recreation grounds were opened at Jones's Road in Drumcondra, suitable for athletics meetings as well as for bicycle and pony races. There were also 'band promenades and what may be called *al fresco* theatricals'.[20] The inaugural meeting of the cycling club was organized by the Constabulary. Bands of the Dublin Metropolitan Police, the Royal Sussex Regiment and the

Duke of Cornwall's Light Infantry played in the recreation grounds. The prizes for athletics and for the cycling and pony races were 'gracefully distributed by Lady Reed, wife of the Inspector General of the Royal Irish Constabulary'.[21] The following year it was reported that the amusements at Jones's Road grounds drew large crowds of pleasure-seekers, and, judging by the popularity of the grounds, it was expected that they would yield a big dividend to the company that developed them. But that was not to be. The sports grounds were not a commercial success and were first rented and then in 1908 sold to the Gaelic Athletic Association, which developed them as Croke Park.[22] In 1893 *Irish Society*, a popular contemporary magazine, reported that 'The band promenades in Drumcondra Park attained to great popularity this year'[23] with many young people coming out from the city to enjoy the bands. In June 1894 it is reported that 'The Drumcondra Light Railway Bill has passed the Second Reading in the House of Lords'.[24] The coming of the railway to Drumcondra was a cause for celebration and Frank and his friends watched the construction of the railway bridge with avid interest.[25]

Frank Duff has described what it was like to grow up as a child in Dublin in the 1890s. Street games were very common among children at a time before roads were filled with motorcars. While the younger children would remain at home with their mothers, the older children would play in the streets, where they often ran barefoot, though Frank himself was never barefooted. At play, the boys tended to keep with the boys and the girls with the girls. Wheeling hoops was a popular game with boys. The bicycle with pneumatic tyres on steel rims had recently been invented. The rims provided the hoops that could be driven with sticks. There was a certain amount of cricket played. Frank describes the general enthusiasm for sports on his road. He recalled a man called Hegarty, a civil service colleague of his father's and a lodger in a nearby house, who would referee their street games.[26]

As a boy Frank enjoyed family trips to the Dunsany estate where his grandfather's work as land steward included charge of farming operations, livestock, crops and sawmills. Frank always made for the farm workshops, where he learned much about farming, including crop rotation. Harvesting was of particular interest, as the Dunsany estate was the first in Ireland to use a reaper and binder.[27] Although the Dunsanys were a landed Protestant family, they were well disposed towards Catholics and conscious that Oliver Plunkett, the Catholic Archbishop of Armagh in the seventeenth century and later a saint of the Catholic Church, had been a member of their family. When the Penal Laws were in force, the Dunsanys had helped their Catholic relatives, the Killeens of Killeen Castle, who had been Earls of Fingall since the seventeenth century – at one time the premier Catholic peers in Ireland – by allowing them to transfer the title of their lands in trust to the Dunsanys, only to transfer it back when the penal code was relaxed. The atmosphere of mutual respect which existed between the Protestant Dunsanys and their Catholic employees, the Duffs, must have impinged on the young Frank, who as a child had listened to tales about Daniel O'Connell as he sat at the fireside in his grandparents' home. The first public meeting of the Repeal Association, which aimed to repeal the Act of Union, took place in Trim in 1843 when O'Connell addressed a crowd of around thirty thousand. Frank's forebears had collected Catholic 'rent' for O'Connell and no doubt the Dunsanys were aware of this, but it never affected relations between them. Throughout his life Frank maintained some contact with the Dunsanys.

Reading was very much a part of Frank's life from his earliest years, first through stories read aloud by his mother and then on his own. His mother's reading aloud included Grimms' Fairy Tales and a series called the *Blue Fairy Book*, the *Yellow Fairy Book* and the *Red Fairy Book*.[28] Charles Perrault, whose versions written in seventeenth-century France gave classic status to fairy tales, observes that fathers and mothers 'deserve praise for giving young children early moral instruction by means of such stories'.[29] Whether or not such was the intention of Lettie Duff, her children enjoyed the tales. Frank described the routine adopted by his mother whereby when she had finished reading she would answer any questions the children might pose and then she would divide sweets between them. She divided the sweets into shares, including a share for herself, which was the same size as that for the children, and then the children would choose in turn on a rota system – by height one day, by lowest age another day, and so on. Frank could never resist print and when he started to read on his own, he used to stay up late at night reading the adventures of Roland Quiz, Tom Pippin or Charon the Charioteer. His mother gave him an *Encyclopaedia Britannica* and together they did general knowledge quizzes in *The* (London) *Times*, Mrs Duff's daily paper. He told a friend that when he was young he had read *The Malay Archipelago* – presumably his mother's copy – and Darwin's *Origin of Species* and that, as a result, he was never troubled in his faith by the theory of evolution. Decades later, when the Jesuit priest Teilhard de Chardin published *The Phenomenon of Man*, Duff wrote an article on de Chardin's book in which he said that more or less everyone, including himself, accepted evolution in some form, but that for the Christian 'to carry lifeless matter over into the order of vegetable life a creative act was required, proceeding from outside, that is from God'.[30]

There was a marked emphasis in the Duff household on developing and using one's talents. Education, then as now, was a route to advancement. In selecting first the Jesuits in Belvedere College and then the Holy Ghost Fathers in Blackrock College for the boys, and the Dominican nuns in Eccles Street and the Loreto nuns in St Stephen's Green for the girls, the Duffs were selecting premier academic schools for their children. In the Duff household, although based on traditional lines of a mother in the home and a breadwinner father, the parents sought the best education for their daughters as well as their sons.

When he was close to eighty years of age, Frank wrote to a friend, 'I have seen a vast number of lives begin and accomplish themselves and end. And I have observed it is in those early days of shaping that the end is determined.'[31] In Frank's own early days, his capacity to build relationships was formed in the secure relationship which he had with his parents, and his talents were identified and began to develop. His home was not an especially religious one. In days when it would have been common for families to recite Grace before and after meals, this was not the case in the Duff household.[32] When the family moved to Kingstown and Frank entered Blackrock College in 1899, daily Mass was routine practice for the boarders. Frank, a day boy, said that neither daily Mass nor family Rosary featured in his family circle, although their Catholic allegiance was never in doubt. At a time when many families, especially large families, had a priest or a nun among the wider group of blood relatives, there were none among Frank's immediate family or among his numerous uncles and aunts. The nearest priest within the wider family was Fr James Reynolds, brother of Mary Reynolds, sister-in-law of Frank's father. León Ó Broin, one of Frank's closest friends, recounts that Frank's mother once remarked to León's wife, Cáit, at the time when Lettie lived with Frank in Morning Star Avenue, off North Brunswick Street, 'The house is full of holy books and I could never read one of them.'[33]

Possibly as early as five years of age, Frank began attending a Dame School, a small private school run by two sisters.[34] At the age of eight he entered Belvedere College, where James Joyce was a senior student and president of the Sodality of Our Lady. In 1899 the Duff family moved to 17 Clarinda Park East in Kingstown following an improvement in family fortunes, including promotion obtained by Jack Duff in the civil service. Also in the mid-1890s Mrs Duff had come in for a substantial inheritance, including American Railway Stock, which passed to her from her Uncle Tom Freehill via her father, who had died in 1892. Tom had emigrated to Nevada in the United States and died there without issue.

Notes to Chapter 1

1. Ó Broin, *Frank Duff*, pp. 80–81.
2. Author's interview with Carmel Duff, 20 May 2008.
3. Máire M. Kealy, OP, *Dominican Education in Ireland 1820–1930*. Dublin: Irish Academic Press, 2007, p. 151. The Trim school later transferred to the Christian Brothers and was subsequently absorbed into the Community School.
4. Note to author from Anne Jensen, British Postal Museum and Archive (undated).
5. Quoted in Rev. C. C. Ellison, 'Richard Butler – Historian of Trim', included in Dean Butler, *Some*

Notices of the Castle and of the Ecclesiastical Buildings of Trim with in addition a short life of Richard Butler by C. C. Ellison, published by Meath Archaeological and Historical Society, 1978.

6. Eugene Alfred Conwell, *A Ramble around Trim amongst its Ruins and Antiquities*. Dublin, 1878, p. 65.
7. *A Memoir of the Very Rev. Richard Butler, Dean of Clonmacnoise and Vicar of Trim* by his Widow, 1863.
8. Diary of James Cahill passed to his son Christy and photocopied by Fr Herman Nolan, CP.
9. *Irish Society*, 20 June 1891, quoted in Dónall Ó Luanaigh, 'Glimpses of Drumcondra in the Time of the Young James Joyce', *Dublin Historical Record*, 50:2 (Autumn 1997), p. 189.
10. Adrian Hardiman, '"A Gruesome Case": James Joyce's Dublin Murder Case' in Felix Larkin (ed.), *Librarians, Poets, Scholars*, p. 283.
11. *Thom's Directory*, 1901.
12. On 22 July 2000 I visited Regan's pub in Newtown near Trim where I met Mrs Kathleen Lynch, whose son owned the premises that had previously been owned by Missy and Marcie Regan. Mrs Lynch had been to school with Carmel Duff. She said that there had been a romance between Tom King and Susan Freehill before Susan became engaged to John Duff.
13. The marriage certificate from the Church lists St Michan's, Halston Street, while the civil certificate lists St Joseph's, Berkeley Road.
14. Transcript of Duff's interview with Fr John Aherne CSSp, in 1968, given to author by Fr Seán Farragher, CSSp, 10 February 2009; henceforth called 'Aherne interview'. The tape of the interview is in LOMA.
15. ibid.
16. *Thom's Directory*, 1891.
17. Bradshaw, *Frank Duff*, p. 52.
18. Bradshaw, tape 132, LOMA.
19. Duff to Brian, 29 April 1975.
20. *Irish Society*, 3 September 1892, quoted in Ó Luanaigh, 'Glimpses of Drumcondra', p. 191.
21. ibid., p. 192.
22. ibid., p. 194. In 1910 approximately four acres were sold to the Jesuit Order for use as the Belvedere College sports grounds.
23. *Irish Society*, 12 August 1893, quoted in Ó Luanaigh, 'Glimpses of Drumcondra', p. 193.
24. *Irish Society*, 2 June 1894, quoted in ibid., p. 194.
25. Dunleavy to author, 21 May 2010.
26. Duff interview with Bradshaw, tape 118, LOMA.
27. Source for this information is from notes taken by Enda Dunleavy following conversations with Duff, referred to subsequently as 'Dunleavy notes'.
28. Duff interview with Fr Bradshaw, tape 118, LOMA.
29. Christopher Betts, *The Complete Fairy Tales by Charles Perrault*. Oxford: Oxford University Press, 2009, p. xiii.
30. Frank Duff, 'De Chardin's Phenomenon of Man', *The Woman of Genesis*. Dublin: Praedicanda, 1976, p. 443.
31. Duff to Dairine, 4 January 1968.
32. Duff interview with Bradshaw, tape 118, LOMA.
33. Ó Broin, *Frank Duff*, p. 3.
34. Mary McAndrew suggests the sisters' surname was Clarke, while Enda Dunleavy thinks it was McVeigh.

CHAPTER 2

Blackrock College

'Before I was nine years of age I had worked through the contents of my father's library – or at least through a considerable portion of it.'
DUFF TO MARY DILLON-LEETCH, 28 APRIL 1973

The move to Kingstown in mid-April 1899 brought many changes, including that of a larger house in more fashionable surroundings. The house contained fine furniture, silver and china, some of which survived subsequent house moves back to Drumcondra, then to Dartmouth Square and finally to North Brunswick Street. At the time of the move to Kingstown, Sarah Geraldine, aged five, was the youngest of the Duff children until Ailish was born in 1902. On the night of the 1901 census there were four children recorded in the Duff household, while Frank was a patient in St Michael's hospital, suffering from 'inflammation of the stomach'.[1] Lettie, who cared for her children and household with the help of a housekeeper, never failed to read *The Times* daily or to complete its crossword. Jack Duff enjoyed physical exercise and swam all year at the Forty Foot bathing spot in Sandycove, a location then reserved for male swimmers. Jack began to take Frank with him on these trips to the sea, where they often swam in the early morning. For holidays the Duff family went to Bray, where they rented a house. One Christmas his parents bought Frank a bicycle. This would become his regular mode of transport and remained so until his death.

Following the move to Kingstown, Blackrock College was an obvious choice of school for Frank, both because of easy access via the new tramway and because Frank's uncle, Albert Walter, attended Blackrock as a boarder and later as a third-level student in the Royal University and Civil Service College, then attached to the College.[2] In the College register Albert's fees were paid by Lettie Duff, who was fourteen years his senior. Blackrock College, which Frank entered on 17 April 1899 when he was almost ten years old, was known locally as the 'French College', having been founded in 1860 by French priests. It followed the French system of education until the Intermediate Education Act 1878 introduced a new approach, a feature of which was that schools and students qualified for public financial support on the basis of their performance in examinations set by the Intermediate Education Board. Teachers were not paid a salary by the government but by the school, from student fees and from money allocated by the Board as 'result fees', which were paid on the basis of examination results achieved. The system was described by Patrick Pearse as 'the Murder Machine', criticizing the concept of 'education as some sort of manufacturing process' in which children were 'raw material'.[3]

There were four public examinations – Preparatory, Junior, Middle and Senior Grade, graded according to age. Preparation for these public tests would dominate Frank's school life for seven and a half years. The emphasis on these examinations is borne out by Senia Paseta, who says in her study of Ireland's Catholic élite before Independence that 'Examinations came to dominate the lives of Catholic students.'[4] Frank said that he and other boys 'were very heavily burdened and from the age of thirteen, twelve or thirteen, I was learning four languages, not counting English – Latin and Greek, French and Irish'. He supposed that 'most young people slacked a bit, but if you did what you were supposed to do you'd have no free time at home. You'd have to work at it from the time you came home and keep at it 'til bedtime.'[5]

In addition to the Intermediate or secondary school, there were two third-level establishments at Blackrock – a university college preparing students for examinations conducted under the auspices of the Royal University of Ireland and a college that prepared students for entrance examinations to the civil service. The 'third-level' college was based in the 'Castle', a separate building. Finally there was a juniorate for students who hoped to join the Holy Ghost Congregation. During Frank's years at Blackrock College, the biggest numbers, over two hundred, were in the boarding school, with between sixty and eighty in the day school, forty in the juniorate and thirty-five in the 'Castle'. One of the students in residence in the Castle at the time Frank arrived was Éamon de Valera. The staff at the time included thirteen priests, eleven 'prefects' or junior (clerical) masters and nineteen brothers, who looked after the material needs of the College, as well as a number of lay teachers.

Frank's earliest friend in Blackrock was Michael Davitt, son of the founder of the Land League. The League, founded in 1879, sought a reduction in rents for tenant farmers and ownership of the land by tenants when, in the words of John Mitchel, 'Land in Ireland is life.' Michael was in class with Frank during his first two years in the College from 1899 until 1901, when he transferred to O'Connell School. During those two years the Davitts lived in Comber House in Dalkey, a short walk to the tram line. Frank travelled by tram to Blackrock each day with Michael. The old horse-drawn trams had been electrified but retained the open structure at the front where the driver sat. According to Fr Thomas Davitt, the young boys sometimes spat down on the drivers from above.[6]

In September 1899, five months after Frank's arrival at Blackrock, a new president of the college arrived. Fr John T. Murphy came from Pittsburgh, where for twelve years he had been rector of the high school, soon to be granted university status as Duquesne University. Fr Murphy, nicknamed 'Jumbo' by the students, was a big man, not only physically, but as a man of vision with ambitious plans for the college. On one memorable occasion the students were party to Fr Murphy's strategy for development. As Queen Victoria's entourage passed the College at midday on 4 April 1900, the students lined the main road under instruction to cheer as the royal carriage passed, and also to cheer when Murphy doffed his large American rector's hat to indicate the carriage of the Earl of Pembroke, the College's landlord. A few days later a successful interview took place between Murphy and the Pembroke Estate agents about the renewal of the College leases and the remodelling of the frontage along the Rock Road.

Fr Murphy introduced two organizations into Blackrock with which Frank Duff would later, but not then, be associated: the Pioneer Total Abstinence Association and the St Vincent de Paul Society. While Fr Murphy planned the future of the College, Frank started his studies in the Elementary course, including French, which laid the foundation of his later competence in the subject. Irish was coming into schools as the second language and the Gaelic League was mounting a campaign to have it included on the secondary curriculum. The Gaelic League had been founded in 1893 by Douglas Hyde, also known by the pseudonym An Craoibhín Aoibhinn [The Lovely Little Branch] and later first President of Ireland. Among Frank's library is a copy of *Trí Sgéalta*, a collection of folklore stories taken down in oral narration by Conor Desmond from Cork and edited by An Craoibhín Aoibhinn.

From the start Frank took to Irish with enthusiasm. A distinctive feature of his outlook on life which goes back to this time was a lifelong passion for the preservation and development of what was best in things Irish, whether it be folklore, literature, music or the natural landscape. Frank's first teacher of Irish was a German, Fr Ferdinand Senger, who had taken 'Celtic' as a subject when he was a student at the college in the 1880s. After Fr Senger, his Irish teachers were Michael Smithwick, close co-operator with Thomas MacDonagh, who had been a former classmate of Smithwick's in Rockwell; Risteárd Ó Foghlú (Richard Foley), alias 'Fiachra Eilgeach'; and Denis Lynch and Thomas O'Nowlan, well known as Irish authors and enthusiastic workers in the Gaelic League.[7] Ó Foghlú (1873–1957), a native Irish speaker, became the first editor of An Gúm, the State publishing company for the Irish language established in 1925. It is said that he was the reader for Browne & Nolan when they rejected the novel *An Béal Bocht*, written by another alumnus of Blackrock College, Myles na Gopaleen (Brian O'Nolan/Flann O'Brien). It was published in 1941.

Frank's teacher in the elementary course for religion was Claremorris-born Br Thaddeus Judge, a legend for his total commitment to the most junior boys, or the 'chicks', as they were called. The religion course covered three categories – Christian Doctrine, Scripture and Church History. Among the religious booklets of the period was *The Student's Manual of Prayer*, published by the College in 1891. Its table of contents included Morning and Night Prayer, Rosary of the Blessed Virgin Mary, Litany of the Blessed Virgin Mary, Prayer before Class, Devotion in honour of St Joseph, Devotion in honour of St Aloysius and Manner of Serving Mass.

Apart from formal religious instruction, the atmosphere of the school was religious. The Holy Ghost Fathers are a missionary order, and Fr Farragher says a main purpose of the college at the time was to provide vocations for the missions. Frank would certainly have had the idea of the Church's mission to spread the Gospel presented to him at Blackrock. Religious pictures hung on the walls; the halls and dormitories were named after saints. Statues of four saints were chosen to make a statement about the college ethos: St Joseph holding the Child Jesus, which overlooked the school and recreation area, reminded all that he was the special guardian of the college; St Patrick's statue – facing east, recalling that he had probably come from Wales – represented the Irish dimension of the faith; St Peter's statue emphasized the link with Rome; while that of St Paul, apostle of the Gentiles, underlined the main purpose of the College in providing vocations for the missions. 'The pride of place in the quadrangle was given to the statues of the Sacred Heart and Our Lady with the Child Jesus. A beautiful new statue of Our Lady entitled *Tutela Domus* – Protectress of the House – was installed at the head of the main hall in 1898, some months before Frank's arrival.'[8] His own portrait hangs beside this statue today.

The school year began with the votive mass of the Holy Spirit – a 'Red Mass', so called after the red vestments worn by the celebrant. Classes were preceded by a prayer recited by teacher and students, a custom that persisted in many Catholic schools in Ireland for at least another fifty years. The insistence on silence between classes, inherited from the French system of education, was meant to foster an atmosphere of recollection.

As was customary at the time, Frank was close to eleven years old when he received First Holy Communion. He retained a vivid memory of his Communion Day on Ascension Thursday, 24 May 1900, and of the retreat in preparation for the sacrament. The retreat was given by Fr John Martin (Mattie) Ebenrecht, a native of Colmar in Alsace,[9] who had arrived at the college in 1862 to take over the functions of bursar and art teacher, becoming director of Sodalities when he had learned sufficient English. In his spare time he studied architecture and designed and supervised the main college buildings, beginning in 1867 with the chapel. Frank, together with nine other day boys and four boarders, received his First Holy Communion in the college chapel with the parents of the day boys present. Fr Ebenrecht celebrated High Mass at 9 a.m. with a Deacon and Subdeacon. The music and singing included Gounod's 'The Redemption'. It is recorded that Fr Ebenrecht took the communion boys to Artane, where Brothers gave them 'a good tea lunch'.[10] On the way to Artane the boys and Fr Ebenrecht stopped off at Werner's studio to have a group photograph taken.

Before First Communion, the boys received the sacrament of Confession. Frank Duff has described his awareness of right and wrong at that early age:

> In the General Confession which I made the day before my First Holy Communion, I shaded off an offence which I confessed. On thinking over it, I became extremely worried in case I had made a sacrilegious Confession. Consequently, on the following morning, when the great mustering was taking place, I had, to my great confusion, to ask for confession. So let no one tell me that very young people do not realise their wrongdoing very precisely.[11]

Two years after his First Communion, Frank received the sacrament of Confirmation, taking the name Stephen. Once again Fr Ebenrecht prepared the boys, some forty of them, mostly day boys, who received the sacrament from the Archbishop of Dublin, William Walsh, in Booterstown parish church on 29 April 1902.

In an interview in the 1960s with Fr John Aherne, a Holy Ghost priest, Frank said that on the day of their First Communion the boys were asked what they intended to be when they grew up. Like many other boys, Frank said 'a priest'. However, he also said that 'the idea never again came back into my mind. Even … by way of a late vocation because I was never in the position actually to do it. My course was terribly clear before me, because I told you about the family reverses caused by my father's retirement.'[12] This did not prevent a friend later suggesting to the thirty-year-old Frank Duff in 1929 that he should consider becoming a Trappist monk.[13]

Fr Farragher considers that the early seeds of Legion of Mary spirituality may have been implanted in Frank Duff at this time, saying that Fr Ebenrecht would certainly have pointed out to the boys the significance of the crest of the Holy Ghost congregation, namely a dove, representing the Holy Ghost, hovering above the Heart of Mary. Farragher also raises the intriguing question of whether Fr Ebenrecht might have told the boys that the founder of the Holy Ghost Congregation, Claude Poullart des Places, had been a boyhood friend of Grignion de Montfort, author of the *Treatise on the True Devotion to the Blessed Virgin*, which became central to the life of Frank Duff and of the Legion of Mary. By coincidence, it was one of Ebenrecht's successors as college architect, Vincent Kelly, who introduced Frank to de Montfort's classic.

Frank's academic record in Blackrock was excellent. In addition to the state examinations, there were also in-house exams preceding the public examinations, rather like the 'mocks' of nowadays. Subjects were grouped in categories: Modern Literary, Classical, and Science and Mathematics. Frank missed the mock examination leading to the Preparatory Grade in 1903, having fallen ill with typhoid fever, as did his father. Both were together in the Elpis Nursing Home in Lower Mount Street, where they were cared for by Dr Thornley Stoker, brother of Bram Stoker, author of *Dracula*.[14] Following the bout of typhoid, Frank's father took him on a sea journey to the Tilbury Docks in London, travelling on the boat from the Custom House in Dublin. While Frank recovered fully, the illness led to his father's retirement from the civil service. Frank was aged fourteen in 1904 when his father was forced to retire, on health grounds, from his job, at the age of forty-three.

In September 1903 Fr James Keawell took over as Dean of Studies (Principal) in Blackrock. He recorded that Frank achieved an honours mark in all subjects in the Preparatory Grade, except Drawing and Science. The teaching of practical science and technical drawing was being promoted at the time, and grants towards the building of science rooms and towards the tuition of each student was sponsored by the Department of Agriculture and Technical Instruction, then under the direction of Horace Plunkett. Frank had availed of this tuition grant for 1902/03 but did not continue in that course, aiming instead for an Exhibition in the Modern Literary group. At this stage Frank actually disliked mathematics and it was only when he was working on land annuities in the Land Commission that he concentrated on the subject.

The academic year 1903/04 was a tough and challenging one for Frank, when his father's enforced retirement was compounded by the collapse in value of Mrs Duff's railway stock. Money became scarce for the Duff family and they were forced to move from Clarinda Park to their old home in Drumcondra, which the family still owned. The daily timetable now faced by the fourteen-year-old Frank was a punishing one. Every morning he left his home at 7.30 to walk the two miles to Westland Row station. Having reached Booterstown station, he had a further walk to the college, often arriving late, and frequently wet. In the course of one journey, Frank indulged in a bit of boldness when he and a friend lit up their cigarettes in a railway carriage in the company of a stern woman traveller who objected to their doing so. She complained to a guard, who had them moved to an adjoining carriage. There they discovered a knot hole in the wooden partition separating the two carriages. They used all their lung-power to blow smoke into the carriage they had left, making a hasty retreat at the next stop.[15] Frank could be a mischievous schoolboy with an irresistible sense of fun and enjoyment of practical jokes, which remained with him as an adult. Because of the amount of time spent on travel, he had little opportunity to enjoy extra-curricular activities and he said that he used to get a pain in his heart on Sunday evenings at the prospect of restarting the weekly drudgery the next morning.

He continued to make academic progress. In the Junior Grade examination in June 1904 he was awarded a first-class exhibition, valued at £20, in the Modern Literary group. To put that figure in perspective, the fee for the day school for the year was eight guineas (£8. 8s. 0d). In the 'house' exams before the public exams, Frank had come first in Irish, winning a book prize. That year he was among the college 'galaxy' of prize-winners who went on an outing to a beauty spot in Wicklow. Because he was underage, Frank was entered again for the Junior Grade in 1905, this time in the Classics group. Once again he won a £20 Exhibition. Years later, Frank would remark how he was only one of a number of bright sparks in Blackrock at the time. He did so in the context of advising a legionary not to underestimate the capacity of young people to understand the Legion of Mary *Handbook*:

> Before I was nine years of age I had worked through the contents of my father's library – or at least through a considerable portion of it. More lately I have often wondered how I understood what I read because of course I encountered a multitude of words which I did not understand and which I did not stop to look up in a dictionary. So in later years I took up some of those books again and went through them and I found that I had gained a very just appreciation of their contents. Do not counter this suggestion by telling me that I must have been an exceptional child. True, I was intelligent and did well in my school career, but I had a very great number of fellow-students who were of my own level. It would have been sheer injustice to any of us to present us with a babyfied edition of the Legion Handbook.[16]

During Frank's years at Blackrock there was at least one brilliantly gifted student in his class, so Frank often had to be content with second place. Stephen Roche from Monasterevin, rated by Frank as the best student he had known, would join the civil service, rising to the rank of Secretary of the Department of Justice. A close contemporary was Cornelius (later Sir Cornelius) Gregg, who finished two years ahead of Frank, completing Senior Grade in 1905. Gregg graduated with a BA from University College Dublin (a constituent college of the National University established in 1908) in 1909, and he also joined the civil service and was posted to London. He was temporarily seconded back to Dublin to help with the establishment of the Irish civil service after the Treaty, in which capacity Frank would work with Gregg for a short period. He would also differ from Gregg in relation to his own claim to promotion in the civil service. In due course Gregg became chairman of the Board of Inland Revenue in the United Kingdom and became known as the man who devised the PAYE system of taxation, introduced in Britain on 6 April 1944.

There was an extensive range of extra-curricular activities in Blackrock. Drama and elocution were organized by Mr M'Hardy Flint. Frank was chosen by M'Hardy to act a leading role in the college production of Shakespeare's *Twelfth Night*, but at an early stage he was afflicted with stage fright and asked to be excused. He said that he was painfully sensitive and shy at this time.[17]

Photography captured the attention of some of the staff members and students at Blackrock. Fr Ebenrecht has recorded in his journal that he and the science teacher, Fr Hugh O'Toole, 'went out to a lecture in Dawson Street on an improved and portable camera.'[18] Some of the developing and printing of the glass negatives took place in the science room, with the involvement of staff and students. In September 1903 the College had a visit from a noted photographer from Paris, M. David, famous for the large-sized albums he produced for schools all over France. Fr Farragher wonders if Frank's life-long interest in photography could have stemmed from this time. He may also have gained some interest in photography from his maternal grandfather, Michael Freehill, one of the earliest photographers in Ireland. It is recorded that in 1857 Michael Freehill took the photograph of Dean Richard Butler at the Model School in Trim, an engraving of which appears in Conwell's *A Ramble around Trim*.

Physically fit, a keen cyclist and cross-country runner, Frank also enjoyed tennis and cricket. A photograph of the junior cricket team shows him sitting in the centre. On one occasion while keeping wicket when he was twelve years old, he was hit by a cricket ball at the back of his left ear and was knocked unconscious. He suffered damage to his ear and was removed to the college infirmary. That blow is thought to have contributed to his partial deafness later in life. Frank does not appear to have engaged in the great Blackrock game – rugby. Perhaps in reaction to the premium placed on rugby at Blackrock, on one occasion he pulled off a remarkable prank. On 14 March 1906 in the semi-final of the Leinster Schools' Cup, Blackrock beat Wesley by 25 points to nil. Fr Ebenrecht recorded 'The Cup will be won or lost next Tuesday with S. Andrews.'[19] In the event, St Andrew's would beat the favourites by 5 points to nil. But on the day following the triumph over Wesley an account appeared in the *Freeman's Journal* purporting to describe victory celebrations at Blackrock, which involved much emphasis on matters 'Irish', albeit the victory was in a 'foreign' sport:

> Last evening at Blackrock College a very enjoyable entertainment was given in honour of the students' victory over Wesley. A large number of cinematograph films on numerous subjects were shown by Mr Joseph Healy, greatly to the enjoyment of the boys. Mr R. Foley, the professor of Irish in the College, gave an interesting lecture on the Gaelic Revival. Songs were sung at intervals by Rev. P. J. McAllister, Bryan Fitzgerald, B. A., and William O'Gara. An Irish jig was danced by John Martyn. At the close of the proceedings three cheers for the Cup Team was proposed by the president and given with zest.[20]

Ebenrecht's diary for 16 March 1906 includes the following: 'Subjoined article was in yesterday's *Freeman's Journal.* A day boy is suspected to have sent it to the paper. It speaks for itself. Not a word of truth is in it.' It is possible that someone from the school called to the *Freeman* and identified the handwriting. In any event, when Frank admitted authorship, his father was 'as proud as punch',[21] despite Frank's first note in his 'judger' book the following week when he received zero for conduct. It is amusing that the earliest publication of Frank Duff was a letter to the *Freeman's Journal*, the contents of which were sheer invention. Perhaps unsurprisingly, some of his teachers, in particular the Professor of Irish, were not amused. According to Farragher:

> His father laughed off the incident, knowing Frank's penchant for the practical joke. But it would appear that some of Frank's teachers did not see the humour of it and may well have made it difficult for him as a result. He had to approach the Dean about some perceived victimisation and, though Fr. Keawell was not particularly noted for catering for students' sensibilities in such situations, he went out of his way to accommodate Frank in his predicament, making alternative arrangements for him.[22]

Irish was the first class in the morning, and as a result of his long journey across the city from Drumcondra, Frank sometimes arrived late. He associated the unfriendly attitude of his Irish teacher towards him with his late arrival at class. Aware of the problem, Fr Keawell proposed that Frank would move to a lower class with a different teacher, but that he would also attend grinds given first by Thomas O'Nowlan in Baggot Street and later by Denis Lynch in Lynch's home in Cabra. Lynch had great faith in Frank's ability in Irish and told him he could win first in Ireland in the subject in Senior Grade. In the event, he came second, beaten by half a per cent and just missing out on the gold medal.

Frank never forgot Fr Keawell's kindness to him and from his early earnings he purchased a gold card case, which he presented to the priest in gratitude for his support. Fr Farragher recounts how, having cycled out to Blackrock one Sunday to present the gift in person, Frank found that Fr Keawell was on priestly duty in Bray for the weekend. The gold card case is now kept in the Blackrock College archives, having passed to Fr Michael O'Carroll. Fr O'Carroll has described how, following Fr Keawell's death, he returned the card case to Frank: 'Some time later at a meeting of the Pillar of Fire Society, I gave the gold card case to Frank. He placed it in my hand and pressed his hand affectionately on it.'[23]

In the 'mock' exam for Middle Grade in 1906, Frank won first prize in History and Geography. His best mark was for Latin and his knowledge of this would prove valuable when he began to recite daily the Divine Office in Latin. His acquaintance with Latin classical literature served as the basis of his choice of nomenclature and organizational system for the Legion of Mary. As he entered his final year at Blackrock, Frank received the news that he had again won an exhibition, though this time a second-class exhibition, on the basis of the Middle Grade Examination.

In his final year Frank opted to cycle to school rather than travel by train. In June 1907 he sat for the Senior Grade Examinations. When the results came in the autumn, he had passed with distinction. He was awarded a first-class exhibition in the Modern Literary course, valued at £40; he gained second place in Ireland in Irish, English and History and Geography, as well as third place in French. His achievement helped to put Blackrock College in joint second place with Royal Belfast Academical Institution in the number of exhibitions gained.

From an early stage Jack Duff had high ambitions for his eldest son, hoping that he would attend university and then enter the higher rank of the civil service, possibly serving in the colonies overseas.[24] In the Indian Civil Service, for example, every year of service counted as two for pension purposes, so that at the age of forty-two or thereabouts one could retire with a two-thirds salary as pension. One could come home as a relatively young man with a good income and pursue a further career, possibly at the Bar, or in business:

> My father had very tremendous notions with regard to us all. He designated me for the higher Civil Service, i.e., what they call Class 1 Examination – it was the plum job of the Service. He had started off originally as what they call a Second Division Clerk. It was a splendid job in those days, the very one I started off with myself later on, but he had gravitated into the Higher Civil Service, what they call Class 1, by promotion; that was a remarkable feat because the aim at the time was to make it a cast iron division. The Class 1 was not for the hoi-polloi, but for the élite … he intended me to start off where he was leaving off.[25]

But this was not to be. There would be no university education for Frank Duff. Instead, he would enter the civil service, specifically the Land Commission as a Second Division Clerk, in 1908. Several of Frank's contemporaries went to university, including Michael Davitt and Stephen Roche. Davitt studied medicine in UCD, where he became Auditor of the Literary and Historical Society. Following his untimely death at the age of thirty-eight, his widow, Mona Farrell, married Patrick Hogan, the Minister for Agriculture, for whom Frank was destined to work. But that was in the future.

In time, Frank would contribute to the support of the younger members of his family. According to Carmel Duff, three of Frank's siblings – John, Sarah Geraldine and Ailish – obtained scholarships at various times for UCD. Evidence of Ailish's success at school is found in a copy of *Great Expectations* in Frank's library. The book was awarded to the sixteen-year-old Ailish as a prize for 'German, French and Mathematics' when she attended Loreto College on St Stephen's Green. John obtained an honours BSc degree in maths and physics in 1914 and entered the civil service as an examiner in the Exchequer and Audit Office in London. Like many public servants, he volunteered in the Great War and was taken prisoner of war in Germany. He was called to the Irish Bar in June 1923 and was appointed principal officer of the Department of Home Affairs in the same year and Secretary of the Department of Justice not long before his death in 1949.[26] Sarah Geraldine and Ailish would both qualify as medical doctors. Frank once remarked that his life had been 'salted with disappointments'. The fact that he was robbed of a university education because of his father's ill health was a blow. Other disappointments would follow, among them the failure to receive adequate recognition in the civil service and lack of support for his Legion of Mary work from some leading clergy in the Dublin Archdiocese.

By the time he left Blackrock, his life had been touched by many who would feature at future stages of his life. Fr Michael Toher, present at the first meeting of the Legion, was a Blackrock man. Fr John Heffernan, later a missionary bishop and Legion of Mary supporter, was an undergraduate teacher when Frank was at school. Frank would encounter Sir Cornelius Gregg and Stephen Roche in the civil service. Matt Lalor, a Dublin tobacconist, would become a guide and mentor. At the Blackrock College centenary dinner in 1960, Dr Dan Murphy, former Provincial of the Holy Ghost Order and Procurator of the Order in Rome, posed the question as to who was the most distinguished alumnus of the school. Six alumni had qualified to have their portraits put on display in the College 'Hall of Fame': President Éamon de Valera, Cardinal John D'Alton, Archbishop John Charles McQuaid, Archbishop Charles Heerey, Onitsha, Nigeria, Dr Alfred O'Rahilly, former President of University College, Cork, and Frank Duff. All six men were photographed together at the celebratory garden party in July 1960 at Blackrock. According to Fr Seán Farragher, who was present on the occasion, Dr Murphy remarked that Duff would be rated 'the finest flower this nursery had produced'.

Notes to Chapter 2

1. Information from 1901 census supplied by Michael McNamara.
2. This chapter draws heavily on the research of Fr Seán Farragher, CSSp, who kindly gave me permission to avail myself of his work.
3. Pádraic H. Pearse, 'The Murder Machine' in *Collected Works of Pádraic H. Pearse: Political Writings and Speeches*. Dublin, Cork, Belfast, 1912, pp. 5–50. Pearse writes: 'Our children are the "raw material"; we desiderate for their education "modern methods" which must be "efficient" but "cheap"; we send them to Clongowes to be "finished"; when "finished" they are "turned out"; specialists "grind" them for the English Civil Service and the so-called liberal professions.'
4. Senia Paseta, *Before the Revolution: Nationalism, Social Change and Ireland's Catholic Élite, 1879–1922*. Cork: Cork University Press, 1999, p. 33.
5. Duff interview with Bradshaw, Tape No. 118, LOMA.
6. Fr Davitt, C M, was told this by his father, Cahir, later President of the High Court and brother of Frank's friend Michael. Fr Davitt asked that the information be recorded.
7. Seán Farragher, CSSp, 'Frank Duff and his Alma Mater'.

8. ibid.
9. Seán Farragher, CSSp, *Irish Spiritans Remembered*. Orleans, Massachusetts: Paracelete Press, 1998, pp. 98, 211 ff.
10. Quoted from the Blackrock College community journal by Fr Farragher in 'Frank Duff and his Alma Mater'.
11. Bradshaw, *Frank Duff*, p. 17 ff.
12. Aherne interview.
13. Columbcille to Duff, 4 July 1929.
14. Author's interview with Fr Herman Nolan, 1 December 2007.
15. Farragher, 'Frank Duff and his Alma Mater'.
16. Letter to Mary Dillon-Leetch, 28 April 1973.
17. Farragher, 'Frank Duff and his Alma Mater'.
18. Diary of Fr Ebenrecht, Blackrock College archive.
19. ibid.
20. Quoted in Farragher, 'Duff and his Alma Mater'.
21. Enda Dunleavy told the author, 21 May 2010, that this was how Duff described his father's reaction.
22. Farragher, 'Duff and his Alma Mater'.
23. Michael O'Carroll, *A Priest in Changing Times*. Dublin: Columba Press, 1998, p. 130.
24. Phyllis Mc Guinness, in a communication with the writer (22 August 2008), said that Duff told her that his father had hoped he might enter the India Service.
25. Aherne interview.
26. Obituary, Mr J. E. Duff, *The Irish Times*, 22 August 1949.

CHAPTER 3

The Civil Servant as a Young Man

'My cast of mind is mechanical rather than literary. I was a Civil Servant.'
DUFF TO SEÁN Ó FAOLÁIN, 16 AUGUST 1944

In order to pass the civil service entrance examination, Frank attended Skerry's College, a 'grinders' on St Stephen's Green, for six months. The College was founded in the 1880s by George Skerry, a prominent mathematician and publisher of commercial arithmetic texts. As well as the college in Dublin, there were Skerry's colleges in Cork, Belfast and in Britain. Courses were provided to prepare students for university matriculation and civil service examinations. A near contemporary of Frank's at Skerry's was William Joseph Shields, better known as Barry Fitzgerald, who, following a period in the civil service and as an Abbey actor, became a Hollywood film star and won a Best Supporting Actor Oscar for his role as Fr Fitzgibbon in *Going My Way* (1944). In Frank's words:

> Of course, after Blackrock, I would normally have proceeded to the university. Now all that had to be jettisoned and … I went to the grinders at Skerry's College … and then I passed into the Civil Service. I got first place in Ireland in the examination, 16th place in the United Kingdom. … From the first minute my money was of great importance. My father died in 1918. He died of cancer and from that moment, and even before it, I had to be the mainstay, but from that moment on, you see, I was head of the house and I was completely necessary and there was no thought in my mind of anything else but attending to that. I had the fullest sense of responsibility for my brother and my sisters. I regarded myself as responsible for them. I had no idea of marriage for instance.[1]

It is worth reflecting that at the age of twenty-nine, when his father died, Duff ruled out marriage for the foreseeable, if not indefinite, future, on grounds of economic necessity, voluntarily embracing celibacy with all the restraint that such a choice implied. One hundred years later, the notion of a young man opting for celibacy is difficult to comprehend, but it was not unusual at the time or for decades afterwards. While economic factors contributed to the low marriage rate and late average age at marriage in Ireland in the early decades of the twentieth century, the Catholic Church played a role, providing a degree of social control, as well as a motivation that supported the restraint associated with late marriage and celibacy.

Duff's life as a civil servant began on 27 May 1908 when he took up duty in the offices of the Irish Land Commission at 23–26 Upper Merrion Street in Dublin as a Second Division Clerk. He started at the bottom of the salary scale for the post, which was £70–£300 per annum, but this was a good job at a time when, for example, a Bank of Ireland clerk started at £45 per annum and a National School teacher earned £100 a year.[2] In the open competitive examination for Second Division Clerks, held two months earlier, on 23 March and following days, Duff, as he said, was placed 16th among 70 successful candidates out of a total number of 1,220 and first among the candidates with addresses in any part of Ireland. Within a few years, having successfully completed university studies, some of his contemporaries in Blackrock College, including Stephen Roche and Cornelius Gregg, would enter the First Division. Knowing the potential advantages of a university degree, Duff made enquiries in 1910 from the recently established National University of Ireland as to the possibility of an external degree by correspondence, but such was not available.[3]

For decades the land question had been at the core of British policy in Ireland and the Land Commission was central to that policy. The Land Commission was established in 1881 as a rent-fixing body, with the objective of supervising rents at fair levels in the wake of Gladstone's 1881 Land Act. When that task was completed, the Commission worked on the transformation of tenants into owner-occupiers. Approximately 400,000 tenants-at-will and their successors came to own the fee simple of the land. Another feature of Land Commission work – the purchase and distribution of untenanted land for the relief of rural congestion – intensified after Independence. In the words of Patrick Sammon, a former civil servant in the Commission, 'The Land Commission was at the centre of this great bloodless revolution',[4] in the course of which around fifteen million acres out of a total of seventeen million acres in the country were transferred from landlords to tenants between 1870 and 1965. The Land Commission was absorbed into the Department of Agriculture in 1978.

Land law was known for its complexity. In a famous comment on the 1881 Act, the Bishop of Limerick wrote to Archbishop Walsh of Dublin, 'since the Apocalypse was written, nothing so abstruse has appeared'. Walsh, who supported the tenants in their struggle, wrote *A Plain Exposition of the Land Act of 1881* (1881). The days of the landlords were numbered, as Standish O'Grady remarked on their behalf: 'The stone which Michael Davitt set rolling now rolls irrecoverably to the abyss.'

A Land Act known as the Birrell Act, after the Chief Secretary Augustine Birrell, was in preparation when Duff joined the Land Commission. The way the land purchase scheme operated was that the government gave landlords Land Bonds plus a cash bonus and financed these transactions by collecting annuities from the tenant purchasers. It was the work of the collection department to which Duff was assigned, to calculate the annuities year by year and to collect the amount due. He has given his impression of his initial encounter with one of the Commissioners: 'I waited on Commissioner Wrench – he looked a pure Cromwellian. He showed what he thought of me and my new consortees.'[5]

A Belfast man, Jack O'Callaghan, who had passed the same examination as Duff, was requisitioned with him to work in the collections department under Mr Crosbie.[6] Duff and O'Callaghan worked as a team until after a short time O'Callaghan contracted tuberculosis. When the method of assessment was explained to Duff and his colleague, neither of them could understand the methodology, so Duff got down to serious study and, never fond of mathematics at school, resolutely set about grasping all the details of the scheme. He developed a novel methodology for the calculation of annuities, sinking fund and interest, which resulted in substantial economies in the hours required for the necessary calculations and attracted the attention of his superiors who, convinced of the value of the method, approached W. G. Turpin in the National Debt Office. Turpin suggested that even further economy could be effected 'by the use of decimals and logarithms in working out the details of the calculations'. On 13 December 1910 Crosbie wrote to J. C. Warman in the Exchequer and Audit Department in London, submitting details of Duff's methodology and enclosing a table illustrating the method. On 15 December Warman replied with enthusiasm, saying that the proposal 'seems to be a very valuable production and Mr. Duff is to be congratulated upon it'.[7] Turpin wrote suggesting a face-to-face meeting of relevant officials. Mr Beard of the Irish Land Commission replied to Turpin, expressing agreement with him 'that the mode of working the calculations could best be decided by an interview with our representative, and we propose sending over Mr. Duff, as you suggest, provided we are given 24 hours' notice'. He said that 'Mr. Duff is quite a junior Second Division Clerk, but he is a man of very considerable ability, and it was he who originated the new method of calculation, which Mr. Crosbie submitted to you.'[8]

The result of these exchanges was that Duff was received at the National Debt Office in London on 2 February 1911 by W. G. Turpin, the Comptroller General, and Mr Ansell, who had charge of the Land Acts Branch. Duff spent three days explaining his methodology and answering questions. Crosbie later sent a memorandum to Beard suggesting an increase in salary for Duff. On 30 May 1911 Beard, in his reply to Crosbie, said that he had been impressed by Crosbie's 'high recommendation' of Duff and was satisfied 'that his good work in connection with the revised method of calculating revisions of annuities deserves some recognition'. However, Beard pointed out that because of Duff's comparatively short service, he was not yet qualified to receive any reward in the shape of an additional increment. Beard continued:

I understood from Mr. Duff some time ago that he would prefer to wait and take his chance of obtaining some permanent advancement rather than to have his case put forward now for a special Bonus which I was otherwise prepared to recommend; and that being so, I shall place on record the fact of Mr. Duff's good service so that his case can be considered with similar cases when the time is ripe.[9]

Beard asked Crosbie to let Duff see the memo and then to return it to him.

The year in which Duff travelled to London to visit the National Debt Office was the year after he had celebrated his twenty-first birthday, and it was a census year. The Duff household returns reveal that on the night of the census in 1911 eight persons were residing at 55 St Patrick's Road: John Duff (48), described as a retired civil servant; Susan Duff (47) – wife; Francis Michael (21) – civil servant Land Commission; Isabel Maud (19) – no occupation listed; John Edwin (16) – scholar; Sarah Geraldine (13) – scholar; Alice Mary (8) – scholar; and Kathleen Mary Tyrell (20) – general domestic servant. The breadwinner in the household and mainstay of the family was Frank Duff, because his father's pension was modest. Isabel was a semi-invalid and the other siblings were attending fee-paying schools. Duff had many family calls on his income, which explains why his rank and salary in the civil service was of such importance to him. In the phase of his life when he battled to carve out a career, there was one determining influence – that of his mother. He cared deeply for her and was rigorous in what he understood as filial duty.

A turning point occurred in Duff's life when Jack O'Callaghan, on his return to work following illness, recruited him into the St Vincent de Paul Society (SVP). Others had earlier proposed membership, but Duff had declined. Then, as he explains, O'Callaghan 'succeeded where others had not succeeded, and that was because I liked him so much. In other words the motives were not one hundred per cent pure, but the normal natural motives God uses.'[10] One of Duff's friends in the Society was Diarmuid Ó hEigeartaigh, whom he succeeded as Secretary of the SVP Conference of Our Lady of Mount Carmel. Ó hEigeartaigh was also a colleague in the civil service and it was through him that Duff attended Sinn Féin lectures in the premises of Conradh na Gaeilge (The Gaelic League) in Harcourt Street,[11] where 'Arthur Griffith was always present, often presided, but was not always the main speaker'. Griffith's capacity for debate made a lasting impression on Duff, who remarked to both Enda Dunleavy and Fr Herman, 'When Arthur Griffith had spoken, there was nothing left to be said.' At the time, Ó hEigeartaigh talked openly of rebellion to Duff, but Duff did not take him seriously, thinking that it was 'all moonshine'.[12] When the executions of the 1916 leaders took place, Duff's reaction was one of revulsion, remarking that Carson, Craigavon and F. E. Smith had rebelled, but 'they had been promoted' for so doing.[13] Fr Tom O'Flynn made the following observation regarding Duff and Ó hEigeartaigh:

> When Diarmuid O'Hegarty, one of Collins' chief aides, was a member of the same Conference of the St. Vincent De Paul Society they often walked home after the meeting together. Diarmuid was up to his ears in the movement at the time but oddly enough never attempted to recruit Frank. This tells something about both men. O'Hegarty's ability was such that he later became Secretary to the government and was generally regarded as its éminence grise. Shrewd and a rock of good sense, he had probably sized up his companion and felt that Frank's service to Ireland and humanity lay along a different path from his own.[14]

Regarding his lack of active involvement in any political movement, Duff simply records, 'I never had the time to take any active part in politics.' His family had been followers of John Redmond, the Nationalist MP, and of the Irish Parliamentary Party that Redmond led. Duff favoured a non-violent approach, as evidenced by a certain distaste for statues of men with guns which sprang up around the country a few decades after the civil war.[15] Fr Herman Nolan, whose father, Jack Nolan, was a Republican arrested during the War of Independence, said that a number of these limestone statues were the work of Leo Broe, a craftsman from Harold's Cross in Dublin. A good example of Broe's work is to be found at the Royal Canal Bank in Phibsborough in the locality where Duff was born. When, in the course of a cycling trip, Nolan pointed out one of the statues to him, Duff merely nodded. But it is worth noting that Duff included in the Legion of Mary *Handbook* an illustrated version of the poem 'I See His Blood upon the Rose' by Joseph Mary Plunkett. Plunkett, son of George Noble Plunkett, Curator of the National Museum, was executed for his part in the Rising of 1916. Referring later to his selection in the civil service to work for Patrick Hogan in January 1922, Duff said that he had never sought the position and 'had no political claim'.[16]

But it was not all work and no relaxation during Duff's Land Commission years of 1908–22, when, despite responsibility as effective breadwinner in his family, he enjoyed social and sporting activities, including swimming, tennis, cycling and athletics.[17] He had a keen competitive side, which led him to have an operation to remove the turbinate bones from his nose. The object was to facilitate a rapid intake of air and improve his athletic performance.[18] In November 1911 he participated in the Donore Harriers' Invitation Race. He finished respectably in the middle of a field of over sixty runners.[19] The following year he was runner-up in the men's singles tennis finals at Drumcondra, one of two tennis clubs to which he belonged – the other was Kenilworth on the south side of the city. According to a newspaper report of the annual 'At Home' of the Drumcondra club, the men's five-set final was well contested, and though only extending to three sets, was a closer struggle than the score suggested. 'F. M. Duff put up a very stiff fight against J. R. Ennis, and with his present rate of improvement it will not surprise many to see the championship come his way very soon.'[20]

On Sunday 31 May 1914 he completed a 155-mile cycle trip in a day. Following early Mass in Whitefriar Street Church, he set out from Drumcondra at 8am and headed for Drogheda, then on to Ardee and Dundalk. He sent postcards to at least four colleagues in the Land Commission en route. The cards which survive are written to A. G. Lewis, Stephen Murphy, S. W. Waters and A. F. Hinton. As he departed Ardee for Dundalk, Duff wrote a card to A. F. Hinton at one o'clock saying that he had had 'a shocking time so far. Rained half the way and blew a gale in my teeth. Had to bend double on the bicycle the whole way.' On the return journey he went through Ardee to Kells and Athboy. From Athboy at 6.30pm he wrote to S. W. Waters, '109 miles. Getting a little tired but expect to knock off another 40 before bedtime. Wind with me from this out.'[21] He passed the family homestead at Freffans outside Trim and went on to Maynooth, Leixlip and back to Dublin, where he arrived at 11.20pm.

Duff's interests included the occasional flutter on a horse. Fr O' Flynn recounted his surprise at Duff's reaction when, driving through Dublin with him in the 1960s, they passed a number of bookmakers' shops:

> Thinking, I suppose, to hear him comment on the evils of excessive gambling, I remarked on the number of bookmakers' shops that we were passing. He went on to talk about backing horses and his thesis was that it was ultimately impossible for anybody betting regularly to end up with a profit. To my surprise he told me that in his early years in the Civil Service he and a number of colleagues had some 'contact' in one of the big stables in England. But, as he put it himself, even with first-hand information they could only break even.[22]

Until his hearing began to fail in his twenties, resulting, it was thought, from the incident at school when a cricket ball had struck him behind the ear, Duff enjoyed visits to the theatre. One show he saw was *The Vagabond King* in the Gaiety.[23] In the closing decade of his life he recalled when he had been told by 'the leading specialist in Dublin' that he was on the way to total deafness. But half a century later he was 'getting on all right, and only using the hearing aid at meetings.'[24] He enjoyed the cinema and often accompanied his mother on visits, usually on Saturday afternoons.[25] Lily Hudson, who knew Duff before he founded the Legion of Mary, recalled how she and her husband met him and his mother one afternoon in O'Connell Street. Duff told them, 'I'm taking my mother to see *The Gay Divorcée* in the Savoy cinema.'[26] He enjoyed the Jeanette MacDonald–Nelson Eddy films and also Laurel and Hardy, once remarking that it was enough for him to hear the theme music of the latter to start laughing. He may also have followed his mother's taste in film when he saw a number of films of 'Latin lover' Rudolph Valentino and he sometimes used the term 'Valentino' when describing a man with allure.

Notes to Chapter 3

1. Aherne interview.
2. Tony Farmar, *Ordinary Lives*. Dublin: Gill and Macmillan, 1991, p. 5.
3. Paperwork regarding Duff's application was pointed out to me by Fr Eamonn McCarthy in the Duff archive.
4. Patrick J. Sammon, *In the Land Commission*. Dublin: Ashfield Press, 1997, p. xi.
5. Duff to Dunleavy, 6 September 1979. Right Hon. Frederick Sterling Wrench, PC, was one the Estates Commissioners in the Irish Land Commission. He was brother-in-law of Sir Henry Bellingham.
6. Aherne interview.
7. Warman to Crosbie, 15 December 1910, Land Commission copy, Duff papers, LOMA.
8. Beard to Turpin, Land Commission copy, Duff papers, LOMA.
9. Beard to Crosbie, Memo, 30 May 1911, Land Commission copy, Duff papers, LOMA.
10. Aherne interview.
11. Enda Dunleavy, 'Assessment of his [Duff's] Work as a Civil Servant', Frank Duff Civil Service (FDCS) Memos, no. 59, LOMA; author's interview with Dunleavy, 4 April 2008.
12. Phrase used by Duff in conversation with Bernard McGuckian, SJ; author's interview with McGuckian, 27 November 2009.
13. Enda Dunleavy noted these comments following a conversation with Duff while on a cycling trip in Connemara on 6 September 1979; author's interview with Dunleavy, 4 April 2008.
14. Thomas O'Flynn, *Frank Duff as I Knew Him*. Dublin: Praedicanda, 1981, p. 56.
15. Author's interview, Fr Herman, 23 November 2007.
16. Draft letter to Sir Joseph Glynn, 1924: FDCS Memos, No. 56.
17. Duff to Casey, 25 July 1972.
18. Memo from Dr Michael McGuinness, 7 November 2008. McGuinness expressed doubts as to the value of the operation and thinks that it may have left Duff prone to ear infections in the days before antibiotics.
19. Newspaper cutting, 11 November 1911. Dunleavy collection.
20. Newspaper cutting, 1912. Dunleavy collection.
21. Photocopy of postcards. Dunleavy collection.
22. O'Flynn, *Frank Duff*, p. 17.
23. Duff to Shaw, 30 November 1929, Ms 31670/2, NLI.
24. Duff to Casey, 25 July 1975.
25. Ó Broin, *Frank* Duff, p. 11.
26. Phyllis McGuinness, 'They Knew Frank Duff in 1916,' *Maria Legionis*, 2/1989, p. 11.

CHAPTER 4

Joseph Gabbett

'Anything that Gabbett would do had to be viewed seriously. He talked away and his thoughts were profound. But Gabbett could only write his name.'

CHARLES T. MOSS (ED.), *FRANK DUFF*

If Edwardian Dublin in the twilight years of the Long Peace before the Great War held many attractions for a talented young man, Dublin was also a city that reeked of poverty; the city of O'Casey's slums and Larkin's 'Lock-Out'. The 'Lock-Out', which lasted from August 1913 to January 1914, was an acrimonious industrial dispute ultimately won by the employers, led by William Martin Murphy. Duff depicted Dublin, apart from the city centre and the main streets, as 'one gigantic tenement district'. In 1926 there were 27,000 Dublin households, comprising 140,000 persons, who lived in one room. Of these, 4,000 of the households, comprising a total of 28,000 persons, were households with six or more persons:[1]

> What were the tenements like? ... The houses would be large – four and five storeys. On every landing there would be two rooms, and those rooms had their specific name. On the ground floor you'd have the front parlour and the back parlour. The next floor would be the front drawing room and the back drawing room. The next would be the two-pair-front and the two-pair-back, and the next would be the top-front and the top-back. Some houses had a return building to them and that meant several more rooms, and every room housed a family.[2]

A big problem at the time was the level of drinking, aggravated by the prevailing custom of paying wages in a public house, which meant that some men would start drinking before they got home to their wives with their meagre pay packets. Labour leader Jim Larkin strongly opposed the payment of wages in pubs and eventually the practice was discontinued. Next to the pub, the pawn shop featured prominently in daily life, with the latter often filling the gap until the next week's wages were paid. A large pool of unemployed ensured that wages remained low. When Frank joined the St Vincent de Paul Society in October 1913, the wage of a builder's labourer was 18s/3d a week, 'or rather it was 17s/9d a week and the Larkin strike of that time got 6d a week added on'. The wages of a tradesman – carpenter, plumber or painter – were 30s/- a week. Prices were accordingly low:

For the best meat obtainable, you couldn't pay any more than 8d a pound. Second rate meat … was 6d a pound. And what they called 'pieces' – that would be cut-off ends to bring a piece within weight, you know, which of course would be just as good as the original thing, but wouldn't have the appearance that certain people would want – that was 4d a pound. That is what the poorer people had if they had the money for meat … . And one thing that people would find very hard to believe, but for which I vouch, is matches. There was a match made by Bryant and May and called the 'Puck match' – it was identical in size with the older Friendly – at a penny for a dozen boxes. That's an old penny, remember. Now that, you see, enabled men's wages to support them. A penny was a sum of money: you could buy a big bag of sweets for a penny.[3]

Duff described himself as a 'very casual Catholic indeed' until he joined the St Vincent de Paul Society. 'I wouldn't miss Mass, but that's all you could say, though, about it. If anybody asked me if I had devotion for the Blessed Virgin, I would have said in those days "Yes." But I knew nothing about her and I couldn't answer a question. I couldn't have answered a question as to why you pray to her.'[4]

On 22 October 1913, at the height of the 'Lock-Out', Duff first attended a meeting of Our Lady of Mount Carmel Conference of the SVP attached to the Carmelite Church in Whitefriar Street in Dublin. The president of the Conference was John T. Lennon, who later became Secretary of the Revenue Commissioners, and the secretary was Diarmuid Ó hEigeartaigh. In the same year Duff was enrolled in the Brown Scapular Confraternity, an association of those who seek to develop Christian lives by drawing on Carmelite spirituality, in Whitefriar Street. The roots of the Brown Scapular devotion go back to the eighth century BC, when the prophet Elias prayed on Mount Carmel in Palestine. León Ó Broin's father was secretary of the Confraternity and Duff recalls that it was there in 1914 'that I met León Ó Broin as a boy of about eleven, then sporting the *fáinne*', an emblem in the shape of a ring which indicated that the wearer was able to speak Irish.[5] In later years Duff told the Carmelite priest Fr Mark Horan, who repeated the fact to John Gavin, a civil servant and legionary who became president of the Legion of Mary, that his first apostolic work was promoting the Brown Scapular.[6]

From the time he became a member of the SVP, Duff's focus in life shifted as his religious commitment began to grow. During Advent in 1913 he made his first enclosed retreat in Milltown Park. Sixty years later, he recalled the event in a letter to his friend, the Jesuit priest Tom Counihan:

Your statement that Milltown Park has ended its career as a Retreat House presents a shock to me. In the Advent of 1913 I made my first Retreat there, and subsequently attended a large number given by our venerated Father Fegan. No word that he spoke ever slipped out of my memory … . After my first Retreat I made myself responsible for filling a couple every year.[7]

Early in 1914 the Whitefriar Street Conference of SVP received a letter from Tom McCabe, a member of the Society in another Conference, regarding proselytizing, which was being carried out at a place known as 6½ Whitefriar Street. The venue had probably been in operation since the minor famine of 1878, when clients were offered various inducements, including meals and accommodation in hostels, in return for taking instruction in the Protestant faith and attendance at services – a form of buying conversions. According to Meath farmer Joe Ward, 'souperism' was particularly prevalent in Mayo, where soup kitchens were set up by evangelical Protestant groups:

> The proselytisers – 'the soupers' – used to boil this yellow meal and dish it out to the poverty-stricken people. It certainly kept them alive for some time, although it was a despicable type of thing to do, because people had to renounce their Catholic religion and become nominal Protestants in order to receive the food.[8]

Historian Lindsey Earner-Byrne states that 'the belief that Protestant or "non-sectarian" charities were only interested in helping Catholics in order to convert them was a potent motivation for the creation of equivalent Catholic charities'.[9] Earner-Byrne points to several letters in the 'Charity Case Boxes' in Archbishop Byrne's papers in which people wrote to the archbishop seeking help and referring to neighbours as 'soupers', meaning that they had accepted charity in return for converting to Protestantism.[10] Among those concerned about proselytism in Dublin were Margaret Pearse, sister of Patrick Pearse, and Lillie Connolly, wife of James Connolly and herself a convert to Catholicism, who both saw the injustice of making the necessities of life conditional on changing faith. Both women belonged to St Joseph's Guild of Rescue, which concerned itself with children of poor unmarried Catholic mothers who might be prevailed upon to hand their children over for adoption by Protestant societies. When Duff started making an annual pilgrimage to Lough Derg, Mrs Connolly was among the group that went with him on a number of occasions. Among Duff's books is a copy of *Labour in Ireland* by James Connolly, which Lillie Connolly gave him.

Duff, whose father was a close friend of and once had been a civil service colleague of Tom McCabe, volunteered to go to Whitefriar Street on the following Sunday, together with John Lennon, the conference president, to find out what precisely was happening. He arrived on a cold Sunday morning and watched as the frequenters of the place began to arrive: 'They were the most awful-looking crowd of poor creatures that could be thought of. Those were the days of alarming poverty and these were the ultimate in the way of misery.'[11] In the course of the visit, Duff was approached by a woman who told him that if he was interested in what was happening he should talk to Mr Gabbett, indicating a tall man who was standing nearby. Gabbett, a Limerick man, was by trade a maker of shoes and boots; in particular he crafted boots for army officers and had served twenty-one years in the army in India. He would have a singular and profound influence on Duff, who would learn from him what it meant to be apostolic. He told Duff that he was planning to open an institution in opposition to the proselytizing one and had rented stables in Cheater's Lane for the purpose. As a result of Duff's encounter with Gabbett, the cooperation of the St Vincent de Paul Brothers, as the members were called, was enlisted. The premises Gabbett had obtained were known as Number Nine Cheater's Lane, a corruption of the word 'Chaytor'. Ó Broin recalls the premises as a stable:

> I saw the stable being cleaned out on a Saturday night, and, early on the Sunday morning, tea being brewed in a copper urn and piles of bread cut and buttered. This was intended for poor dishevelled creatures who were to be diverted from 6½ Whitefriar Street, a proselytising establishment, to a place where, without detriment to their religion, they could have a mug of hot tea to help them shake off the effects of a night spent in an open doorway or a tenement lobby.[12]

Gabbett already had a few men helping him with the work of making the tea and 'a whole bevy of girls, a lot of them out of Jacob's factory', the well-known biscuit factory located in Bishop Street, who used to collect a penny a week for him from their fellow workers to help maintain the work. He called his work 'The Guild of the Immaculate Conception'.

After a while it was not possible for John Lennon to continue the work, but Duff and Gabbett continued together, sweeping and cleaning the venue on a Saturday night and serving breakfast to the men the next morning. Duff and Gabbett became friendly and Duff used to visit him in his workshop, often at around ten o'clock at night when Gabbett would talk while he was working, 'hand-stitching, polishing and smoothing'. He would talk away about God and Mary while Duff would 'sit there drinking it in. I was truly a disciple at his feet and he certainly fired me with the whole business.' Gabbett could read, but could write only his name. Yet Duff was happy to be apprenticed to him in the business of apostleship. In one phrase Duff describes himself as Gabbett's 'sort of lieutenant'.[13] Gabbett was a recovering alcoholic who had joined the Pioneer Total Abstinence Association, founded in Dublin by the Jesuit priest Fr James Cullen in 1898. It was Gabbett who brought Duff, later described by the historian of the Pioneers as 'The public figure most associated with the Pioneers,' into the Association.[14] Duff said that it was Gabbett's 'sporting of the pin [the Pioneer emblem] that first concentrated my own thoughts on the Pioneer Association'.[15] 'Anything that Gabbett would do had to be viewed seriously. He talked away and his thoughts were profound.'[16] Duff described how, following an evening of visitation of homes as members of the SVP, he and his co-worker sometimes 'went off to a pub. I took I think Devonshire cider which was my drink at the time: before the days when I became a Pioneer.'[17] On holiday in Paris with his mother and sister, Duff partook of a bottle of wine with his lunch. The result was that he became drowsy, fell asleep on a bench and missed out on a visit to the Louvre.[18]

The element of personal influence which would become a central feature of the Legion of Mary was evident in the relationship between Gabbett and Duff. Duff explains:

> I was incredibly captivated by Gabbett, because I had never met anybody like him. Now you must understand at that time I was really tremendously casual about my religion. I had been inveigled into the Vincent de Paul Society. I had become a good member immediately: that is, I saw the sense of all that and I began to give more and more of my time to it. I was appointed secretary to the Conference at my third meeting, but I hadn't seen Catholicism of Gabbett's type before.[19]

In addition to his regular Vincent de Paul visitation, Duff undertook additional visitation in the tenements on his own in the course of many evenings after work. Gabbett and Duff, together with some helpers, began to develop other activities in the coach house in Cheater's Lane, including instructing children about the sacraments. Duff ran a class for boys and men, while some women helpers gave classes to girls. Around this time Gabbett purchased a statue of Our Lady of the Immaculate Conception with a penny subscription from girls who were customers in his shoemaker's shop. He set up an altar with the statue in the room where they conducted Catechism classes. In due course the statue would be used at the first Legion of Mary meeting and is now in a special case in the headquarters of the Legion. Among Gabbett's young women supporters were some who would be among the first members of the Legion.

Gabbett led Frank into another work – the calling on soldiers who were suffering from venereal diseases. One day after the outbreak of war in 1914 when Gabbett was in his workshop, a man named Pope came in to see him. Pope was a member of the Church of England (the expression Church of Ireland was not used) and lay assistant to the chaplain in Portobello Barracks. At the time there were two battalions of the Lancashire Fusiliers in the barracks, amounting to two thousand men. Since Lancashire includes the city of Liverpool, which has a large Catholic population, there were many Catholics in Portobello. At the time there was an isolated venereal hospital at the Barracks with about two hundred men. According to Duff's own account, the men were divided as follows: 'one-third C of E (Church of England); one-third RC (Roman Catholic) and one-third NC (Non-conformist)'.[20] The Church of England soldiers had a chaplain who conducted services on a Sunday; the Non-conformists also had a chaplain; and while the Catholics had a chaplain, Fr O' Loughlin from the nearby Rathmines parish, his parochial duties were so demanding that he could do little for the men.

The proselytizing element among the Non-conformists started working among the Roman Catholics, who were aggrieved and receptive enough because of what they perceived as neglect by their own pastors. However, Pope viewed the manoeuvres of the Non-conformists with dissatisfaction, and hearing of Gabbett and his activities sought him out and told him of the position in the hospital. Gabbett got up at once from what he called his 'state of work', put on his coat and went to the barracks. In his capacity as an old soldier, Gabbett gained access, including to the venereal wards. He found great resentment among the men who had not seen a representative of their religion since the time they had been admitted to the hospital. Gabbett reported back to Fr O'Loughlin, who 'with great alacrity, formally appointed Gabbett as his lay assistant, and that entitled Gabbett to wear a uniform'. The uniform looked like an officer's uniform, except there was a Maltese Cross on the hat. Gabbett approached the commanding officer and obtained permission to hold a Sunday Service at the hospital. His next step was to bring a small statue of the Immaculate Conception into the barracks and to announce that a Roman Catholic service would take place at 10 o'clock on the following Sunday morning. On that Sunday, Gabbett, having placed the statue on the mantelpiece in the room allocated to him, put a lighted candle at each side of it. He then started a hymn followed by the Rosary, after which he gave a discourse and concluded with another hymn. Duff remarked that 'A feature of the proceedings was Gabbett's discourse: rough, unpolished but Oh! so effective. He possessed the secret of successful preaching: patent sincerity, and being completely understood.' Looking back, Duff marvelled at Gabbett's enterprise: 'He was fearless, he was resourceful. He had a magic gift of handling people. His sincerity was such that he would give faith to a stick.'[21] On the first occasion, about twenty men attended Gabbett's service. By degrees, the number rose to around seventy. Duff described further developments, which included a striking element of ecumenical co-operation between the Church of England and Roman Catholics. Fr O'Loughlin started going to Portobello on the eve of the First Friday to hear confessions in the hospital, and on the First Friday he gave Holy Communion:

That was a great step forward and then after that a tremendous step took place. They brought over a wooden chapel from the Wellington Barracks and they fitted this up in the hospital. By agreement between Fr. O'Loughlin and the Rev. Mr. Lambe, who was the Protestant chaplain at the time, they furnished it. It was an absolute imitation of a Catholic chapel. Fr. O'Loughlin supplied the Stations of the Cross. Reverend Lambe sent a carpenter into St. Mary's Church in Rathmines to have a good look at the altar and imitate it, and there was an imitation tabernacle on the altar. The Protestant rubrics do not permit a crucifix, so therefore there was a picture of the Crucifixion hung on the wall behind it and on one side of the altar one of the Madonna pictures and on the other a picture of 'Our Lord the Light of the World' – you know Holman Hunt's picture?[22]

Gabbett, having begun with the men in the hospital, gradually extended his work to the general barracks. The departure of many men to the trenches was imminent. Gabbett and Duff approached the Regimental Sergeant Major, Henry Baxter, a convert to Catholicism. Duff remarks, 'Baxter, being a convert, had none of the servility that one of our own people might have had in such circumstances and be afraid to do things. Baxter was not afraid.' He facilitated and encouraged what Gabbett and Duff were doing. They extended their Sunday services to all the men who wished to attend, and Pope, who had been the catalyst for the work, played the organ in an example of ecumenical co-operation. Following Gabbett's abrupt departure in 1916 to rejoin the army, Duff continued the Sunday services until some time in 1918 when the hospital inmates were transferred to Spike Island in County Cork and given their own chaplain. According to Duff, 'The Sunday before they went, every Catholic in the place went to the sacraments … . Then they were gone and I was out of a job.'[23]

The Portobello experience was noteworthy in a number of respects. It began as a result of a principled approach to Gabbett by a member of the Church of England and its unfolding provided an epiphany to Duff on the role of the ordinary Catholic lay person in the apostolate. Gabbett persisted with his various works until Easter 1916. Outraged by the Rising, which he regarded as shocking at a time when England was at war, he rejoined the British army, although he was beyond the age for active service. Duff observes that 'The British army had put an extraordinary mark upon its people. Gabbett was no exception to that, and he saw red at the rebellion.' Gabbett was sent to Aldershot, where he was appointed master bootmaker. He shut down Cheater's Lane abruptly, leaving behind his various items of equipment and statues, including those of the Immaculate Conception and of St Patrick, to Duff, who moved them to Myra House in Francis Street.

With the closure of the Cheater's Lane premises, those who had availed themselves of Gabbett's breakfast began to move back to the proselytizing premises at Whitefriar Street. Looking on in dismay, Duff said to himself, 'Well now, I have to tackle that. Of course, I had got tremendous confidence from Gabbett.' Initially, Duff commenced a picket on the Whitefriar Street premises, walking up and down outside, saying the Rosary, but after a short while, because of the shocking poverty that then existed, he realized that you could not say to a man 'Now, don't go in there.' There was no state support at a time when, according to Duff, some men were forced to live 'like wolves.' There was a threepenny breakfast run in Meath Street by Fr Alphonsus Ryan, and Duff began to give the men the price of the breakfast out of his own pocket. As the numbers increased, the expenditure increased, and Duff enlisted the help of a group from the SVP, including John Lennon, Tom Fallon and Frank

Sweeney. The SVP came in with financial support, the picketing continued and eventually the Whitefriar Street premises closed. The remaining attendees moved to the Metropolitan Hall in Lower Abbey Street, which operated on the same basis of old-styled 'souperism'. That institution was picketed and eventually ceased such activities. The very first occasion on which Duff had picketed the Whitefriar Street premises had almost been his last. He had been approached by a very drunken sailor who pulled a knife on him: 'I was so taken off my guard, so surprised, that I didn't make a move. Only that he was drunk and that he missed his aim – it wasn't my doing, but he just missed his aim because he was so drunk – I think he'd have driven that [knife] into me.'[24]

Around this time Duff started daily recitation of the Rosary and during Lent 1914 he commenced daily Mass attendance, a practice he maintained throughout his life. For a number of years he attended two Masses daily.[25] According to Fr Bradshaw, the amount of time Duff spent at prayer 'was truly astonishing'.[26] His day would start with 7am Mass in the Redemptoristine Convent in Drumcondra. Sometimes he would attend 7.15am Mass in St Francis Xavier's in Upper Gardiner Street on his way to work.

In August 1915, he undertook the first of forty-nine pilgrimages to Lough Derg. On the second occasion in 1916 the pilgrims offered a 'station' involving a number of prayers for Roger Casement, who was shortly to be hanged.[27] Some years, when the weather was cold at Lough Derg, Duff wore the army coat of his brother John from the Great War. His final pilgrimage was in 1963 when he was seventy-four. He did not find Lough Derg easy, as his letter to Fr Agius in 1946 attests: 'I am off to Lough Derg on Sunday and am looking forward to the experience with no manner of pleasure. It is my thirty-second time there, and with each new time it has acquired some additional mental pangs.'[28] 'About 1915' he met and went to confession for the first time to Fr Michael Browne, SJ, at St Francis Xavier's. From then until 1922, when Browne moved from Gardiner Street to Rathfarnham Castle, Duff 'ordinarily went to confession to no other priest'.[29] From 1922, Duff attended confession at St Peter's Church, Phibsborough, but continued to consult Fr Browne until the latter's death in 1933. In Browne he found a man with 'deep devotion to the Blessed Virgin', which was a great help to him at a time when he 'was trying to probe my way in that direction'. He also found that Browne was a man steeped in the writings of John Henry Newman.[30]

Duff began to weave prayer into his working day, adopting the habit of saying a prayer every time he wrote a date. Even before he discovered Louis Marie de Montfort's little book *True Devotion to the Blessed Virgin*, which brought into focus the role of Mary, his habit was to ask the saint whose feast day it was to pray to Mary for him.[31] He also began to read a number of continental writers on the faith, including de Jaegher, SJ, de La Taille, SJ, and Vonier, OSB. De La Taille's writings on the Mass made a particular impression on Duff.[32] Attracted to French writers perhaps because of his education at Blackrock College by a French Order of Priests, in 1926 he wrote in French seeking the work of P. J. B. Terrein, SJ, on The Blessed Virgin.[33] When he worked in the Department of Finance in Upper Merrion Street, Ó Broin recounts:

> Frank's unchanging practice was to go to the Marie Réparatrice convent at lunch-time and at no other time. I got to know the whole operation very well. It began with a brisk march along the corridor swinging a towel, followed by a noisy scrubbing of face and hands, then off on his bike along Merrion Square, and back to his room by the same route within the hour. He would then plug in an electric kettle for a cup of tea, pick a biscuit or two from a box he kept in a bottom drawer of his desk and almost simultaneously dig into a file.[34]

It was in the Marie Réparatrice chapel that Duff first met Mrs Elizabeth Kirwan, a sister of Fr O'Loughlin and later the first president of the Legion of Mary. Mrs Kirwan had been born in Dunedin in New Zealand in 1857. Her father, a barrister, died twelve years later, leaving a widow and three young children. The family moved to Ireland, where Elizabeth trained as nurse. For many years 'religion meant nothing to her (as she declared); she neglected it, she despised it'.[35] Then 'as the phrase goes, she married beneath her'.[36] John Kirwan was a lamplighter with Dublin Corporation. Through his influence, Elizabeth was attracted back to religion. In 1917 she was living in a small flat at 8a Dean Swift Square, off Francis Street, but she worked at the Holles Row dinner centre off Merrion Square. She used to visit Marie Réparatrice convent at lunchtime and it was there that she met Duff. Duff invited her to undertake the running of a children's library in Myra House under the auspices of the SVP. Elizabeth Kirwan also became president of the Pioneer Total Abstinence Association branch in Myra House.

In November 1917 Duff started a League of Daily Mass and began to enlist others who would undertake daily Mass attendance. There is in the Legion archives a bound volume containing the names of over a thousand persons enrolled in the League; the majority of names are in Duff's handwriting. In December 1917, under the guidance of Fr Michael Browne, he began to recite the Divine Office and continued to recite it daily in Latin until the end of his life. He learned to appreciate the Psalms and the Bible readings and said that 'I have looked on the Divine Office as pure communication with God.'[37] At first he found it tiring and time-consuming but with practice he could complete the Office without haste in about one and a half hours. Fr Michael O'Carroll once heard Duff say that he sometimes completed the breviary at four o'clock in the morning when he was 'crazy with fatigue'.[38] He never travelled anywhere without his breviary and would recommend its recitation, or a substantial portion of it, to legionaries.

Notes to Chapter 4

1. Census of Population 1961, vol. VI: *Housing and Social Amenities*, Table 6.
2. Aherne interview.
3. ibid.
4. ibid.
5. Talk on Joseph Gabbett by Frank Duff, tape 35, LOMA.
6. Interview with John Gavin, 17 February 1986.
7. Duff to Counihan, 9 September 1974. Non-residential day retreats continue to be held at Milltown.
8. Ciaran Buckley and Chris Ward, *Strong Farmer: The Memoirs of Joe Ward*, Dublin: Liberties Press, 2007, p. 27.
9. Lindsey Earner-Byrne, *Mother and Child: Maternity and Child Welfare in Dublin, 1922–60*. Manchester: Manchester University Press, 2007, p.75.
10. ibid., p. 87, note 125.
11. Mgr Charles T. Moss (ed.), *Frank Duff: A Living Autobiography*. Dublin, Philadelphia, Manila: *Maria Legionis*, 1983, p. 20.
12. Ó Broin, *Frank Duff*, p. 1.
13. Gabbett and McNally, tape 103, LOMA.
14. Diarmaid Ferriter, *A Nation of Extremes*. Dublin: Irish Academic Press, 1999, p. 129.
15. Talk on Joseph Gabbett by Frank Duff, tape 35, LOMA.
16. Moss (ed.), *Frank Duff*, p. 22.
17. 'Gabbett and McNally', ibid.
18. Duff told this story to Bernard McGuckian, S J. Interview with McGuckian, 27 November 2009.
19. 'Gabbett and McNally', as recounted by Duff to Fr Bradshaw in Mount Melleray, tape 103, LOMA.
20. 'Gabbett and McNally' as told by Duff to Fr Bradshaw, tape 103, LOMA. 'Non-conformist' was a term used for those who did not comply with the Act of Uniformity (1662) in England. Non-conformists include Presbyterians, Baptists and Quakers.
21. Talk on Joseph Gabbett by Duff, tape 35, LOMA.
22. 'Gabbett and McNally'.
23. ibid.
24. ibid.
25. Fred A. Fulton, 'Frank Duff: Legionary Extraordinary', *The Marianist*, November 1959.
26. Bradshaw, *Frank Duff*, p. 45.
27. McGuinness, 'They Knew Frank Duff', p. 11.
28. Duff to Fr Agius, 3 August 1946.
29. Thomas Hurley, SJ, *Father Michael Browne, S. J., (1853–1933): A Man who took Christ at His Word*. Dublin: Clonmore and Reynolds, 1949, pp. 195–97.
30. ibid. pp. 117, 197.
31. Aherne interview.
32. Bradshaw, *Frank* Duff, p. 133.
33. Duff to 'Monsieur', 1 July 1926.
34. Ó Broin, *Frank Duff*, p. 45.
35. Frank Duff, 'Elizabeth Mary Kirwan: Death of Legion's First President', *Maria Legionis*, Christmas 1940, p. 4.
36. ibid.
37. Bradshaw, *Frank Duff*, p. 44.
38. O'Carroll, *A Priest in Changing Times*, p. 138.

CHAPTER 5

Myra House and De Montfort

'You were discussing De Montfort's *True Devotion*, a copy of which had recently been given to you by Mr. Lalor. Your description was vivid and stuck in my mind… . It was definitely that book which threw my life into the Marian channels which it has ever since followed.'

DUFF TO VINCENT KELLY, 13 OCTOBER 1973

In 1915 representatives of the SVP Conference of St Nicholas of Myra in Francis Street asked Duff to take over the presidency of that conference, which was alleged to be in a state of disorder and needing new members. Its president was Pat Gorevan of the well-known Dublin drapery firm in Camden Street. Duff, while retaining membership of his existing conference, prepared to take on the fresh task, bringing along a couple of new members with him. However, when the day arrived for the appointment of the president, Frank Sweeney, distinguished barrister and Blackrock College alumnus, was appointed to fill that role, not Frank Duff. Duff recalled that Sweeney was forty-five at the time but that he regarded him as 'a very senior man' whose coming had a 'galvanic' effect on the conference:

> It was a case of the touch of the master's hand. … All the other members were far older than I was, definitely set in their ways and disinclined to accept teaching from one whom they regarded as a boy. So it proved a very happy thing for the conference that I had not been made president … . In Frank Sweeney I found a great friend and a backer ever after.[1]

Myra House at 100 Francis Street came into the possession of the SVP in 1917 because of a connection between its owner, Mrs Keogh Donnelly, and Sweeney.[2] It had been part of Donnelly's bacon factory until it was leased for use as Lord Iveagh's play centre for children. When the play centre relocated to the Bride Road, the owner gifted the premises to Sweeney, with the intention of passing the house on to the SVP. In the period before passing to the SVP, Myra House had become almost derelict. One room had been used for a local men's club, and on Sunday mornings the large hall in the house was used by a women's committee as a venue for free breakfasts for children. On 2 February 1917 a new conference, the St Patrick's Conference, was established in Myra House, and this time Duff was appointed president. Shortly afterwards Sir Joseph Glynn, an important future ally of Duff's, was appointed president of the Central Council of the SVP. Glynn, another Blackrock College alumnus and thirty years older than Duff, was a solicitor and chairman of the National Health Insurance Commission. St Patrick's Conference grew prodigiously, produced several new conferences and undertook new works. Among its members, John Murray, Jack MacNamara and Jock McGallogly would become members of the first praesidium for men in the Legion of Mary.

Matthew Redmond Lalor, proprietor of tobacconist shops, was also a prominent member of the SVP. Lalor, a native of Moone in County Kildare, had come to Dublin to serve his apprenticeship in Clerys department store. He subsequently established himself as a tobacconist and an importer of cigars and cigarettes, which he supplied under distinctive regimental crests to the British army in Ireland and overseas. If Duff had a pressing problem to resolve, he would often drop into Lalor's shop in Nassau Street for advice. For a period of about ten years from the late 1920s Duff regularly cycled out to Lalor's home in Blackrock for mid-day Sunday dinner.[3] Ó Broin says that 'Matt had a way with him, a shrewdness, a capacity to influence, a diplomatic flair from which Duff benefited. He was a cultivated man, too, a lover of books, secular and spiritual.'[4] A bachelor, Lalor donated substantial sums of money to provide bursaries for the education of priests. A close friendship developed between the two men, which lasted until Lalor's death in 1937.

Another close friendship Duff forged in the SVP was with Ulick McNally, who also worked with him in the Department of Finance. Duff said that McNally taught him the art of home visitation because, no matter how miserable the tenement visited, McNally treated the residents with such respect and graciousness that it was conjured into a palace. McNally, who came from Headfort in County Galway, had an alcohol problem and lost his job in the civil service. Duff's friendship with and affection for McNally never wavered and they carried on an extensive correspondence.

Duff helped to start a Pioneer Centre affiliated to the Central Council of the Pioneers on 27 April 1917. At first only men were enrolled, but by 1919 a branch existed for women. Fr Toher, a curate in Francis Street, where Fr (Canon) John Flanagan was parish priest, became Spiritual Director of both St Patrick's Conference of the Society of St Vincent de Paul and of the Pioneer Centre. Duff, at first a reluctant Pioneer, disliked the idea of wearing emblems and hesitated to 'take the pin'.[5] At the time of applying for membership in late 1916, he had not drunk beer for a few years and no cider for seven months. Nonetheless, he was told that he would have to serve the normal two-year probationary period. He walked away in indignation. On reflection, he realized that he had overreacted and, as he said himself, 'he crawled back'. He was enrolled as a probationer on 27 October 1916 and completed his probation and received his certificate as a full member of the Pioneers on 27 October 1918. In pursuit of what he regarded as an improved version of the

Pioneer badge, Duff commissioned a jeweller to make a special badge for him. When the director of the Pioneer movement, Fr J. Flinn, SJ, heard about this, he told him to wear the ordinary badge like everyone else. However, Duff's Spiritual Director, Fr Browne, took the view that he was entitled to wear the badge he had commissioned and which was a miniature work of art in gold and enamel and a perfect depiction of the emblem. Enrolment of new Pioneers in the Myra House Centre proceeded apace, with between ten and thirty-five applications processed at each monthly council meeting. An article in the *Irish Catholic* in June 1920 told of over 200 Pioneers in the centre and reported that the impact on the 'immense working population' of 'that great labour district' was noteworthy in the amount of income being diverted from alcohol consumption to clothes and household needs.

One of the members of the men's branch of the Pioneers in Myra House was Matt Murray, who started the guild of St Camillus, comprising four SVP brothers. The object of the Guild was to visit the cancer wards in the South Dublin Union infirmary (St Kevin's, now St James's Hospital). The origin of the infirmary derived from the Poor Law in the nineteenth century, which saw the country divided into 130 poor law unions, each with a workhouse. The South Dublin Union area was divided from the North Dublin Union area by the river Liffey. A feature of the South Dublin Union infirmary was that there were separate infirmaries for Catholics and Protestants, staffed by Sisters of Mercy and Church of England Canonesses respectively.

Duff said of Matt Murray that 'Like so many others who have figured importantly as apostles inside or outside the Legion, Matt Murray was weak on learning. He was a shining example of what faith can accomplish independently of worldly possessions and advantages.'[6] As a result of an error he made in completing a dispatch form, which proved costly to his employer, noted wholesale firm Park's of the Coombe, Matt had lost his job. After a period of unemployment, he was appointed caretaker of Myra House. Duff later suggested that, while at one level Matt's move a few hundred yards from Park's to Myra House could be viewed as a disaster, it was also providential: 'God's signposts are often drastic and can leave one disconcerted and devastated in some way or another.'[7] Murray holds a key role in the history of the Legion of Mary, because a report by him on his hospital visitation work would lead to the involvement of some women in similar work and those women would form the nucleus of the early Legion.

On 7 June 1918 a ceremony of Enthronement of the Sacred Heart took place in Myra House. Devotion to the Sacred Heart is central to the Pioneers and it is to the Sacred Heart that the 'Heroic Offering' prayer of the Pioneers, recited twice daily by members, is addressed. It is worth quoting the prayer, since it gives an insight into the spiritual motivation Duff embraced when he joined:

For Thy greater glory and consolation, O Sacred Heart of Jesus, for Thy sake to give good example, to practise self-denial, to make reparation to Thee for the sins of intemperance and for the conversion of excessive drinkers, I will abstain for life from all spirituous [later 'intoxicating'] drink.

The Pioneer Council in Myra House, which comprised both men and women, held meetings on the last Sunday of each month. As soon as the regular Pioneer items on the agenda of the Council had been dealt with, the practice developed of reporting on other activities that had been undertaken by the members of the Council and which were centred on Myra House. The men were engaged in visitation either of homes or hospitals, while the women included among their activities Catechism classes for children. The Council meeting began at 4.30pm, and at 6pm, as the Angelus bell tolled, the Angelus was recited and the meeting concluded. Following the meeting, the members shared a cup of tea and spent time in informal discussion. Those present generally included Fr Toher, Duff, Mrs Kirwan, Misses Donnelly, Murray and Keogh.

The Jesuit philosopher Bernard Lonergan refers to the 'Providence of Books'. He was prompted to use the phrase when he came across Newman's *Grammar of Assent* while he was a student at Heythrop College near Oxford. Newman's analysis of the concept of assent set Lonergan off in a particular direction of philosophical enquiry regarding the compatibility of reason and religious faith.[8] Augustine's life was changed when he heard the words '*tolle et lege* [take and read]' and picked up and read the Epistles of St Paul: 'Let us walk honestly as in the day; not in rioting and drunkenness. ...' (Rom. 13.13–14). Ignatius of Loyola's life was changed from soldier to founder of the Jesuits when, having been hit in the leg by a cannonball in battle, he read during his recuperation the *Imitation of Christ* by Thomas à Kempis, an Augustinian monk. Duff's life was changed when he read, and finally grasped, the *True Devotion to the Blessed Virgin* by Louis Marie Grignion de Montfort.[9]

Louis Marie Grignion de la Bacheleraie was born in 1673 in Montfort-la-Cane in Brittany and was ordained in 1700. The manuscript of his *True Devotion* remained hidden for over a century until it was rediscovered in 1842. Interest in de Montfort and his writings grew during the papacy of Pius IX, who had practised the *True Devotion* since his youth. De Montfort was beatified by Pope Leo XIII in 1888 and canonized by Pius XII in 1947. The worldwide spread of the Legion of Mary contributed to de Montfort's canonization. As Eddie Doherty[10] suggests in *Wisdom's Fool*, the story of de Montfort's influence might begin not in France, but in Dublin in 1921, when the Legion of Mary was founded.[11]

The twenty-nine-year-old Duff was introduced to the *True Devotion* by his fellow Blackrock College alumnus and member of the SVP, Vincent Kelly. In a letter to Kelly more than fifty years later, he spoke of the event as 'something which definitely affected the course of my whole life'. He recalled the way in which some of the SVP members would stay around after their Thursday night meetings to discuss a range of topics. One night Duff noticed a group of the brothers gathered around Kelly. He joined the group and found that they were discussing de Montfort's *True Devotion*, a copy of which Matt Lalor had recently given to Kelly. Duff recalled that Kelly's description of the book 'was vivid and stuck in my mind'. Some days later, 'by a surpassing coincidence', he encountered the book on a second-hand bookstall on Aston Quay. Struck by the coincidence, Duff said that he bought the book for fourpence. It was the first English printing of the work, the translation being that of Fr Faber. The printer was an old and well-known firm in Capel Street – Coyne & Co.:

> I applied myself to the reading of the book with results that may be said to have been far-reaching. It was definitely that book which threw my life into the Marian channels which it has ever since followed; the booklet which I enclose to you gives an account of that development, it will be of interest to you to know that it was you who sparked off the whole process.[12]

The impact of de Montfort was, according to Duff, 'immense':

> Somewhere in 1919 some of us had encountered St. Louis Marie de Montfort's book on True Devotion to Mary. It depicted Our Lady in a devastatingly different dimension to what we were accustomed. The catechism had never shown us anything even remotely like that. De Montfort exhibited her sharply as the Mother of the Christian life, absolutely indispensable, concerned in every grace. The vastness of the role which he attributed to her and the very vehemence of the way in which he described it gave the initial impression of gross exaggeration. Nevertheless he gripped the mind and forced one to read and enquire. At some stage in this process the conviction was gained that the book was justified and that the common presentation of Our Lady was not.
>
> The seriousness of this was like an electric shock. For virtually it meant that we were leaving Mary out.[13]

At the time teaching on the Blessed Virgin in the Catechism placed her in a general section on saints – it was 'lawful' to be devout to her. In relation to this statement, Duff later made the acid comment: 'In other words it was not a sin, a ludicrous description which would almost amount to placing it in the same category as backing horses or moderate drinking.'[14] On a first reading, the *True Devotion* even seemed to Duff to 'border on the absurd'. Then Tom Fallon, a civil servant and member of the SVP who would go on to become a missionary priest in Mexico, where he died aged ninety-six, pressed him to read the book again. Duff tried perhaps half a dozen times with the same result and was engaged on 'the final forced reading' when 'Without any process of thought leading up to it, something which I could but regard as a Divine favour was granted to me. It was the sudden realisation that the Book was true.'[15]

Years later, Pope John Paul II would say that he also found de Montfort's book difficult, but described his reading of the *True Devotion* as a decisive turning point in his life, or rather a long inner journey. Speaking in Rome at the 8th International Mariological Colloquium, the Pope said that it was when he was working at the Solvay factory in Krakow during the Nazi occupation that he 'read and re-read de Montfort' in order to understand it: 'Many times and with great spiritual profit I read and re-read this precious little ascetical book with the blue, soda-stained cover.'[16] Pope John Paul II took his motto, *Totus Tuus* ('I am all thine'), from de Montfort.

Duff's 'epiphany' in relation to de Montfort was the occasion of a rare, perhaps unique, reference by him to a 'Divine favour' being granted. He concluded that de Montfort was writing for a theologically educated class and that he (Duff) lacked a whole field of knowledge that de Montfort assumed to exist in the reader. His own education on the subject took a big step forward when, on 3 April 1920, he made his first visit to the Cistercian Abbey at Mount Melleray in County Waterford in the company of his friend Joseph Gabbett, who had started to drink again following his demobilization from the army and his return to Dublin from Aldershot. Their names and addresses are listed in sequence in the monastery guest book. Duff's address is 55 St Patrick's Road, while that of Gabbett is 40 South King Street. Later in the same year, on 30 September, Gabbett, together with Ulick McNally, went on another visit to Melleray.[17] In the days before alcoholism was recognized as an illness, Mount Melleray operated a version of treatment that was often successful. In Honor Tracy's novel *The Straight and Narrow Path*, the parish priest tells his inebriated curate, 'I'll just tell you the one thing now, Paddy. You'll be off to Mount Melleray in the morning.'[18] Duff was concerned about his friend and gladly accompanied Gabbett on his search for sobriety in Melleray.

In Melleray Duff decided to look for a book on the theology of the Blessed Virgin, and the Guest Master, Fr Brendan, gave him a copy of Fr Januarius de Concilio's *Knowledge of Mary*. De Concilio was born in Naples in 1836 and died in Brooklyn in 1898. As a parish priest in Brooklyn, he looked after an immigrant community of Italians and Irish. In addition to his parish duties, he wrote a number of books, including a play called *The Irish Heroine* for his Irish parishioners. He was honoured by Pope Leo XIII and received a doctorate from Georgetown University, the Jesuit University in Washington, DC. De Concilio's book was the key that opened de Montfort for Duff, who was so exhilarated by its contents that he worked late into the night copying all that he could of the contents of the book. The result was striking:

> As a total transaction I have assigned in my Marian philosophy an equal rating to those two books, de Montfort and de Concilio. It took the second one to open the first one

to me, so that I have always thought of them as interdependent halves in this teaching operation which turned my life upside down.[19]

Cardinal Vaughan, referring to the persevering study of one spiritual book, says of the *True Devotion* that 'We never get a proper hold of a great spiritual doctrine until we have lived it and been saturated by it. The soul must soak in the brine until it has become wholly impregnated with its qualities.'[20] Duff immersed himself in the *True Devotion to Mary* such that it became a lived reality for him.

Notes to Chapter 5

1. Talk by Duff, 'Frank Sweeney', audio tape 34 (a), LOMA.
2. Much of the information in this chapter is based on Duff's own account of events in *Miracles on Tap*.
3. Duff to Mackey, 25 October 1935.
4. Ó Broin, *Frank Duff*, p. 27.
5. Enda Dunleavy, 'Frank Duff and the Pioneers', manuscript given to author by Dunleavy.
6. Talk by Duff, 'Matt Murray', tape 36 (b), LOMA.
7. ibid.
8. Bernard McGuckian, S J, gave this information about Lonergan.
9. McGuckian in a talk at Glasnevin cemetery, 8 June 2008.
10. Doherty was an Oscar-nominated screen writer, thrice-married and later ordained priest in the Melkite Greek Catholic Church.
11. Eddie Doherty, *Wisdom's Fool: A Biography of St. Louis de Montfort*. New York: Madonna House, 1998, p. 17.
12. Duff to Kelly, 13 October 1973.
13. Frank Duff, 'A Great Legion', *Victory through Mary*. Dublin: Praedicanda, 1981, p. 383.
14. Frank Duff, 'St. Louis Marie's Way is also Pope John Paul's', *Victory through Mary*, p. 460.
15. ibid., pp. 461–62.
16. Address by Pope John Paul II to the Participants in the 8th Mariological Colloquium, 13 October 2000, Rome.
17. McNally's address is given as 94 Lower Leeson Street in the Guest Register of Mount Melleray.
18. Honor Tracy, *The Straight and Narrow Path*. London: Penguin, 1960, p. 171.
19. Duff, 'St Louis Marie's Way is also Pope John Paul's', *Victory through Mary*, p. 465.
20. Quoted in O'Flynn, *Frank Duff*, p. 4.

CHAPTER 6

The Legion of Mary Begins

'It was not a thought-out organisation. It sprang up spontaneously.'
HANDBOOK OF THE LEGION OF MARY

Following a Pioneer Council meeting at Myra House during the summer of 1921, some members of the Council, including Duff, decided to hold a special meeting to discuss de Montfort's book. This meeting took place in August 1921, probably on the 14th or 21st of that month.[1] Based on the knowledge he had acquired, Duff was in a position to explain the *True Devotion* to those present. Mary's role was far greater than the 'lawful' devotion accorded to her in the Catechism. It was through Mary that Christ came into the world and through her that humankind continues to receive Christ. In a letter to French legionary Anna Choiseul, he wrote:

> There had been a large amount of casual talk about the True Devotion and it was suggested that a special meeting be held for the purpose of talking it over and learning what it really was. That meeting was fixed for a Sunday midway between two ordinary meetings of that prior organisation [Pioneer Council]. As a result, all those who were present had the full scope of Mary's role in grace fully explained to them and they accepted it all. Apparently that constituted the missing ingredient, because 17 days later the first meeting of the Legion was held.[2]

At the Pioneer Council Meeting on 28 August, visitation of the Union Hospital, a hospital for the poor in the care of the Sisters of Mercy, was discussed. The ladies of the Council agreed to undertake this work and a special meeting to consider the details of the work was planned. The nuns in the Union Hospital would have two Masses a month said for those who were going to visit the hospital.[3] Over the following month four meetings were held and the Association 'placed itself under the patronage of Our Lady of Mercy'.[4] One of these meetings marked the beginning of the organization that in 1925 would become known as the Legion of Mary. According to Duff, a report by Matt Murray at a Pioneer Council meeting was the catalyst for the start of what would become the Legion. Murray described 'a visit paid by him and another brother that very morning to the Dublin Union', strangely enough to the women's hospital, where at the time it was not customary for men to visit.[5] When the formal meeting concluded, two of the young women present asked why they could not undertake similar work. When it was clear that six women present would be interested in the work, a meeting was fixed for the following Wednesday, 31 August, and it was suggested that others might be invited if they were interested. This meeting was preliminary to what in retrospect has been identified as the first meeting of the Legion of Mary, which took place on Wednesday, 7 September in Myra House and at which the officers of the Association were appointed. That first group grew to around 70 members until the second group was started in July 1922.

When Fr Toher, Duff and the women arrived for the meeting on 7 September, they found that an altar had been set up on a table. Standing on a white cloth was the statue of the Immaculate Conception which had belonged to Joseph Gabbett and had been stored in Myra House, two vases with flowers and two candlesticks with lighted candles. The arrangement of the first Legion altar which, with the addition of the Vexillum or Legion standard is identical with the altar at every subsequent Legion meeting, was the work of Alice Keogh. Alice Keogh's niece Patricia (Patty) Kavanagh, who joined the Legion as a young girl in 1937 and was still an active member seventy-three years later in 2010, described how her aunt found the statue of Our Lady on a ledge in Myra House and set up the altar.[6] Alice Keogh herself did not remain with the young organization but joined the Little Sisters of the Assumption, taking the name Sister Brendan Mary. She joined first in Dublin's Camden Street from where she was sent to London, then to New York, and finally to Canada, where she died on the anniversary of the founding of the Legion of Mary – 7 September 1943. She is buried at Ville-Lasalle, south-west of Montreal, on the banks of the St Lawrence.[7]

When the first meeting of the Association of Our Lady of Mercy, later known as the Legion of Mary, commenced, the order followed was that set down on the SVP Prayer Card. The invocation to the Holy Ghost was said, followed by five decades of the Rosary. These prayers were followed by the reading by the chairman of a short passage from St Matthew's Gospel, chapter 25, including Christ's words, 'Just as you did it to one of these my brethren, you did it to me.' Officers were then appointed as follows: Mrs Kirwan, the only woman of mature years present, was appointed president. She was sixty-four years old. Duff said that Mrs Kirwan 'brought the note of poverty into that meeting; she was, undoubtedly, the poorest person in the room. Mrs Kirwan caused the right note to be struck from the first meeting, the real Legion note, the absence of all social and worldly distinctions in the membership.'[8] The absence of social distinction of any kind became a hallmark of the Legion of Mary, and any Legion group around the world might include a blend of men and women, professional and unskilled and of varied ethnicity. Following the selection of Mrs Kirwan as president and the appointment of other officers, the 'sisters', as the women were called in the manner of the St Vincent de Paul 'brothers', were allocated visitation in pairs in the women's wards, including the cancer wards in the South Dublin Union. The practice of visitation in pairs, never as individuals, became another hallmark of the Legion of Mary. Visitation by an individual on his or her own in a Legion capacity is specifically excluded under Legion rules. There were seven pairs, excluding Mrs Kirwan, who does not appear to have been allocated work. The meeting closed with further prayers, following the Vincent de Paul format. A secret collection was made, amounting to fifteen shillings.

In this hidden, almost accidental, manner, the Legion of Mary was born. It came into existence as a parish-based organization. The beginnings of the Legion were veiled in obscurity and poverty: 'The place – top back-room of Myra House, Francis Street, a poor and old part of Dublin.'[9] The support of the locate curate, Fr Toher, and the parish priest, Fr John Flanagan, in Francis Street was essential since diocesan approval would remain in the distance. From the start this was an organization in which the priest had a crucial role and, from the aspect of mobilizing the laity, could become, as Duff would later write, 'the priest's organization, par excellence'. By this he meant that the Legion could be used as an instrument of the priest in his work of spreading the Gospel.

A few problems of factual reconciliation arise with regard to historical accuracy. It says in the minutes for 7 September that the 'Sisters gave accounts of their visits to the union',[10] implying that they had already undertaken work. It seems likely, therefore, that work was agreed at the preliminary meeting on 31 August. A further problem of reconciliation arises regarding the attendance. At a meeting held when the Association was just three years old in 1924, Fr Michael Toher said that there were eight members at the first meeting. It is likely, however, that this refers to the preliminary meeting:

Father Toher, after taking the chair, spoke of the origins of the Association, its small beginning of eight members; its first meeting in a back room of that house [Myra House]; its rapid progress during the three years of its existence, so that now its membership ran into hundreds, and a further extension of its activities to the north side of the City was in contemplation. Its notes had ever been the true spirit of fraternity and a perfect trust in God; with these in evidence in the future as they had been in the past, one could look forward with confidence to a great expansion.[11]

There is no one who possesses a perfect memory, so that it should not surprise that details recalled may vary with the lapse of time. In January 1955 Duff consulted 'first-nighter' Kathleen Hanvey to check what she remembered regarding the attendance at the first meeting. In his letter he writes:

Thank you for the list of names which you give, that is of those who were present at the first meeting of the Legion. I think that you are right in including Miss. Rooney. Certainly Mrs. Leech was there. The number which you supply is thirteen, but I think that the number of the ladies present was fifteen. Of course it is possible that the number of 15 was made up by including Father Toher and myself. But still I think there were 15 apart from the two of us.[12]

While the minutes of the first meeting list fifteen women in attendance in addition to Toher and Duff, in an article entitled 'A Great Legion'[13] Duff says that there were a total of fifteen persons present at the first meeting, including thirteen women:

That evening was the Vigil of the Feast of Our Lady's Nativity; a circumstance not adverted to at the time. At 8 p.m. 15 persons assembled, 13 women, nearly all young, Father Toher and myself. What in the circumstances we could justifiably call a portent met our eyes. For on the table stood the Legion altar as we have it today, but of course without the Vexillum. This was due to the initiative of one of the early comers, Alice Keogh, who later was the first vocation of the group.[14]

Whatever about points of detail, the great adventure had been launched. Within a month, it is reported in the Pioneer Council minutes of 30 October 1921 that a 'gratifying account was given of the work done and contemplated'[15] and that membership had reached thirty-two. It is also recorded that Fr Devane, SJ, attended as a visitor and gave an inspiring address. The role of the Pioneers was critical because it was in the context of a meeting of the Pioneer Council that the catalyst which sparked the Legion occurred. Fr Toher, who was Spiritual Director of the Pioneers, would play a crucial role in the Legion. Duff, Mrs Kirwan, Alice Keogh and some other 'first-nighters' were all members of the Pioneers. For some reason or other, the early links of the Pioneers with the Legion have received little recognition compared with the Legion's early links with the SVP. Duff, who had a dread of addictions of any sort, always encouraged legionaries to promote the Pioneers. He was particularly pleased when, a few decades after the Legion began, the national director of the Pioneers, Daniel Dargan, SJ, granted permission for Legion praesidia to be constituted as Pioneer Councils and to act as such.

Duff maintained that the Legion of Mary was not an organization that had been planned: 'The Legion has always declared that it was an unpremeditated organization. Nobody sat down at the beginning and put on paper what the Legion was intended to be … . The history of the Legion has that character of one step leading to another step.'[16] Not even the name was selected at the beginning, when the association was called the 'Association of Our Lady of Mercy'. Nor was the nomenclature of the Roman Legion adopted at the start. The first groups were called 'conferences', the name used by the SVP for its branches. Later the conferences were called 'patronages' before the title 'praesidium' was finally adopted. On 2 November 1924 representatives of the four conferences of the 'Association of Our Lady of Mercy' met at Myra House. Before the meeting ended, a 'Central Council' of the Association was established. Fr Toher presided. Mrs Elizabeth Kirwan was elected president, Miss Scratton vice-president, and Miss Molly McCarthy and Miss Sally McNamara were appointed secretary and treasurer respectively.[17]

Following the establishment of the central council, the question of a name for the new organization was raised. Mary Duffy, the first Legion envoy, told how in November 1925 members of the Association of Our Lady of Mercy were asked to begin a novena on the Feast of All the Saints of Ireland (6 November) for guidance in the choice of a title for the new movement. 'Bro. Duff expressed the opinion that, while it might be presumptuous to anticipate a wide expansion of the organization, still it might come and that, therefore, the title chosen should be without a national tag.'[18] One evening when Duff was at home looking at a picture of Mary as the 'Morning Star' hanging on a wall, the name 'Legion of Mary' entered his head. Initially this name was rejected by the members, some of whom preferred more traditionally devotional titles, but it was accepted in late November 1925.

By the autumn of 1925 the number of patronages had increased to six. From 1925, Legionaries were required to recite daily the short prayer known as the 'Magnificat' (Lk. 1.46–55). Duff composed a further prayer recited at the conclusion of every Legion meeting. On 8 March 1927 permission was given by the Dublin Archdiocese (*Permissus Ordinarii Diocesis Dubliniensis*) for the printing of the prayers to be recited at Legion meetings. At the Council meeting 15 May 1927, it was proposed to replace the name 'council' by 'curia'. The members agreed on the basis that 'the proposed title was distinctive and appropriate'.[19] In December 1930, other 'distinctive and appropriate' titles were adopted – 'Concilium' and 'praesidium'. The first Concilium comprised in effect the four Dublin curiae then in existence, developing in time into the governing body of the Legion of Mary. In 1929 the picture on the Legion Tessera or prayer leaflet was designed by the artist Hubert McGoldrick.[20] In 1929 too, the Vexillum was added as part of the altar equipment. The Vexillum is the standard of the Legion and is based on an adaptation of the standard of the Roman Legion, whereby the eagle is replaced by the emblem of the Holy Spirit and the portrait of the emperor by one of Mary, Mother of Christ. The Vexillum was made by Sam McKay, a gold and silver chaser who worked for Hopkins and Hopkins, close to O'Connell Bridge. McKay, a Protestant Scotsman and also a musical conductor, became a Catholic later in life. His best-known work was the Sam Maguire Cup, awarded for the all-Ireland county championship in Gaelic football, the design of which was based on the Ardagh Chalice. The Cup was presented for the first time in 1928 when it was won by Kildare.

The stimulus to formulate an embryonic *Handbook* describing the organization of the Legion and its motivation arose with the opportunity for the

Legion to spread outside Ireland into Scotland in 1928 and 'the necessity for having something printed' to explain the organization. The *Handbook* was written based on 'what was in existence'.[21] It sets out the details of Legion organization and explains Legion spirituality. Duff completed the first version of the *Handbook* in the late summer of 1928 and it was printed for private circulation.

Frank Duff did not accept that he was the 'founder' in the conventional sense of having set out to establish an organization. In a letter written in 1951 to Monsignor (later Cardinal) Suenens, the Auxiliary Bishop of Malines, he said, 'As a particular request I would ask that you omit reference to me as "Founder of the Legion" everywhere throughout the narrative. The expression grates on me immeasurably.'[22] Twenty years later, he had accepted the reality that he was everywhere recognized as the Legion's founder. In a letter to the Archbishop of Lisbon, Antonio Ribeiro, written in 1973, he described himself as 'founder of the Legion of Mary and new Vice-President of its Concilium in Dublin'.[23] At a fundamental level, Duff believed that Mary was the Legion's founder. Insight into the role of Mary through a study of de Montfort was the lever on which the movement was launched. As the Legion grew, Duff believed that it remained in the care of Mary: 'Definitely there is in the Legion a principle of orderly growth, of design not of our making, which is both touching and strengthening because it suggests the care of a maternal power.'[24]

Reflection on the nature of 'founders' helps to throw light on Duff's position in relation to the establishment of the Legion. Founders of religious communities tend to be of two main types – 'deliberate' founders and 'accidental' founders.[25] Deliberate founders are men and women who had an idea or vision and founded a community to realize that vision. St Benedict, founder of the Benedictines, and Angela Merici, founder of the Ursulines, are examples of deliberate founders. On the other hand, accidental founders are charismatic individuals to whose personality and mode of life people are attracted. St Francis of Assisi had planned to be a hermit and did not plan to found a community, but the Order of Friars Minor grew out of the attraction of others to his way of life. This was also the case with St Elizabeth Anne Seton, founder of the Daughters of Charity of St Vincent de Paul in the United States. Her community grew out of her school for children and work for the poor. St Philip Neri does not fall into either group, but he is closer to an accidental founder. St Philip denied throughout his life that he founded the Congregation of the Oratory and he refused the title 'founder'. This was conferred on Neri only after his death, when he could not refuse it. Like Duff, he attributed the foundation of his Congregation to Mary:[26] 'St. Philip [said] that he would not have thought of founding the congregation, but Our Lady founded this Institute, so fruitful and peculiar in the church of God.'[27] Fifteen years after the foundation of the Legion, Duff would write:

... the Legion seems to bear innumerable marks of a providential origin and mission. Its beginnings and early growth were not the result of clever framing and planning. It owed nothing to external support, or to the qualities of its own leaders or members, all of whom were most inconspicuous persons ... . Everywhere it produces the same spirit of apostleship and devotion in its members, and the same success in its work for souls.[28]

And yet one finds Duff proposing in the booklet *Can we be Saints?* – written between 6 April and 10 May 1921 and published in 1922[29] – that contenders for holiness should gather others for holy enterprises. So the idea of 'founding' or starting a fresh group had been in Duff's mind. León Ó Broin suggested that the booklet was written some years earlier than 1921.[30] However, since Ó Broin's book was published, evidence has been unearthed which dates the work to 1921. In a handwritten response to Sister Bernard Brennan, requesting permission to translate the booklet into Polish and to publish it in Poland, Duff replies:

Needless to say permission is gladly given. The book was written at the expense of much effort. My life is very busy and it was written for the most part very late at night when I was tired out. Indeed but for a fortunate accident which befell me and confined me to bed, I don't know if I ever would have finished it.[31]

The 'fortunate accident' referred to an occasion when Duff was knocked off his bicycle by a motorcar and sustained injuries. His bicycle was a write-off. Duff's personal civil service file shows very little sick leave, with the exception of a period of over thirty days from 6 April to 10 May 1921 following the accident. A Polish version of the *Can we be Saints?* was published by the Jesuits in Poznan.

Notes to Chapter 6

1. Moss (ed.), *Frank Duff*, p. 13.
2. Duff to Choiseul, 28 July 1967. Seventeen days before the first meeting would fix the date of the special meeting as 21 August. But the mid-point between the Pioneer Council meetings suggests 14 August. The July council meeting was held on 24 July to facilitate those going on pilgrimage to Lourdes.
3. Minutes of Pioneer Council, 28 August 1921, LOMA.
4. Minutes of Pioneer Council, 25 September 1921, LOMA.
5. Duff, *Miracles on Tap*. New York: Montfort, 1961, p.100.
6. Author's interview with Patricia Kavanagh, 26 January 2008.
7. Patricia Kavanagh, 'The Legion Altar', *Maria Legionis*, 3/1987, p. 14.
8. Duff, *Miracles on Tap*, p. 106.
9. 'The Unfolding of Her Mantle', published in first issue of *Maria Legionis*, March 1937; reprinted in *Maria Legionis*, March 1998 to mark sixty years of *Maria Legionis*, 1937–1997.
10. Minutes of meeting, 7 September 1921, reproduced in Moss (ed.), *Frank Duff*, pp. 64–65.
11. Minutes of Meeting of representatives of four branches already established of Association of Our Lady of Mercy, 2 November 1924, LOMA.

12. Duff to Hanvey, 15 January 1955.
13. Duff, 'A Great Legion', *Victory through Mary*, p. 385.
14. ibid., p. 385.
15. Minutes of the Pioneer Council, 30 October 1921, LOMA.
16. Moss (ed.), *Frank Duff*, p. 15.
17. Minutes of a special meeting of representatives of the four branches, 2 November 1924, Minute Book, LOMA.
18. 'Mary Duffy, the first envoy recalls!' *Maria Legionis*, June 1993, p. 11.
19. 'The Unfolding of Her Mantle', first published in *Maria Legionis*, March 1937; reprinted in *Maria Legionis* 1/1998 to mark sixty years.
20. Item on the agenda for the curia meeting of 15 September 1929 refers to thanks to Hubert McGoldrick for design of Legion picture. Information supplied to author by Donal Healy, 20 December 2007.
21. Moss (ed.), *Frank Duff*, p. 15.
22. Duff to Suenens, 1 December 1951.
23. Duff to Ribeiro, 22 December 1973.
24. Duff, 'True Devotion to the Nation', *The Woman of Genesis*, p. 21.
25. These observations on Founders rely on a paper, 'Reluctant Founders: St Philip Neri and Venerable John Henry Newman', delivered by Fr Joseph F. Pearce, CO, at the National Newman Conference in Pittsburgh, 2007.
26. ibid., pp. 2–3.
27. F. W. Faber, *The School of St. Philip Neri*. London, 1850, p. 267.
28. Duff to Riberi, File 1083, 1936, LOMA.
29. The publication date of this booklet was verified as 1922 by Donal Healy, who identified the date in the publication list of the Catholic Truth Society.
30. Ó Broin, *Frank Duff*, p. 9.
31. Duff to Brennan, 1922, a letter brought to author's attention by Phyllis McGuinness.

CHAPTER 7

Work on the Land Act 1923

'What became known as the Hogan Act of 1923 was, to a degree, Frank's work.'
LEÓN Ó BROIN, *FRANK DUFF*

When Jack Duff died two days before Christmas in 1918 he left his wife Lettie, aged fifty-five, two sons and three daughters. Frank was aged twenty-nine. John, twenty-three, had been released recently from prisoner of war camp in Germany. Isabel Maud, a semi-invalid, was twenty-seven; Sarah Geraldine, aged twenty-one, was a medical student at University College Dublin; and the youngest, Ailish, aged sixteen, was still at school.

Frank Duff had already been contributing to the family budget, but now his role increased as he started to fill the 'male head of household' role in place of his father. When Jack and Lettie Duff married, they had opened a joint bank account in the Hibernian Bank, which operated until Jack's death. The account continued in Mrs Duff's name until 1942 when, following an illness of Mrs Duff, Frank's name was added to the account. However, from 1918 until his mother's death in 1950 the account was 'fed almost exclusively' by her son.[1] His mother's dependency on Frank for financial support, especially following the death of his father, until at least the mid-1920s, when Ailish graduated from UCD, is a defining factor in Duff's life. It made him anxious to earn as much as possible from his job in the civil service. It also put the question of marriage out of his head. Years later, when friends asked him about marriage, he joked that if he had married he might have made one woman happy but he would have made several others unhappy. He also said that if he had children of his own he would have wanted to spend every possible moment with them, to the exclusion of other occupations.

The Duff family situation was not unlike that of the Moynihan family, in which two of the brothers, John (Seán) and Maurice, would reach high office in the public service. Their father, Michael Moynihan, also died in 1918, the same year as Jack Duff. Moynihan was survived by his widow, Mary, and six children. Mary's chief support then became her eldest son, Michael, who had joined the civil service in 1910, two years after Duff. On the outbreak of war in 1914 Michael joined the British army and was killed in June 1918, five months before the Armistice. The next son, John, then assumed the breadwinner role, giving up 'hopes of entering the priesthood to support the family'.[2] Nor did John marry.

Duff was aged thirty-two and had worked for over twelve years in the Land Commission when in 1921, three years after his father's death, the Duff family left Drumcondra and moved to 51 Dartmouth Square. The house was two-storey over basement, with the sash windows and cast-iron fireplaces of the period. In 2010 it would sell after auction for €1.2 million.[3] Dartmouth Square was closer to the government offices in Merrion Street and to University College at Earlsfort Terrace where, also in 1921, Sarah Geraldine qualified as a doctor, and where her younger sister Ailish would qualify as a doctor in 1926. The family remained there until 1927 when they moved to North Brunswick Street, beside the Legion hostel for homeless men. The Dartmouth Square years were ones of intense work for Duff. He was stretched on all fronts, although he managed to take his mother on a number of holidays, including one to London, where she had relatives, and where he availed himself of the opportunity to go Wimbledon to see the great French champion Susan Lenglen play.

During 1922 and 1923 Duff was at work on the 1923 Land Act and from 1924 he was in the Department of Finance. Simultaneously, he was carrying out his work in the SVP and making extra visits to tenements in the evenings, guiding the Sancta Maria Hostel for prostitutes[4] and working with the newly formed Association of Our Lady of Mercy, the fledgling Legion of Mary. It was in the house in Dartmouth Square that the name 'Legion of Mary' came into Duff's mind.

In the early years of Independence conferences organized by the Catholic Truth Society held in the Mansion House in Dublin provided an opportunity for the clergy and the laity to engage with 'the problems of the day'.[5] The theme of the 1922 conference was 'Catholics and Citizenship', and in his address to it, which took place as the civil war raged, Bishop O'Doherty pointed out that it was the duty of citizens to respect their duly elected leaders. A major theme at the conference held in October 1923 was the role of the Catholic laity. The opening address was given by Cardinal Logue, who expressed the hope that Ireland would prove to be a 'sound, solid, Catholic nation'. Among the speakers was Sir Joseph Glynn, president of the SVP and vice-president of the Catholic Truth Society, who deplored the lack of organization of the Irish Catholic laity, by comparison with continental countries.

The keynote speaker at the conference in 1923 was the Minister of Home Affairs, Kevin O'Higgins, TD. His address, delivered on the afternoon of 12 October, was entitled 'The Catholic Layman in Public Life'. Dr MacRory, the Bishop of Down and Conor, presided. When O'Higgins rose to speak, he was interrupted by the revolutionary Maud Gonne MacBride and some other women. O'Higgins said that Irish independence had brought weighty responsibilities: 'Liberty meant responsibility in its first and last analysis, and it was an unfortunate fact that large numbers of their Catholic fellow-countrymen had fallen into the old and false doctrine that liberty was licence.'[6] O'Higgins said that national freedom did not mean 'endless holidays'; rather, 'responsibility and hard work'. He asked how 'the Catholic laity could breathe into the nostrils of an Irish democracy the breath of its powerful though dormant life'. It was here that the involvement of the best type of Catholic layman in public and private life was needed. On 13 October at the conference, Fr Michael Creedon addressed it on the subject of 'Catholic Women in Social Service'. Creedon said that the state of woman's work in Ireland aroused in him 'an intolerable sense of unused possibilities'.[7] The vote of thanks to Fr Creedon was proposed by Frank Duff and seconded by Fr Michael Toher. Both the participants and the kinds of discussion at the Catholic Truth Society conferences give a flavour of the type of citizenship expected of Catholics in the new State, where, it was argued, Catholics should, as a matter of responsibility, help to shoulder the burdens of the State.

At the time of the 1923 CTS Conference, Duff had been on loan from the Land Commission to the Department of Lands, Agriculture and Fisheries for nearly two years. The letter that led to Duff's move and which marked him as the first civil servant invited to move from the old British and Irish civil service to the new Irish civil service was signed by P. Sheehan, Secretary of the Ministry of Home Affairs, and was written on paper headed 'Dáil Eireann, 15 Wellington Quay, Aireacht um Gnothaí Duithche Department of Home Affairs'. It ran simply, 'Dear Duff, Could you call to see me this afternoon at 3 or 4 on a particular matter of interest to you?' At their meeting, Sheehan invited Duff to come over to the newly established Provisional government to assist the Minister, Patrick Hogan, in taking over and running the Land Commission. Apart from two brief periods amounting to less than three weeks in 1922, Duff was based in the Department of Lands, Agriculture and Fisheries until 1 January 1924, when he was transferred to the newly established Department of Finance. In Lands, Agriculture and Fisheries he worked directly to the Minister, visiting the Land Commission in Upper Merrion Street only as need arose.

Duff's work for Hogan centred on the 1923 Land Act, which became known as the Hogan Act and 'which was to a degree Frank's work'.[8] In the first systematic analysis of the land question in independent Ireland, Terence Dooley argues that the 1923 Land Act not only ended agrarian agitation but also made a major contribution to ending the civil war. Dooley says that the issues dealt with 'were so complex, as well as numerous and varied, that probably only a very few TDs fully understood the implications of the legislation they were dealing with'.[9] Duff retained a file of over 200 foolscap pages of carbon copies of memos and other material he prepared for Hogan. It is an impressive body of work. In a 27-page memorandum on Irish Land Purchase written in 1922, much of which is of a technical nature, Duff sets out the system of land purchase and the methodology to be followed. Separate memoranda deal in detail with specific issues such as the 'Bonus and Excess Stock'. Some of these matters related to the financial settlement between Britain and Ireland following the Treaty. Side-by-side with Britain's obligations to Ireland in respect of over-taxation, there is the counter-obligation in respect of Ireland's share of war debt. There is also a Note on the 'supposed differences between Article 5 of the Treaty and Article 15 of Document 2' – the latter a proposal of de Valera's. The largest individual document contained in the file is a 52-page memorandum by Duff on the 'Reorganisation of the Irish Land Commission and the Congested Districts Board'. It is an exceptional document and could be read with profit today by anyone interested in public administration. Attention is given to both the efficient delivery of services and to the treatment of staff. It is not without touches of humour: 'The Land Commission is the Paradise of the man with any sort of legal qualifications.'

The file also includes three newspaper articles Duff drafted for the Minister. One was for publication in various American newspapers; the other two were for the *Manchester Guardian* and the *United Irishman*. The article for the American papers deals with 'The Future of Agriculture in Ireland'. One of the difficulties highlighted concerns the raising of credit, in relation to which 'the present insecurity is most unfortunate' – a reference to the difficulties caused by the civil war. In the article for the *Manchester Guardian*, entitled 'Ireland and the Land Acts', tribute is paid to the achievement of the Acts, under which 400,000 homesteads had been established. Behind the statistics lay 'the regeneration of a people'. Duff writes that if 'to-day we can forget the clearances and the emigrant-wards in the New York hospitals and instead look forward and make plans for Ireland, it is in a very large measure the fruits of the Land Acts we gather'. He describes the consequences of the Land Acts as 'a revolution infinitely more complete than the conquest of England by the Normans or Ireland by the Danes … wrought from some old houses in Merrion Street, Dublin'.[10]

In 1923 four million acres, much of it untenanted, remained to be dealt with. A new Land Bill was required because 'For all the good done, the land problem is, after 42 years of attention, still left alive to harass and endanger the government.' Duff, showing a sense of fairness, urged that 'Each of the parties concerned [landlords and tenants] should remember that the others have rights, and all should remember that there are other interests in Ireland besides land which need State attention.'[11] In relation to the Land Conference held on 10 and 11 April 1923, Duff noted: 'Each side tried to controvert statements made by the other.' He recommended an outline Bill on the basis of what both sides were likely to accept and set down 27 suggested Heads for the Bill.

When Duff went to work in the Department of Lands, Agriculture and Fisheries in January 1922, it was in the rank of Junior Executive Officer.[12] It appears that Hogan held out hopes of his substantial promotion. In fact, Duff claimed that Hogan had promised him eventual secretaryship of the proposed new Irish Land Commission. The failure of promotion to materialize became a source of grievance to Duff. High office at a young age was not uncommon in the new Irish civil service. Joseph Brennan (1893–1974) and J. J. McElligott (1887–1963) became Secretaries of the Department of Finance at ages thirty-five and thirty-four respectively in February 1923 and September 1927. When Duff went to work in the Department of Lands, Agriculture and Fisheries in January 1922 he was aged thirty-two. Brennan, who had entered the First Division of the civil service as a university graduate, would be appointed Comptroller and Auditor General in April 1922 and Secretary of the Department of Finance the following year. J. J. McElligott, also a university graduate and a First Division man, would become Assistant Secretary to Brennan in 1923. Cornelius Gregg was in 1922, at the age of thirty-three, Assistant Secretary to the Board of Inland Revenue in London. Gregg came on loan to the Department of Finance in April 1922 and remained there until October 1924 when he returned to the Inland Revenue in London. President Cosgrave showed his esteem for Gregg by granting him the designation 'Secretary for Establishment Matters' and saying that he should be responsible directly to Cosgrave himself, who held the Finance portfolio at the time as well as being President of the Executive Council of the Free State.[13]

In a handwritten memo, Duff tells how, in his interview with Sheehan before working for Hogan, 'it was plainly suggested to me that I was to be the chief man in the new Land Commission. In the meantime, "I was to be our Green."'[14] Duff describes the subsequent interview with the Minister, at which Hogan informed him that he would reward Duff to the extent to which he made himself useful to him. He was expected to possess a good general knowledge of all Land Commission matters, although one of Hogan's first instructions to Duff was to the effect that he was 'not to be running over' to the [old] Land Commission. He adhered strictly to this advice and accordingly was thrown upon his own resources:

> Mr. Hogan came to his new duties knowing very little about Land Purchase, but bent upon knowing about it. He was extremely clever, readily understood anything, however difficult, which was explained to him and absorbed information rapidly. His method of acquiring information was not through the medium of books on the subject, but viva voce. Whatever he wanted to know or follow up, he reached by questioning and by the reading/studying of memos explanatory of points upon which he demanded

information … . During that year [1922], I was his Land Commission, expected to combine in my own proper person every function which a Minister would expect to find in the whole department responsible to him.[15]

A letter on the file in the Department of Finance dated 26 September 1922 from Mr Gregg, Head of Establishment, to Mr Hogan, Minister for Agriculture, requested Duff's transfer to the Ministry of Finance for two weeks from 27 September 1922, but gives no reason for the request, to which the Department of Lands, Agriculture and Fisheries acceded. The Department of Finance letter refers to the fact that Duff had been transferred earlier that year for a brief period to the Department of Defence, located at Portobello. This refers to the days when Duff acted as private secretary to Michael Collins prior to the latter's death. Following the death of Arthur Griffith on 12 August 1922, a reassignment of duties occurred, and in that period it was decided temporarily to suspend work on the Land Act. On18 August Duff was assigned to work for Collins and met with him and new staff on the same day.

On 20 August Duff attended as Collins got into the army car that was to take him to the Curragh and then on to Cork and to his death in an ambush two days later. León Ó Broin recounts how Duff had told him about his attendance on Collins and how, when he went into the office on the morning following Collins's death, he found all the women in tears.[16] Duff described Collins as 'one of our very great men'.[17] Following the death of Collins, Duff resumed his work for Hogan and 'sat in the Dáil during the whole of the passage of the Irish Land Bill, 1923'.[18]

Duff travelled with Cosgrave and Hogan on the Irish delegation for talks arranged in London for 9 February 1923. In his official history of *The Irish Department of Finance*, Ronan Fanning states that the Irish party comprised Cosgrave, Hogan, Hugh Kennedy, the Law Officer, and two civil servants – Brennan from Finance and Gordon Campbell [Lord Glenavy] from Industry and Commerce. He omits to mention Duff, who was, according to Cosgrave's own testimony, a valued member of the delegation.[19] Also omitted is Joe O'Reilly, Cosgrave's aide-de-camp. Before departing for London, Hogan called Duff into his room, where he asked him if he had space in his bag for a quart bottle of whiskey. He then asked Duff if he could use a gun. 'Yes,' Duff replied, 'ordinary revolvers.' A friend's father who owned a pub in Dorset Street had a number of guns and together they had shot rabbits. Hogan produced a 'formidable automatic', which Duff declined, and Hogan then placed it in a drawer.[20] Clearly Hogan thought that the threat which hung over the lives of those who favoured the Treaty would follow them to London and that they might need to defend themselves.

Duff noted that the delegation to London was driven to Dún Laoghaire and given first-class cabins. In London the ministers stayed at the home of Lionel

Curtis, special adviser to the Secretary of State for the Colonies. The others stayed at the Royal Court Hotel in Chelsea. Campbell and Duff were the last to arrive and they noticed that the earlier arrivals had entered false names in the hotel register. Duff then signed in as 'F. S. Mitchel' and Campbell signed as 'C. Henry'. Shortly after arrival, a message came from Hogan for Duff: 'Bring the item' – the bottle of whiskey.

On 1 April 1923 Duff was promoted to Higher Executive Officer on an acting basis. The salary scale was £400–£500. In comparison to other employments, such as secondary teaching, this was a good salary. The Department of Finance authorization for Duff's promotion, dated 18 December 1923 and signed by Gregg, also sanctioned a bonus of £150 per annum for Duff in respect of his period in the Department of Lands, Agriculture and Fisheries. The offer came as a disappointment to Duff since he believed that Hogan had led him to expect greater things. At first he refused the offer, and on 21 December applied to retire from the civil service under Article 10 of the Treaty, which stated that 'the government of the Irish Free State agrees to pay fair compensation on terms not less favourable than those accorded by the Act of 1920 to judges, officials, members of the Police Forces and other Public Servants who are discharged by it or who retire in consequence of the change of government effected in pursuance hereof'. In a memo to Hogan dated 20 December 1923, Gregg stated firmly that if Duff did not transfer into the Department of Finance as a Higher Executive Officer on an acting basis, he would have to return to the Land Commission as a Junior Executive Officer, the rank he held before going to work for Hogan. The options facing Duff were formalized in a letter to him from the Secretary of the Land Commission, dated 28 December 1923. He was told the offer would be withdrawn after 31 December.

In a lengthy draft letter to his friend Sir Joseph Glynn, from whom he sometimes sought advice, Duff explained that he was being asked to decide on Gregg's offer to become Higher Executive Officer on an acting basis *before* the hearing of his application to retire under Article 10. He felt that Gregg was placing him under unfair pressure and he wanted to know if the Ministry of Finance offer could not be suspended until after his case had been heard. He said, 'According to the present arrangement, I am to be made refuse on the 31st, and then, if the Committee decide that I am sufficiently rewarded by the terms, these are no longer extant.' He continued:

I hold that from before the Nominated Day, I have been in everything except official designation a Secretary to a Ministry. I had access to the Minister, charge of a Department with full responsibility for all the correspondence which was signed either personally or by delegation without reference to the Minister; have kept my own hours; and in every other way had to do for the Minister what any Ministerial Secretary is called upon to do. It is now proposed to take away all this and to replace with a H. E. [Higher Executive] position. Is this not making a change in the conditions of my employment which materially alters my position? … I was given every mark of apparent confidence and good opinion. What wonder should there be at my taking seriously a remark to the effect that it was intended to cap my work with the very position to which it seemed naturally to lead.[21]

Duff explained in the draft to Glynn that he had told Gregg of Hogan's offer but that Gregg claimed that Hogan had made no such offer. When he raised the offer of a secretaryship with Hogan directly, Hogan also denied that he had made such an offer. Duff said that he had told friends of the offer but was reproached for the folly of imagining that he could rise so high from his position of Lower Executive Officer. He admitted that it did seem like folly now that the old Land Commission was being reconstituted with all its former officers and he was being offered the next step from his existing grade. Duff said that, in conversation, Gregg 'taxed me with being unreasonable' and said that 'I had backed a loser and was too proud to cut my losses.'[22] These were unusual times and it seems that Hogan had raised Duff's expectations beyond what it was feasible for him to deliver once a civil servant of Gregg's outlook and knowledge of the traditional civil service came on the scene and a 'new' Land Commission was not established.

Duff accepted Gregg's offer by letter on 31 December and began work in the Department of Finance in the Finance and Supply Division, reporting to the Principal Officer, Arthur Dean Codling, an English Methodist, on 18 January 1924 following annual leave from 2 to 17 January.[23]

Notes to Chapter 7

1. Letter from Duff which accompanies file of probate of the will of Susan Letitia Duff in 1950. File marked 'Susan L. Duff', LOMA.
2. Deirdre McMahon, 'Maurice Moynihan (1902–1999), Irish Civil Servant: An Appreciation', *Studies*, vol. 89, no. 353, Spring 2000, p.72. See also Deirdre McMahon (ed.), *The Moynihan Brothers in Peace and War 1909–1918: Their New Ireland*. Dublin: Irish Academic Press, 2004.
3. *The Irish Times*, Property, 1 July 2010, p. 4. A photograph of the house is reproduced in the paper.
4. See chapter 8.
5. Maurice Curtis, *The Splendid Cause*. Dublin: Veritas, 2008, p. 60.
6. *The Irish Times*, 13 October 1923.
7. *The Irish Times*, 15 October 1923.
8. Ó Broin, *Frank Duff*, p. 11.
9. Terence Dooley, '*The Land for the People*:' *The Land Question in Independent Ireland*. Dublin: UCD Press, 2004, p. 57.
10. Duff, 'Ireland and the Land Acts', draft article for the *Manchester Guardian*, Land Purchase File.
11. ibid.
12. On 1 January 1920 the Grade of Second Division Clerk had been assimilated to Junior Executive Officer Grade, nowadays called Executive Officer, with the salary scale of £100–£400.
13. Ronan Fanning, *The Irish Department of Finance, 1922–58*. Dublin: Institute of Public Administration, 1978, p. 77.
14. FDCS Memos, 55, LOMA.
15. ibid.

16. Ó Broin, *Frank Duff*, p. 11. The fact that Duff worked for Collins for a brief period was referred to by the latter's grand-niece, Mary Banotti, at a seminar in Trinity College Dublin on 15 November 2007.
17. Frank Duff, 'Potentialities of Telefís Eireann', *Hibernia*, April 1963.
18. Aherne interview.
19. Fanning, *The Irish Department of Finance*, p. 136 and Cosgrave memorandum written for Joseph Pilendiram, a legionary from Ceylon who had worked with the BBC.
20. Enda Dunleavy, 'Frank Duff and Collins', memo by Dunleavy.
21. Duff to Glynn, FDCS Memos, 56, LOMA.
22. ibid.
23. At the time, the other division in the Department of Finance was the Establishment and Supply Division.

CHAPTER 8

The 'Monto' and the Sancta Maria Hostel

'The Mecklenburgh/Montgomery district of the city, north-east of the Custom House, marked the infamous Monto district.'

MARIA LUDDY, *PROSITUTION AND IRISH SOCIETY 1800–1940*

During most of the 1920s Duff spent his working day in the civil service and many evenings on SVP work, taking on some additional visitation of tenements. One evening in 1922 he knocked at 25 Chancery Lane, where he found a lodging house owned by Mrs Slicker. There were approximately thirty women, mostly young, engaged in prostitution lodged within. Following Duff's visit, Fr Ignatius Gibney, a Passionist priest who was giving a retreat at the time to the women in Francis Street parish, together with Fr Creedon, curate in the parish, called to Mrs Slicker's. Fr Gibney and Fr Creedon spoke to the women, who expressed interest in getting away from their life in prostitution if some other means of survival could be found. There and then Fr Creedon offered to pay Mrs Slicker a sum for maintaining the women until further notice. No one seemed quite clear on the next step when Fr Richard Devane, a Jesuit priest who had opened the Retreat House for men at Rathfarnham Castle, suggested offering the girls an opportunity for a retreat. Duff commented:

> Now Fr. Devane believed in the enclosed retreat. He believed it would cure broken limbs. I never saw such a conviction as he had about the value of a weekend retreat. At that particular time I partially shared his enthusiasm which diminished later … . We thought over a lot of things but the only one that seemed to have promise was Father Devane's suggestion that we gather them together and give them a retreat – a three-day retreat. He volunteered to give the retreat himself.[1]

With the idea of an enclosed retreat in mind, Devane, accompanied by Josephine Plunkett, set out in search of a venue. Earlier in 1922 the Reverend Mother of the Convent of the Sisters of Charity in Baldoyle had introduced Duff to Miss Plunkett and to Miss Scratton, who were staying at the guest house attached to the convent and who wished to undertake some social work. Miss Plunkett's father had been a leading member of the Irish Bar, while Miss Scratton's father, Thomas Scratton, was a former Church of England clergyman who entered the Catholic Church under the influence of Newman and had come over to Dublin with Newman many decades earlier to work with the Catholic University. These two women would shortly form the nucleus of the second branch of the Association of Our Lady of Mercy, which would take charge of the soon-to-be-opened Sancta Maria Hostel, by which time the founding branch numbered over seventy members.

Convent after convent turned down the request of Devane and Plunkett until Mother Angela Walsh, Superior of the Convent of the Sisters of Charity in Baldoyle, then considered a distant suburb of Dublin, agreed to house the girls for the retreat while more permanent accommodation was sought. The retreat was given by a recently ordained Franciscan, Father Philip Murphy. Murphy had become something of a legend, since, in the course of a retreat he had given at 'Adam and Eve's' Church on Merchants Quay, he had tipped the winner of the upcoming Grand National – an Irish contender named 'Sergeant Murphy', which romped home at big odds. But where were the women – whom Duff described as a 'lovely lot of girls, practically all of them young and pretty' – to go after the retreat?[2] Ever practical, Duff realized that some sort of hostel accommodation was required and he turned to the civil, not church, authorities.

On Saturday, 15 July 1922, in the middle of the civil war, when ministers and officials were living in Government Buildings in Upper Merrion Street under armed guard, Duff and Creedon obtained an interview with W. T. Cosgrave, Minister for Local Government and soon to be President of the Executive Council of the Free State, at Government Buildings. E. P. McCarron, Secretary of the Department of Local Government, was also present, and it is likely that he had facilitated the meeting.[3] Cosgrave recalled how 'Frank and Fr. Creedon came to the ante-chamber of the cabinet room while a meeting was in progress – asking to see me. It was then he told me of the efforts of Fr. Creedon and himself on behalf of these friendless girls.'[4] Cosgrave listened intently and asked them to call back for his response in the morning. On the following morning, a Sunday, Duff and Creedon called to Government Buildings, where they were given a letter.[5] The letter, in Cosgrave's handwriting, informed them that premises at 76 Harcourt Street had been placed at their disposal, free of rent or taxes. Duff described what happened when he went into the office on Monday:

> I went into the building and Mr. McCarron, who was then Secretary of Local government, one of the finest human beings that ever drew breath, a noble figure, came to me with the key to Sancta Maria [name given to 76 Harcourt Street] and a cheque for fifty pounds. It was real money in those days.[6]

Number 76 Harcourt Street was not without its own history. In 1919, following the raid on Sinn Féin offices at 6 Harcourt Street, Michael Collins asked his friend, the builder Batt O'Connor, to purchase number 76, where O'Connor built 'a secret closet in the thickness of the walls' where books and papers could be stored.[7] In October 1919 Collins made an escape from the house during a raid via a route designed by O'Connor.[8] In due course, O'Connor's daughter Eileen would become a dedicated member of the Legion and a member of Duff's cycling parties. By an odd coincidence, Thomas Scratton had lived for a time in 76 Harcourt Street when he was Registrar of the Catholic University at St Stephen's Green.

When the women were installed, Joe Gabbett, who earlier had helped to move furniture into number 76, cooked the first meal. In Duff's words, 'Gabbett took off his coat and he cooked the first meal eaten in that place … which is extraordinary if you think of it because we had a professional cook among the women who afterwards gravitated into that very position in the house, a woman called Hannah Reekley.'[9] A large picture of the Sacred Heart, which belonged to Gabbett, was hung on a wall in an 'Enthronement of the Sacred Heart' ceremony, a traditional practice at the time. Afterwards all the helpers got together in what was destined to become the common room and had a tremendous discussion with the girls. It was eleven o'clock that night when, leaving Plunkett and Scratton at the helm, Duff and Creedon set out for their homes.

A sentence in the faded records of the Sancta Maria Hostel for early spring 1923 states that two of the residents, Lizzie Manley and Kathleen Deegan, had left the hostel and gone to live in the notorious Monto area where they were engaged in prostitution.[10] The area was so well known as a centre for late-night drinking in shebeens and for prostitution that it merited a mention in the *Encyclopaedia Britannica* in 1903: 'Dublin furnishes an exception to the usual practice in the United Kingdom. In that city the police permit open 'houses', confined to one street; but carried on more publicly than even in the south of Europe or in Algeria.'[11] Monto derived its name from Montgomery Street, since renamed Foley Street, which runs parallel to the lower end of Talbot Street on the way to what was Amiens Street (now Connolly) Station. According to local historian Terry Fagan, 'The heart of Monto was Mecklenburgh Street (renamed Tyrone Street in 1887, changing again to today's Railway Street in 1911), and the surrounding lanes and alleys, many of which are now gone for ever, subsumed beneath later developments like Liberty House flats.'[12] The Monto was situated in the Pro-Cathedral parish, in which Archbishop Byrne had worked as a curate, and which was one of his own parishes when he became Archbishop. Mary Purcell provides historical background to the settlement near Aldborough Barracks, in the Monto area, of the returning 'Castrensi', or camp followers of the victorious army in the Crimean war. She says that 'The authorities took one look at these foreigners from every country in Europe and promptly shipped them to Dublin.'[13] Professor Maria Luddy, in her history of prostitution in Ireland in the nineteenth and early twentieth centuries, provides an illuminating context for the Monto.[14]

On 22 March 1923 Duff and Plunkett set off for the Monto. They had the name and address of one girl living in the area: Mary Tate at 8 Elliott Place.[15] They had an introduction to May Oblong,[16] a former 'madam' or brothel-keeper, now retired, and owner of a shop at 15 Corporation Street.[17] Mrs Oblong warned them that it would be very dangerous to proceed with their visit. However, they decided to seek out Mary Tate and found her lying ill in bed. They persuaded her to go to hospital and arranged for a horse-drawn cab to take her to the Westmoreland Lock hospital for venereal diseases in Townsend Street, where she lived for another six weeks. When she died, her funeral was one of the biggest ever seen in the Monto. According to Fagan, all the prostitutes from the Monto and the Sancta Maria Hostel turned up for Mary Tate's funeral to Glasnevin Cemetery.

When she had been taken to hospital, Duff and Plunkett continued their visit in the area. At first they met 'very neat, well-dressed girls', but soon encountered another category – 'the battered type that had been on the streets for a great number of years and who had sunk with every day, perpetual drinkers, clad in rags, whose appearance was generally dreadful'.[18] They saw a group of about eight women seated in a ring passing around methylated spirits and water. Duff and Plunkett managed to converse with the women and invited them over to Sancta Maria for a retreat, as a preliminary to moving out of the Monto. At that stage Duff and his colleagues regarded the retreat as a necessity, but they changed that view. 'We were in the grip of something that we now repudiate – we attached a sort of undue influence to the retreat.'[19] For the initial retreat in Sancta Maria, many of the 'Monto' women said that they would attend, but did not have any decent clothes to wear other than garments hired from the 'madams', so Duff and his colleagues provided clothes. Several of the women attended the retreat and were helped to establish lives outside prostitution. One of those was Maggie Ballard:

> Maggie Ballard was known as Queen of the Spunkers. Spunk is a cant expression for methylated spirit. Normally it's slang for courage but it is also used to designate methylated spirit. She was called the Queen of the Spunkers and had been 22 years down there [the Monto]. She was originally from Glasgow and she was one of those who turned up and who was a perfect restoration from the first second and never looked back. After she had been with us for some time, we set inquiries on foot and managed, with her aid of course, to restore her to her family in Glasgow.[20]

In 1925 the Lenten Mission in the Pro-Cathedral was conducted by three Jesuits – Fathers Devane, Mackey and Roche – and was attended by many Monto residents. Duff and his helpers continued to visit the Monto and made contact with a number of the madams and some of the men who acted as 'bullies' (pimps). A number of madams agreed to close their premises if they received some financial compensation for their loss of business. One of them had seven children to support and Duff said of her, 'She was a fair person. If her trade could be justified, she was an admirable person.'[21] He accepted the economic realities of Monto life and came to a financial arrangement with the madams. A date was set for closure of the brothels. But when he felt he was being held to ransom by one of the madams, Duff approached the Garda Chief Commissioner in Dublin Castle. A large-scale police raid was organized for midnight on 12 March 1925 under the supervision of Colonel David Neligan and Captain Ennis of the Detective Branch. Of the 120 people arrested, only two were charged. One served a six-week sentence.[22]

The work of the Sancta Maria Hostel centred on 'a large body of voluntary workers' who on a weekly basis visited women's lodging houses, the venereal hospital, the women's casual ward of the Union and any other locations where women might be found who could be helped with accommodation in the hostel.[23] The Sancta Maria depended for its existence on fundraising and voluntary contributions from well-wishers. An example of fundraising was the 'Violetta Fête' at which the Metropolitan Garda Band performed. An advertisement for 'The Violetta Fête and Sale of Work, Lr. Leeson Street, August 6 and 7' appeared in the *Evening Herald* of 30 July 1927. In a letter from Duff to the director of the Band, he explained that the fête was in aid of 'work for the prostitutes, carried out at 76 Harcourt Street'. He said:

> ... our work has been along new lines. It was an effort to get at that large number of girls for whom the Magdalen Asylum exercised no appeal ... . The centre of the work is of course the Hostel at 76, Harcourt Street, which tempers considerably the requirements of the Magdalen Asylum, giving some liberty, allowing some cigarettes, and imposing no uniform.[24]

One of the women who lived in the hostel from time to time was Elizabeth or Lily O'Neill, better known as 'Honour Bright', who usually lodged with another young woman, Madge Hopkins, at 48 Newmarket in Dublin. Duff and his helpers befriended her in 1922. Lily O'Neill was brutally murdered at Ticknock in the Dublin Mountains on 9 June 1925. Ó Broin recounted how, one evening, Duff found her swinging on the old chain rails which used to surround the corner of St Stephen's Green opposite the Shelbourne Hotel, and how he pleaded with her to go to the hostel. She replied, 'I'll come back tomorrow. I promise I will, Mr. Duff.'[25] Another woman with a Sancta Maria association, Lily Casey, was murdered in December 1926. Casey, who had been married in Francis Street parish, was working as a prostitute when she met some legionaries. They introduced her to Fr Michael Creedon, who was Spiritual Director of the Legion of Mary and a curate in Francis Street. Creedon referred Casey to the Sancta Maria Hostel in Harcourt Street on 12 May 1926. In August she got a job as a maid in Newcastle Sanatorium, a hospital for TB patients in County Wicklow. Following a drinking spree in October, the matron refused to have her back. She returned to her husband and they lived together at 37 Francis Street where they had procured a room. There early one December morning she was found dead following an alleged beating by her husband, who then absconded. He was apprehended but acquitted.[26] The rumour was spread in the archdiocese that Creedon was indirectly responsible for Lily's death because he was forcing men to marry girls from 76 Harcourt Street. In a written statement, Creedon said that he 'had nothing whatever, direct or indirect, to do with her marriage which took place as will be observed from the particulars herewith – 1 year and 188 days before I was transferred to Francis Street'.[27]

As Duff struggled with the double burden of his day job in the Department of Finance and Legion work, including responsibility for the Sancta Maria Hostel, his commitment to daily Mass, the recitation of the Divine Office and the Rosary provided his oxygen. Hard at work in the Department and burdened with other responsibilities, Duff wrote on one occasion to Fr Creedon describing his exhaustion. 'I am writing this at 2 am. Last night in bed at 4.40 and the previous night at 5.10. I am feeling very done up. …'[28] What Duff needed more than anything at the time was a sustaining word of encouragement from the archdiocese and the acceptance of his work. But that was slow to come.

The late Monsignor Michael Nolan, Professor Emeritus of Psychology at University College Dublin, took a special interest in Archbishop Byrne and was familiar with the Diocesan archival material in relation to the Archbishop. He maintained that Byrne's disposition was non-confrontational and that his letters were very polite. It was Nolan's belief that Byrne, having served as Vice-Rector of the Irish College in Rome, could have pursued an ecclesiastical career in Rome, but opted to return to Dublin, where he was appointed Titular Bishop of Pegae in August 1920 and Archbishop of Dublin one year later. Byrne's reign in Dublin lasted for twenty years until his death in February 1940. However, for much of his tenure he suffered from a debilitating disease and the work of the archdiocese depended on the vicars general.

Nolan thought that Byrne was present in the Pro-Cathedral on the Saturday evening at the end of the retreat which preceded the closure of the Monto and was upset that he had not been given prior notice of the Garda raid that led to the closure of the brothels there. The Monto was in the Pro-Cathedral area and Byrne felt let down by his own administrator there.[29] According to Thomas Morrissey, SJ, 'Duff was criticized for involving priests like Frs Creedon and Toher in a movement that was undermining the clergy's responsibility for the care of souls.'[30] Morrissey suggests that Byrne

> … seems to have viewed the whole operation as unwise and excessive. He had served for years in the Pro-Cathedral and knew and respected the people of the parish. The

priests had endeavoured to adapt to the reality of the situation, even to having an understanding with the proprietors of the red light area that if any customer or other person became gravely ill a priest would be called. He would stand at the door of the premises and attend to the sick person form there.[31]

A possible reason for the wariness of certain prelates in the archdiocese towards Duff and his work was suggested by Archbishop (Cardinal) Desmond Connell.[32] He believed that in the 1920s and 1930s priests would have recalled what they saw as the high-risk strategy of the nineteenth-century British prime minister, Gladstone, visiting prostitutes with a view to their rescue. The clergy would have been wary of engaging in such work, or of allowing lay people to engage in it.

Notes to Chapter 8

1. Moss (ed), *Frank Duff*, p. 30.
2. ibid., p. 35.
3. Ó Broin, *Frank Duff*, pp. 20–21.
4. Cosgrave memorandum written for Joseph Pilendiram, private papers.
5. The framed letter hung for many years outside the Oratory of the Regina Coeli Hostel, close to a large drawing of W. T. Cosgrave by Seán O'Sullivan.
6. Moss (ed.), *Frank Duff*, p. 36.
7. Fanning, *The Irish Department of Finance*, p. 18.
8. ibid., p.18.
9. Moss (ed.), *Frank Duff*, p. 37.
10. Duff, *Miracles on Tap*, p. 113. In his account of the 'Monto' area, Duff uses the pseudonym 'Bentley Place'.
11. Terry Fagan, *Monto: Madams, Murder and Black Coddle*, undated; Duff, *Miracles on Tap*, p. 117; *Encyclopaedia Britannica*, Tenth Edition, Vol. XXXII. The article in the *Encyclopaedia* is by Dr Arthur Shadwell.
12. Fagan, *Monto*, p. 9. On 19 May 2009 I participated in a guided tour of the 'Monto' given by Terry Fagan.
13. Mary Purcell, *Remembering Matt Talbot*, 1954, reprinted Dublin: Veritas, 1990, pp. 13–14.
14. Maria Luddy, *Prositution and Irish Society 1800–1940*. Cambridge: Cambridge University Press, 2007.
15. In Moss (ed.), *Frank Duff*, p. 44, Duff speaks of 'Mary Kate at Number 8', while in *Miracles on Tap*, p. 128, he speaks of 'Mary Lyne of number nine'. In Moss (ed.), *Frank Duff*, p. 45, Duff explains that Mary Kate is described as Mary Lyne to 'conceal her identity'. Ó Broin, *Frank Duff*, p. 23, speaks of 'Mary Lyne of ninety-nine'. Enda Dunleavy has confirmed that the correct name was Mary Tate and that 'Kate' was a misprint in Moss.
16. Named 'Mrs Brewster' in *Miracles on Tap*.
17. Fagan, *Monto*, p. 94.
18. Moss (ed.), *Frank Duff*, p. 46.
19. ibid., p. 47.
20. ibid., p. 48.
21. ibid., p. 51.
22. Fagan, *Monto*, p. 99.
23. Duff to Director of Metropolitan Garda Band, 19 September 1927.
24. ibid.
25. Ó Broin, *Frank Duff*, p. 18.
26. *Evening Herald*, 2 and 3 May 1927.
27. Statement by Creedon, LOMA.

28. Duff to Creedon, 26 September 1926.
29. Author's conversation with Mgr Nolan, 13 July 2008.
30. Morrissey, *Edward J. Byrne*, p. 227.
31. ibid, pp. 227–28.
32. Meeting of author with Archbishop (Cardinal) Connell, 12 August 1999.

CHAPTER 9

The Morning Star and Regina Coeli Hostels

'I've never altered the opinion I formed then, namely, that Frank Duff concerned himself exclusively with the good – real or potential – in all those with whom he made any kind of contact.'

NIVARD FLOOD, 'MY MEMORIES OF FRANK DUFF'

In 1926, at a time of severe poverty and dire housing conditions in Dublin, the government established a Commission to investigate the conditions of the poor. Duff, who was known as someone working among the poor, was invited to give evidence. In a detailed statement, he said that many of the existing lodging houses were 'swarming with vermin'.[1] He pointed to the existence of an even less fortunate group than those who lived in the lodging houses – the 'Down and Outs', whose life was 'shocking in its hardship'. Most of the 'down and outs' were in the position of 'not seeing the way clear for another meal' and it was impossible for a man who fell into that state 'to secure any ordinary description of employment, if indeed he had the heart to seek it'.

On the basis of police data and figures for those needing free breakfasts, Duff reckoned that the number of 'down and out' men in Dublin amounted to at least 600. He argued that the state approach to the problem under Poor Law regulations had been a failure: 'The remedy is *not* within the reach of the Poor Law or other secular administrative machinery and a lodging house of some kind or another is manifestly indicated.'[2] He proposed the establishment of a hostel with a yard attached, to give the men the opportunity to contribute towards their keep by chopping firewood. The hostel would be staffed by voluntary workers. And then the astonishing part – side by side with care for basic necessities, 'an intimate and personal acquaintance' was to be built with each man. He stressed the duty of Christians to take responsibility for their fellow people. To suggest that Duff relied for the remedy of social ills on 'a morally interventionist state' is mistaken and misleading.[3] By his work, Duff showed clearly that he did not believe reliance on the state, either in its laws or its services, could substitute for Christian obligation. He described as 'disaster' the 'supposition that the state has to do everything itself'.[4]

A breakthrough in the hostel proposal occurred when Duff talked 'to an old school-fellow, William Dwyer, the City Commissioner'.[5] In May 1924 the

Council of the Corporation of Dublin had been dissolved owing to a failure to duly discharge its duties and coincidentally on foot of a report on the finances of the Corporation, which Duff had carried out in the Department of Finance. Dwyer, together with Seamus Murphy and P. J. Hernon, were appointed Commissioners of the County Borough of Dublin to perform the duties of the said Council.[6] The Commissioners remained *in situ* until October 1934 when, following legislation, a new Council was elected. Dwyer succeeded in interesting his colleagues in Duff's hostel proposal, with the result that premises were offered on condition that the SVP would make itself responsible for the work. The Vicar General, Mgr Wall, on behalf of Archbishop Byrne, discouraged SVP involvement and the project stalled.[7] However, the government, eager to move on the proposal, then made the premises of the North Dublin Union directly available to Duff and a committee, under certain conditions, including personal financial pledges from Duff.

In 1918 the North Dublin Union had been merged with the South Dublin Union, the joint Union being named the Dublin Union and based at the South Dublin Union site. A few years later the North Dublin Union premises was taken into military use and provided a headquarters building for the 'Black and Tans.' The name derived from the black and tan uniforms worn by the paramilitary police force, drawn from the ranks of World War I veterans sent to subdue the Irish rebels during what became known as the 'Tan War.' The war was waged from spring 1920 to the truce in July 1921.

In early March 1927 Duff wrote to Archbishop's House requesting an interview with the Archbishop. The letter, dated 9 March 1927, is the first to appear in the Dublin Diocesan Archives (DDA) from Duff to Archbishop's House and is addressed to Dr Dunne, Secretary to the Archbishop.[8] In the event, Duff would have to wait eight years, until 24 January 1935, for a personal interview with Dr Byrne. The letter of 9 March 1927 is marked in pencil in the Archbishop's handwriting: 'Kindly put in writing what he wants [presumably, at the requested interview].' Accordingly, just one week later, a second letter is sent by Duff saying that he was seeking permission for a private Mass in the new Morning Star Hostel for derelict men on the day of its opening, provisionally 25 March, the Feast of the Annunciation. The plan was to have a Mass followed by enthronement of the Sacred Heart. The small number of guests would include President Cosgrave and Sir Joseph Glynn, chairman of the National Health Insurance Commission, who often acted as a conduit for communication between the Archbishop and Duff. Proceedings would be private; there would be no member of the press. The archbishop declined Duff's request for a Mass at the opening. Duff's letter setting out his request for permission to have a Mass celebrated is marked 'No.' That simple word summarizes the attitude of negativity in the Archbishop's House towards Duff and the Legion of Mary during the Byrne years.

The hostel opened its doors and began to welcome its residents. A small daily payment was required from each man on admission. Duff saw the payment as serving two purposes. Firstly, together with donations from legionaries and those who supported the work of the hostel, the daily tariff helped to defray the expenses of the hostel, but secondly, and more importantly, it was a guarantee of a resident's independence. It placed the volunteer workers in the position of providing a service rather than running a free charity. Shortly after the Morning Star Hostel opened, Duff wrote to Celia Shaw, thanking her for a financial donation and referring to the 'nightly tariff':

> The Morning Star continues its course – storms without, but peace within – frustrated by the ecclesiastical authorities (or rather by one of them) but obviously blessed by Heaven. It is a great argument in favour of the theories on which the place was opened, that not one man has so far failed in payment of the nightly tariff.[9]

Three months later Duff was able to report to Creedon that 'The Morning Star now has 65 guests, all conducting themselves excellently. The Labour Yard has been opened and has over 30 employed.' He said that a magnificent statue of the Sacred Heart had been received and that they had an 'Enthronement' of the statue on the Feast of the Sacred Heart by the Jesuit priest Tom Murphy. The Society of Jesus (the Jesuits) 'is standing to us well and send priests whenever asked.'[10] He also mentioned that Bob Tyson of the men's outfitters in Grafton Street had promised at least £100 for 76 Harcourt Street.

One year after the opening of the Morning Star Hostel, the small cul-de-sac off North Brunswick Street, where the hostel was located, was named Morning Star Avenue, which it has remained ever since. It is thought that the name was given by the Commissioners of the County Borough of Dublin as a result of a chance meeting on a city street between Duff and Dwyer. The two men agreed that the poor of the city would be helped by a definite address when seeking to locate the hostel.

The opening of the Morning Star Hostel in March 1927 was the occasion for the establishment of the first Legion of Mary praesidium for men. The Cistercian priest Nivard Flood has provided a vivid account of the early days in the Morning Star. In 1929, when he was a Leaving Certificate student in the Christian Brothers' School in North Richmond Street and a member of the SVP, he became a 'student helper' in the hostel. When he first heard of the 'Morning Star', he thought it was a minibus, not a hostel for down and out men, because in Dublin in the late 1920s the transport system was enlivened by privately owned minibuses with names such as St Francis, St Thérèse and Morning Star. Flood's first impression of the hostel was formed in the kitchen, which at the time also served as dining room, recreation room and general clearing-house for most of the hostel business. Flood recounts how he cut endless loaves of bread, using an old-fashioned bread-cutting machine, and how he manned the 'Iron Maiden' fumigator, in which clothes were hung on sliding racks of hooks with lighted sulphur employed. When there was an outbreak of turbulence among the men, Duff was able to restore order in a calm and quiet way. According to Flood, Duff always looked for the best in people. Flood recalled one phone conversation during which Duff described as a 'nice type of man' someone who had served several periods in jail for minor crimes.[11]

Flood recalled the dedication of the Legion Brothers – Carey, White, Desmond, Rutherford, Kirwan and Ryan and the legendary full-time 'indoor brothers' who roomed in the hostels and were provided with subsistence – Tom Doyle and Brendan Crowley. Doyle, who was born in Rathvilly, County Carlow, in 1905 joined the praesidium that staffed the Morning Star in 1929 and remained a key figure in the life of the hostel for sixty years. He took the radical step of giving up his job at a time of economic depression and becoming an indoor brother, making the hostel his own home. When he became hostel manager in 1931, he had two elderly indoor brothers and one praesidium to help him to care for 150 residents. He established another praesidium, which in turn led to others. The great majority of hostel legionaries are 'outdoor' brothers who combine hostel service with other commitments in their daily lives. According to Stephen Redmond, SJ, Doyle had a daily routine of two early Masses in the nearby Capuchin church. Personal attention to each man was his watchword:

> A favourite 'indulgence' of his was presiding at afternoon tea and a favourite priority was personal attention to the residents. He once said: 'There is a danger that we may fall short in our service by not giving full personal attention to each man. We should get to know them intimately, share their interests and as friends show an interest in their hopes and desires.'[12]

When Doyle died in 1992, there were many calls to Gay Byrne's radio show to speak about him. The man who chose to be buried in the Morning Star plot in Glasnevin cemetery together with former hostel residents might well have been amused by his celebrity.

Legionaries organized a range of activities, which included indoor and outdoor games, a debating society and amateur theatricals for the residents of the hostel. Ó Broin recounts how he spoke to the debating society and gave some help to the drama group, which was preparing a play for a local feis (festival). Another who helped the drama group was the Abbey actor Seamus Forde. Ó Broin remarked that there was talent in the group, some of whose members had spent time in jail. When for financial reasons the feis abandoned the competition in dramatic art, the Legion organized its own feis.

The adjudicators for the plays were Andrew E. Malone, critic from *The Irish Times*, and Ó Broin.[13] In a report on the business of the Dublin Union in 1930, *The Irish Times* referred to the fact that the commissioners had furnished a portion of the old North Dublin Union and 'handed them over to Mr. Frank Duff and his co-workers for the reception of males heretofore entering the workhouse'. *The Irish Times* declared, 'The experiment has so far been a complete success.'[14]

Poverty was a feature of life in the Morning Star, not only among the residents. The indoor brothers lived very simple lives. But the atmosphere was cheerful. Among the residents were to be found a few professional men, even including the occasional priest. Flood recalls a doctor and a solicitor, both of whom had fallen into difficulties and for whom the hostel provided special support in the form of a room for study to enable them to get back to their regular lives.[15] Fr Michael O'Carroll has told of a medical student who had completed his studies, but because of a 'problem' had not sat his final examinations. He came to the Morning Star Hostel, where it was ascertained that he was eligible to sit a later examination. O'Carroll said that he passed the examination and so became 'the first doctor to graduate from a Legion of Mary hostel'![16] Less successful was Duff's attempt to get one resident back on his feet by hiring an ass and cart at a cost of £3 10s to give him an opportunity to trade. Unfortunately, the beneficiary sold the ass and cart and ended up before the courts.[17]

Just before the official opening of the Morning Star Hostel on 25 March 1927, Duff persuaded his family to leave Dartmouth Square. On 23 March 1927 the Duffs moved into the house adjacent to the hostel that had previously been occupied by the doctor in charge of the North Dublin Union Hospital. It must have been a difficult move for Mrs Duff, who was sixty-three at the time, and for her son John, who enjoyed the St Stephen's Green Club where 'the bar and snooker room' were 'more in his line'.[18] Sarah Geraldine married fellow doctor Vincent Monahan the year the family left Dartmouth Square and went to live in Navan, while Ailish, recently qualified as a doctor, took up a post in England. Lettie did her best to keep the family together and to maintain her household in a cul-de-sac off North Brunswick Street, quite a come-down from Dartmouth Square.

Duff's cousin Carmel has recounted the intimacy of the Duff household when she visited with her father and mother as a child in the 1930s, usually coming for lunch or high tea or sometimes both. Present were Aunt Lettie, Frank, sometimes his brother John, occasionally Geraldine, and Ailish if she were home on holidays from England, where she was an eye specialist in Walsall, outside Birmingham. Frank's sister Isabel, who was frequently ill and suffered from chronic asthma, might come downstairs from her bedroom.

Carmel recalled how Frank always included her in general conversation, even though he and Carmel's other cousins were much older. When Carmel came to work with the Lucan Dairies in Dublin in the 1940s she stayed in the Holy Child Hostel in Harcourt Street and went to lunch daily with the Duffs for a period of two years. When later she moved to work with Aer Lingus, she came to lunch on Mondays. Other members of the family were invited on Tuesday and Wednesday; Mrs Duff did not have lunch guests on Thursday or Friday.[19] On one occasion when Mrs Duff was looking for her copy of *The Times*, the housekeeper told her that she had given the paper to Carmel, to which information Mrs Duff replied, 'You know Miss Carmel does not read *The Times*.'

On 5 October 1930, 'Rosary Sunday', a hostel for 'derelict women', the Regina Coeli, opened beside the Morning Star. In 1926, four years before Duff opened the Regina Coeli Women's Hostel, there were over a thousand unmarried mothers with their babies in county homes.[20] The work had been carefully planned in advance. The first meeting in connection with the women's hostel was held in January 1929, almost two years before the hostel opened. The meeting was attended by five women legionaries, Duff and Morning Star Brother Metcalfe.[21] As with other Legion activity, all work was undertaken on a voluntary basis, with a number of legionaries opting to live in the hostels as full-time 'indoor sisters'. These 'indoor sisters', like the indoor brothers, were provided with subsistence in the hostel. Every woman would pay a small contribution towards her keep, and a 'task system' of laundry or domestic work would be avoided at all costs. If the women could not afford the tariff, bottles or jampots, which could be redeemed for money in those days, would be accepted. The object was to create 'a home-life feeling about the place'.[22] Duff stressed that the surroundings should be as beautiful as possible because 'The silent influence of beautiful and artistic surroundings is incalculable.'[23] He said that the 'conduct of the women will in great measure be governed by their surroundings'.[24] The women should be encouraged to take an interest in their appearance and Miss Mortell suggested the introduction of several panel mirrors.

In the first week fifteen women were admitted to the hostel. Soon after the opening, a pregnant woman sought admission. Her entry to the hostel and keeping her child led to the inauguration of the '*Mater Dei*' aspect of the hostel, a type of hostel within a hostel specifically organized on the basis of units for mothers and children. One of the mothers in each unit elected to stay at home and care for the children, while the others took jobs to pay for household costs. Thus began a revolutionary system for assisting lone mothers to keep their children. By Christmas 1930, a couple of months after the hostel opening, the minutes report that residents were going to the Coombe Hospital for the delivery of their babies.[25] Duff's special sympathy for unmarried mothers was at odds with the mores of the time, when the consequences of an extra-marital birth were disastrous, rendering both mother and child social outcasts. In his powerful novel *Esther Waters* (1894), in which he tells the story of a mother's fight for the life of her illegitimate son, George Moore wrote, 'Hers is a heroic adventure if one considers it – a mother's fight for the life of her child against all the forces that civilisation arrays against the lowly and the illegitimate.'

In a memorandum entitled 'The Amendment of the Criminal Law', which Duff wrote in preparation for the evidence he gave to the Criminal Law Amendment Committee (Carrigan Committee, 1931), he emphasized his concern for unmarried mothers. He compared the harsh treatment of mothers with that of those who fathered children outside marriage. He said that English law was 'considerably in advance of our Irish law on this matter and it is relatively an easy matter to get an Affiliation Order in England'.[26] He also pointed out how easy it was for a young unmarried woman who became pregnant to be recruited into prostitution, because she lacked any form of financial support. Duff described her fate: 'the girl in trouble leaves home, if not driven out by her friends'. After a period of great stress when she is unable to work because of her pregnancy, she enters the workhouse, is confined, leaves with her baby, but has no home to return to. If she finds a job as a domestic servant, the 'child must be supported and she herself clad on the miserable wages of the ordinary domestic servant.' Duff details the costs of a 'nurse-child' (a wet nurse) and other expenses and concludes 'it is not a matter of wonder' that the girl ends up on the streets.

When the Regina Coeli began to accept pregnant women and unmarried mothers and their babies, there was no state institution where an unmarried mother could keep and continue to rear the child herself. St Patrick's Home at Pelletstown in north Dublin, which was the responsibility of the Dublin Board of Assistance, was the main refuge for pregnant unmarried women. However, women desirous of going to Pelletstown were obliged to go through the Union, the old workhouse, a place they dreaded. In the Union the women were housed in the 'Healthy Yard'. Women would transfer to Pelletstown before entering a maternity hospital for their confinement. Following confinement, the women could return to Pelletstown for a period until the children were either adopted – a process arranged informally prior to the Adoption Act, 1952 – or sent to Industrial Schools. According to the 1949 Report of the Consultative Health Council, unmarried mothers generally remained in institutions such as Pelletstown for between eighteen months and two years for the 'purposes of house and laundry work'.[27] Only Dublin City women were admitted to Pelletstown, so girls who came to Dublin from the country in the hope of hiding themselves would not be admitted, even if they were prepared to enter the Union first.

Duff disapproved of the housing of unmarried mothers in a section known as the 'Healthy Yard' in the South Dublin Union, describing those who came to this place in large numbers as 'many simple decent girls from the country', but from where because of their 'predicament … the streets obtain many of their recruits'.[28] Nor was Duff an advocate of Industrial Schools, where children could be sent as young as two years of age. Writing to a priest on the subject, Duff attributed difficulties encountered by the children when they left these schools as being attributable to 'the absence of the children's mothers during a period of life when such is necessary to the children. The consequence is that a peculiar and unnatural life is lived by those children.' He referred to a nun whom he considered one of the best superiors of these schools, but who had confided in him that 'she does not believe in the schools, but only acquiesces in them as a necessary evil'.[29] Duff said that to think of the children as in some way 'weak or warped' by virtue of their origin 'is untrue – utterly untrue' and he cited the tremendous results that had flowed from the work in the Regina Coeli. 'They live the ordinary life of the community; attend the ordinary schools and churches and move about in the city as they are brought up by their mothers.' Writing to his friend Celia Shaw, a UCD graduate and one of the first women to hold administrative rank in the civil service, Duff reported in late 1930: 'The Regina is doing excellently. The unmarried mother is the great development in connection with it. We will have to make fuller provision in this particular direction.'[30]

The carefully kept minute books of the Regina Coeli praesidia provide a unique record of life in the hostel. They are filled with detail of specific cases of women and their babies. The mothers showed varying degrees of interest in their babies, from the very committed to the occasional mother who left her baby in the hostel and disappeared to another mother who was found washing her baby under a cold tap. General issues of administration and finance are also covered. It is clear that making ends meet was a huge task and for decades there are references to bazaars, flag days, 'Rosetta Days' when paper flowers were sold, Beetle Drives and even a special night of greyhound racing at Shelbourne Park stadium. On one occasion an iced cake was presented for a raffle by the manageress of Woolworth's Cafeteria. Funds also came from donations from relatives of hostel residents and from friends of Duff and supporters of the Legion. The minutes note contributions from W. T. Cosgrave and his sister Miss May Cosgrave and, in the 1940s, from Archbishop McQuaid.

The health of the mothers and babies is a constant issue. There are frequent mentions of women going to the Lock Hospital in Townsend Street for tests and of children being brought to St Ultan's, Temple Street, Harcourt Street and other city hospitals. Frequently the hospitals are full and the children cannot be admitted. The hostel sisters encourage breast-feeding and there are references to attempts to get supplies of orange juice and cod liver oil supplement. The problem of supplies was particularly acute during World War II, when the sisters were asked to be sparing in their use of sugar and to ensure that the lights were turned out. On one occasion in 1942 there is reference to the fact that 'Two cwt. [hundred-weight] of blocks daily is at present being used to boil the water for the washing of baby clothes.'[31]

The Regina Coeli was not without its critics. The writer Seán Ó Faoláin questioned its work in an article in the June 1944 issue of the magazine *The Bell* in which he implied that, in contrast to himself, the Legion of Mary was not interested in the slums. This annoyed Duff, who wrote to Ó Faoláin telling him that 'it was unquestionable that you keep talking about the slums, while legionaries were actually visiting them continually'. This evoked a response from Ó Faoláin in which he described the Regina Coeli as a slum.[32] Duff responded that a rough definition of a slum would be a place that is very poor and overcrowded, and he agreed: 'Yes, the Regina Coeli conforms to that definition.' He then went on to ask whether Ó Faoláin was dishing out the old shibboleths about 'dulling the revolutionary edge of poverty'?

> A girl comes to us in trouble – most of them almost demented – and we should refuse her because of some doctrinaire stuff or other! Likewise we should let the down and out man or the prostitute rot in the interests of world revolution, or of a future reform of the system! As you are over forty, I decline to believe you are serious.[33]

In answer to Ó Faoláin's distinction between 'charity or justice', Duff responded:

> This is a false antithesis. For the one must never exclude the other. Indeed rightly viewed they are the same thing. But even if they were not they would be strictly complementary. Charity without justice would be a crime. Justice without charity would be … hell on earth! But this is like a school lesson, and you are no child, though you are pretending to be one for the sake of having a slap at the Legion and the Vincent de Paul Society.[34]

The exchange between Ó Faoláin and Duff took place in wartime, when poverty was rife. In 1941 a wages standstill was introduced, while the cost of living soared. Maternal and infant mortality were extraordinarily high by today's standards. This was particularly so in Dublin where, in 1945, almost 12 per cent of children were either born dead or had died by the age of one. The infant mortality rate was significantly worse for illegitimate children – the overall rate was 66 per 1,000 births, while it was 194 per 1,000 for illegitimate births.

In general, the relevant public health authorities were supportive. During a bad outbreak of enteritis among babies in Dublin in 1942, Dr Tom Murphy of the Department of Local Government and later President of UCD tried to help with supplies of medicines from the chemists Messrs May Roberts.[35] Dr Robert Collis, a noted paediatrician at the Rotunda Hospital, claimed that conditions at the Regina Coeli Hostel were very poor and that babies were dying there. Dr James Deeny from the Department of Local Government and Public Health went along to see for himself. He described how he had met 'an extraordinary little man called Frank Duff. His brother was a friend of mine in the Stephen's Green Club and was Secretary of the Department of Justice.'[36] Deeny confirmed that some of the babies did have enteritis. His secretary, Miss Howett, organized a 'whip-around' in the Custom House and collected £25 'and with this I prevailed on Frank Duff to give me a little room, which we furnished as a kind of quarantine station'. In this way the problem was gradually solved. Deeny wryly observed, 'We soon found that when babies did show green diarrhoea or enteritis … many of them came from or had just been discharged from the Rotunda.' Later in the year Dr Collis visited the hostel himself. Afterwards he wrote to Duff saying that, although he had worked with the poor since his youth, he had never seen anything like the work of the hostel, and looked upon it as 'the work of Christ'.[37] But he regarded overcrowding in the dormitories as 'a menace to health'.[38]

Both the Legion of Mary and the Regina Coeli Hostel were praised in a letter dated 18 June 1945 from the Parliamentary Secretary of the Department of Local Government and Public Health to the Private Secretary to the Taoiseach, regarding the provision of homes for unmarried mothers and their children. The letter provides an overview of existing institutions, including St Patrick's Home, Pelletstown. It states that the problem is greatest in Dublin since girls came from all parts of the country to the city in order to hide their pregnancies from people in their locality. The letter continues, 'The Regina Coeli Hostel under the auspices of the Legion of Mary performs admirable work for the unmarried mother but the resourcefulness of the administration of the hostel is often sorely tried by the pressing need for additional accommodation.'[39]

In the late 1940s, following a number of inspections of the Regina Coeli, officials in the Department of Local Government and Public Health expressed admiration for the work carried out in the hostel. In September 1946 medical inspector of the Department of Local Government and Public Health, Dr Michael Daly, visited the Regina Coeli in connection with an enteritis outbreak. Daly reported that the staff consisted of seven permanent voluntary workers, with no trained nurses. Since there was no doctor attached to the hostel, patients attended the Benburb Street Dispensary. He judged that 'The voluntary effort, beyond doubt laudable, in my opinion is unable to cope with the situation in a satisfactory manner.'[40] In July 1948 a further inspection was carried out by Dr O'Sullivan, who reported that there were 85 babies in the hostel at the time. His recommendations included refurbishment and re-equipment, along with the appointment of a visiting paediatrician.[41]

Despite a determination on the part of the hostel workers to safeguard the privacy of its residents and the conscious avoidance of publicity, word of the work of the Regina Coeli spread. A surprise visitor in October 1948 was Seán MacBride, the Minister for External Affairs, who accompanied Mgr Suenens from Belgium. McBride, who had initially intended a brief visit, remained for two hours, expressing his approval of keeping mothers and babies together.[42] In November 1948 another report entitled 'Regina Coeli Hostel' and initialled possibly by Dr Conor Martin, Director of the Maternity Section in the Department, repeats the need for a visiting children's doctor, trained nursing staff and for the provision of equipment:

> This hostel is not an ideal home for mothers and babies. It has, however, since its inception, filled a want, and it does something which no other home in Eire succeeds in doing. It keeps mother and child together … . Were it not for the existence of the hostel these children would be for the most part in Industrial Schools. Separation of mother and child would in most cases be complete. The hostel has kept mother and child together and has saved the State the cost of maintenance of the children in Ind. Schools.[43]

The report went on to say: 'The spirit of self-sacrifice which motivates the Legionaries who work in the Hostel is to my mind the fine flowering of a selfless humanity. It is certainly not something which may readily be replaced by paid labour.'

In February 1952 twenty-three social science students from TCD visited the hostel and it was noted that the student who showed the greatest interest in the work was 'Egyptian Mohammedan'.[44] Later in the same year there was a visit from the Vicar General of the Vatican and Papal Sacristan, Most Revd Dr van Lierde, who celebrated mass in the oratory.[45]

Early in 1953 Duff wrote to the Dublin Board of Assistance seeking financial help with basic renovation of the hostels. At the time there were 200 men in the Morning Star, and 170 women together with 150 children in the Regina Coeli. He explained, 'We are able with effort to keep the hostels going [to meet the running costs] but we are not able to raise capital sums.'[46] In his *Memoirs* the Chief Medical Officer of the Department of Health, James Deeny, described when he told Jim Ryan, who was Minister for Health 1951–54 and also a medical doctor, how he had earlier set up a quarantine room at the Regina Coeli, Ryan expressed an interest in visiting the hostel. Deeny accompanied him on the visit. According to Deeny, he and Ryan walked about looking at everything, and since 'Dr Ryan said nothing, one could see Frank Duff growing increasingly uneasy and wondering what we were up to and fearful lest we might close the place down. The place was pretty grim … . It had been handed to the Legion in a semi-derelict state.' Deeny continues:

Here and there through those great empty workhouse wards, the women had made little private areas. An old bed, a cradle made from an orange-box, a couple of other such boxes for a bedside table or a stool, a rag of a floor rug, pin-ups and holy pictures and a clothes line and this was their home. The women went out to work as cleaners and suchlike and the children were cared-for. As they grew up, Frank saw to their schooling and eventually found them jobs or apprenticed them to trades.[47]

Deeny described how, on the point of leaving, Dr Ryan suddenly turned and said, 'Frank, I'll give you £30,000 sweep money [proceeds of Hospitals' sweepstake established to provide funds for hospitals]. Give each woman a decent cubicle, fix up the sanitation and the heating and so on, and when you have finished let me know and I will come and see it.' According to Deeny, Duff 'nearly fainted with joy. He got so excited that he turned off his hearing aid and did not know whether he was coming or going.'[48]

Decades later, Lindsey Earner-Byrne, in a study of mother and child welfare in Dublin, acknowledged the unique role of the Regina Coeli, saying that there was practically no official attempt to support the mother-and-child bond in the case of the single mother and her infant: 'With the notable exception of the Legion of Mary, no organisation sought to empower the single mother to retain guardianship of her child.'[49] Earner-Byrne claimed that any preference for Pelletstown rather than the Regina Coeli Hostel 'ignored the psychological and emotional benefits of the policy operated by the Regina Coeli hostel'.[50]

In a lengthy letter written when the Regina Coeli Hostel had been in existence for just over forty years, Duff explained his thinking on the position of the unmarried mother and her child:

> As far back as one's knowledge goes this was always a torturing problem. Its older aspect was that a girl in trouble either went to England or into her own Union or into one of the specialised Homes ... the system operated uniformly to separate mother and child, the latter going off into fosterage and then into the Industrial Schools. ... So we began to work for a place which would provide for the mother keeping her child. On 1st October, 1930, the Regina Coeli Hostel was opened and it sought as part of its work to provide for that particular problem.
>
> At once it was found that it met a dire need .... The success of the method has been positively incredible. About three thousand five hundred children have been dealt with in the intervening time. All but the handful at present resident in the Hostel have gone out into the world and have been living the ordinary life of the community.[51]

Duff described how many of the Regina Coeli women married and how their husbands accepted the illegitimate child. He detailed a tiny minority of problem cases among the hostel children, including three boys who got into trouble over theft and looked as though they might 'be heading for crime', but were now living 'without fault'. Some of the residents had further illegitimate children, but Duff remarked, 'Usually those girls show themselves to be admirable mothers, and bring up their flock well.' He said that the fruits of the system of enabling the mother to retain her child were so striking that one would imagine it to be impossible that any sensible person would gainsay them:

But the fact is that almost everybody seems to be in opposition. This has been the lesson of our forty years of work. This opposition is not based on the idea that adoption is now available and is a solution to the problem, because in our earlier days adoption was not the feature that it now is and nevertheless there was the same resistance to our method. Then it took such forms as declaring that because we did not possess the amenities of a costly Hospital, or staff of doctors and trained nurses, we were unfit to have the custody of infants … .

But here I make our position perfectly clear. We are not insisting that a girl be forced to keep her child; that would in practice be impossible. There are cases where it [adoption] will be the best way out of a difficulty. What we are protesting against is a method of such determined solicitation that a mother is almost impelled to part with the child. This is the present position whereas the stress should be thrown in the opposite direction … . We are <u>not</u> suggesting the abolition of adoption which can to-day fulfil an excellent role.[52]

Duff concluded his letter with a reference to the pressures on young women to have abortions:

I find it a little difficult in my own mind to make a broad differentiation between the determined separating of the unmarried mother from her child and the relieving of the unmarried mother from her unwanted child by way of abortion. Deep down it seems to me that those two processes have an identical root. This root would be the denial of the fact that a spiritual relationship of the supremest order exists between a mother and her child, inclusive of the unborn child.[53]

But those observations were in the future.

Notes to Chapter 9

1. Statement of Evidence by Mr Frank Duff to the Commission on the Relief of the Sick and Destitute Poor, Dublin, 1927.
2. Shortcomings in the Poor Law were highlighted, for example, in the Debate on the Second Stage of the Poor Relief (Dublin) Bill, Seanad Eireann, Volume 13, 11 December 1929.
3. Philip Howell, 'Venereal Disease and the Politics of Prostitution in the Irish Free State', *Irish Historical Studies*, vol. xxxiii, no. 131, May 2003, pp. 320–41.
4. Duff, *True Devotion to the Nation* (1971 edition), Introductory Note.
5. Duff to Byrne, 23 November 1928.
6. *The Irish Times*, 21 May 1924.
7. Duff to Byrne, 23 November 1928.
8. Dr Patrick Dunne (1891–1988), was Secretary to three Archbishops of Dublin between 1919 and 1943. His tenure covered the final years of Archbishop Walsh, the entire reign of Archbishop Byrne and the opening years of Archbishop McQuaid's reign. In 1946 Dunne was appointed Titular Bishop of Nara and Auxiliary Bishop of Dublin. He was appointed Parish Priest of Haddington Road in Dublin in 1947.
9. Duff to Shaw, 31 March 1927.
10. Duff to Creedon, 30 June 1927.

11. Nivard Flood, 'My Memories of Frank Duff', 10 July 1982, manuscript, LOMA.
12. Stephen Redmond, SJ, *So Great a Cloud*. Dublin: Veritas, 2009, p. 159.
13. Ó Broin, *Just like Yesterday*, p. 128.
14. 'Dublin Union Changes', *The Irish Times*, 17 October 1930.
15. Flood, 'My Memories'.
16. O'Carroll, *A Priest in Changing Times*, p. 134.
17. *The Irish Times*, 21 May 1930.
18. Ó Broin, *Frank Duff*, p. 15.
19. Author's interview with Carmel Duff, 1 May 1982. During some of the period when Carmel worked in Aer Lingus, John Leydon, friend and former colleague of Frank, was chairman.
20. *Report of the Commission to Inquire into Child Abuse*, Dublin 2009, chapter 3, p. 8.
21. Minute Book of Regina Coeli, 27 January 1929, Myra House.
22. ibid.
23. Regina Coeli Minutes, 3 March 1929.
24. Regina Coeli Minutes, 27 January 1929.
25. ibid., 5 December 1930.
26. Duff, Memorandum on the Amendment of the Criminal Law, 1930. An Affiliation Order is a court order requiring the father of an illegitimate child to make child-support payments.
27. Earner-Byrne, *Mother and Child*, p. 189.
28. Statement of Evidence by Mr Frank Duff to the Commission on the Relief of the Sick and Destitute Poor, 1927, p. 38.
29. Duff to Langan, 18 December 1948.
30. Duff to Shaw, November 1930, NLI Ms 31, 670/2.
31. Minutes of Regina Coeli, 15 May 1942, Myra House.
32. Ó Faoláin to Duff, 19 July 1944.
33. Duff to Ó Faoláin, 27 July 1944.
34. ibid.
35. Minutes of Regina Coeli, 12 June 1942, Myra House.
36. James Deeny, *To Cure and to Care: Memoirs of a Chief Medical Officer*. Dublin: Glendale, 1989, pp. 96–97.
37. Minutes of Regina Coeli, 11 December 1942, Myra House.
38. ibid.
39. Record 15950, Department of Taoiseach, 18/6/45, s 108154, Adoption of Children general file.
40. Memo by Dr Michael F. Daly, 'Regina Coeli Inspection and Enteritis', 6/9/46, HLTH/ M 34/60, NAI.
41. Memo by Dr O'Sullivan, 30/7/48; recommendations added 4/Oct/48, HLTH/ M 34/60, NAI.
42. Minutes of Regina Coeli, 1 October 1948, Myra House.
43. Memo 'Regina Coeli Hostel', initialled, 12-11-48, HLTH/ M 34/60, NAI.
44. Minutes of Regina Coeli, 1 and 8 February 1952.
45. Minutes of Regina Coeli, 19 September 1952. It was Van Lierde who administered the last rites to both Pius XII and John XXIII on their death beds.
46. Duff to Secretary Dublin Board of Assistance, James Street, 21 January 1953, LOMA.
47. Deeny, *To Cure and to Care*, p. 161.
48. ibid.
49. Earner-Byrne, *Mother and Child*, p. 224.
50. ibid., p. 201.
51. Duff to Mahon, 13 October 1970.
52. ibid.
53. ibid.

CHAPTER 10

A Finance Man

'The Irish State was being built up and in the Department of Finance you were in the very centre of things.'

DUFF, AHERNE INTERVIEW

Duff 'liked the work immensely' in the Department of Finance, describing it as 'all thinking' and constructive work.'[1] But although he enjoyed the work in the Department, he was not always happy with his treatment there. In April 1925, Duff's appointment as Higher Executive Officer (Acting) was made substantive. But on 15 October he sent a minute of protest to Joseph Brennan, Secretary of the Department, via the Assistant Secretary, J. J. McElligott, about his reassignment as an assistant to John Leydon, then an Assistant Principal Officer (APO) in the Finance Division.[2] While there was no question of any personal criticism of Leydon, for whom Duff had a high regard – he was best man at his wedding[3] – he claimed that his reassignment was a 'degradation in status'. Since he had come to Finance nearly two years earlier, he had, although a Higher Executive Officer, an independent status equivalent to that held by the Deputy Principals and he had been engaged upon work of appropriate quality.

> In the circumstances to deprive me of the status I have had, treating me as if I were a raw entrant from the Junior Cadets Examination, is contrary to every usage of the old civil service. It is an action unprecedented in the recollection of either myself or of my colleagues in this Department.[4]

There is no record of a written response to this minute. In December, Duff, as spokesman for staff, wrote to McElligott regarding what he saw as the unfair staffing structure between the Finance Division, which he maintained was understaffed, and the Establishment Division:

> Our grievances have been greatly accentuated recently by the action of the Establishment Division in making additions to their own staff, while doing nothing for the Finance Division which was in a relatively much worse position … . We append a Table of the staffs working in the various divisions, which we believe is approximately accurate. Paper staffs are no good to us.[5]

In 1925 a competitive examination to recruit university graduates to fill administrative posts was introduced, which would impinge on the promotion prospects of Duff and others of his rank.[6] The first competitive examination for the grade of Junior Administrative Officer (JAO), open to both women and men, was held on 14 April 1925. Three of the seven recruited at the examination, John Garvin, Maurice Moynihan and León Ó Broin, went on to become Secretaries of Departments, while a fourth, L. M. Fitzgerald, became an Assistant Secretary. Ó Broin was placed first in the examination. As the introduction of a graduate élite of JAOs affected the promotion prospects of the HEOs who were not graduates, they formally protested to Brennan in July 1927. H. P. Boland, the Assistant Secretary in charge of Establishment and Supply, was keen on the idea of a graduate administrative corps, even though he himself had entered the Office of Public Works (OPW) in 1895 as a Second Division Clerk. Boland's belief in a *corps d'élite* 'found expression in private dinner parties which he held for them in the Gresham'.[7]

In a minute dated 17 December 1928, Boland recommended Duff's promotion, on a temporary basis, to the rank of APO at an annual salary of £550. The vacancy arose because of Leydon's appointment as secretary of the recently established Economic Committee, which met for the first time on 5 December 1928. The memo notes that Duff had been a HEO since 1923. The recommendation was accepted by the Minister, Earnán de Blaghad (Ernest Blythe), and became effective from that day.

Duff's reason to believe that he was poorly treated in Finance must be set in the context of a Department which was then a young man's country. In 1923, when Duff, aged thirty-four, was a HEO, Joseph Brennan, two years his senior, was Secretary of the Department. McElligott, who was thirty in 1923, would become an Assistant Secretary that year, and then Secretary of the Department in 1927 at the age of thirty-four, succeeding Brennan, who resigned as Secretary to head the Currency Commission at the age of thirty-nine. Both Brennan and McElligott had entered the civil service as First Division men with university degrees, although McElligott had been dismissed for his part in the 1916 Rising and returned to the newly established Irish civil service from his post as editor of the financial journal *The Statist* in London. Leydon, like Boland and Duff, had entered the civil service as a Second Division Clerk. Leydon, six years younger than Duff, commenced work in the War Office in 1915, having taken first place in the Customs and Excise examination the previous year. He worked in the Ministry of Pensions in London from 1917 until 1923, when he was appointed HEO in the Ministry of Finance which preceded the Department of Finance established under the Ministers and Secretaries Act, 1924. Later in 1923 Leydon was appointed Assistant Principal in Finance at the age of thirty-two.

An illuminating comparison may be made between the career paths of Duff and O. J. Redmond, who was two years younger than Duff and who succeeded McElligott as Secretary of Finance in 1953, having entered the civil service as a boy clerk in 1906, aged fifteen. In 1910 he became a Second Division Clerk, following competitive examination, as Duff had done two years earlier in 1908. Redmond was made a higher executive officer in 1923 when Duff, in the same year, on his return from working with Hogan on the Land Act, was offered higher executive officer on an acting basis. By the beginning of 1926 both Redmond and Duff were HEOs, but in the course of 1926 Redmond was promoted to Assistant Principal. Duff did not become an Assistant Principal, and then only on a temporary basis, until the end of 1928. His position as Assistant Principal was made permanent in August 1930. Duff would retire from the civil service at the rank of Assistant Principal in 1934. Redmond was promoted to Principal in 1932, Assistant Secretary in 1944 and Secretary in 1953.[8]

Following his promotion, on a temporary basis, to Assistant Principal in 1928, Duff was assisted by two Administrative Officers, León Ó Broin and P. J. McDonogh. Ó Broin described how, following an 'office shuffle' in 1928, Duff replaced Larry Lynd as his boss. He said that it was a 'privilege to share Frank's company in this way and to be given an opportunity of seeing something of the double life that he was living'. Duff believed that his career in the service had suffered as a result of the view held of him by Cornelius Gregg. Gregg, who knew Duff from Blackrock College, was loaned from the Board of Inland Revenue in London during 1923/24 to assist with the organization of the new Irish civil service. According to Joe Lee, Gregg 'ensured that the service would bear the stamp "made in England"'.[9]

It was Gregg's view that Duff had too many outside interests. This is clear from a letter Duff drafted in 1929, but, on the advice of Fr Michael Browne, SJ, did not send to the Department of Finance. His failure to obtain a permanent post of Assistant Principal when one came up in 1929 led to the drafting of the letter. Faced with what he regarded as unfair treatment based on false assumptions, the contents of his letter amount to an *apologia*. In the draft letter, Duff wrote that Gregg had said, 'in circumstances of sufficient publicity to go out over the city', that he would not give Duff advancement because his 'centre of gravity' was not in the Department of Finance. Duff said that if that meant he did not attend to his work, it was factually incorrect. He admitted to 'some laxity in the matter of early morning attendance but this has been completely made up by the end of the day'. He said that in the matter of sick and privileged leave (i.e. half-days or hours off), he had an exceptionally favourable record. Furthermore, aware of the rumours regarding his 'outside interests', he had been timid to take even hours off and believed that the amount he owed on that score could not amount to a day a year. Duff continued by saying that the variant to the charge that he was wasting official time was that his mind was so occupied or his body so weakened by 'outside interests' that he was producing work of poor quality. He firmly denied both these charges: 'As regards bodily condition, I can only refer to my sick leave record: as regards the quality of my work – it is there to look at if anyone is so minded and I venture to claim – that on the whole it is of good quality.' He continued:

It seems to me however, that genuine fault is not being found with me along lines such as any of the foregoing, but that the reason lies in the fact – belief – announced by Mr. Gregg, the late Establishment Officer – that my centre of gravity was not in this Dept. My answer to this might well be that, if I had been so circumstanced as to have no mental relief from my intolerable (as it seems to me) official experience since 1922, I would now be in an asylum.

However, if it were an absolute fact that my chief interests lie outside the office, I contend that that does not deprive me of the right to normal promotion in the office, if my services are satisfactory there. I do not think any government office has a right to 100 per cent of the serious mental activities of its officers, nor indeed is that claim advanced. Outside interests are everywhere permitted and encouraged – provided they be of an unobjectionable character, and the fact that an absorbing interest in these directions does not impair office efficiency is evident on all sides in the higher ranks of the Civil Service.[10]

Soon after the Economic Committee ceased at the end of July 1929, Boland raised with McElligott the temporary nature of the appointments of Lynd and Duff. McElligott directed that in both cases their acting appointments should end on 1 April 1930 and that Duff and Lynd should revert to their previous grade of HEO and Assistant Principal respectively, with reduced salary. This appears harsh by today's standards, but it reflected both frugality in public expenditure and the absence of strong public service trade unions. On 31 July Boland noted the permanent promotion of Duff to Assistant Principal in the Supply Division, where he would work for the remainder of his civil service career.

By the early 1930s it was clear to Duff that his double life would have to end. He could not continue in a demanding day job and give the attention required – and which he desired to give – to the Legion of Mary. Duff wished to retire on a pension, if possible, without recourse to Article Ten of the Anglo-Irish Treaty, which provided for persons whose positions had been affected by the Treaty to leave the public service. In 1932, when there was a change of government, he hesitated to seek retirement since he did not want it to appear that he was leaving because of political change. When he decided to leave in 1934, John (Seán) Moynihan, who had been appointed Secretary to the new government in 1932 and who was a committed member of the Legion of Mary, convinced de Valera that Duff should present himself to the Article Ten Tribunal.[11] In a letter to his friend Ulick McNally, referring to his decision,

Duff wrote, 'I have taken the terrible step of resigning (or trying to resign) under Clause 10 [Article Ten]. I never realised how painful a process it was to tear up one's roots.'[12] By the time Duff resigned, his youngest sister, Ailish, was thirty-two and established in her medical career, so his earnings were of less vital consequence to his family. Nonetheless, he ran an enormous risk in giving up an enviable job in the midst of a very severe economic recession, and when the Legion had not yet received official sanction from the Dublin archdiocese, nor had the Archbishop even agreed to meet Duff. The risk he took represented an act of pure faith.

On 1 October 1934 Duff retired from the civil service under Section 14 of the Civil Service (Transferred Officers) Compensation Act 1929. His pension was £378 per annum, plus a supplement of £86. 4s. 4d. He had completed twenty-six years as a civil servant. Another person who retired under the Act was the actor Barry Fitzgerald. The chairman of the Tribunal which assessed Duff's case for retirement was Cahir Davitt, brother of his school friend Michael Davitt. At the time Davitt, who would later become President of the High Court, was a circuit court judge. Davitt was a contemporary and friend of Duff's brother John, and John Duff was godfather to Cahir Davitt's son, Brian.

Research by Kieran Kennedy and his co-workers in the National Archives provides evidence that Duff, following the pattern set by leaders in the Department, including Joseph Brennan, J. J. McElligott and John Leydon, carried an extremely heavy workload. In addition to a considerable volume of work which might be described as routine, Duff wrote a number of substantial memoranda on a range of subjects.[13] These include *Post Treaty British/Irish Financial Settlement* (1924), *Examination of Dublin Corporation Accounts for 1922/23* (1924), which led to the suspension of the Corporation, *Electricity Supply* (1926), the *Foreign Investment of State Funds* (1929), *Irish in the Garda Síochána* (1930) and *Breaking the Link with Sterling* (1933).

In a memorandum on the Post Treaty Financial Settlement, Duff started with the stipulation in the Treaty that (i) Ireland should take over its proportion of the National Debt of the United Kingdom and (ii) that the financial claim of Ireland against England can be raised, the determining of these amounts to be by arbitration. Duff put a strong case for reducing the burden on Ireland. He maintained that it was unfair to attempt to justify a level of taxation in Ireland because of a certain level of expenditure in Ireland, because the expenditure was not of the people's choosing – for example, the expenditure might be to increase the size of the Royal Irish Constabulary or to pay the 'colossal salary' of the Irish Lord Chancellor. He also pointed out that it was wrong to apportion a burden on the basis of a single year. To do so 'for a single year – and that an abnormal year – is a wild-cat proceeding'. Duff's memorandum displays mastery of the facts and an ability to present his argument in cogent terms, together with a keen grasp of the concepts involved, such as taxable capacity and burden of debt.

In examining the Dublin Corporation Accounts, Duff highlighted two aspects: wasteful expenditure and the nature of the services. He focused in particular on expenditure on housing, arguing that the corporation schemes were failing the poorest and that problems stemmed from the lack of a proper system of control and auditing rather than from corruption. He recommended greater control, possibly by the Department of Finance, but reform should not become obsessed with economy: 'For one thing, if reform is undertaken under an obsession of economy, harm may result, and to the class least able to bear it – the poor.'[14]

Another economic memorandum of particular interest is that on the Foreign Investment of State Funds. Any student of Irish economic history for the first five decades of the state will know that the question of the investment of Irish funds abroad, effectively in British government securities, was a key political as well as economic issue. These investments were made both by private institutions, chiefly the commercial banks, and by the state. At the start of his deliberations, Duff sought to establish 'a few first principles' regarding the movement from British and foreign Stocks into Saorstát (Free State) securities. Firstly, he pointed out that money externally invested was 'at work' outside the country and that the dividends that returned home were of slight value compared with the 'work' the money was doing abroad. Employment was being lost at home. Secondly, he argued that there was plenty of money in the country, but that it was flowing overseas, and so the third National Loan achieved only £20 million:

> This enables us to see external investment as an evil, because it is preventing the getting of money for, say, the Shannon Scheme or a great Housing scheme, or in any case making us timid about 'looking for it' – which is the same thing. If it is prejudicing national interests, it seems the reverse of a commonsense proceeding for the government itself to join the throng of money exporters.[15]

Duff made the further point that by increasing the demand for British government securities and reducing the demand for Irish securities, the relative price of the securities was affected: 'British government securities are made the world's premier gilt-edged securities in part by the investment in them of Saorstát money.'[16] Duff further demonstrated with an arithmetical example that it actually cost more to obtain an equivalent return from a British security than from an Irish one. Among Duff's papers is a long letter, dated 29 January 1930, from Mr Douglas in the Irish Land Commission to whom, presumably, either Duff had sent his memo directly for comment or to whom it had been referred by Lynd. The general tenor of Douglas's reply was that, while Duff's case might be all right in theory, it was not practical. Douglas, painting a picture of troublesome workers and incompetent if not dishonest management, argued that 'the record of enterprises in the Saorstát held out "no inducement to investors to put their money into native enterprise just yet. …"':

A flourishing Paper Mill is operating in Clondalkin under the management of a capable expert, but because the manager happens to be a Saxon, a Strike is organised and the whole enterprise closed down and the mills left derelict. A Dead Meat Company is established in Drogheda and apparently there is no good reason why it should not be a great success – but owing to inefficient (if not dishonest) management the company has to go into liquidation and the Shareholders lose their money … . I therefore come to the conclusion that it is vain to expect Saorstát capital to flow into Saorstát enterprises until such time that a source of security and confidence in the honesty and capability of business managers, workers and others has grown up … but that happy state of affairs is not yet.[17]

Nor did Douglas see any merit in scrapping investment in British government securities. He pointed out that banks and insurance companies invested in British government securities to protect their reserves. He asked disbelievingly:

Are we to be told that Banks and other companies are wrong in protecting their financial positions by investing their Reserves abroad? They must do so at present as they have not sufficient suitable Securities in the Saorstát to serve their purpose and investment in unsuitable and doubtful home stocks (if available) might result in insolvency.[18]

It would be decades before Duff's recommended policy was implemented, albeit in changed times. Likewise, his recommendation regarding breaking the link with sterling, as set out in a memo dated 19 April 1933, would come to fruition. In this memo Duff presented the case for an independent currency at a discount against sterling, arguing in favour of devaluation rather than protective tariffs. Commenting on Duff's paper, Dermot McAleese, Emeritus Whately Professor of Economics in Trinity College Dublin and former Board Member of the Central Bank, described the memo as 'thoughtful, percipient and concisely argued'.[19]

It is clear that Duff's work in the civil service was substantial. Nonetheless, the question may be asked whether or not he could do a complete day's work in the civil service at the same time as undertaking a heavy load of voluntary activity. This is an important question, because Duff never endorsed the least neglect of what were basic duties for the sake of Legion work. In the Land Commission before the establishment of the Free State, Duff said that he kept regular hours and finished work at 5 p.m.[20] During possibly the most crucial period in the life of the Legion, 1922–23, when Duff was working on the Hogan Land Act, he explains, 'I have kept my own hours.' If he took time from the office, or if he arrived after the customary hour in the morning, he was careful to make up for any time taken. He says that he 'took no holiday for two years and never left the office until approximately 7 o'clock'.[21]

Not many judgements are available on Duff's civil service career, but the few that are are significant. Thus within a couple of years of his entry to the Land Commission, Mr Beard, a senior official, described him as a man of 'very considerable ability' while he earned the 'high commendation' of another senior official, Mr Crosbie. When on 1 October 1934 Duff retired from the civil service, the head of the Establishment Division, H. P. Boland, gave the following assessment: 'Mr Francis M. Duff, Assistant Principal Officer, has served with diligence and fidelity to the satisfaction of his superior officers.'[22] Of particular interest are the comments of W. T. Cosgrave, who attested to Duff's mastery of Land legislation in a memo written for Joseph Pilendiram from Ceylon (now Sri Lanka) when he sought Cosgrave's opinion of Duff in July 1960. Pilendiram, who had worked as a reporter for the BBC on Asian affairs in the 1950s, was a member of the Legion of Mary and went as Legion Envoy to East Africa, covering Kenya, Uganda and Tanzania, in 1959.[23] He did not lose his reporter's instincts. He asked Cosgrave if he could throw a light on Duff's life, 'particularly during the twenties when not only Ireland took its proper place in the world but also Ireland gave a mighty apostolic organisation to the whole world'.[24] He sent Cosgrave a series of questions, saying that he sought those particulars so that we can 'preserve for posterity one of the greatest men of the twentieth century'.[25] Cosgrave explained how Duff was part of the delegation that travelled to London to discuss financial matters early in 1923:

> On that expedition, Mr Duff came over with the Secretary of the Finance Ministry. At the time, early in 1923, I held the Finance Portfolio as well as President. Mr Duff would have required to have mastered the details of the Land legislation in all details and his selection emphasised the standing he had achieved.[26]

According to one of Cornelius Gregg's sons, Dr Thomas Gregg, who was born in 1921, his father was discreet and did not speak of civil service matters to his family. Dr Gregg did, however, recall that his father referred to Duff as a 'respected man'.[27] J. J. McElligott, former Secretary of the Department of Finance, suggested that the Department lost an organizational genius when it lost Duff.[28] T. K. Whitaker joined the civil service on 10 October 1934, ten days after Duff left. When Whitaker was assigned to the Department of Finance in 1938, his desk was in Duff's former room. At times Whitaker had cause to look through old files dealing with compensation claims for damage done to property during the 'Troubles'. Claims were submitted to the Compensation (Ireland) Commission and eventually passed to the Department of Finance for payment of the Irish share of compensation.[29] Whitaker remarked how Duff emerged as 'very human', while John Leydon adopted the tougher 'Finance' line.[30] Maurice Moynihan,[31] one of the outstanding Irish public servants of any era, who joined the Department of Finance in 1925, declared that, with Duff, he knew he was 'dealing with a saint'.[32]

Hard work did not dampen Duff's sense of fun or his love of practical jokes. Such humour provided a safety valve of sorts. León Ó Broin tells how the room in the Department of Finance in which Frank worked, along with Paddy O'Kelly and Jimmy Smith, 'all three hard workers', was called 'The Tivoli' after a well-known music hall on Burgh Quay famous for its comedy acts, and later occupied by the *Irish Press* newspaper. When Paddy O'Kelly, a relative of J. J. McElligott, Secretary of the Department, was promoted, Frank wrote a paper on how to apply the Theory of Relativity, which was being discussed in scientific quarters at the time.[33] Sarsfield Hogan, who worked for a time as Duff's Junior Administrative Officer, also recalled Duff's humour and how when Paddy Fay, the Department messenger, used to come around with envelopes containing salary cheques, Duff would say 'You are the master of our destiny. Only for this we would not be here at all.' But Hogan recalled something else about Duff. He said that towards the end of 1930, when his daughter Mary was seriously ill, he had called into a convent chapel on Merrion Square when he met Duff coming out. Hogan asked Duff to go back in to pray for his daughter. That evening, Hogan's daughter had shown a dramatic improvement.[34]

According to Ó Broin, Duff gave up his job without any fuss, setting himself free for 'monumental activities'. Ó Broin believed that 'Frank had what the Germans called *fingerspitzgefühl* (tip-of-the-finger feeling), a sense of opportunity allied with clearness of mind and a decisive purpose.'[35] Perhaps the most painful aspect of his decision to resign was the reaction of his mother, whom he loved dearly. Having experienced the reduced circumstances resulting from her husband's enforced early retirement and knowing that Duff's income would be reduced subsequent to his own early retirement, she remarked, 'Isn't it hard to be going back again to the old times?' Even though the remark wasn't meant to hurt, Duff felt it very much.[36] Members of his family did occasionally express anxiety that the Legion was taking over his entire life. Writing to Bessie O'Meara, a legionary in Ottawa, in 1952, he wrote:

> My own dear mother was in the main placid in regard to my activities, but on one occasion long ago she permitted herself an outburst: 'Oh how I hate this octopus which has taken possession of your life.' And more recently, my surviving sister emitted a similar plaint: 'Your whole life had been sacrificed to this Moloch.'[37]

Duff was forty-five when he left Finance, two years older than his father had been in 1904 when he retired owing to ill-health. He had served at a critical period in Irish history. In the apt words of Ronan Fanning, 'These were days, moreover, when much was done by few.'[38] Frank Duff, Sarsfield Hogan, John Leydon, Maurice and John Moynihan and León Ó Broin belonged to that 'first generation of post-independence civil servants who were imbued with profound loyalty and commitment to the public service'.[39] Duff's leaving affected a varied staff in a personal way:

Those who knew him best admired him greatly and, in that company, were messengers as well as men who were subsequently to reach the heights of distinction. Frank, too, must have felt a twinge at leaving. He never forgot that he was 'a Finance man', and would always talk affectionately of the happy times he had had there.[40]

Notes to Chapter 10

1. Aherne interview.
2. Duff's Personal File, ES, 283, Roinn Airgid (Department of Finance).
3. Ó Broin, *Frank Duff*, p. 44.
4. A copy of this memo was typed by Seán Cromien, former Secretary-General of the Department of Finance, from a photocopy he possessed of the original document in the Department of Finance.
5. Duff to McElligott, December 1925.
6. Fanning, *The Irish Department of Finance*, pp. 75–77, 537. According to Fanning, three appointments were made to the Junior Administrative Officer grade *before* the first examination. The three appointed were Sarsfield Hogan, Leo MacCauley and Tommy Coyne. Their appointment was as a direct result of contact between Joseph Brennan and the Provost of Trinity College and the President of UCD.
7. ibid., p. 542. H. P. Boland was the father of F. H. Boland, who became President of the General Assembly of the United Nations in 1960/61. Boland was also the father-in-law of Sarsfield Hogan, who became Assistant Secretary in the Department of Finance.
8. Summary of Redmond's civil service *curriculum vitae* from Fanning, *The Irish Department of Finance*, pp. 535–36.
9. J. J. Lee, *Ireland 1912–1985: Politics and Society* Cambridge: Cambridge University Press, 1990, p. 105.
10. Handwritten draft letter written by Frank Duff to Department of Finance in 1929. The letter is marked 'Not sent in – on advice of Fr. M. Browne'. (1929) FDCS Memos, 35, LOMA.
11. Ó Broin, *Frank Duff*, pp. 43–44.
12. Duff to McNally, 5 May 1934.
13. He told Enda Dunleavy that he attempted to do one 'ideas' memorandum every year when he was in Finance.
14. *Memorandum on Accounts of Dublin Corporation*, 1922/23, FDCS Memos, LOMA; also File 1/3868, NAI.
15. *Memo on Foreign Investment of State Funds*, 4 December 1929, FDCS Memos, LOMA.
16. ibid.
17. Reply by J. Douglas, 28 January 1929 to Duff's memorandum *Foreign Investment of State Funds*. FDCS, LOMA.
18. ibid.
19. Written communication to Kieran Kennedy, 3 September 2004, seen by author.
20. Aherne interview.
21. Draft letter to Sir Joseph Glynn, FDCS Memos, 56, LOMA.
22. Duff, Personal File, Department of Finance, ES. 283.
23. On his return to England from East Africa in 1962, Pilendiram worked as a Probation Officer. He received a Papal Knighthood in 2007.
24. Pilendiram to Cosgrave, 6 July 1960, author's copy.
25. ibid.
26. Memo given to author by Enda Dunleavy, who received it from Joseph Pilendiram.
27. Author's telephone conversation with Dr Thomas Gregg, 16 July 2008.
28. Ó Broin, *Frank Duff*, p. 46.
29. The Compensation (Ireland) Commission, known as the Shaw Commission after its chairman,

Lord Shaw of Dunfermline, was established in May 1922 by the British government to deal with claims for compensation for damage to property between January 1919 and July 1921 in Ireland, excluding Northern Ireland. The expenses of the Commission were borne in the first instance by the British government, subject to recovery from the government of the Irish Free State in such proportion as might be agreed upon.

30. Author's conversation with T. K. Whitaker following a meeting of the Statistical and Social Inquiry Society of Ireland, 6 May 2004.
31. See McMahon, 'Maurice Moynihan'.
32. This judgement was pronounced by Maurice Moynihan to his brother, Fr Anselm Moynihan, OP, and was repeated by Moynihan to Fr. Bede McGregor, OP, who told the author on 5 August 2008.
33. Ó Broin, *Just Like Yesterday*.
34. Notes by León Ó Broin of an interview with Sarsfield Hogan on 28 January 1981, when he was preparing his book on Duff.
35. Ó Broin, *Just Like Yesterday*, p. 127.
36. Bradshaw, tape 132, LOMA.
37. Duff to Bessie O'Meara, 5 August 1952.
38. Fanning, *The Irish Department of Finance*, p. 629.
39. McMahon, *Maurice Moynihan*, p. 71.
40. Ó Broin, *Frank Duff*, p. 45.

CHAPTER 11

Rome and Dublin Approve

'Without the moral support of Your Grace we are exercising but a fraction of our potential influence.'
DUFF TO ARCHBISHOP BYRNE, 25 FEBRUARY 1929

Although he might complain privately to friends, Duff's constant response to the rejection of his requests by the ecclesiastical authorities in the Dublin archdiocese was to accept the rejection in a spirit of obedience. His close collaborators were of like disposition. When Duff shared the news with his friend Matt Lalor that permission for celebration of Mass at the opening of the Morning Star Hostel in March 1927 had been refused, Lalor urged him to 'embrace the cross lovingly. Obedience comprises all the virtues.' In 1928, when Duff asked Lalor's opinion of a letter he proposed writing to the Archbishop, Lalor's advice, posted from Milltown Park where he was making an enclosed retreat, began by saying:

> The object, the sole object of course, is the Glory of God and the good of souls. Therefore the first thing you have to do before you sit down to write, is to open the window, throw out self completely and then close the shutters and bar them and keep them so till you are finished … . The tone of your letter ought to be as humble and as respectful as possible.[1]

The root cause of the difficulties Duff encountered in the archdiocese of Dublin sprang, at least in part, from his understanding of the role of the laity in the Church, which was far in advance of the restricted one then held by the diocesan authorities and many clergy. In the twenty-first century it may be difficult to grasp that in the Catholic Church in Ireland in the 1920s and 1930s the Legion represented a revolutionary concept of stunning dimensions, anticipating, as it did, the teaching of the Second Vatican Council.[2] In the 1920s and 1930s there was an abundance of priests, and many clergy viewed the idea of laymen and laywomen engaging in apostolic work as a threat rather than an opportunity. For example, in November 1928 Fr Toher felt obliged to write to the Vicar General in the archdiocese, Mgr Wall, 'to remove a serious misconception that I have been "caught up" by a few "most indiscreet" laymen, who are out for the "laicization" of the Church. Nothing is further from the truth.'[3]

The Byrne era covered momentous events for the Legion from its foundation in 1921, including the opening of the Sancta Maria, Morning Star and Regina Coeli hostels, the acceleration in the growth of the Legion overseas which followed the Eucharistic Congress in Dublin in 1932, Duff's first visit to Rome, where he was received by Pius XI in 1931, and his reception by Pius XII in 1939. The central issues that arose in the Byrne era were the approval for the Constitutions of the Legion, which was applied for in November 1928 and not finally granted until January 1935, and the *imprimatur*[4] for the *Handbook*, which was delayed even longer. The constitutions were set out in a short booklet of sixteen pages, comprising the outline of the Legion system, the role of the Spiritual Directors and the relation of the Legion to ecclesiastical authority. The booklet makes numerous references to the *Handbook*, indicating that the latter existed when the constitutions were drawn up.

Recurring problematic issues with diocesan authorities included permission for Masses and retreats in the hostels as well as the organization of Legion functions. For example, in October 1928 Fr Hayden, who had replaced Fr Flanagan as parish priest in St Nicholas of Myra, Francis Street, wrote to Elizabeth Kirwan, President of the Legion of Mary, saying that, having consulted Mgr Wall, he could not lend the Church for the annual reunion for 'the Association called by you "The Legion of Mary" unless you are able to show me that this Association has the formal approval of His Grace the Archbishop, nor can I consent to the holding of the Social in Myra House referred to in your letter'.[5] Hayden stated that since the Legion had not been formally recognized in the archdiocese, the praesidium of Our Lady of Mercy should clear out of Francis Street. In an ironic twist, Jim Larkin, the trade union leader, provided alternative accommodation for the Association in the premises of the Transport Union at 78 Thomas Street and later at Unity Hall in Marlborough Street. Replying to a query regarding the activities of communists in Dublin from a Jesuit priest, Joseph Ledit at the Pontifical Congregation for the Orient in Rome, Duff said that he was unable to supply any information, but mentioned the generous practical support given to the Legion by Jim Larkin, a supposed communist:

> I may mention that a couple of branches of the Legion of Mary enjoy the hospitality of the Union which is popularly supposed to represent the high-water mark of communism i.e. James Larkin's Unity Hall. They [the legionaries] have nothing to pay for rent, heat or light and James Larkin himself has been very solicitous as to their comfort.[6]

According to Duff, Larkin would look into the room in which the legionaries were meeting 'to see if they were quite comfortable'.[7] The two men shared common cause in working to overcome the abuse of alcohol in the days when some 'men almost swam in drink'.[8]

When the earliest version of the *Handbook* became available in 1928, a copy was sent to Archbishop Byrne with a request for an *imprimatur* so that its compliance with the faith and morals of the Roman Catholic Church could be acknowledged and the book could be circulated publicly. Byrne told Sir Joseph Glynn that he was placing the *Handbook* in the hands of the Diocesan Examiner (censor) with a view to possible approval. Towards the end of the year, Duff decided to seek formal approval for the Legion of Mary also, and he wrote to Byrne in late November 1928. In the letter his feelings of alienation in the archdiocese are expressed with intensity. At the outset he said that he had learned from a number of persons that the Archbishop regarded him 'with considerable disfavour'. Since the Archbishop had refused to see him to tell him 'the grounds of complaint', it was 'left to hearsay to ascertain them'. Duff said that 'all concerned were afraid to approach you' and that as a worker in the diocese since 1913, which involved fifteen years of 'unremitting labour', he believed he was 'entitled to treatment from the Archbishop which an ordinary parent would give his child. Instead not one kind word has ever come my way.'[9] He stated his belief that the Legion was 'destined before long to exist in every quarter of the globe', a remarkable belief at the time as the first praesidium of the Legion outside Ireland had been started only a few months earlier in Scotland.

On 29 February 1929, the centenary of Catholic Emancipation, Duff asked for permission to hold a one-day retreat for the residents in the Morning Star Hostel. This was refused 'for various reasons', including the fact that there were retreats available in city churches. But Duff had provided a list of reasons why these were not suitable, including the extreme poverty of many of the men, some of whom had just been released from jail, the fact that others had held good positions and included ex-Army officers, men who would be shy about appearing in a public place while resident in the hostel. As well as seeking permission for the retreat, Duff made the following request:

> May I suggest to Your Grace that some mark – however informal or small – of Your Grace's regard would be intensely appreciated by all of us in our rather desperate struggle, and moreover would have important reactions on the whole under-world of Dublin … . Without the moral support of Your Grace we are exercising but a fraction of our potential influence.[10]

Early in 1929 Mgr Walsh, who was one of the diocesan vicars and also parish priest in St Joseph's Parish, Glasthule, County Dublin, invited Duff to meet him. The meeting took place on 30 January at 3pm at the Vicariate, 47 Westland Row. Duff's note of the meeting records that it was Walsh's intention, having read the *Handbook*, to recommend approval. However, two months later, Walsh expressed his fear that approval was not imminent and stated as his 'private opinion' that he could not express 'any hopeful view', and that 'if you want extra copies of the handbook in the very near future, I would advise you not to await diocesan approval in Dublin'.[11]

On 29 June 1929 Duff again wrote to the Archbishop explaining that the draft *Handbook* was the only document available to give to interested enquirers and that the absence of the *imprimatur*, or official declaration by the hierarchy that a work is free from error and is in accordance with the Faith, 'at the very outset of the Legion's foreign developments may, if not at once rectified by the appearance of an approval on the handbook, have fatal consequences'. Duff also asked that approval for the Legion of Mary be placed on the agenda for the next meeting of the bishops, with a view to gaining their united endorsement. He expressed optimism that if given sanction by the Irish bishops, and then approved by the Pope, 'the Legion of Mary will exist all over the world within the next decade and eventually form another great contribution from Ireland to Christianity'.[12] Commenting on the contents of Duff's letter, Thomas Morrissey, SJ, says: 'To an admirer and friend it was prophetic language; to critics among the archbishop's colleagues, on the other hand, it must have seemed unreal, the excessive aspirations, even hubris, of an ambitious and difficult man.'[13] There is no record of any reply to this letter, nor was the matter of approval for the Legion of Mary placed on the agenda of the next bishops' meeting.

On 2 October 1929 an urgent request for approval of the Legion was submitted to the Archbishop, since in the absence of formal approval the development of the Legion was being impeded overseas, including in Britain, where it was beginning to spread rapidly and where Duff had been warmly received by a number of bishops and archbishops, including those of Westminster and Liverpool. Duff wrote, 'But for the fact that difficulties have arisen which your Grace alone can remove, I would not venture to address to you this request that you will, if at all possible, now give your approval to the Legion of Mary'.[14] In the diocesan archives the letter is simply marked 'File?' There is no record of any reply.

Duff resorted to his friend President Cosgrave, who in turn approached the Papal Nuncio, Paschal Robinson, and recommended the Legion to him in the highest terms. Robinson had been born in Ireland in 1870 but went to the United States as a young man. A successful journalist before studying for the priesthood and becoming a Franciscan, he was Professor of Medieval History at the Catholic University of America and later entered the Vatican diplomatic corps. Robinson travelled from Italy to Ireland via England and Wales, arriving by boat on the evening of 14 January 1930 at Dún Laoghaire,[15] where he was greeted by Archbishop Byrne, President Cosgrave and Patrick McGilligan, who was Minister for both Industry and Commerce and External Affairs.

Owing to renovation work in progress at the Nuncio's intended residence in the Phoenix Park, he was driven to the Shelbourne Hotel. Keogh furnishes the details:

> The government had taken a 'nice suite' in the Shelbourne. This included a large reception room (no. 60, where the 1922 constitution had been drawn up), a small sitting room, a bedroom and a bathroom. There was also a further bedroom in the suite in case the nuncio brought a secretary.[16]

A handwritten letter, undated but clearly written shortly after Robinson arrived in Ireland, from Paul Banim, the President's Secretary, to Duff, says, 'You are to be in Room 58 Shelbourne Hotel at 5 o'clock this evening sharp. The President has made the appointment you sought. Ring me.'[17] The letter is initialled 'Appointment with the Nuncio, F.D.' Notes by Duff in preparation for his meeting with the Nuncio included the fact that he was not getting help from the Church as represented by the ecclesiastical authorities, but rather was being 'impeded in every possible way'. Instead, he had to look to the government for sympathy. He claimed that Dublin was 'the root of the whole trouble: The rest of Ireland is marking time – waiting for its lead.' The sequel to Duff's meeting with Robinson was his reception in private audience by Pius XI and the declaration by the Pope of 'his desire that the Legion would spread over the whole world'.[18] Duff's successful resort to Robinson would not have gone down well with Archbishop Byrne, who, in the words of historian Dermot Keogh, 'had suffered a double disappointment in 1929. He had to accept – very reluctantly – the presence of a nuncio in his Archdiocese. He had also lost his only chance of being made a cardinal.'[19] The red hat went to Cardinal MacRory in Armagh in 1929.

After Robinson's death, Duff wrote an article about him in the *Franciscan College Annual* in which he referred to their first meeting. Duff said that at the time of the meeting 'The Nunciature was in the tedious grip of the Board of Works, and the new Nuncio had to live some weeks in a hotel.' He recalled that the Nuncio was 'extraordinarily kind to me that day in the hotel. He gave me two whole hours in which we talked about a lot of things. He gave me, too, what I sorely needed, interest and encouragement – things which he kept on tap for me ever after.'[20] Put in context, this was an extraordinary meeting. At the time Duff was a forty-year-old layman, a civil servant engaged in a variety of social and apostolic works, including the maintenance of two hostels, the Sancta Maria and the Morning Star, and a third, the Regina Coeli, shortly to open, but he was *persona non grata* with the diocesan authorities in Dublin. Access to the Nuncio was entirely due to W. T. Cosgrave, who was on good terms with Archbishop Byrne, but who, at the same time, clearly had faith in Duff. The welcome Robinson extended to Duff set a pattern for a continuous supportive relationship with him and his successors, as well as with staff at the Nunciature. Archbishop (later Cardinal) Riberi, who was Nuncio in Dublin from 1959 to 1962 and exceptionally supportive of Duff and the Legion, first met Duff when he spent time working at the Irish Nunciature as Secretary to Paschal Robinson.

Approximately eighteen months after the Shelbourne meeting, Cosgrave accompanied Duff to the Nunciature on 7 May 1931. In a letter to Celia Shaw written the same day, Duff said, 'The President brought me up to the Nuncio today and we had a great talk over the Roman trip. I will tell you the result.'[21] He enquired if she had 'a good guide book to Rome and a pocket dictionary?' Two weeks later, on 23 May 1931 at 11.30am, Duff was received by Pope Pius XI. He was accompanied by Monsignor O'Brien from Liverpool, the diocese in which Dr Downey was Archbishop and with whose episcopal blessing he travelled to Rome. The Pope discussed the Legion with them for about twenty minutes. Writing to Shaw from Marseilles on 31 May on his journey home, Duff recounted that they came away from Rome very satisfied with 'some marvellous endorsements':

> His Holiness is rather severe in manner and did not smile even once during the interview. He asked many questions. Monsignor did very well. No reference to our condition in Dublin, although I was in a state of nerves on this point. It must have been the first thing which struck the notice of the acute gentleman, Monsignore Pizzardo, the assistant Secretary of State, who saw us twice before our audience was fixed and who went into details of the subject matter of the interview. I read into this that the Dublin position is appreciated at its true value in Rome.[22]

Duff described the events of the visit to Rome formally in a letter to Cardinal MacRory, Archbishop of Armagh and Primate of All Ireland, written shortly after his return. He said that in addition to the private audience with the Pope, he was received by Cardinal Pacelli, later Pope Pius XII, Secretary of State. He also had two interviews with Cardinal Marchetti, one of which took place before the meeting with the Pope, while the second followed the meeting. Duff also had two interviews with Cardinal Lepicier. In the second interview, Lepicier said that he had read the *Handbook* with deep interest and would discuss it that evening with the Pope.[23] In writing to thank him for the report of his Roman visit, MacRory promised, 'I shall try to have a talk with the Archbishop of Dublin, within the next week, on the position of the organisation.'[24] Writing from the Gresham Hotel in Dublin later in the month, the Cardinal told Duff that he had spoken to Archbishop Byrne: 'As promised, I spoke of you and the Legion to the Archbishop of Dublin, but I was unable to get from him anything definite.'[25] Three months later Dr Dignan, Bishop of Clonfert, invited Duff to lunch on 12 October at the Royal Hibernian Hotel, where Dignan was staying. Duff's memo, written after the lunch, recorded that

Dignan said that he could not use the Legion of Mary in his diocese without approval for the Legion from the Archbishop of Dublin or the Pope, unless without using the name of the Legion, which Duff observed 'was hardly the [appropriate] thing.'

Frank Duff never forgot his, and the Legion's, debt to Cosgrave. When Cosgrave's government was replaced in 1932, Duff wrote to him:

> You have won the deep respect of all and you have made Ireland respected everywhere.
>
> Personally, I could not possibly express the extent of my regard for you and for your work. You have placed me under immeasurable obligations to you, which can never be repaid. You actually never refused me any request I ever made of you.[26]

Speaking of Cosgrave over thirty years later, he made clear the depth of his feeling. He said: 'W. T. Cosgrave was one of the noblest figures that could be imagined. Whenever I think of him it is with sheer emotion.'[27]

In 1930, the year in which Duff first met the Papal Nuncio, a threat of closure from the Dublin ecclesiastical authorities hung over the Sancta Maria Hostel. According to Ó Broin, when information regarding closure had come from the Archbishop via Sir Joseph Glynn, Duff reacted by saying that he would close the hostel, but according to Ó Broin he asked Glynn to 'Tell the Archbishop to put it in writing, and I'll nail his letter to the street door.'[28] A letter written on 3 March 1930 by Glynn to Dr Dunne, secretary to the Archbishop, is in a diplomatic vein:

> Without mentioning any names I conveyed the purport of what you told me yesterday to Frank Duff. As I expected he said 'at a word from His Grace 76 Harcourt Street will be closed'. However he hopes that His Grace will depute someone to enquire into the working of it before ordering it to close.[29]

The letter is marked 'Will give no word. They know what he thinks.' The hostel remained open for five decades until 1974 when a changed economic environment, including the introduction of a state allowance for unmarried mothers in the previous year, lessened the need for such a facility. Duff's contemporaneous memo on the Sancta Maria Hostel testifies to deep faith: 'The Legion system with its completely spiritual outlook, backed by infinite patience and thoroughness, cannot eventually be deprived of the object of its pursuits.' The memo gives a different picture of 'Catholic Ireland' to that widely assumed to have existed at the time. It refers to the visitation of the lodging-houses of prostitutes, of the venereal hospitals, the women's casual ward in the Union, the prison, the Bridewell and the proselytizing centres.[30]

The official diocesan attitude to the Legion at this time is illustrated in a letter in September 1931, four months after Duff's meeting with the Pope, from one of the Vicars, Mgr Waters, to a priest of the diocese, Fr Flood, who had enquired about the status of the Legion in the diocese. Waters said that he had the 'pleasure of informing you that the "Legion of Mary" has no diocesan approval i.e. from His Grace and I think therefore that you ought to take no official part in its promotion in Howth. The time has not come for formal approval.'[31] Negativity and refusals of one sort or another continued to mark the reaction to the Legion by the diocesan authorities. One typical refusal was that in November 1932 to a request from May Mortell, Vice-President of Concilium and the first President of the Regina Coeli Hostel, to hold a religious ceremony in the Pro-Cathedral associated with the annual Legion reunion. In March 1933 Esther Lawrence of Ailesbury Road in Dublin, an auxiliary member of the Legion, asked permission for the erection outdoors at the Regina Coeli Hostel of a set of Stations of the Cross which she wished to donate, since she thought they would provide an attractive and prayerful amenity for the residents. Her letter to Archbishop's House is marked 'Some difficulties in the way.' In the same month Fr Hayden, parish priest in Francis Street, declined a request made by a legionary to offer Mass, saying 'nor can I accede to your request with reference to Mass on Friday. I return your pound note.'[32]

Meanwhile the *Handbook* was translated into Italian with the help of Mother Perry, a nun in Rome. In April 1932, Fr Hugh O'Connor, writing from San Silvestre in Capite, expressed impatience to Duff: 'You really *must* do something about this "Imprimatur"[33] if you can't get it for the original copy how do you expect us to get it for the translation? … So please get a move on. …'[34] If O'Connor was not fully in the picture in Rome, another one of the Dublin vicars, Mgr Fitzpatrick, who was sympathetic to Duff and his work, certainly was, as is clear from his letter to Duff around the same time: 'I know how keenly you feel the difficulties of your present position, and that a work of God seems about to be broken on these rocks that block its route.'[35] On 24 May 1932 Duff wrote to Waters setting out the facts since 1928 when a copy of the *Handbook* had first been sent to Byrne.[36] There is no record of a reply. The position then was that, eleven years after the founding of the Legion, no diocesan approval had been granted either for the organization or for the *Handbook*. Nor had Duff ever been received in interview by the Archbishop, although he had been received by the Pope. Replying to a letter from Archbishop Harty of Tuam in June 1932, Duff said, 'I myself have never spoken to His Grace. All applications either direct or through Sir Joseph Glynn and Mr Lalor were refused.'[37]

Early in 1933 the relationship between Duff and the diocesan authorities was put under further strain when Waters made a false charge, claiming that Duff had been sent scurrying from Rome in 1931. Duff wrote to Mgr O'Brien, who had accompanied him at the audience with Pope Pius XI:

A rather serious position has come about which I hasten to tell you of. Monsignor Waters, one of the Vicars General of the Archdiocese of Dublin, told an assemblage of persons at a Clondalkin convent (i.e. there were Priests there and the nuns and possibly some of the laity as well) that we had gone out to Rome to advance the interests of the Legion: that we were asked first thing what the Archbishop thought about it all, and when we stated his attitude, we were at once kicked out and packed off about our business. There is no mistake about this. Our informant is the local Parish Priest Father O'Ryan, who was present on the occasion … .

It is everywhere known that you and I were on the trip and to charge a Domestic Prelate of His Holiness with faking a story of a favourable interview, whereas in reality, we had been unceremoniously kicked out, is going beyond the beyonds.[38]

Since Duff had already provided Waters with a full account of the Roman visit, the statement was not the result of a lack of information. When Duff's friend Matt Lalor taxed Waters about the remark, Waters said that he had made the statement only 'as a joke'.[39]

Towards the end of 1933, still with no approval in sight, Duff turned again to Rome. On 30 August 1933 he wrote to the Nuncio, Dr Robinson, about the forthcoming Holy Year pilgrimage of 300 legionaries and 20 priests to Rome where they were due to have an audience with Pope Pius XI. At the audience on 16 September 1933 the Pope gave the endorsement of the Legion, which was printed on the first page of the *Handbook* when an edition was finally published with the Dublin *Imprimatur* dated 7 March 1937. The Pope begins, 'We give a very special blessing to this beautiful and holy work – the Legion of Mary. Its name speaks for itself.'

The following year, 1934, was the landmark one when Duff resigned from the civil service and threw himself completely into the work of the Legion. It was also the year of the first Legion pilgrimage to Lourdes. In the summer of 1934 definite progress was reported regarding approval. In May, Waters presented to Duff proposals for a constitution for the Legion, drafted by the Dublin vicars, and invited Duff to discuss the constitution with himself and Mgr Cronin. Duff wrote that he was 'grievously disappointed at the contents of the Draft Constitution which was enclosed with your letter of yesterday's date. For I recognised therein little of the Legion of Mary.'[40] The vicars' draft commenced by limiting the membership of the organization to women. Men were to be explicitly forbidden from membership. 'Praesidia of men, and much more mixed praesidia are forbidden in the Diocese of Dublin.' The Spiritual Director was to have a veto on all proceedings. Despite this expression of disappointment at the contents of the Archbishop's proposals, Duff accepted the invitation to meet with the Monsignori, saying that he proposed to bring with him Miss Mortell, Miss Shaw and Mr Tom Cowley, who occupied representative positions in the Legion. Waters replied, swiftly rejecting the suggestion that Duff should be accompanied to the meeting, saying that 'colleagues' agree that their idea is to see Duff alone as 'the founder of the Legion of Mary'.[41] Duff's rejoinder was unambiguous. He said there was no official position in the Legion of Mary as that of founder. Whatever status he had in the organization depended on his position as president of the Concilium or central council of the Legion:

That I should represent, alone, the Legion, in a conference proposed (prima facie) for the purpose of sweeping away every distinctive feature of the Legion and of setting up something completely different, which is to be clothed with the name of the Legion is a responsibility which I shrank from assuming voluntarily. I therefore consulted with those who occupy with me the chief offices in the Legion and they insist that I should not attend the proposed conference alone.[42]

Duff then suggested that he and Mortell would meet the vicars. Waters accepted the compromise, saying 'You may bring Miss Mortell with you to your interview with Mgr. Cronin and myself tomorrow evening at 6 oc.'[43] In turn Duff replied, 'I am obliged for your letter. Miss Mortell and I will be in attendance this evening.' He dated his letter 'Feasts of Corpus Christi and Our Lady Mediatrix of All Graces'. The meeting had been set for that evening and in 1934 those two feasts coincided on 31 May. The venue for the meeting was 87 Iona Road, Glasnevin, where Waters lived. It was inconclusive and was adjourned to 6 June. The participation of Miss Mortell proved to be significant. Writing to Duff later in June, May Dunne, a legionary and friend of both Duff and Waters, referring to Miss Mortell and to Duff, said 'I got a good report of both of you just now. Miss M. has captured him [Waters]!'[44]

Insight into the scale of difference between the protagonists can be gleaned from Fr Creedon's response to Duff on receipt of the constitutions which the vicars had proposed on behalf of the Archbishop. Creedon described these as 'shallow, badly worded, lack unity and cohesiveness and have not the Legion grip on them'. He continued:

I am in agreement re one document. That would be a decided advantage to have agreed emendations made in the Handbook by you and sent to the Censor. Even though our hand will be in the dog's mouth. However Our Lady will see us through in her own way. Notwithstanding everything I am glad that you found the interview pleasing and satisfactory and also charmed to note a real optimistic tone in your letter. The chat with Nuncio and Secretary was also very consoling. Am pleased you got a bit of your own back on Mgrs. – they and their Chief are in a worse hole than we are and please *play for time*, as Nuncio says, all along the line.[45]

Two days later, Creedon sent a telegram to Duff: 'Advise Caution Writing Fully – Creedon.' In his letter he drew a revealing contrast between the attitude of the Irish hierarchy in general to the Legion and the particular difficulties in Dublin:

On Sat evg when I wrote at end of my letter that 99% of the Irish hierarchy had not asked for such a veto, but were satisfied with the status of ecclesiastical authorities and

S. D. [Spiritual Director] as outlined in the handbook, I intended to develop that point further and put the whole matter before Irish Bishops (who have been generally always so kind and helpful to us) rather than leave decisions to people who have not the foggiest notion (witness their silly statutes) of Catholic Action and who were always so hurtful to us … .

So if we wait for Bishop's Meeting and nothing done we would still be in the grip of Dublin and most likely they would have the final word.[46]

A further meeting was required and this was planned for 18 June. However, this meeting had to be deferred to the next day because it coincided with Prize Day at Clonliffe College. A Dublin legionary, Muriel Wailes, wrote to Duff on 21 June 1934 with the news that she had heard from the 'Venerable Archdeacon Peter' that the Legion was being examined by two of the vicars with a view to its being recognized as an Association of the Church. Wailes told the Archdeacon she would like the Archbishop to know that the legionaries were absolutely loyal to him and that, speaking for herself, and she was sure also for all legionaries, 'if Dr Byrne said tomorrow that he wished us to leave the Legion, not one of us would attend another meeting. That this was the spirit inculcated in the Legion.'[47] Some details still remained, and following a delay of some weeks owing to the priests' retreats in the archdiocese, a final meeting between Duff, Mortell and Mgrs Waters and Cronin took place on 27 July.

On 14 August Waters wrote to Duff saying that he was returning the draft constitution. 'It is quite correct. This draft is final as far as Mgr. Cronin and I are concerned, and I am confident there is no one among us who wants it changed.'[48] Formal approval for the Legion of Mary in Dublin was granted on 3 January 1935. On 6 January Duff wrote to the Archbishop expressing his thanks. 'I am sure it is not necessary for me to say that it has brought me, as it will bring the whole Legion, joy. On behalf of all my fellow-Legionaries I offer your Grace our sincere thanks.'[49]

On 7 January the *Irish Independent* published a report entitled 'Legion of Mary approved by Archbishop', accompanied by a photograph of Byrne. The printed letter of approval read as follows:

My Dear Mr Duff,

I have received from Mgr. Cronin and Mgr. Waters an account of their conversations with you regarding the constitutions for the Legion of Mary. They have submitted to me the draft constitutions agreed upon by the Monsignori and yourself. I have examined them carefully and am now happy to convey to you my approval of them.

I feel that the Legionaries, working in accordance with these constitutions and in the spirit of ecclesiastical authority which they inculcate, will be abundantly blessed by God. The Divine Assistance is assured to them by their devotion to Mary, their Special Patroness.

In conveying to you this formal approval of the constitutions of the Legion of Mary, I wish you and the Legionaries every blessing from God.

The Legion of Mary organization had finally gained diocesan approval in Dublin but the Dublin *imprimatur* for the *Handbook* would not be granted for a further two years. The earliest *imprimatur* for the Legion *Handbook* was given by the Archbishop of Melbourne, Dr Mannix, in May 1934. Mannix, who was born in Cork, had been a professor in Maynooth before he went to Australia, where he became a figure of importance in Church and public affairs. When on 17 May 1934 Ruth Gavan Duffy wrote from Australia to inform Duff that Mannix had granted an *imprimatur*, Duff in turn sent word to Fr Creedon, who replied by telegram: 'Thanks. Handbook now unassailable. Mediatrix wins again. Creedon.'[50]

The first edition of the *Handbook* to be printed with the *imprimatur* of the Archbishop of Dublin is dated 7 March 1937. The *nihil obstat* is that of Michael L. Dempsey. This indicates that a document has been examined by the censor, in this case Dempsey, and nothing has been found to stand in the way of an *imprimatur*, or of granting permission to publish. In the process of censoring the *Handbook*, Dempsey sought guidance from Dominican theologian Thomas Garde, OP who was *Socius* or Assistant to the Master-General of the Dominicans and who came from Castlemartyr in east Cork. Early in January 1937, Garde wrote to Dempsey from Santa Sabina in Rome:

I had hoped to send you my opinion on the hand-book of the Legion of Mary before this, but more urgent duties compelled me to lay it aside for a week.

I read carefully all the passages dealing with Mary's privileges and devotion to her. Moreover I discussed certain propositions with competent authorities here. The general impression is excellent. The expression of devotion to Mary is similar to that which we find in the writings of B. Grignion de Montfort, Colin, Chaminade etc. Just a few phrases seem to need correction. I have set them down together with my own comments on them, leaving the final judgement to yourself. [There follow several paragraphs in Latin and French].[51]

Notes to Chapter 11

1. Lalor to Duff, 16 November 1928, File 1309, LOMA.
2. See, for example, McGrath's 'Introduction' to Bradshaw, *Frank Duff*.
3. Toher to Wall, 12 November 1928.
4. See Glossary.
5. Hayden to Kirwan, 10 October 1928, File 1322, LOMA.
6. Duff to Ledit, 1 May 1935.
7. Quoted in Donal Nevin, *James Larkin: Lion of the Fold*. Dublin: Gill and Macmillan, 1998, p. 476.
8. Duff to McGuckian, 22 December 1973.
9. Duff to Waters, 24 May 1932, File 1083, LOMA.
10. Duff to Byrne, 25 February 1929, LOM file, DDA.
11. Walsh to Duff, 22 March 1929, File 1083, LOMA.

12. Duff to Byrne, 29 June 1929, File 1083, LOMA.
13. Morrissey, *Edward J. Byrne*, p. 233.
14. Duff to Byrne, 2 October 1929.
15. Dermot Keogh, *Ireland and the Vatican*. Cork: Cork University Press, 1995, p. 72.
16. ibid. p.70.
17. Banim to Duff, undated, File 1083, LOMA.
18. *Maria Legionis*, 1966.
19. Keogh, *Ireland and the Vatican*, p. 69.
20. Frank Duff, 'Paschal Robinson', *Franciscan College Annual*, 1952, pp. 51–52.
21. Duff to Shaw, 7 May 1931, National Library of Ireland, Ms 31,670/2. Researched by Donal Healy.
22. Duff to Shaw, 31 May 1931, NLI, Ms 31,670/2.
23. Duff to MacRory, 9 June 1931, File 1083, LOMA.
24. MacRory to Duff, 18 June 1931, File 1083, LOMA.
25. MacRory to Duff, 26 June 1931, File 1083, LOMA.
26. Duff to Cosgrave, 8 March 1932, File 1187, LOMA.
27. Aherne interview.
28. Ó Broin, *Frank Duff*, p. 49.
29. Glynn to Dunne, 3 March 1930, DDA.
30. Memorandum by Duff, 1930, LOM file, DDA.
31. Waters to Flood, 22 December 1931.
32. Hayden to Murray, 14 March 1933.
33. See Glossary.
34. O'Connor to Duff, 27 April 1932, File 1083, LOMA.
35. Fitzpatrick to Duff, 11 May 1932, File 1083, LOMA.
36. Duff to Waters, 24 May 1932, File 1083, LOMA.
37. Duff to Harty, 7 June 1932, File 1083, LOMA.
38. Duff to O'Brien, 28 February 1933, File 1083, LOMA.
39. Noted on a letter from Duff to Waters, 16 March 1933, File 1083, LOMA.
40. Duff to Waters, 28 May 1934.
41. Waters to Duff, File 1180, LOMA.
42. Duff to Waters, 30 May 1934.
43. Waters to Duff, 30 May 1934.
44. Dunne to Duff, June 1934, File 1180, LOMA.
45. Creedon to Duff, 9 June 1934, File, 1180, LOMA.
46. Creedon to Duff, 11 June 1934, File 1180, LOMA.
47. Wailes to Duff, 21 June 1934, File 1083, LOMA.
48. Waters to Duff, 14 August 1934, File 1180, LOMA.
49. Duff to Byrne, 6 January 1935, File 1180, LOMA.
50. Creedon to Duff, 12 June 1934, File 1180, LOMA.
51. Garde to Dempsey, 8 January 1937, File 1309, LOMA.

CHAPTER 12

Building the Legion

'The Legion of Mary represents the first completely original organisation which this country has produced which has become international.'

DUFF TO SEÁN MACENTEE, 3 JULY 1933

The earliest legionaries were all women. Men came into the Legion with the opening of the Morning Star Hostel in 1927. In December 1929 the first two praesidia for men, named respectively 'The Morning Star' and 'Our Lady of Knowledge', were affiliated to the Central Council of the Legion. From the start, women exercised roles of authority and leadership. This in itself is noteworthy because in the 1920s women were not only excluded from many employments but also from certain voluntary work within the Church. For example, full membership of the St Vincent de Paul Society was confined to men until 1967. Duff's mother was a woman of ability and two of his sisters were medical doctors, so he easily accepted the ability of women to assume a variety of leadership roles. An early legionary and helper in the Regina Coeli was Emma Bodkin, one of the first women to qualify as an accountant in Ireland. Bodkin was the sister of Thomas Bodkin, Director of the National Gallery in Dublin and later of the Barber Institute in Birmingham. Of those who joined the Legion in the early days, a key group came from the civil service. Celia Shaw, a contemporary and close friend of Ailish Duff while at UCD, remarked that she 'listened to Ailish talking about him [Frank] for years before I knew him'.[1] Together with Patricia Boyne [Browner], Shaw was prominent in student life in UCD in the 1920s. In the *Centenary History of the Literary and Historical Society* it is recorded, 'Of the daring few [women] who talked, Celia Shaw was the doyenne … more than willing and able to deal, in no uncertain manner, with James Dillon himself, had he not been wily enough to be always on her side'.[2] As is clear from their extensive correspondence, Shaw became a confidante of Duff's.

When the Legion was opened to men, several of those who joined were also civil servants. John Murray from the Board of Works (now the Office of Public Works), John (Seán) Moynihan, later Secretary to the government, and León Ó Broin, later Secretary of the Department of Posts and Telegraphs, were among those who joined in the 1930s. Murray became president of the Concilium, as did other civil servants, John Gavin and Enda Dunleavy. James Dillon, when leader of Fine Gael, remarked about Moynihan, 'anyone seeing the Secretary of the government tending a Legion of Mary book barrow in O'Connell Street at night would recognise a supernatural force at work'.[3] According to Ó Broin, 'Frank Duff in time was to say that Seán Moynihan was the most apostolic-minded man he ever met.' The book barrow work was started in the summer of 1935, when:

On 23 June 1935, the barrow, fully licensed for hawking and street pedalling [*sic*], set off from the Legion's Morning Star Hostel and commenced operations at the junction of O'Connell Street and Cathedral Street. It maintained its presence in the street, weather permitting, every evening from 7.30 to 10.15, and on Sunday mornings.[4]

While several Secretaries of Departments of State, prominent businessmen and women, and many persons in the fields of education and entertainment are, or have been, Legion members, Duff was particularly pleased with the accolade of Mgr Montini (Pope Paul VI) in 1952 that the Legion had learned to use the 'little people'. Such, it could be said, were the Apostles. The Legion's plan of campaign 'builds motive and means into a whole and seeks to be helpful to all sections and parties without affiliating to any'.[5] Duff saw that politics had its own important sphere, but he did not want politics to enter the Legion. The first President of the Irish Free State, W. T. Cosgrave, was a Laureate member. Legion membership covered the spectrum of political opinion. Its membership included Jock McGalloghly, who travelled from Glasgow to take part in the Easter Rising, later giving an account to the Bureau of Military History of how he and his fellow insurgents, led by Joseph Mary Plunkett, boarded a tram in Terenure to reach their post. It included Lady Mary Kerr, whose husband served with the Crown Forces in Ireland, and whose son Philip, Lord Lothian, was British Ambassador in Washington during World War II.

Nuns often played an important role in the extension of the Legion. In 1927 the Legion first set down roots outside Dublin as a result of a letter to Duff from a nun in the Ursuline Convent in Waterford. Soon Duff was on his way to Waterford to start a praesidium. Later in the same year, Mrs Mahony of the Blarney Mills in Cork invited Duff to Cork to give a talk on the Morning Star Hostel. This visit led to the establishment of the first praesidium in Cork, with Belfast following as the pace of expansion quickened. In reply to a letter in May 1945 from Sister Camillus, a member of the Holy Rosary order of nuns, Duff noted that her letter to him had been written on 23 April, the Feast of St George. He wrote, 'You may not realise that that day has keen memories for us. It was on that day that I started off to Scotland in 1928 on the trip which was destined to found the first branch outside Ireland.'[6] The establishment of that first branch outside Ireland required much effort. On a visit to the convent of the Sisters of Charity in North William Street in Dublin during 1927, Duff met Sister Josephine, who was interested in the Legion, and who in turn spoke to Sister Brendan, the superioress at Wilton Crescent in Glasgow. Some time later Sister Brendan wrote to Duff saying that a meeting had been arranged for him with the Archbishop of Glasgow.

Duff travelled to Glasgow for a meeting on 12 August 1927, but found that the Archbishop was not ready to see him. Not wishing to give up, and displaying customary perseverance, he wrote an eight-page letter to the Archbishop explaining his mission. He left the letter with the Vicar General and then took the train to Edinburgh, where he knew another nun who was based at the Sacred Heart Training College at Craiglochhart. In Edinburgh he discovered that the bishop was away on holidays and so he set out again for Glasgow. In Glasgow Duff received two phone calls, one from Archbishop's House in Glasgow inviting him to meet the Archbishop, and the other from Lady Mary Kerr, who was living in Edinburgh and who was a friend of one of the nuns he had visited there. On 14 August, Duff had a meeting with the Archbishop of Glasgow, Dr Mackintosh, who promised to speak to the Pope about the Legion. The following day he met Lady Mary, who offered him every possible help.[7]

On 23 April 1928 Duff set out for Glasgow once more. The following day he had an interview with the Archbishop, Dr Mackintosh, who received him graciously and expressed his strong desire to have the Legion established in his diocese.[8] A patronage was formed in the parish of St Peter, Partick, under the title of 'Our Lady of Lourdes'. It held its first meeting, which was attended by Duff, a local priest, Fr Conlon, and twenty-four women, on 26 April. Its work included visitation of the Western and Children's Infirmary and the jail. The next day Duff went to Edinburgh, where he spoke to women students in the Craiglockhart Teacher Training College. He had a two-hour meeting with the bishop, Dr Graham, who gave every encouragement for the establishment of the Legion there. Duff then moved on to London, where he met Bishop Brown and Cardinal Bourne. Together with Matt Lalor, he made a three-day retreat at the Carthusian Monastery at Parkminster in West Sussex, before meeting Cardinal Bourne for a second time. Bourne gave full sanction to Duff and promised 'to pray earnestly' regarding the introduction of the Legion into his diocese.[9] The first praesidium in England was started in Brook Green parish in London on 31 May 1929, the Feast of Mary Mediatrix of all Graces, by Mother Mary Woodlock of the Sacred Heart Convent in Hammersmith. A Polish woman, Philippa Szczepanowska, was the first president. In the same month, the Concilium minutes noted the request for a *Handbook* from Hyfrydle in north Wales.

Although it still lacked official approval from the Archbishop of Dublin, by the end of the 1920s the Legion was well established in Ireland, with several praesidia in parishes throughout the country, north and south. The Sancta Maria and Morning Star Hostels were fully operational and the Regina Coeli Hostel would open shortly. The Legion had also put down roots in Scotland and England. The Legion system had taken shape and it was ready to spread across the world. In June 1930 Duff was elected president of the Concilium, in succession to Mrs Kirwan. In August his appointment as Assistant Principal in the Department of Finance had been made permanent. His workload was heavy on all fronts. In October the Regina Coeli Hostel for homeless women was opened. Also that month, Edel Quinn, the future Legion Envoy to East Africa, joined. In November 1930 Duff travelled to Paris with Monsignor O'Brien from Liverpool, a fluent French speaker. They had an appointment to see Cardinal Verdier, a meeting that led to the granting of permission to start the Legion in France, although the first praesidium in France was not started until a decade later in Nevers. The introduction to Cardinal Verdier had come via Cardinal Bourne of Westminster, as Duff acknowledged in a letter to Celia Shaw: 'Cardinal Bourne has sent me a note of introduction to Cardinal Verdier. This should work wonders. Isn't he very good?'[10] While in Paris, Duff visited the convent in the Rue du Bac where he met an American nun, Mother Elizabeth Reeves, and gave her a copy of the *Handbook*.

Among the delegates at a chapter meeting of the Vincentian Order in Paris in 1931 was Fr Joe Donovan. Donovan met Mother Elizabeth Reeves and she passed him the copy of the *Handbook*. It sparked his interest in the Legion and Fr Donovan visited Dublin, where he met Duff. On his return home to St Louis he wrote an article entitled 'Is this the long-looked-for Church society?' in the *Denver Register* and the *American Ecclesiastical Review*. Fr Nicholas Schaal, a priest in Raton, New Mexico, read the article in the *Denver Register* and set up the first praesidium in the United States in the parish of St Patrick in Raton, known for the Raton Pass on the Santa Fe trail along the Colorado–New Mexico border, with a population of about 6,000.[11] The chief economic activities in Raton were coal-mining, rail-roading and cattle-raising. There were two parishes: one for the Spanish–Americans and the second, St Patrick's, for the other nationalities, including Irish, German, Italian and French. The first praesidium in America, founded on 27 November 1931, was named 'Our Lady of Mercy'. Soon a second praesidium was founded in one of the mining camps in Van Houten. Fr Donovan, the author of the article which sparked interest in the Legion, founded a praesidium for women at St Louis in May 1932. The Legion quickly spread to Chicago, Los Angeles, Boston, San Francisco and other cities of the United States.

The Legion reached beyond Europe for the first time when a praesidium was established in Mylapore, a suburb of Madras in India, by Mrs Mackenzie-Smith in 1931. She had been a member of the patronage at Brook Green in Hammersmith. Within a few decades the Legion was in almost every diocese in India. Mackenzie-Smith, having joined the Legion in London, had met Duff when he was visiting London and told him that her husband had been appointed Sheriff in Madras. Duff urged her to start the Legion there and she did so successfully. The early members of the Legion in India included Portuguese, Eurasians, Indians and British.[12] In May 1932, one of the Madras legionaries started the Legion in Calcutta. As the spread of the Legion continued to Bangalore, New Delhi, Ceylon and Burma, no problem ever arose with regard to colour or caste.[13] An Italian missionary priest working in Madras, whom Mackenzie-Smith had introduced to the Legion, wrote the following arresting account in *L'Osservatore Romano*:

> I am a parish priest in Madras, in charge of a parish of 2,000 Catholics out of a total population of 50,000 people … as compared with four mosques and thirty-five Hindu temples … . The President [of the Legion praesidium] gathered together about ten of my women parishioners and spoke to them as she knows how to do. … I have been able to baptise children, men, women, entire families who have been brought into the church by these women … . Women who have the courage to do this, who go into hospitals and prisons and even into leper hospitals, who succeed in convincing and converting – do they not remind us of those other women mentioned in the Acts of the Apostles whom St. Paul praises in his Epistles.[14]

The thirty-first International Eucharistic Congress, held in Dublin from 21 to 26 June 1932, has been described by Duff as the 'Epiphany of the Legion.'[15] The Congress was significant in displaying Ireland's identity as a Catholic nation, part of the universal Catholic Church, differentiating Ireland from the British Commonwealth, of which it still formed a part. An Act, the Eucharistic Congress (Miscellaneous Provisions) Act, 1932, was passed by the Irish government to facilitate the event. The major buildings, including the General Post Office, Trinity College and Government Buildings, were illuminated as Dublin became the 'city of lights'. Among the events was a huge garden party in the grounds of Blackrock College. Foremost among the visitors was the Papal Legate, Cardinal Lorenzo Lauri. Legionaries visiting Dublin for the Congress, together with legionaries from other parts of Ireland and abroad, along with other interested persons, were invited to visit the Legion hostels and the Concilium office. The 3,000 people who visited the headquarters of the Legion included a cardinal, two archbishops, fifteen bishops, two abbots and 'God knows how many priests'.[16]

Many of those who visited Dublin for the Congress returned from where they came bringing the Legion of Mary with them. Among the visitors was Ruth Gavan Duffy, wife of a descendant of Sir Charles Gavan Duffy, Prime Minister of Victoria, and connected through marriage to Louise Gavan Duffy, already a member of the Legion in Dublin. On her way back to Australia, she visited Madras and Calcutta and saw the Legion in operation there. When she arrived back in Australia together with a copy of the *Handbook*, she found that Fr Bakker, who had also attended the Congress, was already in the process of starting the Legion. A parish priest from Melbourne, Bakker started the first praesidium in Australia at Ascot Vale, Melbourne in November 1932. Gavan Duffy started a second praesidium in May 1933. Dr Mannix, Archbishop of Melbourne, became a strong supporter. The Legion was taken to New Zealand by a priest from Dunedin who had come to Dublin to do postgraduate studies. From Dunedin, which had been the home of Mrs Kirwan, the first President of the Legion, it went to Christchurch. A chain reaction was established and twenty years later two Australians, Agnes Orlebar and Charles Kenny, would respectively extend the Legion to Japan, New Guinea and the Solomon Islands.

The system of Legion envoys whereby a legionary volunteers to work full-time for the Legion in a particular area began in 1934 as a result of an initiative by a wealthy American businessman, Bartley Oliver, who lived in San Francisco. Oliver read an article on the Morning Star Hostel written by Alice Curtayne, which appeared in an American magazine. He then wrote to the Legion in Dublin inviting a representative to come over to San Francisco to explore the possibility of starting a similar hostel there and offering to pay the expenses of the representative. Because it seemed from Oliver's letter that he thought the Legion was an organisation specifically for running hostels, a reply was sent explaining that this was just one aspect of the Legion's work. Oliver, on whom Laureate membership of the Legion would later be conferred, replied with renewed interest and enclosed a payment to cover the expenses of sending someone from Ireland to explain the Legion further.[17]

As a result of Oliver's intervention, Celia Shaw went to the United States on a fact-finding mission in October 1933. When the possibility of Shaw travelling to the United States on behalf of the Legion arose, she was working as one of the organizers of the Central Savings Committee attached to the Department of Finance. Duff wrote to the Minister for Finance, Seán MacEntee, requesting that Shaw be released from the Department for a period of nine weeks (forming with her ordinary leave a period of twelve weeks or three months) 'on the condition that her salary during that period would be refunded in full'. It is clear from Duff's letter that, even at that early stage in the Legion's life, he had no doubt regarding the future worldwide expansion of the Legion. He began by stating that 'The Legion of Mary represents the first completely original organisation which this country has produced which has become international.' He continued by saying that it promised to be 'the most considerable organisation of its kind in the world' and that it appeared to afford to Ireland 'the opportunity to play as a world influence a part even greater than that played in the post-patrician times'.[18]

In the course of her exploratory mission to the United States, Shaw covered a large area and started a number of praesidia. When she met Oliver in San Francisco, he offered to finance a full-time Legion volunteer in North America. In this way Mary Duffy became the first envoy of the Legion of Mary, leaving Ireland in June 1934. Her 'territory' comprised Canada and the western states of the US. In 1936, two more envoys, John Murray and Una O'Byrne, were appointed. Murray concentrated on the eastern and southern states of the US, while O'Byrne helped in both regions. On completion of his envoyship, Murray decided to follow Duff's path and give up his job in the civil service to work full-time for the Legion.

Meanwhile, Fr Joe Donovan had met the rector of a largely black parish in New York. Donovan was interested in starting a praesidium in this parish and was supported by Cardinal Hayes. Elsewhere in New York a white praesidium began, but a year later, when Murray visited, he found among the whites four black faces. This was at a time when the race question was acute and when, in a white church, objections would be made about a black altar boy.[19] The ease with which persons of different race and colour integrated in the Legion became one of its hallmarks. Duff subsequently expressed pleasure when marriages occurred between legionaries of different colour, claiming that difference of colour was a minor matter and that Legion experience had shown how artificial such barriers were. Furthermore, he said, 'It is sheer folly for the white race to take up an attitude of superiority towards the others, because in fact they are not superior.'[20]

American Indians soon followed black Americans into the ranks of the Legion. In 1932, a missionary priest and a member of the Company of Mary, the Order founded by de Montfort, heard of the Legion, read the *Handbook* and decided to put it to the test. He was working among the Cowichan at Vancouver Island in British Columbia, Canada, a majority of whom could not read. Overlooking these problems, he invited all the Indian braves to attend a trial meeting of the Legion. They came and were deeply impressed. Then he risked another trial meeting, conducting these meetings exactly as described in the *Handbook*. He assigned work, but told the braves that they did not *have* to do this work as these were only trial meetings. But some of them decided to try it. When he saw they meant business, he 'called a real meeting on the Eve of Our Lady's Nativity and received five men into the "Mother of God" praesidium of the Legion of Mary'.[21] Some time later one of the envoys visited the praesidium of Native North Americans at Tzouhalem on Vancouver Island, which she described as follows:

There were five members: Abel Joe, Timothy Joe, George Jack, Moody Joe and Timothy George. Their meeting was a revelation to me. Each Legionary does his bit. In the last year they had about eight baptisms, four marriages, several people instructed in their prayers, and about ten funerals. The Legionaries are the officials now at all funerals. They dig the graves, act as pallbearers, and say the prayers … . I enjoyed the meeting and will look upon it as one of the most interesting experiences of my Legionary life.[22]

The Legion was introduced into the West Indies in 1932 by a priest in Caguas in Puerto Rico who had read an article on the Legion in another American magazine, *The Sign*. He was supported in establishing the Legion there by the Bishop of San Juan, Edwin V. Byrne. Another priest established the Legion in the British West Indies in the Port of Spain Archdiocese in Trinidad. The Archbishop of Port of Spain, Revd Finbar Ryan, OP, said that the Legion was 'nothing less than the inspiration of Our Blessed Lady herself. Nothing could be a more clear act of Providence than the starting of the activities of the Legion of Mary.'[23]

Soon after reaching the West Indies, the Legion took root in Ceylon and Panama. In 1933 Fr James Moynagh from the diocese of Ardagh started the first praesidium in Africa at Ifuho in Nigeria. Moynagh was parish priest at St Anne's Mission in Ifuho and later became Archbishop of Calabar in Nigeria. He was nicknamed 'Eyen Mary' or 'Mary's Child' by the local Christians. Michael Ekeng was the first president of the first praesidium in Africa. Born in a tiny village in the district of Arochuku in eastern Nigeria, he and his brother were captured and sold as slave boys in the market in Calabar, but his slave master, a Protestant, gave him the opportunity to attend Bible classes and gain an education. Eventually Ekeng trained as a teacher, purchased his freedom and became a Catholic.

The first praesidium of the Legion in West Africa was composed of men, but soon women were brought in. Referring to the status of women when the Legion began in Africa, Duff said:

The status of women was altogether depressed at the time. It was universally held that women should have no public life, and in fact should not open their mouths in mixed assemblies. Note this: immediately after the start of the Legion, the male members brought in the women. Then the women gravitated into officerships.[24]

The Legion took root in South Africa where the first praesidia were founded almost simultaneously at Johannesburg and at Port Elizabeth, the latter by the Prioress of the Dominican Convent there, who had been one of the early legionaries in Dublin. The praesidium at Port Elizabeth comprised past pupils of the Dominican school, who were white. A second praesidium was started in Port Elizabeth, this time for non-white men. In 1934 a legionary from Belfast, Ruby Dennison, who had a brother living in South Africa, was appointed envoy and remained in South Africa until 1938, doing extension work all over the country.

In a report in January 1936 the Spiritual Director of the Legion in Johannesburg wrote, 'I think we can safely present the Legion of Mary as the ideal society of Catholic Action.' He said that 'it exercises some kind of magnetism which it is difficult to describe, but which is none the less real.'[25] Ruby Dennison, who was white, belonged to praesidia which included members of different ethnic backgrounds. By 1958, a little over two decades after the arrival of the Legion in South Africa, the aim was that the standard praesidium in South Africa should be mixed race, which was against the law and a challenge to racial segregation.[26] But mixed-race praesidia were started and were ignored by the authorities.

Duff was emphatic on the question of racial integration. In 1939 he wrote to Mrs Mackenzie-Smith in India recommending the appointment of an Indian as President of the Senatus there:

> The Legion started and grew up free of racial barriers. Great numbers of Indians have flocked to the standard and are doing splendid work. Now I cannot help feeling that the time has arrived for yet another step forward in that direction … . You will notice how easy comparatively speaking it has been to spread the Legion in Burma and in Central Africa. In both of these places it may be said to be going like wildfire. The reason which I see for this is that in both of these territories the organisation is predominantly native – in fact in [Central] Africa exclusively so.[27]

Notes to Chapter 12

1. Conversation between Bradshaw and Shaw, Tape 110, LOMA.
2. John Farrell, 'Curfew 1916–1923', in James Meenan (ed.), *Centenary History of the Literary and Historical Society 1855–1955*. Dublin: A&A Farmar, 2005, p. 140.
3. Ó Broin, *Frank Duff*, p. 43. The 'book barrow' was a mobile stand used to display Catholic literature.
4. Eamonn Dunne, '"A Combined Barricade and Ammunition Wagon": The Legion of Mary Book Barrow', *History Ireland*, Autumn 2000, p. 8.
5. Duff, 'The Gospel to Every Creature', *Woman of Genesis*, p. 49.
6. Duff to Camillus, 3 May 1945.
7. Duff to Creedon, 14 August 1927.
8. Concilium minutes, 3 June 1928, LOMA.
9. ibid.
10. Duff to Shaw, NLI, Ms 31, 670/2.
11. Jinny Sicking, 'The Legion Comes to North America', *Maria Legionis*, December 1984.
12. Cecily Hallack, *The Legion of Mary*. London: Frederick Muller, 1940, p. 97.
13. ibid. p. 97.
14. Quoted in Hallack, *The Legions of Mary*, pp. 101–02.
15. Frank Duff, 'The Future of the Legion', *Mary Shall Reign*. Glasgow: J. S. Burns, 1961, p. 183.
16. Ó Broin, *Frank Duff*, p. 51.
17. Hallack, *The Legion of Mary*, p. 107.
18. Duff to MacEntee, 3 July 1933, File No. 1572, LOMA.
19. Hallack, *The Legion of Mary*, p. 109.

20. Duff to Coleman, 18 December 1968.
21. Hallack, *The Legion of Mary*, pp. 111–12.
22. ibid., pp. 114–15.
23. ibid, p. 125.
24. Duff to O'Connor, 21 May 1954.
25. Quoted in Hallack, *The Legion of Mary*, pp. 133–34.
26. Duff to McGrath, 3 May 1958.
27. Duff to Mackenzie-Smith, 4 January 1939.

CHAPTER 13

Rivalries

'The essence of Catholic Action in the 1920s and 1930s was that it should be initiated by the Hierarchy, or at least by the clergy.'
MGR JEROME CURTIN, 9 SEPTEMBER 1999

When Cardinal Newman was in Ireland in the 1850s he reflected on the state of the laity, writing that the Irish clergy think 'that then only Ireland will become again the Isle of Saints, when it has a population of peasants ruled by a patriotic priesthood patriarchally'.[1] Not much seemed to have changed by the 1920s. According to Mgr Jerome Curtin, a prominent priest in the Dublin Archdiocese during the episcopacy of John Charles McQuaid, the essence of Catholic Action in the 1920s and 1930s was that it should be initiated by the hierarchy, or at least by the clergy. Because of this restricted understanding of Catholic Action, it was difficult for some clergy to recognize a movement initiated by lay people. According to Thomas Morrissey, SJ, Catholic Action 'was confined to designated lay groups mandated by the local bishop. The mandate was essential.'[2] Among those who refused to have the Legion of Mary in their parishes were leading clerical lights in the Archdiocese of Dublin, including Dr Dunne, Canon Gallen and Mgr Glennon.[3] In Dublin, then a city of widespread poverty and deprivation, it was easy for the clergy, who formed an educated caste, to underestimate the apostolic potential of their 'flock', most of whom had little formal education.

In 1936 Fr Kieran, SJ, Provincial of the Irish Jesuits, carried out a survey among Jesuits regarding Catholic Action and a report was prepared.[4] Some of those surveyed were critical of the diocesan priests, claiming that they were 'not imbued with the true spirit of their calling'. One contributor, the well-know writer Fr Robert Nash, was extremely critical, saying that he had 'written freely, from conviction'. He thought that some secular clergy basked in a comfortable life and showed little interest in Catholic Action. He cited the case of a parish priest who had a 'magnificent house, sumptuously furnished with all sorts of modern conveniences'. Yet the priest refused an increase in wages to his chauffeur/gardener/handyman, a married man who was paid ten shillings a week. Nash said that 'Many people complain bitterly of their clergy, of their wealth, their worldliness etc. This complaint may indeed be sometimes due to prejudice, but it is certain that it is very difficult at times to defend the clergy against such attacks.'[5]

Frank Duff told many people, including John Gavin, that during the 1920s he lived in dread of the day when he would be told that the Legion was being closed down. He said it was 'a nightmare'.[6] But why should clergy oppose the Legion? Gavin believed it was because of fear – fear of the laity by the clergy; fear that the laity would assume too much power. Fr Nicholas Casey, parish priest in Kilbeggan, County Westmeath, who had been in the Irish College in Paris and who saw the value of the Legion, told Gavin that he could well remember when parish priests lived in fear of it taking over their parishes. This was at a time when more priests were being ordained in Ireland than 'jobs' were available and some of them had to serve for a time in England and Wales before a position became available in Ireland. Fear of laymen 'usurping' priests' jobs may also help to explain why some priests wanted to restrict membership of the Legion to women.

The idea of Catholic Action had begun with Pope Leo XIII in his encyclical *Rerum Novarum*, in which he said that Catholic Action should be directed towards 'the practical solution of the social question according to Christian principles'. Catholic Action became the broad umbrella term for many groups of lay Catholics who were attempting to further Catholic influence in society. In the nineteenth century such groups were strong in countries, including Italy and France, which had experienced anti-clerical regimes. Both Pius X and Pius XI wrote encyclicals on Catholic Action in Italy.[7] Pius X recommended that Catholic Action 'employ all those practical means which the findings of economic and social studies place in its hands'. He urged priests that their 'proper field of action is the Church' and that the priest should be cautious about taking part in 'tasks harmful to himself and the dignity of his office', a warning against the involvement in political movements. In France Action Catholique Ouvrière (Workers' Catholic Action) grew for a time but the French bishops became somewhat disillusioned by it, turning their attention to the Moral Rearmament Movement. The allegation of the politicization of Catholic Action in Italy was strongly rejected by Pius XI, who wrote that 'Catholic Action, both from its very nature and essence ("the participation and the collaboration of the laity with the Apostolic Hierarchy") and by our precise and categorical directions and orders is outside and above party politics.'[8]

A group of laymen – the Knights of Columbanus – endowed a Chair of Catholic Action and Sociology in Maynooth, to which Fr Peter McKevitt was appointed in October 1936. In 1939 McKevitt published a report entitled 'Proposals for the Initiations of a Scheme of Catholic Action in Ireland'. Historian Maurice Curtis judges the report as follows: 'The McKevitt Report reflected the hierarchy's wariness of lay initiative, and especially the view of

Archbishop Byrne of Dublin. In fact the whole report seems to reek with a tone of suspicion vis à vis lay organisations.'[9]

The experience of official Catholic Action varied from country to country, with the hierarchies of some countries granting more latitude to the laity than others, but a common thread was a tendency to draw more on the educated groups in society than on the ordinary people, with an emphasis on the intellectual and the theoretical. In 1957 Duff wrote to a legionary in Linz in Austria about his interview with the Papal Nuncio in Dublin, Archbishop Levame, who spoke of the tendency of Catholic Action to be 'aristocratic', that is to have a select membership, intellectually and technically, whereas the Legion drew on the whole membership of the Church, aiming particularly at 'a working-class representation'.[10] This membership across class lines in the Legion made a big impression on Celia Shaw when she joined the Legion in Dublin in the 1920s, since she believed that poorer people, especially in rural Ireland, were becoming disaffected and anti-clerical owing to a perceived preference of some members of the clergy for association with the better-off people.[11]

Duff's term of office as President of the Concilium ended in 1936 and Jack Nagle replaced him. Early in 1939, Nagle and Duff were invited to the Vatican by Cardinal Pizzardo, Head of the Central Bureau for Catholic Action. However, the Pope died in February and the visit was postponed for a few months. Some time before leaving Dublin for Rome, Duff received a message from the Papal Nuncio in Dublin asking him and Nagle to call to the Nunciature. There they met Dr Gilmartin, Archbishop of Tuam, who requested them to bring to Rome a wooden box containing documents from the commission investigating the apparitions at Knock. This they did gladly.

When Pizzardo invited Duff to Rome in 1939, the Legion requested a formal letter of recommendation from Archbishop Byrne. The letter, dated 13 April 1939, was literally drafted on the back of an envelope. It went as follows:

My Lord Cardinal

I have the honour to present to you Mr. Frank Duff and Mr. Jack Nagle of the Legion of Mary. They are going to Rome in obedience to an invitation of Your Eminence received some short time ago. I can recommend them in every way to Your Eminence's kindness.

[As far as I know][12] They are devoted to forwarding the work of God in the souls of the faithful here in Ireland and elsewhere. I am sure your Eminence will find in them everything you desire in their zeal to forward the apostolic work of the Hierarchy.

Duff found the attitude in the Vatican strongly supportive of the Legion. When he and Nagle met Cardinal Fumasoni-Biondi, Prefect of Propaganda, he told them that the Legion had his 'whole-hearted support', assuring them of the help of the Apostolic Delegates, saying 'Why should they not support you, are they not Apostolic men?'[13] While in Rome, Duff received the first consignment of the Italian translation of the *Handbook*. The Italian edition bore the *nihil obstat* of Mgr Canestri, who described it as 'a gem of Italian literature'. The private audience with Pius XII took place on 28 April. Duff told the Pope that the Legion embodied the principle of search: it sought out individual souls.

The next day Duff wrote to Fr Creedon:

I think things have worked out successfully yesterday (L. de Montfort's Day). We had a long interview with the General of the Jesuits at 10 o'clock – I think it was favourable. He said he would do all possible to wipe out the regrettable differences. Secondly, the Italian Handbook was published yesterday. Thirdly, we had our audience with the Pope. The latter was indescribable. I started right away that we had come to seek his special aid. Then I spoke with great freedom and covered every inch of the ground. He listened with the greatest sweetness. It was a pleasure to talk. He let me go ahead without any sense of limitation. When I had finished he asked several questions … . The Pope assured us three times of his favour. 'I want to help you.' We gave him a copy of the Italian Handbook. He looked through it and said 'I will read through it carefully' – then he looked again and added 'I will read it in a fatherly way.'[14]

In his letter to Creedon, Duff remarked on the great help he had received in Rome from Dr Percy Jones of the Archdiocese of Melbourne and from Dr MacSherry, Archbishop of Port Elizabeth. Duff said that he had already spoken on the Legion to the students of Propaganda and of the Irish College:

[At the Irish College] Dr McKevitt and Dr Kyne abstained from attending the lecture, although everybody else in the College was there plus Dr MacSherry and Dr MacShane (Armagh) … . Tomorrow I address the English College, Monday the Beda, Tuesday the Scots College.[15]

In May 1939, shortly after Duff and Nagle had been received by the Pope, permission for Mass in the Morning Star Hostel was still being refused. When a request was made to the Archbishop's secretary, Dr Patrick Dunne, by Dr Michael Dempsey of Clonliffe College for permission for Mass in the Morning Star on Sunday during the Whit retreat, permission was refused for Sunday Mass, but granted for Monday. At the time attendance in one's own parish for Sunday Mass was customary. But refusal for Sunday Mass was made despite the fact that Duff had earlier argued that this facilitated a return to the sacraments for men who might be obliged to seek work on Mondays. A further request for Mass to celebrate the ordination of a former voluntary staff member of the hostel was granted on condition that it was not a Sunday Mass and that there was no publicity. Following the death of Archbishop Byrne, a letter from Jack Nagle requesting permission for Masses in the Morning Star and Regina Coeli Hostels during retreats was marked 'leave granted for weekdays of these Retreats but not for Sundays' and signed F. J. Wall [Mgr Francis Wall].[16]

A different source of difficulty for Duff and the Legion arose during the 1930s from a misunderstanding with the Jesuit Order, the result, it appears, of a belief at the highest level in the Order that the Legion was distracting Jesuits from work with their own Sodality of Our Lady. Duff's first encounter with a religious order had been with the Jesuits in Belvedere College when he was a boy. Fr Michael Browne, SJ, of whom Duff said 'He gave me the greatest encouragement and endorsement at all times, and until his death he always heard with delight of the growth and of the work of the Legion; and I know that it had his potent prayers,'[17] held a special place in his affection. From 1913, when Duff made an enclosed retreat given by Fr Scanlan, SJ, at Milltown Park, he became a regular attender at retreats there. He was very friendly with and often consulted individual Jesuits, including Fr Mackey and Fr Tom Counihan. The Council of the Pioneer Movement at Myra House, a movement founded by the Jesuit Fr Cullen, was the crucible within which the Legion was born. In a letter to Mackey in 1928, Duff wrote, 'I am very grateful to the Jesuits. They were the only <u>body</u> that stood by me in the bad time.'[18] In a letter to Tom Counihan, SJ, in 1938, Duff contrasted the difficulties then being experienced with happier days: 'The position is the most awful imaginable – especially to me who remembers that the Jesuits stood more by us in the early difficult days than any other section of the Priesthood.'[19] Five years earlier in 1933, in a letter to Aubrey Gwynn, SJ, Duff said that he had found friends 'who were always true' among the Jesuits.[20] Three Jesuit priests, Fathers Devane, Mackey and Roche, played a role in closing down the Monto brothels. Of Fr Mackey, Duff said, 'Fearless, single-visioned, and utterly spiritual – that is Father Ernest Mackey, SJ, in tabloid form!'[21] Duff's problems with the Jesuit Order never interfered with his admiration for, and gratitude to, individual Jesuits. For example, in 1968 he spoke in the highest terms of a Jesuit priest based in Gardiner Street: 'I could not recommend anybody to you who would be better than Fr McCarron.'[22]

The root of the problem seems to have been the degree to which Jesuits were required to support their own sodality in preference to the Legion of Mary. The issue merits reflection because it provides an example of how people with the shared goal of spreading the Good News of the Gospel could come into conflict. Such conflicts are commonplace in Church history and have emerged within religious orders themselves. The name 'sodality' comes from the Latin 'sodalitas' meaning comradeship or fellowship, 'sodalist' being the word for comrade. The Sodality, a lay association under the authority of the Father General of the Jesuits, dating back to the early days of the Jesuits in the sixteenth century, was founded by a Belgian Jesuit, Jean Leunis, who had known Ignatius Loyola. The first members were students who sought to integrate their studies with their Christian faith, choosing as their patron

Our Lady of the Annunciation. Membership of the Sodality grew and the commitment of membership which was rooted in Ignatian spirituality included attendance at a weekly meeting and the undertaking of some apostolic activity.

When the Jesuit Society was suppressed in 1773, there were over 2,000 sodalities, some of which continued under the local bishop. By the time the Jesuit Society was restored in 1814 a huge number and variety of sodalities existed, many removed from the original idea of their founder. One hundred years later, in 1922, Fr Ledóchowski, Father General of the Society of Jesus, saw the need for renewal of the Sodality and summoned forty Jesuits, all Sodality directors, to a meeting. A central secretariat for the promotion of the Sodality was established in Rome but over succeeding decades the original component of apostolic work was not emphasized. Following the Second Vatican Council and an initiative taken in France, the Sodality found new expression in 'La Vie Chrétienne', so that the Sodalities of Our Lady would re-emerge as Christian Life Communities.

Duff set out his account of the difficulties in a memo written in 1938. In the first ten critical years in the life of the Legion, that is until 1931, the Jesuits were very favourable to the Legion. In November 1931, a few months after the publication of the encyclical of Pius XI on Catholic Action, *Non Abbiamo Bisogno*, Fr John C. Joy, SJ, editor of the Jesuit journal *The Irish Monthly*, wrote a very favourable article about the Legion as a true example of Catholic Action.[23] Jesuit supporters of the Legion included Laurence Murphy, SJ, Rector of Loyola College in Madras, who helped Mrs Mackenzie-Smith to launch the Legion in India. In Calcutta, Fr De Staercke, SJ, started the first and second branches in that city. Fr Piers Smith, SJ, was probably the first priest in England to discern the value of the Legion and, according to Duff, 'In Ireland the Jesuits gave conspicuous help to the Legion – more than conceded by any other body of the clergy.'[24] Deep roots for a link between the Legion and the Jesuits might be found in the fact that Louis Marie Grignion de Montfort, whose book on the *True Devotion to the Blessed Virgin* played a vital role in the founding of the Legion of Mary, had spent eight formative years in Jesuit education between the age of twelve and twenty.

In 1931 contact took place between members of the Jesuit Order and the Legion of Mary on the subject of effecting a working arrangement between the Jesuit sodality and the Legion. The discussions progressed favourably and reached their climax in a letter from Père Villaret, SJ, based at the Central Secretariat of the sodality in Rome, to Duff on 28 October 1931.[25] While this letter was being discussed by Legion authorities, the latter learned that another letter had been issued by the Father General of the Jesuits in which the Legion was mentioned in an appreciative way, but at the same time it stressed that the sodality was the work to which the Jesuits were to give priority. The Father General of the Jesuits at the time, Wlodzimierz Ledóchowski (1866–1942), from Poland, held this post from 1915 to his death in 1942, that is for twenty-seven years spanning the period between the two world wars. According to Fr Fergus O'Donoghue, Archivist of the Irish Province, Ledóchowski, in the spirit of the times, tended to be 'controlling'.[26] The Head of the Irish Jesuit Province during the period when relations between the Legion and the Jesuits were difficult was Fr Laurence Kieran. He was Provincial from 1931 to 1941: his normal six-year term as Provincial was extended by Ledóchowski because, in the view of Fr O'Donoghue, Ledóchowski liked Fr Kieran's style of leadership.

Ledóchowski's letter to Kieran, written on 13 November 1931 in Latin, as was customary in communications from the Father General, while describing Duff as 'a most pious man', constituted a reprimand to those Jesuits who were giving priority to the Legion over the Jesuit sodality.[27] Ledóchowski said that he had heard of those 'among our own who are inflamed with zeal for this association, and show themselves ready to promote it, as if they were unaware of our beautiful Marian Congregations' and that he considered it his 'grave duty' to draw Kieran's attention to this 'lamentable negligence of some of our men, to whom divine providence has entrusted so beautiful an instrument for saving souls, and who have allowed it to slip from their hands, by their own fault'. Ledóchowski said that he was advising Kieran to take steps to redress this negligence among some Jesuits, 'not on account of any egotistic spirit, so to speak, which might lead to reserve some apostolic works to ourselves, but on account of the common good of souls'. He pointed out that 'Our congregations',[28] although they did not bear the customary fruit in some regions, have been 'approved for centuries, praised by Pontiffs'. By contrast, he said that those new associations, whose existence and advancement depend on the zeal of some individual, no matter how pious, at the outset 'may produce a certain artificial fire, quickly fade away and perish to the real detriment of souls, which are compelled to return to the ancient and approved Congregations, not without difficulty'.[29]

The letter from Ledóchowski was construed by Duff as a 'warning off' of Jesuits to the Legion and he reacted accordingly. Irish Jesuits continued to be helpful but in other places a diminution in the interest and support of Jesuits in the Legion was notable. As a result of the letter, discussions regarding any possible affiliation between the Jesuit sodality and the Legion ceased. By 1933 relations between the Legion and the Irish Province of the Jesuits had deteriorated so that the Society in general did not weigh in behind the Legion in Ireland as it had done until then. In a letter to the Provincial written in December 1933, Fr Aubrey Gwynn stated:

The plain truth is that the legion has at present got into its ranks almost all the women and a great many of the young men whom we would naturally count on for support in our attempt to make the sodalities more active. This is undoubtedly true in Dublin, and the reports I have seen or heard from other parts of the country give me the same impression … . This means that in a very large and important area all the S. J. connection has already been recruited for the Legion. Any attempt to get them back again from the legion to the Sodality (which they have never left but which is doing no active work of its own) would lead to an endless amount of quarrelling, suspicion and jealousy; and would almost certainly kill the present initiative for Catholic Action.[30]

In 1935 the Irish Episcopacy constituted the Catholic Young Men's Societies (CYMS) as the official Catholic Action organized in Ireland with Mgr Waters as Spiritual Director. By definition, women were not included. Two years later, in June 1937, Fr Egan, SJ, whose sister, Mrs O'Meara, was a 'keen worker in the Legion', wrote to the Provincial expressing his concern about relations between the Jesuits and the Legion because 'I think so highly of the Legion and its work and it seems to me to be what the needs of the time call for so much that I would feel it to be a great pity that there should seem to be any misunderstanding between it and the Society.'[31] In his reply to Fr Egan, the Provincial, Fr Kieran, said that there was 'no opposition of a real nature between the Society and the Legion'. Referring to Egan's proposal that the Provincial or some other Jesuit should talk with Duff, Kieran claimed that 'If your Reverence knew Mr Duff I think you would realise that it would be quite useless for me or any other Father of the Society to talk this matter over with him: he sees no point of view but his own and is quite intolerant of the views of others.'[32]

In February 1938, Kieran issued a confidential circular setting out directions to Jesuits in regard to their association with the Legion:

Ours may, with permission, render spiritual assistance to the Legion of Mary when asked to do so (without however taking part in its organisation or becoming permanently attached to it), just as they render spiritual assistance to other pious associations over which they have no control.

They are not, however, falsely imagining the Legion to be but another form of our own Sodality, to favour it and promote it rather than the B.V.M. Sodality. Nor are they (acting with prudence and charity) to allow the Legion to invade the territory occupied heretofore by our sodalities.

In future no one may become the Spiritual director of a praesidium of the Legion without leave of the Provincial.[33]

In March 1938, when Fr Laurence Murphy gave up the Spiritual Directorship of the Senatus of India, Duff wrote to him on behalf of the Concilium of the Legion 'to express our very deep sense of sorrow'. He said that Fr Murphy had been 'the foundation stone of the work of the Legion in India' and that the work had grown greatly and had been much blessed. Duff said that far more important than the actual growth of the Legion in India was the fact that 'the spirit which fills it seems to be of the purest kind'. He said that from the start colour and race distinctions did not enter in and as a result he believed that they could 'look forward with the greatest hope to its future work, and for all this we must thank you with all our hearts'. He regretted profoundly that Fr Murphy could not have continued to guide the Legion in India, and he concluded with the 'hope that future events will permit your return to the work which owes so much to you'.[34]

In May 1938 Fr Tom Counihan, SJ, wrote to a fellow Jesuit regarding the rows with the Legion, saying 'It's a great pity and will do us untold harm.'[35] He went on to pay a tribute to Duff: 'What would Ignatius think of the zeal of Frank! Probably as much as he did of the zeal and stuff of his own Frank Xavier.' When Counihan wrote those generous words, the Legion had been in existence for fewer than seventeen years, while Francis Xavier was a renowned sixteenth-century missionary who travelled vast distances to spread the Gospel in Asia and had been a saint in the Catholic Church since the seventeenth century. It was a surpassing endorsement. As it happened, Francis Xavier was a saint Duff would describe as 'an object of my particular admiration'.[36]

A year later, when Duff and Nagle were in Rome to meet Pius XII together with Revd Dr Percy Jones, they met the Jesuit General. Also present was Fr Joy, SJ. According to a note on the meeting by Jones, Duff cited cases where Jesuits had opposed the Legion. Duff said that there were hundreds of Jesuits waiting for the assurance that they could assist the Legion after they had satisfied their consciences regarding their obligations to the Sodality. According to Jones's memo, the Father General said he would do all in his power to fix the current breach if it were possible.[37]

Over the succeeding years good relations were restored. A number of events occurred in the 1940s which contributed to developments in the relationship between the Jesuits and the Legion. Ledóchowski died in 1942. Because of the war, it was not possible to hold a General Congregation of the Order to appoint a new Father General, so the Vicar General, Fr Alessio Magni, was at the helm from 1942 to his death in 1944, when he was succeeded as Vicar General by Fr Norbert de Boynes. Fr John MacMahon replaced Fr Kieran as Irish Provincial in 1941. Following MacMahon's appointment and Ledóchowski's death, Archbishop McQuaid contacted the Jesuits and invited MacMahon for interview. Shortly before the interview with McQuaid, a consultation was held in the Irish Province. Fr Fergal McGrath, SJ, author of the classic work *Newman's Idea of a University*, although he was unable to attend the consultation because ill health, asked that his letter be read to the consultation. Stressing that he thought it was the most important consultation during his ten years as consultor, he expressed his 'earnest hope that, as suggested in the letter of V. Rev. Fr Vicar, a *modus vivendi* may be established between the Sodalities of the Blessed Virgin Mary and the Legion of Mary'. He said that this was an intention he had been 'recommending most earnestly to God in my Masses for years past'. He hoped that a solution would be found which 'on the one hand will preserve the independence and safeguard the activities of the Sodalities, and on the other, will enable our Fathers to cooperate in a work which has been the means of the salvation and sanctification of thousands all over the world'.[38]

At the meeting between McQuaid and MacMahon on 28 May 1943, McQuaid rowed in strongly on the side of the Legion and sought a declaration of support from the Jesuits. In response, MacMahon asked to submit to McQuaid a draft of his report to the Vicar General of the Jesuits, Fr Magni. When McQuaid received the draft, he reacted robustly to its suggestion that MacMahon did not think that the Society of Jesus 'could send an authentic declaration affecting the whole Society to so young and so undeveloped a group as the Legion of Mary'. McQuaid replied that he

> ... should be grateful if you made very clear to your Vicar General the attitude I have outlined in this letter, and I should prefer if you sent this letter. I should equally be grateful if you explained my earnest desire that a situation, which is very human but very inimical to the good of religion, were adequately and equitably solved.[39]

In his letter to the Vicar General, MacMahon expressed concerns about the Archbishop's wishes. He said that the Archbishop wanted to appoint Jesuit Fathers as Spiritual Directors of some branches of the Legion but that under existing conditions did not like to do so. He alluded to the suggestions of a widely held belief that

> ... there are difficulties existing between the Archbishop and the head of the Legion – Mr. Frank Duff. A Jesuit Father, placed between the two, would be in a very difficult position and as he would be bound to carry out the Archbishop's directions, he might find himself in conflict with a very excellent but very obstinate man in Mr. Duff.[40]

With changing personnel at the helm in the Jesuits and the onward march of the Legion, relations between the Jesuits and the Legion of Mary improved. In its *Handbook*, the Legion encouraged participation in the Jesuit Sodality and the Pioneers.[41] The Jesuits had given sterling support to the Legion in its critical early years. It was understandable that the Jesuits should wish to prioritize the work of their own sodality. But Duff saw the Legion as possessing features of apostleship not intrinsic to the sodality and was distressed by the Jesuit position.

In an important interview with two members of his Order on 7 March 2008, two days after the General Congregation of the Order at which he was appointed Father General of the Jesuits, Fr Adolfo Nicolás said that one of the factors in the socio-cultural change currently being experienced 'is that we are reaping now the bad harvest of a bad sowing. We have not helped the laity as much as we should have in the past and in our own pastoral attitudes.'[42] Nicolás referred to a study by the American priest–sociologist Andrew Greely regarding 'clerical culture', in which Greely says the worst effect of this clerical culture is that the service of the laity is very poor. A more hopeful note sounded in an article written in the *Homiletic and Pastoral Review* by Hugh Thwaites, SJ, who said that the Legion 'awakens priestly or religious vocations which are lying dormant'.[43]

Notes to Chapter 13

1. Stephen Dessain (ed.), *Letters and Diaries of John Henry Newman* vol. XVII. London: Thomas Nelson, 1967, pp. 385–86.
2. Morrissey, *Edward J. Byrne*, p. 224.
3. Author's interview with Mgr Jerome Curtin, 9 September 1999.
4. Report on Catholic Action, written manuscript; typescript in Latin, IJA, ADMN/3/30.
5. ibid.
6. Author's interview with John Gavin, 15 June 1995.
7. Pope Pius X, *Il Fermo Propositio*, 11 June 1905; Pope Pius XI, *Non Abbiamo Bisogno*, 29 June 1931.
8. Pope Pius XI, 29 June 1931.
9. Curtis, *A Challenge to Democracy*, p. 156.
10. Duff to Ubi, 10 January 1957.
11. Discussion between Bradshaw and Shaw, tape 110, LOMA.
12. This is written but then crossed out in the draft text.
13. Account of visit to Rome given by Duff at Concilium Meeting, 21 May 1939, LOMA.
14. Handwritten letter from the effects of Fr Michael Creedon, 29 April 1939, LOMA.
15. ibid.
16. 28 November 1940, Legion of Mary File, DDA.
17. Hurley, *Father Michael Browne*, pp. 195–97.
18. Duff to Mackey, 12 December 1928.
19. Duff to Counihan, 11 January 1938.
20. Duff to Gwynn, 20 May 1933.
21. Moss (ed.), *Frank Duff*, p. 51.
22. Duff to Dairine, 4 January 1968.
23. John C. Joy, SJ, 'Catholic Action in Ireland: the Legion of Mary,' *The Irish Monthly*, LX, 704, November 1931, pp. 671–84.
24. Frank Duff, memorandum re Jesuits, 8 April 1938, Jesuit file, LOMA.
25. Villaret to Duff, ADMN/3/21 (3), 28 October 1931, JAD.
26. Observation of O'Donoghue to author, 19 May 2008.
27. Ledóchowski to Kieran, ADMN/1 (59), 13 November 1931, Letters Generalate to Ireland, JAD. This letter was translated for me by Fr Gerard Deighan.
28. Reference to Sodality Branches.
29. Ledóchowski to Kieran, 13 November 1931, JAD.
30. Gwynn to Kieran, ADMN/3/21 (4), 18 December 1933, JAD.
31. Egan to Kieran, 22 June 1937, ADMN/3/21 (9), JAD.
32. Kieran to Egan, ADMN/3/21 (10), 26 June, 1937, JAD.
33. Circular letter from Kieran to members of Irish Province of Jesuits, 21 February 1938, ADMN/3/21 (21), JAD. Kieran's letter echoes strongly a letter addressed to him by Ledóchowski in Latin on 25 November 1934, ADMN 1, (65, 66), JAD.
34. Duff to Murphy, 8 March 1938.
35. Counihan to 'Father John', probably John Coyne, ADMN/3/21 (30), 4 May 1938, JAD.
36. Duff to Painter, 13 December 1975.

37. Dr Jones's account of interview with Father General of the Jesuits, 28 April 1939 in Rome. Also present Fr Joy, SJ, John Nagle and Frank Duff, 14 May 1939, File 1348, LOMA.
38. McGrath to Fr Provincial, ADMN/3/46(3), 13 May 1943, JAD.
39. McQuaid to MacMahon, 6 July 1943, ADMN/3/46 (8), JAD.
40. MacMahon to Magni, ADMN/3/46 (18), undated, JAD.
41. When attending a Patrician meeting in Dublin on 21 January 2008, Fr Micheál MacGreil, SJ, spoke of the support given by the Legion to the Pioneer Movement, especially in Africa, at the present time.
42. *Irish Catholic*, 31 July 2008, p. 16.
43. Hugh Thwaites, SJ, 'How the Legion of Mary can Benefit Parishes,' AD 2000, 20/8, September 2007, reprinted from the *Homiletic and Pastoral Review*.

CHAPTER 14

The McQuaid Era

'I have never yet received a personal favour from this diocese.'
DUFF TO FR CHRISTOPHER MANGAN, 25 MARCH 1943

Archbishop Byrne died on 9 February 1940 following a lengthy illness, during which the archdiocese was effectively run by the Vicars General. Byrne's illness and the role of the Vicars contributed to Duff's difficulties because some, in particular Monsignors Wall and Waters, had little time for him or the Legion. On Byrne's death, Wall was elected Vicar Capitular, or administrator, of the vacant diocese by the Cathedral Chapter. Duff, increasingly concerned about the leadership in the archdiocese, drafted a letter to the Papal Nuncio, Dr Robinson. He began by saying that he was enclosing a letter from Dr Stafford Johnson, a friend of both the Taoiseach Éamon de Valera and Dr McQuaid, which had been brought to him by Dr Lea-Wilson.[1] Lea-Wilson, a medical graduate of Trinity College, was a friend of McQuaid. (It was Lea-Wilson who gave the painting, subsequently identified as 'The Taking of Christ' by Caravaggio, and now on permanent loan to the National Gallery of Ireland, to the Jesuit Fathers.) Duff said that he was enclosing the letter because he believed it was essential that the nuncio was aware of every opinion with regard to the vacant archbishopric. In Johnson's letter it was claimed that de Valera was anxious for the appointment of McQuaid, but Duff expressed astonishment at this claim because, he said, 'it is the general rumour that the Irish government is pressing for Dr Browne' (Bishop of Galway). Lea-Wilson conveyed verbally to Duff an invitation from Stafford Johnson to accompany him at once on a deputation to de Valera to urge the merits of McQuaid. Duff said that he excused himself from going 'on the grounds that such would bid to compromise the Legion of Mary'.

In his letter to Robinson, Duff suggested that Robinson himself should take up the archbishopric. He said that if it were utterly impossible for Robinson to fill the role, then 'perhaps the appointment of Dr McQuaid of Blackrock College would be a possible solution. But I feel intensely that the former suggestion should be considered profoundly.' Duff stated his belief that the situation in the Dublin Archdiocese constituted an emergency:

I believe a state of emergency to exist in regard to it. If any of the Dublin 'favourites' are appointed, namely, Dr. Wall, Mgr. D'Alton, Mgr. Boylan, Fr. Dunne (the Archbishop's Secretary), Fr. Michael Murphy, it will mean, I respectfully hold, the condemning of the Diocese to a continuance of the existing stagnation. This it cannot withstand, as the discontent among the people with the regime has been profound; it can only turn into open anti-clericalism if it continues and a crisis of some kind presents itself.[2]

Duff expressed concern that the clergy in Dublin had confined their work to the provision of 'education and church services'. By contrast, 'The Gospel paints the Good Shepherd as one who does not hesitate to leave the fold and to go out after the sheep that was straying. The Dublin church has not in practice understood that view.' He cited examples of the derelict man, the derelict woman, prostitution and the proselytism-free meal system, among others, as problems deserving attention. He also referred to restrictions on permission to say Mass in the Morning Star and Regina Coeli Hostels – hostels that were catering for 200 men and 130 women with 60 babies at the time. Together with Stafford Johnson's letter, Duff said that he was enclosing a copy of an extract from a letter from the Legion envoy in America and a letter from the secretary to Cardinal Pizzardo, who was responsible for the Vatican Bureau for Catholic Action.

The Nuncio replied swiftly in a firm tone, returning the enclosures sent to him. Robinson said that he knew that Duff would pardon him 'if I deem it necessary to express my disapproval of any attempt – such as your enclosures suggests – to interfere in regard to the nomination of a successor to the late Archbishop of Dublin'. The nuncio said that the question of filling the Archdiocese 'should be left entirely to the judgement of the Holy See'.[3]

When the appointment of McQuaid took place in November 1940, Duff wrote expressing hope for his reign. McQuaid responded, saying 'Your immediate note of good wishes was one of those which I most cherish.'[4] McQuaid's first Mass as Archbishop was a private one of thanksgiving, celebrated in the Fitzwilliam Square home of Dr Lea-Wilson, and attended by Duff. The Archbishop shared Duff's Marian devotion and Blackrock College was a common bond. The Legion presented the Archbishop with a chalice in celebration of his appointment. Jack Nagle, then President of the Legion, wrote to one of those who contributed to the chalice: 'I understand that His Grace hopes to use the Chalice for his daily Mass' and asked that the information regarding the chalice be kept private since he thought that would accord with 'His Grace's wishes'.[5] The December 1940 issue of the official Legion journal, *Maria Legionis*, published for the first time in 1937, showed a photograph of McQuaid together with an appreciative report, which referred to the fact that as president of Blackrock College he had started a praesidium of the Legion of Mary in the College and that on any occasion when he was approached 'he opened wide the College doors and made its facilities available to the Legion'.

The welcoming of McQuaid by the Legion of Mary contrasted with the attitude of many diocesan priests. According to Mgr Jerome Curtin, McQuaid's appointment was not generally popular with diocesan priests. Dr Dunne, a keen admirer of Archbishop Byrne and close ally of many diocesan priests, playing Bridge on a regular basis with a number of them, was replaced as secretary to the Archbishop by Fr Christopher Mangan. In 1946 Dunne was appointed Auxiliary Bishop of Nara and the following year was sent to Haddington Road as parish priest when a vacancy arose there following the death of Monsignor Wall. According to Matt Russell, whose family resided in the parish, Wall was nicknamed 'The Bull Wall' by parishioners. Dunne died in 1998, a few months short of his ninety-seventh birthday.

In the early days of his episcopacy, McQuaid consulted Duff on a variety of matters. For example, he asked Duff for names of persons with whom it might be appropriate for him to make contact. In February 1941 Duff replied suggesting 'a couple more names – John Moynihan and Joseph P. Walshe. Both have an outlook which is purely Catholic.'[6] On 4 June 1941 McQuaid wrote to Duff regarding the work of the National Society for the Prevention of Cruelty to Children (NSPCC) and their referrals of children to Industrial Schools. He enclosed the Report of the National Society for the Prevention of Cruelty to Children (Dublin Branch) for 1939/1940, requesting Duff to have 'a look through the specimen cases in the enclosed booklet?'[7] Anyone who reads the six specimen cases encountered by the Society in Dublin that year would be struck by the poverty and suffering described. In one example a man and his wife were charged with wilful neglect of their daughters, aged six, four and three. The man was absent from home at work from six in the morning until six in the evening, but he said his only interest was his children. He was sentenced to a few hours' imprisonment, and was released on the rising of the Court. The woman, who admitted she had neglected her children for one day, was imprisoned for fourteen days. The three children were sent to Industrial Schools. Duff replied on 12 June, expressing serious disquiet. Clearly, poverty was a major factor, and 'no proper attempt is made by the Society to restore or keep a home together'.

Frank Duff was one of the few contemporaneous voices critical of Industrial Schools, as pointed out by Dr Eoin O'Sullivan of Trinity College in his evidence to the Commission on Child Abuse.[8] Duff also queried the role of the NSPCC in the too-easy committal of children to the Schools, a feature questioned again in a recent book by writer and journalist Bruce Arnold.[9] In his letter to the Archbishop, he expressed his reservations about the manner in which children were being 'shovelled' into Industrial Schools on the recommendation of an Inspector of the NSPCC:

I profoundly distrust every word and action of one of the Society's Inspectors, Mrs. Clarke. I go further and I say that I regard her as a danger. She is quite capable (by which I mean she has already done it) of distorting facts to suit any point of view she is trying to make. She exercised an ascendancy over ex-Justice Little, and between them they simply shovelled children into Industrial Schools.[10]

The Report of the Commission of Inquiry into Child Abuse, 2009 (Ryan Report) refers to the interaction between Clarke and Little.[11] Mrs. Hannah Clarke had been an Inspector for the NSPCC for many years when in 1927 she was accused of theft in the course of an inspection, which she carried out in the home of a children's wet nurse. Under the heading 'Baby Farming in County Kildare', the *Evening Herald* on 16 July 1927 reported that, as a result of Clarke's inspection, Ellen Shiels was jailed for two months for neglect of two babies in her care. Michael Shiels gave evidence that Clarke had stolen a ring and a letter from a drawer. Clarke swore she saw no ring or other valuables, but admitted that she had found a letter.

It was not long before the initial good relationship between Duff and McQuaid became strained. In May 1941 a letter drafted in McQuaid's hand, signed by Christopher Mangan, newly appointed secretary, to Jack Nagle, President of the Legion of Mary, expressed the decision of the Archbishop 'that no priest is to be allowed to attend regularly the meetings of the Praesidia of the Legion of Mary in the Diocese of Dublin, unless he enjoys the Faculties [permission] of this Diocese'.[12] As Nagle was sick, Duff replied, 'Your Grace's direction will be acted upon.'[13] The honeymoon period came to an end following the November 1941 meeting of the Concilium, which McQuaid addressed. The address, subsequently printed in the *Standard*, referred to 'indiscretions and mistakes' by the Legion without specifying or giving any examples. Duff defended the Legion against this comment. He wrote to the Archbishop saying that he was very sorry to see the reference to 'indiscretions and mistakes' of legionaries, since it was a charge which was being 'kept steadily in motion against the Legion, and which has done injury'.[14]

In his reply to Duff, McQuaid claimed that he had no knowledge of the particular rumours cited; rather that he had in mind the 'mistakes' of some of the greatest saints, giving a different gloss to the passage in his address to the Concilium, which had referred to 'indiscretions and mistakes' by legionaries:

It is a matter of deep regret to me that my first official contact with the Legion of Mary should have resulted in a letter which is, at least, a protest, if not a challenge to explain my words. I wish to believe it is not meant in either sense.

I think that my entire attitude, more especially my actions, should have prevented such a letter from being sent to me, immediately after my attending your Concilium.

I consent, in this instance, to explain. I made a passing reference to 'mistakes and excesses'.

I mentioned your mistakes as a Legion, because I know that no human institution can avoid mistakes. One sentence of my address – which I omitted – gives my thought: "He knows little of the authentic lives of the greatest Saints of God, who is ignorant of their mistakes' … . Your regret that I should have been to some extent impressed by talk, to which you had not had a chance of replying, gives me to feel that you doubt my sense of justice.

I feel it, then, necessary to say that it is my hope and my resolution never willingly to fail in justice, as an Archbishop, towards your organisation or any other group of the Faithful in this Diocese.[15]

Despite the fact that Duff replied, expressing his distress at McQuaid's letter, and that McQuaid in turn accepted 'very willingly your explanation', a jarring note had been struck in the relationship. Both men had been stung: Duff by what he had taken for a rebuke at a time when he had hoped for affirmation; McQuaid by what he had taken for a challenge to his sense of justice.

McQuaid took two decisions in the early 1940s which in the first instance curtailed the work of the Legion and in the second instance curtailed knowledge of the work. These concerned the Mercier and Pillar of Fire Societies[16] and the censoring of a series of articles in the Legion journal, *Maria Legionis*, dealing with Legion work in the prostitution area of Dublin. Notwithstanding these decisions, and the resulting tensions, Duff and the Legion continued to co-operate with McQuaid in carrying out a range of works McQuaid had asked them to undertake. These included work for mothers and children and work for emigrants. In 1939, the year before he became Archbishop, McQuaid had written to Archbishop Byrne expressing concern about the lack of a Catholic presence in maternity and child welfare. He warned Byrne that the Civics Institute and other 'non-sectarian' organizations in Dublin were involved in child guidance, home visiting, playgrounds and nurseries. The Civics Institute was a philanthropic body concerned with the development of citizenship. Earner-Byrne maintains that McQuaid's correspondence with Byrne indicates that his motives for establishing services for mothers and children derived in part from a fear that the field of care was being left open to non-Roman Catholic agencies. 'McQuaid believed that Catholics should administer charity to Catholics, and Protestants to Protestants; he was convinced that the shared administration of care would lead to confusion of principle.'[17] McQuaid held similar views in relation to health services, as demonstrated by Margaret Ó hÓgartaigh in her account of the work of Dr Kathleen Lynn, the daughter of a Rector of the Church of Ireland, and the establishment by Lynn of St Ultan's Hospital for Sick Children in Dublin.[18]

McQuaid recommended the establishment of a Catholic committee which 'could make effective the directions decided on for various branches of social activity, and thus maintain a loyal co-ordination with the Archbishop.'[19] On

97 Phibsborough Road. House where Frank Duff was born 7 November 1889. Anne Brady drawing.

Frank Duff as best man at his uncle's wedding 1917. In the picture are the groom and bride Francis Duff and Mary Reynolds, Fr James Reynolds, Duff and Kathleen Reynolds.

A Legion day out 1932, Fr Creedon, spiritual director of Concilium, centre back.

Duff with Carmel Duff mid 1950s.

Blackrock College Centenary Garden Party 1960. Left to right: Dr Charles Heerey, CSSp, Mgr Alfred O'Rahilly, Cardinal D'Alton, President Éamon de Valera, Dr John Charles McQuaid and Duff – all Blackrock College men.

Duff with W. T. Cosgrave, Mary Cosgrave and Frank Flanagan, 1965 (4 months before Cosgrave's death).

Duff with Paul VI at Vatican II 1965.

Fr Herman Nolan and friend at Horn Head 1968. Picture taken by Duff.

Duff on bicycle scaling mountain peaks. Drawing by Mary McAndrew.

Duff with Susan and the late Phyllis McGuinness, 1977.

Jack Nagle, Bishop Moynagh and Duff with Sisters of the Medical Missionaries of Mary.

De Montfort House, Morning Star Avenue where Duff died 7 November 1980. Anne Brady drawing.

becoming Archbishop, he established such a committee – the Catholic Social Service Conference (CSSC). In the preamble to the constitution of the CSSC, drafted in 1942, he set out his reasons for Catholic charity for Catholic people, saying that it would be 'utterly wrong to acquiesce in, recommend or accept economic or social teachings that are not in harmony with our religious principles'. Hence he said that Catholics could 'best fulfil the work we have set out to do by pursuing the age-old policy of the Church of developing our own machinery of Social Service'.[20] The CSSC encompassed a number of diocesan charities and programmes and sought both to co-operate with the state in the provision of services and also, by encouraging voluntarism among Catholics, to avoid undue dependence upon or interference by the state. Such an approach was in accordance with the Social Encyclicals of the Church, in particular *Rerum Novarum* and *Quadragesimo Anno*. The CSSC carries on to the present day as Crosscare.

In 1942 McQuaid established the Catholic Social Welfare Bureau (CSWB)[21] to tackle a range of other problems, including the care of emigrants. Duff was a member of the founding board of the Bureau but submitted his resignation in March 1943 because he found it difficult to fulfil the task of board member to his satisfaction in view of his heavy workload. In 1942 the Emigrants' Section of the CSWB was established. This was followed by the Playground Section in 1943, the Primary Schools' Welfare Section in 1944 and the Family Welfare Section in 1945. McQuaid entrusted the operation of the CSWB to the Legion of Mary.[22] Henry Grey, a legionary who was employed on the afforestation programme in the Land Commission, had particular responsibility for the CSWB and frequently travelled on the boats to Britain as part of emigrant care work.

One of the works undertaken by the Civics Institute was the provision of children's playgrounds. During the 1920s and 1930s, in response to the fact that large numbers of Dublin children played unsupervised on city streets, the Civics Institute established ten playgrounds where children between the ages of four and fourteen could play after school and during holidays under the guidance and supervision of play leaders. McQuaid took steps to have playgrounds for Catholic children in the care of Catholics and he summoned the co-operation of Duff and the Legion of Mary. Arrangements were made for the Legion to take over the running of a number of playgrounds at a meeting between representatives of Dublin Corporation and the Legion in March 1943.[23]

Another work carried out by legionaries with McQuaid's approval was the aftercare of girls placed in employment through the Employment Exchange in Beresford Place in Dublin. In a letter to Fr James Robinson, McQuaid told him that it would be helpful for legionaries engaged in that work to be 'trained in a course of properly Catholic lectures'.[24] In his reply, Robinson told the Archbishop that a little more than a year earlier legionaries had arranged a course of lectures by Dr Vaughan on the youth problem at the Dominican Convent, Eccles Street, and that the response was 'quite satisfactory', with an attendance of 350–400 legionaries.[25] At the time the vast majority of young people left school without second-level education to enter dead-end jobs or to face unemployment.

At the same time as the Legion and the Archbishop were collaborating in regard to city playgrounds and other matters, Duff and McQuaid were at loggerheads over the ecumenical outreach of the Legion. In the spring of 1943 Duff and McQuaid clashed over censorship. The clash occurred when the Diocesan censor decided to censor for a second time Duff's booklet *The De Montfort Way*, which had been passed at an earlier date under Archbishop Byrne. He also refused permission for the publication of the final parts of a series on Bentley Place, a pseudonym for the Monto, in *Maria Legionis*. When Duff received the news, which was relayed to him through intermediaries, he wrote to McQuaid saying 'I implore Your Grace not to let Dr Kelly [the acting censor] drive a wedge between us.' Duff pointed out that *The De Montfort Way* had been passed by the previous archbishop, but that Kelly was now demanding changes, and that when Duff had an interview with Kelly he was received 'in a most violent manner'. The series of articles in *Maria Legionis* that had been running since 1937 – for six years – were drawing to a close. Dr Dempsey, the original censor, had fallen sick and his work had passed to Kelly, who proceeded to make trouble, although Duff remarked that Kelly had been rendering good service to the Legion as a Spiritual Director.

The Archbishop's reply came as a bombshell. He said that the decision to halt publication of the Bentley Place series was his own decision. Duff was shattered. Extracts from the exchange of letters between the two men show that the Archbishop maintained that, in virtue of his office, he had to be 'gravely careful'. In his letter written on 23 March 1943, McQuaid, stung once more by what he saw as a slur on his sense of justice, expressed regret that Duff should have written 'imploring that Dr Kelly should not be allowed by me to drive a wedge between us'. McQuaid denied such a possibility, asserting that Kelly had never attempted any such action. McQuaid continued, 'it might be fairly left to me as Archbishop to maintain such balance of justice as to prevent the effect you fear being achieved'.[26] Duff replied the same day, admitting that he had made erroneous assumptions because he felt 'unable to believe that such an action, fraught with disastrous consequences for myself personally, would proceed from Your Grace personally'. He said that he had not been given any indication in advance on the subject 'to soften the impact of the blow; which was made to come [to] me in the crudest possible way, through no less than three intermediaries'.[27]

The following day, 24 March, Fr Mangan replied on behalf of McQuaid, expressing regret that Duff had been informed of the censor's decision in what Duff termed 'the crudest possible' manner, implying that Duff may be under 'strain' partly as a result of works entrusted to him and the Legion by the Archbishop and which they have 'generously accepted'.[28] On 25 March, Duff makes a final plea: 'I have never yet received a personal favour from this diocese. I now ask one. It is that Your Grace would in all the peculiar circumstances of the case permit the 'Bentley Place' series to proceed to its conclusion. This would entail the appearance of only a few more installments'.[29] On the same day, Mangan wrote once more on behalf of the Archbishop, expressing 'his regret that he does not find it possible to reconsider his decision in regard to the series in question'.[30]

Two months later, in May 1943, Fr Toher wrote to the Archbishop about Duff. The exchange of letters between Toher and the Archbishop is illuminating because it contains contemporaneous judgements by both men on Duff. At the time, the Archbishop had transferred Toher from Dublin City to the remote parish of Barndarrig near Arklow in County Wicklow, rendering him in those wartime years well nigh inaccessible to Duff. Fr Creedon, another close confidant of Duff, had been moved out to Dalkey as a curate, also at some distance from the nerve centre of Duff's operations on the north side of Dublin City. Toher pointed out that it was a great disadvantage to Duff that he had been cut off from easy access to both himself and to Creedon. Duff had to a degree become isolated by the relocation of two staunch priest friends who had been accustomed to meet and pray with him and discuss all Legion matters. Toher wrote:

> A gigantic character such as his needs some such intimate body to turn to, for various reasons, but if for no other, as a safety-valve … . I have been dealing with Mr. Duff for about 23 years, and every time I part from him I feel as regards him what the Second Nocturn says of St Catherine of Siena? 'Nemo ad eam accessit qui non melior abierit'.[31] Frank Sheed (of Sheed and Ward) once described him (I believe with perfect truth) as 'the greatest living Catholic layman'. In my opinion he is also the greatest living practical Mariologist, clerical or lay. His faults are the faults of his greatness. He is, above all, the nearest thing to the ideal of sincerity, integrity and moral courage, combined with a deeply true sense of moral values.[32]

McQuaid's reply to Toher begins with an acknowledgement that Toher is well placed to assess Duff:

> Mr. Duff is, I am sure, all that you say, for you have known him a long time and are a shrewd judge.

> My opinion is not based on so long an experience, but I give it as justly as I can and for the purpose that you may assist me, in the measure possible to you.
>
> Mr. Duff is very intelligent; in fact, unusually so. He has been a Civil Servant of much distinction, entrusted with work of special confidence. He has been a very deep and wide student of Mariology. No man would dream of contesting his genuine love of Our Lady, his personal devotedness to the limit of utter self-sacrifice. In addition, his organising ability has seen how to array great forces of workers in the cause of the Church's apostolate, on a basis of system, efficiency and discipline, and with true emphasis on personal sanctification.[33]

But the letter, while representing a tribute to Duff, also claims that 'Mr. Duff lacks a sense of Ecclesiastical authority' partly 'due to lack of Theological training'; also that he lacks 'due respect for intellectual training in Catholic workers'. McQuaid asks Toher to try to effect in Duff a 'genuine humility in regard both to achievement and aspiration in Legion activities'. McQuaid accepts that Duff is prepared to yield to authority: 'When it is brought home to Mr. Duff that he must yield, he certainly gives in at once.'

Toher's twelve-page reply to McQuaid deals with the issue of humility by first citing several extracts from the *Handbook*, which emphasize the paramount importance to the legionary of humility. Toher goes on to say that Duff's three outstanding features are '1. A limitless zeal for the Kingdom of God; 2. A heroic constancy of soul and 3. An intrepid courage – *neminem timet sed Deum solum*.'[34] Such qualities 'exercised to a fault' can produce respectively: '1. A certain impatience to brook opposition, as being something impeding God's work; 2. An unwillingness to give in, under any circumstances, as being a sign of weakness and 3. At least an apparent lack of due respect for those in high stations.' Toher said that Duff had had many unhappy ecclesiastical experiences, which he attributed mainly to Mgr Wall. He said that in the early days of the Legion, when Mgr Fitzpatrick and Mgr Hickey dealt with Duff on behalf of Archbishop Byrne, all went smoothly, but that from the day Mgr Wall came on the scene there was constant trouble. He said that as far as the Legion was concerned, Wall 'proved himself a real *advocatus diaboli*, and all the elements hostile to the Legion have ranged themselves behind him'.

Toher told the Archbishop that Duff was 'a chosen soul, with a great mission, and endowed for the purpose with very special gifts, natural and supernatural' and maintained that he could not be judged according to ordinary standards: 'he belongs to that class of people of whom Our Lord said "A prophet has honour except in his own country."' Toher said that the dominant wish of Duff and of the whole Legion was 'to spend under your guidance and encouragement, every particle of energy they possess'. He suggested a compromise to the Archbishop whereby he send for Duff and give him permission for the publication of just one further article. There is no record of a reply from the

Archbishop to Toher. Permission to publish any further article in the Bentley Place series was refused.

Duff's experience of ecclesiastical censorship gave him an insight into the literary censorship then at its height and a burning issue for Irish writers. León Ó Broin told how he and Frank Duff, together with Peadar O'Donnell and Seán Ó Faoláin, met one night at dinner to discuss the rigours of censorship. In a memo later written by Ó Faoláin he said that the origin of the 'Common Ground'

> ... was a meeting at Leon Ó Broin's house between Frank Duff, Frank McManus, Roibeard O'Farachain, and myself, on the invitation of Leon Ó Broin. I found F. D. interested and sympathetic towards the position of writers like myself and Frank O'Connor in relation to the censorship.[35]

Ó Broin maintained that in other countries a *modus vivendi* had been worked out between literature and the Church, but not in Ireland. There, he said, 'in an abnormal society, literature was outlawed, and writers were developing a psychosis of bitter frustration which was damaging to Irish life as a whole, and most damaging to the influence of the Church itself'.[36]

Meetings of Common Ground were held from early 1943 in a number of hotels – the Gresham, the Hibernian and Jurys – until mid-1944, when the meetings found a home at Newman House, 86 St Stephen's Green. Speakers in 1943 included Maurice Walsh, Peter O'Curry, Roibeard O'Farachain, D. J. Giltinan and Francis McManus. The talk in April 1944 on 'The Function and Scope of Criticism', which was given by Prof J. J. Hogan of University College Dublin, attracted a dose of sarcasm from Myles na gCopaleen, who had received an invitation, saying that he could 'not recall in recent months a more virulent eruption of paddyism'.[37] By autumn 1944 it was decided to hold a formal inaugural meeting, at which Seán Ó Faoláin spoke on the topic 'Literature – its Loyalties?' and Roibeard O'Farachain presided. The explanatory note on the invitation was signed by ten writers: Seán Ó Faoláin, Francis McManus, Frank O'Connor, Peadar O'Donnell, Richard Hayes, Lennox Robinson, León Ó Broin, Brinsley MacNamara, Peter O'Curry and Austin Clarke. The invitation said:

> The Club has been initiated by the undersigned with the idea of bringing into artistic life in Ireland more candour, more liberality of thought, and more responsibility, and above all, to break down those frustrating suspicions and antagonisms which too often surround the work of artists in this country. There will be no formalities, no Minutes, no Press Reports and no Subscriptions. In fact there will be only one Rule – Courtesy.[38]

Common Ground continued until the spring of 1945 when it is recorded that a talk was given by Donat O'Donnell (Conor Cruise O'Brien). Unfortunately the group appears to have foundered on a matter of courtesy as Ó Faoláin made charges against Frank Duff and his associates who, he claimed, were in effect 'capitalist cash-boys' propping up a rotten capitalist system with their patchwork charity for unmarried mothers and down and outs. He claimed, 'Among business-men Religion pays. It pays firstly because to be thought in any way opposed to it does not pay, and secondly, because on social matters, the Church in Ireland is very backward. That suits big business.' In a letter to León Ó Broin, Ó Faoláin referred to 'We few chaps from the so-called LEFT,' and continued:

> The whole point is that the Church is a mystical body which takes human shape. We never complained about the mystical body, or the faith. It is the human Church that we think has gone rotten. No amount of purely apostolic work will hide that basic sham.[39]

The emphasis McQuaid placed on intellectual training seems to have been at the root of his understanding of the skills required for apostolic work. He said that Duff had not 'set sufficient store' in the Legion on intellectual training of workers and that if he intended to make contact with non-Roman Catholics and answer their difficulties – especially in public – 'then he must use for the purpose persons truly qualified by theological knowledge'.[40] In the context of the times when the vast majority of the Irish people left school with, at most, a Primary Certificate, the Catholic clergy had a higher-than-average level of formal education. But Duff, who valued knowledge immensely and who created a mechanism for the deepening of religious knowledge via the Patricians,[41] had been 'soul-apprenticed' to Joseph Gabbett and had seen what people like Gabbett, 'weak on learning', could achieve.

Notes to Chapter 14

1. Lea-Wilson, neé Ryan, was the wife of Percival Lea-Wilson, a District Inspector of the Royal Irish Constabulary, who was shot dead by the IRA in June 1920.
2. Duff to Robinson, 22 February 1940.
3. Robinson to Duff, 24 February 1940.
4. McQuaid to Duff, 21 November 1940.
5. Nagle to Flanagan, Christmas 1940, author's possession.
6. Duff to McQuaid, 13 February 1941. At the time, John, or Seán, Moynihan, a legionary, was Assistant Secretary in the Department of Finance; Joe Walshe was Secretary of the Department of External Affairs (Foreign Affairs).
7. McQuaid to Duff, 4 June 1941, DDA.
8. Evidence by Dr Eoin O'Sullivan to the Commission of Inquiry into Child Abuse, 21 June 2004.
9. Bruce Arnold, *The Irish Gulag*. Dublin: Gill and Macmillan, 2009.
10. Duff to McQuaid, June 1941, LOM file, DDA.
11. Ryan Report, 2009, chapter 3, p. 27.
12. Mangan to Nagle, 26 May 1941, LOM file, DDA.
13. Duff to McQuaid, 12 June 1941, LOM file, DDA.
14. Duff to McQuaid, 18 November 1941, LOM file, DDA.
15. McQuaid to Duff, 19 November 1941, LOM file, DDA.
16. See Chapter 15.
17. Earner-Byrne, *Mother and Child*, pp. 91–92.

18. Margaret Ó hÓgartaigh, *Kathleen Lynn, Irishwoman, Patriot, Doctor*, Irish Academic Press, 2006, pp. 96-105.
19. McQuaid to Byrne, 17 March 1939, quoted in Earner-Byrne, *Mother and Child*, p. 91.
20. ibid., p. 92.
21. Later subsumed into Crosscare.
22. Earner-Byrne, *Mother and Child*, p. 93.
23. Duff to McQuaid, 19 March 1943.
24. McQuaid to Robinson, 29 December 1943, LOM file, DDA.
25. Robinson to McQuaid, 2 January 1944, LOM file, DDA.
26. McQuaid to Duff, 23 March 1943, LOM file, DDA.
27. Duff to McQuaid, 23 March 1943, LOM file, DDA.
28. Mangan to Duff, 24 March 1943, LOM file, DDA.
29. Duff to Mangan, 25 March 1943, LOM file, DDA .
30. Mangan to Duff, 25 March 1943, LOM file, DDA.
31. 'No one ever encountered her without being the better for the encounter.'
32. Toher to McQuaid, 29 March 1943, LOM file, DDA.
33. McQuaid to Toher, 1 May 1943, LOM file, DDA.
34. 'Fears none but God alone.'
35. Seán Ó Faoláin, Memorandum, 'Towards a Common Ground.' Common Ground file, undated, LOMA.
36. Ó Broin, *Frank Duff*, pp. 67–68. See also O'Carroll, *A Priest in Changing Times*, p. 145.
37. Myles na gCopaleen, 'Cruiskeen Lawn,' *The Irish Times*, 26 April 1944.
38. From invitation to Inaugural Meeting, Common Ground file, LOMA.
39. Ó Faoláin to Ó Broin, undated, Common Ground file, LOMA.
40. McQuaid to Toher, 1 May 1943, LOM file, DDA.
41. See Chapter 19.

CHAPTER 15

Ecumenism

'But the insistence by either party on his own point of view would make it impossible to have a neutral ground on which both could meet and agree that Catholicism and Protestantism would once again be united in a single stream.'

DUFF TO FR MURPHY, 27 SEPTEMBER 1943

In a talk broadcast on the Athlone Radio Station on the Feast of the Assumption, 15 August 1935, just months after the Legion of Mary had received approval in the Archdiocese of Dublin, Frank Duff asked for the prayers of his Protestant fellow-countrymen for the Legion of Mary. He said that while the appeal of the Legion would apply chiefly to Catholics, 'the organisation had a claim as well to their Protestant fellow-countrymen .... If they could not become members they could follow it with their regard and their prayers.'[1] The keynote of Duff's approach to those who were not Roman Catholics was one of friendship. He gladly accepted an invitation to speak to a meeting of the Society of Friends (Quakers) in Dublin in February 1938. The topic, 'Hostels and Clinics', was based on his experience of the Legion hostels.[2]

In 1939 Duff proposed a 'League for the Reunion of Christendom'. The League would have a leaflet with a prayer for reunion and persons of different Christian faiths who undertook to say the prayer would be enrolled as members. He designed a leaflet and devised a prayer in which each phrase was linked to a passage in Scripture. In a letter in August 1943 to Mary Duffy, Legion envoy in the USA, Duff described how he had checked the quotations 'over and over again with the Douay Version and with the Protestant Revised Version'.[3] He hoped that the prayer might be used widely in Northern Ireland, but he encountered obstacles. The Bishop of Down and Connor, Daniel Mageean, wanted a more dominantly Catholic prayer. Mageean also wished to change the name of the League to 'Crusade for the Unity of Christendom', a title which embodied a different approach from that intended by Duff. In a letter to Fr Murphy, a priest at Clonard Monastery in Belfast, who was helping to promote the idea of the League, Duff wrote:

> Of course the Catholic has one notion of what reunion means, and the Protestant has another. But the insistence by either party on his own point of view would make it impossible to have a neutral ground on which both could meet and agree that Catholicism and Protestantism would once again be united in a single stream.[4]

Despite prolonged discussion, it did not prove possible to reach agreement with Bishop Mageean without altering the essence of Duff's proposal. Duff did not pursue the project in Belfast, but early in 1941 he wrote to Dr Heenan (later Cardinal), Spiritual Director of the Legion in Liverpool, presenting the case for approaching those who were not Roman Catholics. Duff said that the Roman Catholic Church in England had more or less become a chaplaincy to its own members with little outreach to those who were not members. 'As one would expect in such circumstances, this chilly policy has not been able to warm even our own people so that they tend to fall away.'[5] The use of the prayer leaflet was a means of providing contact: 'The contact is the main thing.'[6] Duff's prayer for the reunion of Christendom first received an *imprimatur* in 1942 in the Archdiocese of St Louis.[7] In 1943 it was approved by the Cardinal of Boston.[8] Other American dioceses followed and the League was also taken up in the Archdiocese of Melbourne.[9] By 1948 the *imprimatur* had been obtained in the Diocese of Cork.[10]

In 1941 the Mercier Society was inaugurated following an invitation from Dr George Otto Simms to Duff to give a lecture to his divinity students in Trinity College on the subject of the Mystical Body of Christ. Michael Ferrar, Dean of the Divinity School in Trinity, Professor W. B. Stanford, Regius Professor of Greek and later Chancellor of the University of Dublin, Dr Edward Leen, CSSp, León Ó Broin, Desmond FitzGerald, a minister in the Cosgrave government and father of the future Taoiseach, Garret FitzGerald, and Bernard Sheppard, founder of St Conleth's College, were among the participants in the Society. Mrs Godfrey, a convert to Roman Catholicism and wife of Professor La Touche Godfrey, a Fellow of Trinity, also took part. The Mercier Society was formed for mutual understanding between Protestants and Catholics and operated on the basis of the presentation of talks in alternate months by Roman Catholics and members of other Christian denominations. The Society was named after Désiré-Joseph Cardinal Mercier, who in the years 1921–27 held conversations with Anglican theologians, notably the future Lord Halifax. These 'Malines Conversations' foreshadowed later dialogue with Anglicans and secured Mercier's place as the pioneer of ecumenism. The Mercier Society had a Catholic Committee and a Joint Committee of Catholics and Protestants. The Society met for a time in the Merrion Square rooms of the lawyer Frank Sweeney before moving to Newman House on St Stephen's Green to cater for the large numbers attending. Meetings were held monthly from 1941 until the suspension of the Society in 1944 following intervention by the Archbishop of Dublin. The attendance, which grew to over one hundred, attracted among the participants Christopher Hollis, a convert to Catholicism, later a Conservative MP and author of several books, Canon W. C. G. Proctor and John Betjeman, then press attaché at the office of the British representative in Dublin. One of the meetings was addressed by Dr W. R. Matthews, Dean of St Paul's.[11] In a meticulously balanced account of the Mercier in his *Memoirs*, Professor Stanford says that 'one member on the Protestant side was constantly aggressive. Eventually when Dr. Edward Kissane, President of Maynooth, read a paper on the inerrancy of the Bible, this person criticised it with little respect or restraint.'[12] This news no doubt travelled back to Archbishop McQuaid, fuelling his fears about the Mercier Society.

At a time of marked anti-Semitism, Duff wished to reach out to Jews and listen to them as well as presenting Catholic ideas, and so he started the Pillar of Fire Society in October 1942. In the same year, a confrère of McQuaid's, Fr Denis Fahey, CSSp, founded an organization called Maria Duce (With Mary as our Leader). The adherents of Maria Duce believed that a Judeo-Masonic conspiracy was impeding the spread of the Kingdom of Christ in the world and they sought to base Irish law on Catholic teaching. Sister Mary Christine Athans, a member of the Congregation of the Blessed Virgin and a writer on religious anti-Semitism in the United States, interviewed Duff in 1979 on the subject of the Maria Duce movement. Duff told her that, from the start, he believed Fahey was 'writing and teaching views that were dangerous'.[13] Legionaries were urged to aim at dialogue with the Jews, never to attack them – an approach that brought the Legion into conflict with adherents of Maria Duce. Duff said that some of Fahey's associates

> … tried to capitalise on the similarity of their title with that of the Legion of Mary. Indeed, at one point, two branches of the Legion became 'infiltrated' with *Maria Duce* adherents. It was learned that Legionaries from these groups who were making home visitations were attacking the Jews, and that the 'book barrows' set up by the Legion operated by these two groups placed 'Maria Duce' signs above them, and were giving out anti-Jewish literature.[14]

In his capacity as President of the Legion of Mary, Duff called in the presidents of those two branches and asked them to desist from what they were doing. Duff said, 'They were very fine fellows, you know; of course, that was the trouble. They were trained to believe that all evil was proceeding from the Jews.'[15] They did not desist from their activities, so they were asked to leave the Legion. Sister Athans asked Duff if he had talked to Fahey about the problem. He answered, 'No, I never did … . You could not reason with him.' McQuaid was close to Fahey, but by 1954 McQuaid said that the name of Mary should not be associated with the work of Maria Duce. Fahey died that year and the group continued in existence for a further decade under the changed name Firinne (Truth).

In the early 1940s, a Legion of Mary praesidium entitled 'Joy of Israel' was formed for the purpose of contacting members of the Jewish community. Fr Michael O'Carroll, Spiritual Director to the praesidium, described it as 'the seedbed of the Pillar of Fire Society'.[16] Members of the praesidium included John Burgess, proprietor of Lafayette Photographers, and John Moynihan, then Assistant Secretary (Establishment Officer) in the Department of Finance. In a paper by Moynihan on 'The Legion and the Jews', he referred to some dozen praesidia in nine countries which were then concerned with visiting Jews.[17] It was hoped by the Catholics that some Jews might consider becoming Christians. In the event, some did, while two Christians espoused Judaism. The response of the Jewish community to the idea of joint meetings where Jews and Christians could listen to each other in a friendly atmosphere was enthusiastic. This is clearly expressed in a letter from Laurence Elyan, civil servant and actor, to León Ó Broin regarding the proposed meetings:

> I cannot tell you how delighted I was to get your letter .... I feel sure, too, that it would not be difficult to arrange some sort of liaison between the types of Catholics and Jews you speak of. My own reaction is in perfect accord with the whole of your letter, and I am convinced that we would be doing God's work in promoting a better understanding between our respective co-religionists.[18]

O'Carroll noted that Elyan, in the course of a visit to Blackrock College, had expressed the hope that the Pillar of Fire idea might spread to other areas of the world where the Legion existed.[19]

A delegation from the governing body of the Jews in Ireland attended the inaugural meeting of the Society held at 18 Westland Row, Dublin, in October 1942. At that meeting León Ó Broin spoke on 'The Mind of the Catholic'. In November, a distinguished Dublin Jew and medical doctor, Dr Leonard Abrahamson, gave the talk on 'The Mind of the Jew'. Other speakers on the Jewish side were Laurence Elyan, Dr Bethel Solomons, a gynaecologist, and Mr Newman, a solicitor. Dr Solomons' brother Edwin, a stockbroker, who was also present, had attended the consecration of Archbishop McQuaid. The Catholic speakers were Ó Broin, P. J. Little, Minister for Posts and Telegraphs and later first Chairman of the Arts Council, Dr Thomas Bouchier-Hayes, Frank Duff and Dr Michael O'Carroll, CSSp. Another participant was Abbey actor Gabriel Fallon, a friend of Laurence Elyan.

Dr Abrahamson talked about how anti-Semitism had affected him when he was a growing boy and how he had studied it as an adult. He was educated in Newry by the Christian Brothers and paid special tribute to Brother Dempsey. The Jews as a whole, he said, had got a bad reputation because of the money-lending activities of some individuals. In the discussion, the subject of money-lending was treated by P. J. Little, who was the sponsor of the Moneylenders' Bill then being debated in the Houses of the Oireachtas (Parliament).

According to Ó Broin, only two meetings of the Society took place prior to its suspension, following the intervention of the Archbishop. However, in the Legion files there is a printed invitation to a meeting in February 1943 at which

Senator Desmond FitzGerald was due to be the principal speaker. Twenty years later, O'Carroll recalled that FitzGerald, at one of the Pillar of Fire Meetings, quoted the famous remark of Pius XI: 'We [Catholics] are spiritually Semites.'[20] In the same article O'Carroll pointed out that his own congregation had been founded by a Jew, Francis Liberman, and described the background to the Pillar of Fire Society at a time when the Nazis were launching an assault against European Jewry.

The Pillar of Fire Society represented the first organized exchange of social and religious views between Catholics and Jews which took place in Ireland and it operated in a spirit of mutual respect and sympathy. In a letter to McQuaid following the second meeting, Ó Broin said that it was even better than the first. The Jews, he opined, feared persecution and wanted 'justice and sympathy'.[21] McQuaid, however, believed in a disciplined form of instruction for Jews, as is clear in his reply to Ó Broin. McQuaid stated that 'The chief value of the Society seems to me that it offers an occasion of exposing Catholic doctrine to the Jews.' He continued, 'The chief value of the Society, in Jewish eyes, is a chance of staving off persecution or expulsion, by making friendly contact with the dominant element in our State, the Catholics. Their purpose, however it be masked by an appearance of suavity and accommodation, is and will remain, material. I have small confidence in the enterprise.' He concluded by saying that the results achieved by the Society would be 'visible when the Jews have sat under a series of Conferences on Catholic doctrine, by recognised Catholics of competence'.[22] In a letter from Ó Broin to Mangan (the Archbishop's secretary), Ó Broin referred to his assumption, 'which apparently His Grace does not share, that the Pillar of Fire Society can only be successful by giving the Jews equal opportunity with ourselves of saying what they think as well as a fair share in running this Society'.[23]

The Mercier Society operated for about a year before McQuaid invoked Canon 1325, paragraph 3, of the Church's code of canon law, the text of which states: 'Catholics should avoid having any debates or encounters (*disputationes vel collationes*), especially in public, with non-Catholics without the permission of the Holy See or, if the situation be urgent, of the local Ordinary.' McQuaid's worries sprang from a fear that questions raised about Catholicism by Protestants might not be fully answered by the Catholic members. A memo written by Professor M. O'Connell, Professor of Dogma in Clonliffe and one of those appointed by McQuaid to attend the Mercier and to report back, gives some insight into McQuaid's mind. The memo is of a conversation on 28 September 1942 between O'Connell and Edmund Leen, another priest whom McQuaid had appointed to the Mercier. O'Connell identified the inclusion of a Protestant (or Protestants) on the Joint Committee as a cause of anxiety. O'Connell told Leen that the controversial character of the discussions seemed to the Archbishop to conflict with the provisions of the code of canon law.[24] According to O'Connell, McQuaid was strongly opposed to any more lectures by Protestants. Leen agreed with McQuaid that all controversy should be excluded and that papers should be read by Catholics 'for the sole benefit of non-Catholics of goodwill who seek enlightenment and honestly desire the solution of their difficulties'. He considered that the Society should concern itself solely with those non-Catholics 'who come for instruction without any controversial intent'.[25]

At a meeting of the Mercier Society Committee held on 2 October 1942, all members of the committee except three priests, Fathers Leen, O'Carroll and O'Connell, were unanimous that it would mean the end of the Society if Protestant speakers were excluded. The Dominican priest Fr John Heuston believed that Canon 1325 was not relevant. Described as 'a theologian long associated with the Roman Angelicum',[26] Heuston was a regular attender at the Mercier. Named Michael from birth, he was a younger brother of Seán Heuston, who had been executed for his part in the 1916 Rising. Fr Heuston had taken his brother's name, John (Seán), when he joined the Dominican Order.[27] Heuston proposed that Canon 1325 was irrelevant, saying that he had looked up 'Vermeersch and Wernz-Vidal' (experts in canon law) and that the Mercier meetings were not public in the canonical sense. A similar view was expressed in a letter from Duff to McQuaid in which he wrote 'I read a commentary in Blat, OP, which seems to suggest that there is obligation to get permission of the Holy See only in case of *public* disputations, etc.'

On 5 October 1942, a full report on the Mercier Society, prepared at the request of the Archbishop, was forwarded to him by Duff. One month later, on 6 November, the Archbishop acknowledged receipt of the report and went on to say that he could not see his way 'to sanction the development of the Society, on my own authority', claiming that the matter lay beyond his competence. He said that in accordance with the terms of Canon 1325 of the Code of Canon Law, he was pointing out that if the proceedings of the Mercier Society were to be continued on their present basis, 'you must petition the Holy See for leave to continue'. On 16 November the Archbishop wrote to Duff restricting the participation of priests in the Mercier, saying that 'No priest has my permission to speak without the previous knowledge and consent of the V. Rev. Chaplain, Dr Leen and Rev Dr O'Connell, even though that priest holds the Faculties of the Diocese.'[28] In the same letter he ordered the praesidium which had made contact with some young communists 'to avoid all encounters with [them]'. Two days later Duff replied expressing complete acquiescence with the Archbishop's wishes.[29]

On 19 November Duff's Petition to the Holy See, addressed to Cardinal Marchetti-Selvaggiani, regarding the continuance of the Mercier Society, the Pillar of Fire and the Overseas Club, where many of those who participated were not Catholics, was submitted to the Archbishop. It comprised a Memorandum of one and a half pages, accompanied by a one-page letter. The Archbishop forwarded the Petition to Rome accompanied by a lengthy memorandum of his own in which he first set forth the facts, as he understood them, regarding the Mercier, Pillar of Fire and Overseas Club, and then offered an opinion with suggestions. The Archbishop said that the Mercier was small at first but that soon about seventy Protestants, both clergy and lay folk, attended. The atmosphere was one of great courtesy and cordiality. 'This is a singular achievement on the part of the Legion of Mary, in view of the Calvinist bitterness that so frequently marks the attitude of Irish non-Catholics. …'

When the Society seemed to me to begin to come under the provision of Canon 1325 par. 3, at once, after consultation with the Vicar General, I appointed four Priests, all expert in their subjects and graduates of the Roman universities, of whom three are secular priests, two being Professors in my seminary and one is a Religious Superior of a House of Theology.[30]

The duty of these priests was to attend meetings, watch over the interests of the Faith, answer objections, set forth Catholic doctrine and report back on all the proceedings to the Archbishop. According to McQuaid, the four priests were unanimous in stating that the Society had done and was capable of continuing to do great good to a 'certain class of educated Protestants'. He said that 'Already a group of five young Protestant clergymen have asked a Dominican priest to give them privately conferences on the doctrines of the Faith'.

The Archbishop was unenthusiastic about the Pillar of Fire, despite the fact that one lecture on the faith aroused 'a quite astonishing interest among the more educated Jews of the City … on hearing that a prominent Jew was to give a conference, in turn, I at once interposed but gave due permission, in order not to damage gravely the good impression created'.[31] McQuaid ordered that, pending a decision by the Holy See, the Society could meet only on a two-monthly basis, with lectures given only by the Catholic members. Such restrictions altered the essential nature of the Society, which was suspended in 1943. Following the suspension, a number of the members kept in friendly contact, hoping, perhaps, that the Society might be regenerated at some stage. For example, in March 1945, O'Carroll and Ó Broin went along one night to Abrahamson's home where they met representatives of the Jewish community – Laurence Elyan, Victor Waddington, the art dealer, Herman Good, a lawyer, and Louis Spiro, proprietor of Imco, a dry-cleaning business. In a letter to Duff, O'Carroll described the meeting as 'a tremendous success – extremely cordial and easy … . They all spoke with extraordinary warmth and esteem of you.'[32] He also mentioned that they were fresh from discussing 'a somewhat anti-Semitic debate in U.C.D. at the L & H (Literary and Historical Society) sometime recently'. The reference to the debate in UCD is borne out in a memoir by the historian Oliver MacDonagh, who was a member of the L&H at the time. He describes some pro-German members of the L&H as follows:

> Most, though not quite all, pro-Germans were extreme republicans, some went the length of wearing leather jerkins or long black raincoats like a Nazi admiral, or swastikas in their lapels, for though they were quite in earnest, there was something schoolboyish about it all.[33]

In an interview on RTÉ television in September 2009, former President of the High Court and Attorney General Declan Costello remarked on the level of anti-Semitism in UCD when he was a student there in the 1940s.[34] Ten years later, anti-Semitism was still at large, as John Moynihan remarked in a letter to Frank Duff in which he says, 'The existence of anti-Semitism among Catholics is undoubtedly one of the big obstacles to be overcome.'[35]

The Archbishop's memorandum to Rome also outlined the work of the Overseas Club, a social club run by the Legion for African and Asian students, including Muslims, Buddhists and Hindus. Before World War II there were usually between fifty and sixty Asiatic and African students attending universities and other third-level educational institutions in Dublin. The Asian students, mostly Indians, were usually either Hindus or Muslims, while the Africans generally belonged to one of the Protestant Churches. The students spent between three and six years in Dublin before returning to their home countries, where they were frequently destined to hold influential positions as doctors, lawyers, and teachers and so on. The main idea of the Club, founded in 1940 under the aegis of the Legion, was to organize monthly meetings which would combine entertainment, talk and a general discussion.

The first meeting of the Overseas Club was held on Saturday 13 July 1940 at the Catholic University School (CUS) in Leeson Street. Ten students were present representing Nigeria, India, Burma, China and Thailand. A film on the Manila Eucharistic Congress was shown, after which Duff spoke. The young Nigerian student who was first to respond to Duff's opening address was Jaja Anucha Wachuku, later to become Federal Minister for Foreign Affairs in the Nigerian government. The following month the speaker was Professor Eoin McNeill, former Minister for Education. He spoke on 'Early Irish Saints and Monasteries'. The following month Anucha Wachuku spoke on 'The African in his Home'. Other speakers in the first couple of years included Frank Gallagher, Director of the Government Information Bureau, who spoke on Abraham Lincoln; S. Chatterji, who spoke on 'Educational Problems of India'; K. Sombuntham on 'Thailand', accompanied by a cine film; and Seán O'Sullivan on 'Irish Folklore compared with Indian and African'. Friends and supporters of the Club included Paddy Little, Minister for Posts and Telegraphs, and F. H. Boland, then Assistant Secretary in the Department of External Affairs.

A report in *Maria Legionis* in 1941 set out the purpose of the Club:

> Its primary purpose as announced at the first meeting is to enable the African and Asiatic students attending the Universities and other educational institutions in the city to acquire a sympathetic understanding of Catholicism and of the Catholic attitude towards social and moral questions. This is all important to those able young students who in due course will be returning to their own countries to play most prominent parts. There they will find large and growing communities of Catholics. If they do not view these understandingly, they will not handle them successfully.[36]

While the earliest meetings of the Club were held in the Catholic University School in Lower Leeson Street, in October 1940 the Knights of Columbanus placed a room at 7 Ely Place at its disposal and the meetings were held there every second Saturday from November of that year. From December the Club was used for recreational purposes on the other Saturdays. A billiard table was provided, table-tennis, cards and chess were also available and a library was established. The Club opened several nights a week, with the formal meeting continuing on a monthly basis. Some years later the question of providing accommodation for overseas students arose as some of the students had experienced discrimination and were not always welcomed by traditional 'landladies'.

In his memorandum, the Archbishop maintained that since the Overseas Club was more a social club than a society for the exposition of the Faith to non-Catholics, less danger existed, but nonetheless he thought that the same regulations as proposed for the Mercier Society should be enforced. The Archbishop stated that, following long inquiry and consultation with the Vicars General, it was his opinion that the 'Associations can, with certain safeguards, achieve a good that it is otherwise impossible to obtain, in the peculiar circumstances of our country; and that they may prudently be allowed to continue by way of experiment.'

McQuaid then listed conditions he thought should be required of the Mercier Society. He wished that selected priests who would guide the choice of subjects and speakers should be present at the meetings and one of whom would report back to him after every meeting. No layman or visiting priest should be allowed to speak without the consent of the priest in charge. All controversy should be strictly excluded and 'only exposition or defence of the Faith be allowed'. Entrance of Catholics to the meetings should be strictly controlled.

With regard to the Society for Jews, the Archbishop believed that 'very much less good will be done to Jews than to Irish Protestants, because of their general character, attitude to the Faith and foreign nationality'. He conceded, 'A certain good can be done to Jews of good-will and of better education. The number of educated Jews in Ireland is, on their own admission, remarkably small.' The Archbishop recommended that the same regulations as suggested for the Mercier Society should be applied to the Society for the Jews, with the added condition that Conferences by Catholics only, and not on alternate occasions by Jews, be allowed and that Jews who wished to state their opinion could do so only after the Catholic had spoken. He then proceeded to give his opinion on the Legion of Mary in general. He praised legionaries for their exemplary lives, their docility to authority and the achievement of good, which it was impossible for priests on their own to obtain. Their defect was a lack of intellectual training. McQuaid recommended as a remedy to what he judged Legion shortcomings 'a systematic course of instruction by Priest-Directors, obligatory on all Members of the Legion, during and after the period of probation and suited to the type, education and work of the Legionaries'. The Archbishop judged a positive feature of the Legion's recruitment the increasing number of boys' secondary schools which were forming praesidia with 'young men who have been trained in the excellent five-year course of Religion in the uniform Bishops' Programme'.

In November 1943 Cardinal Marchetti-Selvaggiani forwarded the judgement of the Sacred Congregation on Duff's Petition to McQuaid:

The matter is to be committed to the prudence of the Most Reverend The Archbishop of Dublin, who, by way of experiment only and for a period of five years, is empowered to grant leave to the Association of the Legion to proceed in its enterprise of propagating the light of Catholic Truth among non-Catholics, in such wise however that, the Authorities of the

1). Association of the Legion of Mary sedulously take care that lay Catholics who, together with priests, meet non-Catholics, especially in Conferences, be altogether trustworthy in respect of Faith and Catholic teaching; and

2). further, that the said Authorities, in every subject-matter and conduct of affairs, comport themselves with docile attention and fidelity to the commands of the Ordinary.

Protestants, however, who assist at these meetings, while they seek for declarations of doctrine, must not, on any occasion, dare to defend the teachings and opinions of their own sect.

In his covering letter, which accompanied Rome's response to the Petition, dated 26 January 1944, McQuaid asked Duff to submit the measures he deemed advisable 'in order that I may judge their conformity with the Decree of the Holy Office'. On 20 February, Duff forwarded a thirteen-page scheme of draft regulation for the Society. It had been drafted by Fr Heuston, in collaboration with the Catholic Committee of the Mercier. Duff said it was their belief that the scheme would 'provide for the continuance of the Society and at the same time secure that the requirements of the Holy See be fulfilled'. His letter opened with an expression of gratitude, saying that the Committee of the Mercier Society wished to convey its thanks to the Archbishop for what he had done to secure a favourable outcome to Duff's petition. McQuaid's reply on 6 April was stern:

> The Decree of the Holy Office is not an answer to your petition. Your petition is not even mentioned, it is an answer to me as Ordinary of this diocese … . The Decree allows me as Ordinary, if I consider it advisable, to tolerate for a period of five years, in this particular Diocese, the existence and work of the Mercier Society, on certain conditions of which I am the competent judge.

McQuaid thought that Duff's proposals were inadequate to meet the requirements of the Holy See. The regulations proposed by the Legion could not in practice succeed in averting the defence by non-Catholics of their doctrines and opinions, and accordingly, he could not sanction the Draft Regulations of the Mercier Society. In his response, Duff said that having put the Archbishop's letter before his collaborators in the Mercier Society, 'We all accept Your Grace's decision with docility.' This was immediately acknowledged by the Archbishop in a letter to Duff, which he signed 'Your faithful servant in Christ'. He thanked Duff, as President of the Legion of Mary and the Committee of the Mercier Society, 'for the immediate and admirable docility with which my decision has been accepted'.

Duff and McQuaid held distinct views on ecumenism. The background of the two men is important in understanding their different approaches. McQuaid was born in Cootehill, County Cavan, a Border county. He would have been conscious of the prayer in the Mass for the Ordination of Priests, which then referred to those who did not accept the full deposit of faith as 'heretics and schismatics'. Both Duff's father and mother had attended a State Model School where different Christian denominations were educated together and Duff supported an environment in which Catholics and non-Catholics could meet on 'a neutral ground' and strive for 'mutual understanding'. In contrast with the approach of McQuaid, it was the opinion of George Simms, later Church of Ireland Archbishop of Dublin and of Armagh and a leading figure in the Mercier Society, that the Society was memorable 'for its prophetic touches and wide vision' and important in that, like 'other much later ventures, it proved that sharing and rapprochement were possible before all the doctrinal differences had been sorted out'.[37]

Duff's approach to ecumenism was based, like the Legion system, on personal contact. As one person listened carefully to the other's story, that person gained the right to present his or her own story and beliefs. True ecumenism could not begin with a 'Catholic lecture' to a 'non-Catholic'. Duff's attitude to the attendance of Catholic students at Trinity College in Dublin, during the years when Catholics were forbidden to attend, illuminated both his approach to ecumenism and his belief that Catholics could not 'live in hot-houses'. Trinity College was founded in 1592 by Elizabeth I so that students might be educated 'free from papish influence'. Catholics were not accepted until 1793. In 1944, the Catholic hierarchy in Ireland again introduced a ban on Catholic students attending. They could, however, work there. During the years of the ban on the attendance of Catholics, Duff was conscious of pastoral neglect of Catholic students as well as missed ecumenical opportunity. He was an enthusiastic supporter of the establishment in the 1950s of a Legion of Mary praesidium for students from both Trinity and the National College of Art & Design then located in Kildare Street. Meetings were held in a house in Mount Street. The Trinity–College of Art praesidium had a lively Patrician Group, which met in a café in Molesworth Street, 'The Turf Fire', where the proprietor was Máire Gavan Duffy, daughter of Mr Justice George Gavan Duffy.

In June 1970, the Catholic bishops removed the ban, partly in response to the announcement in 1968 by the Minister for Education, Brian Lenihan, of a 'merger' between Trinity College and University College Dublin to take effect from autumn 1969.

Notes to Chapter 15

1. Reported in *The Irish Times*, 16 August 1935.
2. *The Irish Times*, 10 February 1938.
3. Duff to Duffy, 5 August 1943.
4. Duff to Murphy, 27 September 1940, LOM file, DDA.
5. Duff to Heenan, 12 February 1941, LOM file, DDA.
6. Duff to Peters, 25 May 1946.
7. Duff to Curry, 11 February 1942.
8. Duff to Duffy, 5 August 1943.
9. Duff to Peters, 25 May 1946.
10. Duff to Michael, 30 December 1948.
11. Cooney, *John Charles McQuaid*, pp. 178–79.
12. William Bedell Stanford, *Memoirs*. Dublin: Hinds, 2001, p. 77.
13. 'Fr Fahey and Irish Catholicism', *Ballintrillick Review*, 28, 1990, p. 14, unsigned.
14. ibid.
15. ibid.
16. O'Carroll, *A Priest in Changing Times*, p. 134.
17. J. Moynihan, 'The Legion and the Jews', file 1350, LOMA.
18. Elyan to Ó Broin, 27 September 1942, LOM file, DDA.
19. O'Carroll note, file 1350, LOMA.
20. O'Carroll, 'The Jews', *The Leader*, Christmas Number, 1963, p. 13.
21. Ó Broin to McQuaid, 4 December 1942, file 1350, LOMA.
22. McQuaid to Ó Broin, 8 December 1942, LOM file, DDA.
23. Ó Broin to Mangan, 7 January 1943, file 1350, LOMA.
24. O'Connell, memorandum, 28 September 1942, LOM file, DDA.
25. ibid.

26. Ó Broin, 'Steps Towards Unity', *Catholic Herald*, 30 January 1970.
27. According to Fr Bede McGregor, OP, Fr Michael Browne (later Cardinal), who was Master of Novices at the time, took Heuston to see his brother Seán in Kilmainham jail before his execution.
28. McQuaid to Duff, 16 November 1942, LOM file, DDA.
29. Duff to McQuaid, 18 November 1942, LOM file, DDA.
30. Memorandum by McQuaid accompanying the Petition, November 1942, LOM file, DDA.
31. ibid.
32. O'Carroll to Duff, 18 March 1945, file1350, LOMA.
33. Oliver MacDonagh, 'The New Physics (1939–1955)', in Meenan (ed.), *Centenary History of the Literary and Historical Society*, p. 230.
34. *One to One*, RTÉ television interview with Declan Costello by David McCullough, September 2009.
35. Moynihan to Duff, 11 August 1954, file 1350, LOMA.
36. 'The Overseas Club', *Maria Legionis*, 1, 1941, p. 23.
37. 'In My Time', interview broadcast by Radio Éireann, 1981, quoted in Lesley Whiteside, *George Otto Simms: A Biography*. Gerrards Cross: Colin Smythe, 1990, p. 38.

CHAPTER 16

Battle for an Imprimatur

'It really is an *emergency* ... '

DUFF TO MONSIGNOR SUENENS, 15 NOVEMBER 1952

If the relationship between Duff and McQuaid was marked by highs and lows, possibly the lowest point coincided with the long delay in obtaining the *imprimatur* for a revised edition of the *Handbook*. The first edition of the Legion *Handbook*, which had been passed by the Diocesan censor in 1937, was reprinted in 1941 just after McQuaid became Archbishop of Dublin, so that an edition of the *Handbook* had been authorized by Archbishops Byrne and McQuaid.[1] When, in 1951, Duff wished to issue a revised and extended edition to include a new section on 'Our Lady and the Holy Trinity', permission for an *imprimatur* was refused. The refusal came at a time when Duff had experienced a series of deaths in his family, including that of his mother.

Drained after the deaths of his sister Isabel and his brother John in 1949, his mother in 1950 and his sister Ailish in 1951, Duff set off with a group of companions for the West of Ireland on a cycling holiday. When he and legionaries Brendan Crowley, Tom Doyle and Jack Nagle placed their bikes on the Galway train, Duff was sixty-one and the eldest member of the group. For the succeeding week the four friends cycled through the glorious Connemara countryside, through Westport and Leenane, to Kylemore Abbey, Clifden, Maam Cross and on to Galway. They stayed in bed and breakfast accommodation, including two nights in the guest house run by the nuns at Kylemore Abbey. From that time cycling holidays became a feature of Duff's life, permitting him to unwind, recharge his batteries and return refreshed to further endeavours.

Early in 1952 Cahills, the printers of the *Handbook*, submitted the proofs for censoring. The proofs were entrusted to Fr Cornelius Lee, who quickly gave the *imprimatur* for pages 1–105 in February 1952. But Lee was concerned about some of the remaining material, suggesting 'that its emphases are somewhat forced and its piety "cerebral"'. He was 'therefore reluctant to take responsibility of giving the "nihil obstat"'.[2] In July McQuaid wrote to Dr Dempsey and asked him to censor the revised *Handbook*. At the outset Dempsey expressed anxiety to McQuaid, saying that when he had censored the original edition, he had received help from the Dominican priest Fr J. E. [Thomas] Garde, who resided at Santa Sabina in Rome. The original edition was the one on which the Legion of Mary had been built, and had been accepted by hundreds of bishops. Dempsey commented that, in view of that acceptance, any change in the *Handbook* was 'to my mind a very serious matter'.[3]

Two weeks later Dempsey wrote to McQuaid that he did 'not like the part about Mary and the Blessed Trinity, nor the alleged excerpt from Scheeben, who, I think, has not yet been understood'.[4] Two months later, a somewhat worried Dempsey wrote again to McQuaid, referring to the great development in Mariology over the past ten years, saying 'that no one could keep up with it'.[5] In a further lengthy letter to McQuaid, written on 27 September 1952, Dempsey said that he did not wish to give the *imprimatur* to the *Handbook*, but neither did he wish to face all the possible consequences of refusing it, so he suggested that Duff be asked to withdraw the text and to resubmit it. McQuaid read the draft carefully and wrote his own six-page memorandum on its contents. The points he noted included the analogy between Eve's relationship with Adam and Mary's relationship with Christ, which he regarded as 'an extremely difficult thesis'; the legionary and the Holy Trinity, a section which he regarded as 'very seriously defective in dogmatic accuracy; in fact, it is quite untenable'; and he definitely did not view it as correct 'to take the exhortation of B. Pius X to the *Catholic Clergy* and apply it to the trivial task of a Secretary [in the Legion of Mary] writing minutes'.[6]

At the time McQuaid wrote his memorandum, the Legion was spreading rapidly in many parts of the world, including China, and this was being impeded by the absence of the revised *Handbook*. For example, the German *Handbook* was out of print, and a new translation was required for the revised edition.[7] As the delay dragged on in Dublin, concern was expressed in Rome where, following an inquiry from Mgr Montini, the future Pope Paul VI, to the Papal Nuncio in Ireland, Dr O'Hara, the nuncio raised the delay with McQuaid. In his reply, McQuaid said that a new section had been added to the *Handbook* 'in which certain modes of expression do not please me'. He told the nuncio that his own views were conservative, but that he wished to obtain the best opinion possible from those who were qualified in that aspect of theology.[8] When McQuaid received Dempsey's report a short time later, he wrote once more to the nuncio, telling him that Dempsey's report bore out his own beliefs:

> He bears out what I myself believed: the Draft, instead of keeping to ascertained Catholic doctrine in Mariology, makes an excursion into speculative Theology, and the result is not altogether happy … .
>
> I am convinced that the Editors of the Draft have, in excellent good faith, overstressed aspects of Our Lady's relation to the blessed Trinity and mediation, in a quite new section of the Handbook.

It remains to have these blemishes quietly withdrawn by the consent of the Editors. Accordingly I am requesting the President, Mr. Frank Duff, to have the Draft brought into line with the emendations that I shall set forth.[9]

On 18 October 1952 McQuaid wrote to one of his Vicars General, Mgr O'Reilly, telling him that he could not see his way to granting the *imprimatur* to the *Handbook* in its present state, and requesting him to notify the chaplain of the Concilium of his decision 'and to request that he would have the necessary corrections made before presenting the work again for my *imprimatur*'.[10] McQuaid's refusal of the *imprimatur* was relayed by O'Reilly to Toher, who passed it on to Duff. In reply, Duff pointed out to O'Reilly that it was forty weeks since the proofs had been submitted for censorship and that the Legion still did not know what requirements might be asked regarding them. He said that he did not think 'that this can be called considerate treatment of the Concilium of the Legion of Mary'.[11] Duff enclosed a brief personal note, indicating that he realized that O'Reilly was not the source of the trouble, saying 'You have always been encouraging and kind to us.' In turn O'Reilly replied, 'May God and His Blessed Mother be always your Guide and may your great work continue to prosper.'[12] That personal exchange is significant for it indicated that while O'Reilly was formally complying with the instructions of the Archbishop, he recognized Duff's 'great work'.

Almost at the same time as McQuaid refused the *Imprimatur* for the *Handbook*, Duff received a summons to Rome for the purpose of an interview with the Pope. He was in the throes of preparing for the visit when he received a letter from McQuaid seeking further clarification 'upon the basic character of your Association, in relation to the Handbook of the Legion of Mary'. In his reply Duff said that he fully appreciated the immensity of the Archbishop's burden, 'but the Legion of Mary has a great burden too, and that burden has not been made lighter by the *Handbook* delay. Unfortunately I have to say that this hold-up of 41 weeks has caused us dislocation and injury throughout the whole world.'[13]

On the same day that Duff replied to the Archbishop, McQuaid replied to an inquiry from the Papal Nuncio regarding his opinion of the Legion of Mary. The nuncio sought McQuaid's assessment in order to pass it on to the Holy See in advance of Duff's visit there. McQuaid paid singular compliments to the Legion, including a comparison with 'Communist associations'. He said that the most remarkable aspect of the Association was the solid sanctity that it habitually engendered in its members, who could be called upon to do work for which no other group is prepared: 'Time after time, I have myself requested the Legion to undertake difficult tasks of a permanent nature and in no instance has it failed.' He said that the members, both men and women, had as a matter of ordinary duty given proof of a persevering devotion that 'would put to shame many consecrated Religious and Priests'. He also remarked that the Legion in its organization and methods and approach to problems, and particularly in its genius for making contact with individuals, resembled, in his opinion, 'more closely than any other group the Communist associations'.[14] McQuaid admitted that if individual legionaries were guilty of gaucheries owing to misplaced zeal, such individual faults were attributable in many instances to a failure on the part of the priest-directors. The single example which the Archbishop gave of something objectionable, in his view, among Legion undertakings, concerned the Mercier Society, which he claimed he had successfully dissolved. He said that while the effort of the Legion in regard to the Society was inspired with 'commendable zeal', it 'failed to take into account the historical attitude of Protestants in this country, their bitterness and the opportunity unknowingly offered them by the Mercier Society of propagating their heresy in the presence of Catholics'. However, McQuaid continued that once he had been empowered by the Holy Office to put into effect the measures that he considered necessary for dealing with the situation, 'the Legion accepted every proposal that I made and the Mercier Society was dissolved without any difficulty or publicity'. He concluded with the following tribute to the Legion:

> Given the attitude of the Legion towards Ecclesiastical authority, its discipline and outlook, its willingness to undertake the most difficult as well as the most monotonous tasks, and especially, its pursuit of personal sanctification, the Legion appears to me to be, in our present circumstances, an unusually powerful instrument of the apostolate.[15]

Exactly one week after writing to O'Hara in praise of the Legion, McQuaid sent his comments on the *Handbook*, together with his judgement and his instructions, to Mgr O'Reilly:

> The doctrine in the Handbook is so gravely inaccurate in its concept and wording, in some sections, that I would ask you to direct Father Toher to have the entire document revised under guidance of Reverend Dr. Michael Dempsey.[16]

The unexpected then occurred when on 13 November Toher wrote to McQuaid enclosing the *imprimatur*, signed by Fr Cornelius Lee, which Lee had already granted to the printers, Cahills, for pages 1–105 of the *Handbook* ten months earlier on 18 February 1952. In his reply McQuaid appeared to withdraw the sanction already granted by the censor for those first 105 pages. At that stage, printing of those pages was underway and binding of the first section had begun in Louisville, USA, at 'immense labour and expense'.[17] Notwithstanding, McQuaid said that he would 'investigate the error by which any portion of the *Handbook* has been released, with signature dated 18 February 1952', and he said that nothing in the formal notification sent concerning the *Handbook* was 'to be modified by any of the circumstances set forth in your letter of 13 inst'.[18]

Despite what must have come as a huge blow, Toher replied, 'The directions laid down by Your Grace in regard to the Legion Handbook will be carefully observed.'[19]

An indication that the work regarding the *Handbook* was taking a toll on both McQuaid and Duff is implicit in the opening paragraphs of a letter from McQuaid to O'Reilly, written shortly after Duff's departure for Rome. Other sections of the letter are important in shedding light on the basis of McQuaid's objections to the *Handbook*, and on Duff's preparedness to 'accept any change or omission in doctrinal matters with complete docility'. McQuaid said that they would both (O'Reilly and McQuaid) 'have a rest' because 'Doctor Dempsey is very safe and … in charge of all Legion products' and because 'Mr. Duff is gone to Rome.' McQuaid said that he had explained to Duff that some of his comments on the *Handbook* were based on material from O'Reilly, while some were doctrinal:

> The doctrinal matters, I insisted, were my chief concern and must be changed according to the Censor's ruling. The other matters of organisation, wording of the old Handbook and even Legion devotions were not my anxiety. I was prepared in view of previous authorisation of the old Handbook by my predecessor and myself to allow wording to stand, unless a doctrinal issue were involved.[20]

McQuaid added that, in the course of conversation, Duff had stressed 'the approval of a Mgr. Canestri for the old Handbook in its Italian form'. McQuaid got the impression 'that Mgr. Canestri's opinion was more valuable than that of the Ordinary of Dublin. Mr. Duff would not put it that way, but I shall, on his return, ask for an explanation. I may be mistaken.'

Before he left for Rome, Duff wrote a long letter to Mgr Suenens. He started by thanking Suenens for agreeing that the Legion would publish his *Life* of Edel Quinn, the young Irishwoman who had been Legion of Mary envoy in East Africa. He went on to apologize for the delay in answering a query about Moral Rearmament in regard to which Duff discouraged condemnation. He referred to the difficulties over the *Handbook* and suggested that perhaps Mgr van Lierde (later Papal Sacristan), a fellow Belgian and a member of the Roman Curia, would be able to help in the 'emergency'. 'It really is an *emergency*, for the drastic revision which the Archbishop is trying to bring about would have the effect, so far as I can gather, of making radical alterations in the Legionary system.'[21]

In Rome, Mgr Montini, on hearing of the difficulties regarding the *imprimatur*, told Duff to consult the Dominican theologian Dr Michael Browne. This consultation was discussed at a meeting between Duff and McQuaid on 12 December following Duff's return from Rome and was the subject of a letter from McQuaid to Duff immediately following their meeting. In his letter McQuaid queried the implication of the referral of the *Handbook* to Browne: 'Am I to conclude that your consultation of Father Browne, at the direction of

Mgr. Montini, is tantamount to an appeal from me as the Ordinary responsible for censorship?'[22] Duff replied that the Legion did not appeal to the Holy See but that Browne had gone through the *Handbook* together with other material, which included articles Duff had published and which had earlier been passed by the censor. Browne did not find any error, but suggested 'for the sake of propitiating a conservative point of view, the toning down of some of the phrases'.[23]

There is no record of McQuaid's reply to this letter but he at once instructed Dempsey to 'proceed with the censorship in the normal way', saying that he was prepared to allow pages 1–105 to stand.[24] Dempsey's reply included an affirmation of the success of the Legion:

> Your Grace says you fail to see why recherché and risqué opinions should be put forward. I think the reason is to be found in the success of the Legion abroad: this has constituted a challenge to the people here and they are afraid of losing the initiative. I know this to be so: it is the crisis of success.[25]

By 14 March 1953, the *imprimatur* had still not been granted, and Duff wrote to Cardinal D'Alton in Armagh, providing an update on what he had earlier told the Cardinal. He did not request action from D'Alton but explained the damage to the Legion as a result of the continuing delay:

> Few more serious blows could have been delivered to the Legion than thus to deprive it completely of Handbooks over a very great portion of the world's surface. The American edition is exhausted for over a twelvemonth. All the other editions in English, with the exception of the Australian one, are likewise out of print, and a condition of chaos has been caused. The German and Spanish handbooks have likewise become exhausted, and reprinting has been held up by the waiting for the new edition. The Portuguese translation has been finished for months now and is being eagerly clamoured for, but its printing has been held up by the necessity for bringing the translation into line with the new revisions. I do not think it represents an extreme statement to say that a degree of harm has been done to the Legion by this withholding of the Imprimatur to its Handbook which Mao in China has not been able to inflict. The instrument which has been used to inflict this deadly damage upon the Legion has been the ecclesiastical Censorship. That Censorship is one of the main instruments for preserving the purity of doctrine and therefore it is a sacred thing. To abuse the Censorship has surely a sacrilegious character.[26]

Duff's opinion of McQuaid's actions or inaction had clearly reached rock bottom by this point. In a memorandum written on 10 June 1953, Dempsey set out a chronology of events regarding the *imprimatur* from November 1951 when Duff showed him the proofs of the *Handbook*. Dempsey's reaction on reading the proofs is important, because he found new material he judged to be of a speculative nature, including some items which, if he were to act as censor, he would not pass, and indeed he said that issuing a *Handbook* with novel material could amount to a 'confidence trick'. Accordingly, he decided to formulate a case against the new *Handbook*:

I was very perturbed by the new handbook. The Legion had spread thro' the world and had been adopted by hundreds of bishops on the basis of the old handbook, and to present them now with something novel and, to my mind, unacceptable, would be something in the nature of a confidence trick. I decided to formulate a case against the new Handbook.[27]

He noted that on 27 December 1952, 'On His Grace's instructions I took up negotiations with Mr. Duff on correction of Handbook draft.' These discussions led to Duff making a number of changes. In January 1953, Dempsey suffered a severe haemorrhage and was brought to the Mater hospital. The proofs were given to Fr (later Archdeacon) Cathal McCarthy. Some weeks later McCarthy was knocked down by a taxi and was also brought to the Mater hospital, where his leg was amputated. Following McCarthy's accident, Dempsey volunteered to complete the task of censor. Still in hospital, Dempsey eventually gave the *nihil obstat* to the *Handbook*, dated 25 March 1953.

The difficulty regarding the *Handbook* had partly arisen because of Dempsey's initial decision to 'formulate a case against the new Handbook', even though it was he who had granted the *imprimatur* for the first edition. The crux of the matter hinged on the fact that Dempsey and McQuaid were both more conservative in their Mariology than Duff. Once it became clear that a theologian of repute in Rome, Dr Michael Browne, saw nothing objectionable in the contents, and that most of the new material had already been passed by the censor for publication in articles in *Maria Legionis*, the way was cleared for the *imprimatur*. Duff saw the role of Browne in the resolution of the problem as central. In a letter to Browne on 1 May 1953, some weeks after the *imprimatur* was received, he set out an account of events and Browne's role:

The Censor did not send for me until the 24th December. And not until 2nd January did he see me on the second occasion … .

At long last I notified the Nunciature. Immediately there was a rapid sequel. A further list of amendments was presented to us, and to these I agreed. We were then notified on Holy Thursday that the Imprimatur would be given … .

Our gratitude to yourself is extreme. Your looking through those documents was the turning point of the whole situation … . The first copy of the Handbook which comes off the printing press I shall have pleasure in forwarding to you as a keepsake.[28]

Duff believed the *Handbook* to be a 'complete Catechism of Catholicism.'[29] He regarded the Maynooth Catechism, then in use, as deficient in that 'it does not teach that the Christian has an active duty of apostleship'. He maintained that 'The most important paragraph in the whole *Handbook* is that one which insists that the Legion without active work is not justified.'[30] The *Handbook* 'gives an adequate exposition of the doctrine of the Mystical Body which has been acclaimed to be the central dogma of Christianity, but which none of the Catechisms describe.' In regard to the position of Mary, Duff argued that the *Handbook* supplemented de Montfort's *True Devotion* by emphasizing the necessity of apostleship:

But you will observe that in the whole book he [de Montfort] does not say a single word about apostleship. The person who has really imbibed his teaching will take that for granted, but it is unsafe to do that. Because very many others will not take it for granted; they will just leave it out and suppose that it has no place. I was one of those who just took it for granted. I was carrying on an apostolate and I always understood the True Devotion as requiring such. In all the earlier editions of the Handbook this was supposed to be evident from a reading of the Treatise, but at a certain stage the contrary was made evident to me. One of the circumstances which enlightened me was my first acquaintance with Cardinal Suenens.[31]

Cardinal Suenens had pointed out to Duff that there were many thousands enrolled in devotional confraternities in Belgium who, while indulging in devotional practices, did not engage in any form of the apostolate. It would not be until after the Vatican Council (1962–65) that the idea of the apostolate of the laity would be recognized widely in the Church. Following the Council, Duff said that 'This notion [the obligation of apostleship] which used to be regarded as a Legion fad has been taken up wholesale and set forth in the eighth chapter of the *De Ecclesia* Decree.'[32]

Approval for the revised *Handbook* was the final 'battle' between Duff and the archdiocese. A feature of the 'battles' regarding the censorship of his writings, both in regard to the Bentley Place series and to the *Handbook*, was the fact that other Legion work and associated relations with the archdiocese proceeded simultaneously without reference to the contentious matters. For example, not long after the resolution of the censorship of the *Handbook*, Duff and McQuaid were engaged in friendly dialogue regarding an important work the Legion was to undertake with the support of the archdiocese among Irish emigrants in England. In April 1954 Duff acknowledged a financial contribution towards the expenses of two legionaries going to England for this purpose.[33] In July of the same year Duff invited the Archbishop to the meeting in the National Stadium to welcome home Fr Aedan McGrath, following his release from jail in China.[34]

Notes to Chapter 16

1. McQuaid to O'Reilly, 18 November 1952, LOM file, DDA.
2. Note written by Lee and sent by O'Reilly to Mangan, 29 March 1952, LOM file, DDA.
3. Dempsey to McQuaid, 4 July 1952, LOM file, DDA.
4. Dempsey to McQuaid, 18 July 1952, LOM file, DDA. Matthias Joseph Scheeben, a German theologian, was the author of several books, including the classic *Mysteries of Christianity* and *Mariology*.
5. Dempsey to McQuaid, 12 September 1952, LOM file, DDA.
6. Handwritten memorandum by McQuaid on the *Handbook*, undated, but probably late September 1952, LOM file, DDA.

7. Firtel, *A Man for Our Time*, p. 89.
8. McQuaid to O'Hara, 16 September 1952, LOM file, DDA.
9. McQuaid to O'Hara, 1 October 1952, LOM file, DDA.
10. McQuaid to O'Reilly, 18 October 1952, LOM file, DDA.
11. Duff to O'Reilly, 27 October 1952, LOM file, DDA.
12. O'Reilly to Duff, 1 November 1952, file 1316, LOMA.
13. Duff to McQuaid, 3 November 1952, LOM file, DDA.
14. McQuaid to O'Hara, 3 November 1952, LOM file, DDA.
15. ibid.
16. McQuaid to O'Reilly, 10 November 1952, LOM file, DDA.
17. Toher to McQuaid, 13 November 1952, LOM file, DDA.
18. McQuaid to Toher, 14 November 1952, LOM file, DDA.
19. Toher to McQuaid, 16 November 1952, LOM file, DDA.
20. McQuaid to O'Reilly, 18 November 1952.
21. Duff to Suenens, 15 November 1952, file 1316, LOMA.
22. McQuaid to Duff, 12 December 1952, LOM file, DDA.
23. Duff to McQuaid, 17 December 1952, LOM file, DDA.
24. McQuaid to Dempsey, 17 December 1952, LOM file, DDA.
25. Dempsey to McQuaid, 28 December 1952, LOM file, DDA.
26. Duff to D'Alton, 14 March 1953, LOMA.
27. Memorandum, by M. L. Dempsey, 10 June 1953, LOM file, DDA.
28. Duff to Browne, 1 May 1953, file 1316, LOMA.
29. Duff to Maureen, 16 November 1967.
30. Duff to O'Connor, 21 May 1954.
31. Duff to Maureen, 16 November 1967.
32. ibid.
33. Duff to McQuaid, 8 April 1954, LOM file, DDA.
34. See Chapter 17.

CHAPTER 17

Edel, Fr Aedan, Alfie

'You will be my witnesses in Jerusalem, and in all Judea and Samaria, and to the ends of the earth.'

ACTS 1:8

The ranks of women envoys in the Legion, which already included Mary Duffy, who remained in the USA and Canada from 1934 to 1946 throughout World War II; Ruby Dennison, who worked in South Africa from 1934 to 1938; and Una O'Byrne, who worked in the USA from 1936 to 1939, were augmented in 1936 by the singular Edel Quinn, who remained in Africa until her death in Nairobi in 1944 at the age of thirty-seven.[1] What is remarkable about this galaxy of fearless young women is that they travelled abroad, alone, and on the most challenging work in the context of the Catholic Church in which men were, and continue to be, the dominant figures. They did not have the security of convent life, where they might form part of a community. They reached out alone into the unknown at a time when the expectation for a young woman in Ireland was that she would marry and take care of her home.

The sending of Edel Quinn as envoy to Africa, where she completed an odyssey as striking as any in the annals of the Church, demonstrated both the remarkable potential of the Legion of Mary and the extraordinary ability of this young Irishwoman. As the liner, the *Llangibby Castle*, drew out from Gravesend, Quinn went to her cabin and wrote a letter to Duff:

> I would like you to remember always, whatever happens, that I am glad you gave me the opportunity of going. I realise it is a privilege and also that only you persisted I, personally, would never have been sent … .
>
> Have no regrets, I am not going to refer to this again. I am glad you let me go – the others will be glad later.[2]

Edel Quinn had joined the Legion through her friend Mona McCarthy, soon becoming president of a praesidium which visited women's lodging houses and cared for prostitutes. At the time she was employed by the Chagney Tile Company, where the manager, a Frenchman named Pierre Landrin, proposed marriage to her, but Edel had already decided to join a Poor Clare Convent. Then, in 1932, came the discovery that she had tuberculosis and she was admitted to Newcastle sanatorium in County Wicklow, where she remained for eighteen months.

When Quinn left hospital she rejoined the Legion. In 1934 she travelled to Lourdes as an invalid; in 1936 she returned there as a helper. In 1936 Edel, together with Muriel Wailes, set off on Legion extension work. They started in Shrewsbury in England and then moved to the Diocese of Menevia in Wales where they worked for two weeks before returning to Ireland. Meanwhile, Ruby Dennison, the envoy in South Africa, was seeking extra help. It was agreed at Concilium to send Quinn, because the South African climate would possibly be good for someone who had suffered from tuberculosis. Then Archbishop Heffernan, the Archbishop of Zanzibar and Nairobi, wrote to the Concilium seeking a Legion envoy, saying that the needs in Nairobi were great. Clearly recognizing the qualities which she possessed, Duff supported Edel's envoyship to East Africa, even though it was opposed by many in the Concilium as being too risky. Quinn spent seven years in Africa, covering vast distances and travelling as far afield as South Africa, where she spent time in hospital in Johannesburg, and Mauritius. Having established the Legion in the Nairobi region, she undertook punishing journeys to establish the Legion throughout Kenya, Uganda, Nyasaland and Tanganyika. She travelled in an old jeep with a Muslim driver, a young woman completely energized by the desire to spread the news of Christ. She died in Nairobi in 1944 and is buried there. Duff who had a deep affection for Edel, described the 'anguishing moment' when he conveyed the news of her death to her mother.[3]

Before Edel Quinn left for Africa, Archbishop Riberi, Apostolic Delegate to Africa, visited Dublin where he met Duff, whom he already knew, and Edel Quinn and expressed his pleasure that she was going to Africa as Legion envoy. A few years later Riberi visited West Africa, inspected the work of Michael Ekeng and the pioneer African legionaries and then addressed a letter to all the bishops of Africa regarding the Legion of Mary. Riberi recommended strongly that they should avail themselves of the Legion in their dioceses and expressed the hope that 'Africa becomes a country of Legionaries'.[4]

Shortly after Edel Quinn reached Africa, the Legion reached China, where it was introduced by the Columban priest Fr Joe Hogan. The first praesidium established in Hanyang included among its members a cook, two workers in the Central China Munition Factory, a fisherman, a boatman, a carpenter and an embroidery worker. The Legion Tessera was translated into Chinese by the Bishop of Nanking, a distinguished scholar.[5] Meanwhile, another Columban priest, Fr Aedan McGrath, who was working in T'sien Kiang, where he lived with a Chinese family and served his twenty-four missions on foot, asked his bishop for another priest to help him. In response, his bishop, Edward (Ned) Galvin, sent him a Legion of Mary *Handbook*. McGrath said, 'In those days we obeyed bishops! I called in six men with no particular qualifications. I did not think it would work; I intended to give the book back to the bishop when it failed. To my utter amazement, those ordinary lay men were able to do many things that I could not do. The Lord was telling me that if I wanted to get anywhere, I must use lay people.'

In 1948, as McGrath was embarking on an intensive campaign to spread the Legion in China at the request of Riberi, then Nuncio to China, ahead of the communist advance, Duff wrote a long letter to McGrath. The following extract contains the essence of how he saw the role of the priest in relation to the laity:

> The more we think over things, the more we are intrigued by the prospect of your mission … . Here is a mass experiment … the mobilising of an entire native people in the work of evangelising their inconceivably vast country. Furthermore it is an experiment based on the right lines, i.e., that of placing before the people from the first moment the authentic outlines of Christianity, which necessarily includes the waging of an apostolate.[6]

Between 1949 and 1951 McGrath's work resulted in the establishment of 1,000 praesidia in China. When the communists gained power, priests connected with the Legion, including McGrath, were imprisoned. The Bishop of Shanghai, Ignatius Kung, spent twenty-seven years, one-third of his life, in prison. During his incarceration, and following the election of Pope John Paul II, the Pope secretly (*in pectore*) named Kung a cardinal. When a frail Kung, then aged ninety, visited the Vatican in 1991, his nomination as cardinal was made public. His obituary in *The Times* of London said that Kung would 'inspire thousands to offer their lives up to God'. The obituary continued:

> In defiance of the government-sponsored China Catholic Patriotic Association, Kung invigorated the Legion of Mary. The government responded by declaring it to be an illegal society that was engaged in espionage and demanded that all members either register with the Public Security Bureau and acknowledge that the legion was counter-revolutionary, or risk imprisonment.
>
> Kung instructed his followers not to comply … with the exception of very few, the members refused to sign the registration, choosing instead to risk arrest in the name of their bishop, their God and their Church. Hundreds of members, including many students, were arrested and sentenced to hard labour.[7]

According to American historian James Myers, on 14 September 1955 Radio Beijing warned that Catholics who did not withdraw from the Legion of Mary would be 'very severely punished'.[8] McGrath was arrested on 7 September 1951 on the charge that the Legion of Mary with which he was working was 'an anti-revolutionary and secret organisation'.[9] He was sent to Lokawei prison, where he remained until 28 April 1954 when he was released and expelled from China. McGrath was refused permission ever to return to a people he had grown to love.[10]

In post-war Japan, some Australian priests established the Legion, while in Korea the last volleys of the war (1950–53) were echoing when Fr Harold (later Archbishop) Henry and his colleague of St Columban's Society, Fr Thomas Moran, founded two praesidia in a South Korean port town. The inspiration for this initiative had come from a talk on the Legion given by the wife of an American colonel stationed in Japan. One year later, Fr Edward McElroy, recently expelled from Shanghai, came to Korea to help spread the Legion. By the mid-1970s there were some 10,000 legionaries active in nearly every diocese in South Korea.[11]

In July 1953 Seamus Grace and Alfie Lambe departed for South America, where Lambe remained until his death six years later. Lambe, from Tullamore in County Offaly, had entered the Novitiate of the Christian Brothers, but had to leave because of ill-health. He had served as an indoor brother in the Morning Star Hostel when preparing for envoyship. Lambe quickly learned Spanish and some Portuguese and began his South American apostolate by setting up a network of praesidia in Ecuador, which included prisoners and lepers.[12] He died from cancer on 21 January 1959 in Buenos Aires. He had been known throughout the regions he visited as 'el cordero' or 'el corderito' (the lamb/lambkin). Comparing Alfie Lambe with Edel Quinn, Duff said, 'They were both wise, charming, lovable, without kinks – models for modern youth.'[13]

Alongside the epic stories of Quinn in Africa, McGrath in China and Lambe in South America, hundreds of remarkable Legion stories unfolded as it spread around the globe. Sometimes the Legion started as a result of a legionary from one country moving to work in another, as was the case in Sweden when a young woman from Dublin went to work in the Irish legation (diplomatic mission) in Stockholm and started the Legion there in 1949. Duff recounted how an excellent start to the Legion had been made in Stockholm, where 'The instigator is Roisín O'Doherty, one of the Secretaries [diplomatic officials] of the Irish Legation there.' He said, 'She drove like the prow of a ship through all the waves of difficulties and objections which were proposed at the outset.' The praesidium O'Doherty started consisted of ten members, of whom four were Swedes. The others were of different European nationalities, including two Irish.[14] One year earlier, on 31 July 1948, the first praesidium of the Legion was started in Poland.[15]

In the 1940s the first non-Irish Legion envoys were appointed. They included Maria Diepen from the Netherlands, who went as envoy to the Dutch West Indies, and Hilde Firtel from Vienna, who went as envoy to Germany. Firtel, a Jew, had become a Catholic while studying music in Milan. She was an official translator at the Nuremberg Trials. Later, she got a job in Liverpool, where she joined the Legion. Two young women from the Philippines,

Joacquina Lucas, a university lecturer, and Pacito Santos, a lawyer, both from Manila, went respectively as envoys to South America and to Spain. A Chinese girl, Teresa Su, went as envoy to Indonesia. When Joacquina Lucas crossed the frontier into Mexico at the start of her mission on 5 September 1946, Duff noted, 'She is our first coloured Envoy – a circumstance which should attract special graces upon her mission.'[16] Duff expected much from the envoys. In a letter to one, he wrote, 'I think that one has to be so resolute on one's mission that if the alternatives present themselves: "the mission or my life", one has to choose the mission.'[17]

As the Legion spread and strengthened, Duff experienced personal losses. His brother John died in 1949. His mother died in February 1950 at the age of eighty-seven: they had been very close. In the summer of 1950, Fr Michael Creedon, Spiritual Director of the Concilium, died. Blanaid O'Rahilly, a Dublin legionary, remembered Creedon as curate in Dalkey when she was a young girl. She said that he was never made a parish priest and that he chose to die in a County Home.[18] One year later, Duff's beloved sister Ailish died. Duff and other family members were at her bedside. Fr Toher, who was Spiritual Director of the Concilium, having succeeded Fr. Creedon, died in 1954. From 1950, when his mother died, until his own death thirty years later, Duff would live alone, taking his daily meals, for which he paid, with the indoor sisters in the Regina Coeli Hostel. For a number of years when his mother was alive, she and Frank would spend time in Christmas week in the home of her daughter Geraldine and Geraldine's husband, Vincent Monahan, in Navan. After his mother's death he spent Christmas Day in Navan, visiting his cousin Carmel and her mother on St Stephen's Day. Carmel's mother, who was about ten years older than Frank, died in 1971. Following Geraldine's death in 1975, Duff spent his last Christmas Days with Carmel.

In July 1954 a large public event was held in the National Stadium on South Circular Road in Dublin to celebrate the return home of Fr Aedan McGrath, following his release from jail in China. Duff introduced McGrath to a brimfull stadium, which included the President, Seán T. O'Kelly. The Taoiseach, John A. Costello, the Lord Mayor, Alfie Byrne, TD, and the leader of the Opposition, Éamon de Valera, were among the speakers who welcomed McGrath. According to the *Irish Times* report of the event, de Valera said that 'In his dreams of the past he had thought of Ireland's destiny in the Europe of the future being like what it was in the Europe of centuries ago, but he never imagined that Ireland would be destined to deal with the larger Asiatic communities.'[19]

One of the mechanisms Duff developed for supporting legionaries around the world was that of 'Concilium correspondents'. These correspondents are responsible for maintaining contact with the Legion Councils (Senatus/Regia)[20] all over the world and do so by writing regular letters to the councils. According to Fr Michael O'Carroll, based on his own experience of correspondence with Duff, his letters were 'optimistic, articulate, always urging a courageous spirit'.[21] He urged the same approach for the Concilium correspondents. The system of Legion correspondents had, like much in the Legion, unplanned beginnings. When envoys first went overseas, Duff wrote a monthly letter to them as a group, filling them in with home news and Legion developments in general. For example, in one letter he reported on the opening of the Regina Coeli Hostel in Glasgow, the first outside Ireland; in another he reported on the opening of a Sancta Maria Hostel in London.[22] In the early 1930s, Jack Nagle, who had tried his vocation with the Dominicans and was at something of a loose end, undertook the role of correspondent. The Nagles were known to the Duffs, as Jack Nagle's sister, Jenny, was a doctor in England and a friend of Ailish. Duff, who until then had dealt with Legion correspondence himself, gave Nagle a Legion *Handbook* and a pile of letters and asked him to take care of them. Jack Nagle got a table and chair and opened the first Concilium Office in an upstairs room in the Regina Coeli Hostel. This was in 1932, coinciding with the Eucharistic Congress, at which time Nagle's name appeared in the visitors' book which is now kept in the Concilium Offices of the Legion.[23]

Duff envisaged a vital role for the correspondents in the Legion system, later saying that

> … the fate of the Legion throughout the world depends on the Concilium Correspondents. They are the links between the Concilium and every directly related council in the world, which in turn transmit the Legionary idealism to the bodies below them … . Our reliance is upon that approximation to personal contact which the Correspondent represents.[24]

Having stressed the importance of the role of the correspondent, he outlined the tone that should be adopted in letters. It provides a clear insight into his approach:

> Never dictate. Your method must be that of patient explanation. Let your opposite number understand the reason for everything that is put down as required by the Legion system. Never merely come down on people. If they are put into a bad mood they will tend to resist, and perhaps to defend a wrong point of view. A blunt 'no' will be resented whereas if you say that 'no' in a thousand words, showing that you have taken trouble, it will be cheerfully accepted. This attitude of taking trouble pays rich dividends. Show it in every way in your letters. The more trouble you take with your letters the more they will be appreciated at the other end.[25]

Duff's advice to the correspondents encompassed both the prayerful and the practical. He stressed the 'profound importance' of practising ourselves what we are trying to teach. 'Among the lessons which we seek to impart is the chief one of prayerfulness which is the very centre of the Legion.' He said that while the proverb places cleanliness next after godliness, he would prefer to assign that 'honourable place to reliability and punctuality – without which no organisation can hope to function properly'.[26]

Testimony to Duff's skill as a correspondent is given by one former envoy with whom he corresponded. Tadhg McMahon, a Dublin schoolteacher, went to Brazil as Legion of Mary envoy in 1959 when he was aged twenty-four, remaining there for three years. During that time, Duff acted as McMahon's Concilium Correspondent, writing to him about every ten days. McMahon described Duff's letters to him as 'absolutely terrific'.[27] When in Brazil McMahon was nick-named 'Timoteo' – a variant of Timothy meaning 'God's honour' – by the locals, and so Duff began his letters 'Dear Timoteo'. The letters to Timoteo were encouraging, grateful for the work being done by him, and meticulous in dealing with any points raised by McMahon in his own letters. In this latter feature, the mark of the first-class civil servant in responding in a systematic way to the issues raised is evident. In addition there would sometimes be a suggestion regarding a possible new challenge. For example, Timoteo was not long in Brazil when Duff enquired about the position of the members of the Orthodox Church there. The letters never failed to show personal interest, whether in regard to vaccinations, or the type of clothing appropriate to the climate, or travel arrangements.

Another strand of communication developed by the Legion was based on the Legion Journal, *Maria Legionis*. León Ó Broin, who edited the journal for the first ten years of its existence, described how he came to be involved. In the mid-1930s he was president of a praesidium which, with Fr Senan Moynihan, the Capuchin, as its Spiritual Director, had begun with a number of artists, writers and actors comprising most of its ordinary members. After a while Moynihan and some of the members left to concentrate on a yearly publication, the *Capuchin Annual*, which contained substantial articles on religion, history, culture and other topics. Among those who remained in the praesidium were Peter Nolan, an Abbey Theatre player, and Gerard O'Byrne, a stained glass worker who painted the altar backdrop in the oratory in the Morning Star Hostel and did the illustration for Joseph Mary Plunkett's poem 'I See His Blood upon the Rose' in the *Handbook*. Jack Nagle, who was President of the Concilium at the time the journal was first published, commented that a long-felt want was satisfied with the appearance of *Maria Legionis*.[28] In the first issue of the journal, Nagle wrote an article entitled 'The Legion Depends on the Spirit Which Animates it'. He said 'It was spirit, and not material resources of any kind, which has made the Legion a vital force in Catholic Action … . But history teaches us how infinitely delicate is the spirit of a religious society; how hard it is to find and how easy to lose.'[29]

Among the early contributors to the journal was Professor Thomas Bodkin, who had moved from Dublin to become Director of the Barber Institute of Fine Arts at the University of Birmingham. In issue after issue, Bodkin selected a picture or sculpture of Mary and wrote an accompanying commentary. For example, in the Christmas issue 1939, Bodkin's selection was 'The Crowning of Our Lady', a rare fourteenth-century work by English alabaster carvers.

Duff was also a regular contributor to *Maria Legionis*, but like all works in the Legion of Mary he never allowed it to become dependent on him. In a letter to a legionary in 1949, he expressed his belief that 'the Legion is no creature of accident or coincidence or of human planning'.[30] Responding to a friend's enquiry on the possible fate of the Legion of Mary after his death, he remarked that it had been placed in Mary's hands at its beginning and it would not be removed from her hands when he died.

Notes to Chapter 17

1. Biographers of Edel Quinn include Cardinal Suenens and Fr Desmond Forristal.
2. Edel Quinn's first letter as an envoy, reproduced in Moss (ed.), *Frank Duff*, p. 62.
3. Moss, p. 60.
4. H. E. Mgr Antonio Riberi to the Ordinaries of Africa, 25 June 1937, reprinted *Maria Legionis* 3/2010, pp. 22–23; Hallack, *The Legion of Mary*, p. 145.
5. Hallack, p. 147.
6. Duff to McGrath, 13 March 1948.
7. *The Times*, 13 March 2000.
8. James Myers, *Enemies without Guns: The Catholic Church in China.* New York: Paragon, 1991, p. 140.
9. *The Irish Times*, 30 June 1954.
10. *Aedan McGrath: From Navan to China – the story of a 'Chinese Irishman'*, compiled and edited by Fr Eamonn McCarthy and Michael Walsh. Dublin, 2008.
11. Patrick O'Connor, 'Frank Duff: Missionary', Praedicanda, reprinted from *Ensign*, undated.
12. Ó Broin, *Frank Duff*, p. 102.
13. ibid., p. 103.
14. Duff to Ingoldsby, 29 October 1949. Roisín O'Doherty, a sister of Rev Professor Feichin O'Doherty, later married Bob McDonagh, who became Secretary of the Department of External Affairs and Ambassador to Italy and the United Nations.
15. Duff to Peters, 7 September 1948, LOMA.
16. Duff to O'Brien, 5 September 1946, LOMA.
17. Firtel, *A Man for Our Time*, p. 75.
18. Author's conversation with Blanaid O'Rahilly, 2 February 2008. The County Homes were former Poorhouses.
19. *The Irish Times*, 26 July 1954. The 'centuries ago' was a reference to the sixth, seventh and eighth centuries when monks from Ireland spread the Christian faith across Europe.
20. See Glossary.
21. O'Carroll, *A Priest in Changing Times*, p. 138.
22. Duff to 'My Dear Envoys', 20 February 1936 and 17 November 1937, LOMA.
23. Information supplied to author by Enda Dunleavy, 20 December 2007.
24. Duff, *The Concilium Correspondents*, Address delivered to Correspondents on 19 January 1975, Concilium of the Legion of Mary, undated, p. 1.
25. ibid., p. 2.
26. ibid., p. 7.

27. Author's interview with Tadhg McMahon, 9 June 2008.
28. Reprinted in *Maria Legionis*, March 1998, p. 3.
29. ibid., pp. 4–5.
30. Duff to Ingoldsby, 29 October 1949, LOMA.

CHAPTER 18

Peregrinatio Pro Christo

'As between that Peregrinatio and your own there is an infinite gulf. Nevertheless, the outline resemblance is there.'

DUFF, *MARIA LEGIONIS*, 1976

Frank Duff rarely travelled outside Ireland but he had an unbounded interest in developments in Church and State throughout the world. The keen interest he took in the travels of friends and legionaries is apparent from his correspondence. Eleanor Butler was a Dublin architect, member of the Irish Senate 1948–51, the Labour Party and the Legion of Mary. In 1959 she married the Earl of Wicklow, also a friend of Duff and a regular attender at a Patrician group in a private house in Blackrock, County Dublin. In a letter to a Danish legionary, Ellen Moller, in 1956 he refers to some of Butler's travels, which were much more exotic over fifty years ago than they would be today:

> One of our legionaries here in Dublin, Miss Eleanor Butler, will be journeying through Denmark and Sweden and Norway in the very near future. She is an organiser under the Kellogg Foundation. The idea is that she will travel all through Ireland helping the housewives with advice as to their homes. It is in connection with this work of hers that she is now paying a visit to Scandinavia.[1]

This would be a fairly typical expression of interest in the travel which recurs in Duff's correspondence. He directed a special focus on the travels of those who came to be known as '*peregrini pro Christo*' – voyagers for Christ.

In the mid-1950s some students at University College Dublin, members of the Legion of Mary, took an initiative which developed into one of the Legion's most remarkable works: *Peregrinatio Pro Christo* (voyaging or adventuring for Christ), known in short as PPC. At the time there were a number of student praesidia in UCD, including one named *Sponsa Spiritus Sancti*, which continued to operate during the summer months among students who remained in Dublin. Michael McGuinness, then a medical student and later Medical Director of a Dublin psychiatric hospital, became president of *Sponsa Spiritus Sancti* in 1953 when the previous president, Seamus Grace, set off as Legion Envoy to South America. McGuinness remained president until his graduation in June 1956. Early in 1954, a Marian year (a year specially dedicated by the Church to Mary), a number of students, including

McGuinness, started a study group centred on de Montfort's *True Devotion*. In March that year some of the students made an act of consecration to Mary, placing themselves at her disposal on the lines recommended by de Montfort. In this way, it might be said that, like the Legion itself, de Montfort was the catalyst for the *Peregrinatio*.

During the 1950s it was customary for several hundred students to work in canning factories and other employments in England during the long summer vacation in order to earn money for fees and living expenses. During the Easter vacation in 1956, two UCD legionaries, Michael McGuinness and Aoife O'Toole, together with two other legionaries who were not students, Aileen Flattery and Eamon O'Toole, volunteered to work alongside legionaries in England. The four met at Westland Row (Pearse) Station in Dublin and arrived in London on Easter Saturday morning where they attended a briefing meeting with English legionaries. McGuinness was assigned to work in the diocese of Portsmouth and Aoife O'Toole was assigned to Norfolk.[2] According to McGuinness, the key figure in the start of the PPC was Hugh Brady, later a prominent Dublin architect and principal in the firm of architects and town planners Brady, Shipman and Martin. McGuinness thought that the first idea for 'holiday apostolate', whereby students combined apostolic work with summer employment, may actually have come from Brady's brother, Donal. The name 'holiday apostolate' was used until the concept evolved further and the title *Peregrinatio Pro Christo* was proposed by Duff.[3]

At the end of the summer holidays in 1957, one of the students, Martin Holland, placed a card from Fr Paul Boland, an emigrant chaplain in England, on the table after a Legion meeting. Boland had passed his card to Holland, saying that he would be happy to meet students from UCD at any time when they were in England. Brady picked up the card, which spurred him to extend his horizons.[4] Teachers as well as students had long summer holidays and Brady wondered how they too might be drawn into the holiday apostolate. A Legion praesidium had started some time earlier, comprised of students in Trinity College and in the National College of Art & Design, while a praesidium for teachers had also been established. Tadhg McMahon and Brady's sister and brother, Mairead and Donal, were officers in the teachers' praesidium and they promoted the idea of holiday apostolate among teachers. A series of discussion meetings was arranged to prepare students for such a possibility. One of the discussions was led by Fr Dermot Lane, a theologian in the Dublin Archdiocese, later President of the Mater Dei Institute and parish priest in Balally in Dublin. In the course of these discussions, the idea developed further and the students decided to approach Duff.

Hugh Brady met Duff for the first time in 1957 when he, Michael McGuinness and some other students went to see him. Brady says that he found Duff to be extraordinarily accessible, which made a deep impression. Accessibility and openness to good ideas were qualities Duff valued in others.[5] Duff was taken with the holiday apostolate idea and came to UCD to talk to students. He was accompanied on the occasion by another legionary, Tom Cowley. He spoke to the students about the early Irish monks and how they had spread Christianity, a subject on which he had recently written an article for *Maria Legionis* under the title '*Peregrinatio Pro Christo*'. Duff, who had earlier spoken at the Divinity School in Trinity, attended a further meeting of students held in the rooms of the Laurentian Society, the society of Catholic students at Trinity. The Trinity student who set up that meeting was a sister of Martin Tierney, later a priest in the Dublin Archdiocese, then a student at UCD.

As the summer of 1958 beckoned, the vital element of a team approach was formed. It was decided that ten UCD students who were going to England would offer their services as a 'team' in a parish where they would attend a weekly Legion meeting. Before the ten set out from Ireland, they went on retreat together to the Cistercian monastery in Roscrea, County Tipperary. The ten UCD students were joined by a couple of legionaries already in London, bringing the total number in the group to twelve, thus comprising a band of twelve 'holiday apostles'. The students obtained a range of jobs in cafés, bars, factories and elsewhere while joining existing Legion praesidia in London. They tried to promote some joint ventures, such as meeting the 5.30am 'emigrant' train at Euston Station, the recitation of a public Rosary at Hyde Park Corner and selling Catholic papers at Marble Arch. Fr Aedan McGrath, together with a number of emigrant chaplains, including Fr Boland, who would shortly return to UCD as a chaplain, played an important role in the work. The work of approaching emigrants, helping them to find accommodation and sustain their faith in a new environment, was never-ending. For example, there were thousands of Irish people working in the hotel industry in London at the time and thousands more in building, construction and other economic activities. It was the era of the 'Kings of Kilburn Road'.[6]

On their return to Dublin, the students took a key decision to hold a promotional conference at Hallowe'en in 1958. They undertook a series of rallies around the country, targeting the universities in Cork, Galway and Belfast. They also visited seminaries to inform clerical students about the *Peregrinatio*. In 1959 the number going on the holiday apostolate increased to ninety-six, among them Anne Allen, also an architect, who would marry Hugh Brady a few years later, and Maurice Foley, who would become Chief Executive of the Guinness Peat Aviation Group (GPA) and Chairman of the Irish Museum of Modern Art (IMMA). In 1960 the total number going on the holiday apostolate increased further and included Seán Donlon, later Irish Ambassador to Washington, and Liam Convery, a dental surgeon. Donlon and

Convery went not to London, but to the Scottish Islands. This adventure 'gave wings to the whole experience', since it showed that the holiday apostolate did not have to be confined to large cities like London.

Among the core group of early *peregrini*, Mairead Brady became Legion of Mary envoy in Portugal, Tadhg MacMahon became envoy in Brazil and Kathleen Coyle became a Columban Sister in the Philippines. Donal Brady joined the air corps and was killed tragically in an air accident. Brian McKeown, who joined the Legion as an eighteen-year-old in Belfast, took part in one of the earliest *Peregrinatio* projects in 1961 in Nevers in France. Aged twenty-two, McKeown became Legion envoy in the Belgian Congo, where he remained for four years, becoming interested in Third World development. He later helped to establish Trócaire, the agency of the Irish bishops to assist development in Third World countries.

The concept of *peregrinatio* quickly developed on a broader basis. To accommodate non-students, the period spent on *peregrinatio* was reduced to one or two weeks, during which legionaries worked full-time in parishes to which they were invited. It was appropriate that UCD was the cradle of the *peregrination* because the Catholic University that was the remote ancestor of UCD had been founded by Cardinal Newman, who in his book *University Sketches* wrote an evocative chapter entitled 'The Tradition of Civilization: The Isles of the North'. This essay recalled the story of the early peregrination of the monks in the sixth, seventh and eighth centuries. Over one hundred years later, speaking to legionaries, Duff said:

> As between that Peregrinatio and your own there is an infinite gulf. Nevertheless, the outline resemblance is there. Underneath what you do lie great reserves of faith and readiness to give if needed. As such it will be taken hold of as the older Peregrinatio and used to accomplish eternal purposes.[7]

A remark made by Fr Granville, an emigrant chaplain from the Dublin Archdiocese, at a farewell party for the PPC teams in London in 1959 was the spark which led to the introduction of another new work in the Legion – the *Viatores Christi*. Granville said to the students that they would return home, but 'for the rest of us [priests] it's a long-term commitment'. The students began to think of how they might respond to the challenge implicit in the comment and commit to work for longer periods of time. At a meeting in the Brady family home in January 1960, the idea developed that emigrants might decide to give extra time to the local church in addition to Legion activities. The idea began to take on a complexion distinct from the Legion in so far as volunteers for work overseas did not necessarily belong to the Legion, although the promoters of the idea were all members. In 1960, one young woman went to Africa, McGuinness went to England and Brady would have gone to Brazil but for the fact that he was knocked down by a double-decker bus and hospitalized.

Discussion began with Duff and other Legion officers to see how the overseas volunteer work might be integrated into the Legion system. It was Duff who coined the term 'Viatores Christi'. A central praesidium, 'Regina Viatorem', was established in 1962. The membership included Hugh Brady's sister, Mairead, Seán Donlon, Maurice Foley and Ivo O'Sullivan.[8] Hugh and Anne Brady, who were married in 1962 following Hugh's discharge from hospital, were not involved since they had left Ireland to work as architects in Brazil and later in the US. As more viators went abroad, the organizers realized that there was a clear difference between spending one or two weeks on *peregrinatio* in a developed country and spending one or two years working in the Third World. In the era of expensive air travel, a volunteer might be away from home for a relatively lengthy period of time. The organizers put together a training programme for volunteers. Following a disappointing experience for four viators in Peru, where promised jobs did not materialize, it became clear that work contracts and health insurance would have to be cleared before viators left Ireland.

When the Bradys returned from Brazil, they found that tensions had emerged between key personnel in Viatores Christi and the mainline Legion. It would not be the first time that religiously minded people in religiously motivated organizations were at loggerheads. It was a fairly frequent occurrence in religious orders. Following his return to Dublin, Brady was president of the viatores from 1968 to 1974. He felt that the viatores were under scrutiny and that their *bona fides* were called into question, including the suggestion that they were not acting openly as legionaries. Unfortunately no provision had been made in the Constitution of Viatores 'for a direct or regular system of communication between the parent praesidium and Concilium'. Brady says that during this period he met Duff several times: 'He was always his usual friendly self toward me and to anyone in my presence, generous with his time – but firm in his views.' During Brady's presidency two meetings were held between Viatores and Concilium officers. At one of these meetings, Brady pleaded strongly for a communication arrangement to be formalized, in response to which Duff put forward an 'interesting but complex proposal regarding the training of prospective Viatores'. The adoption of the combined suggestions of Brady and Duff might well have provided the solution, but in the event Concilium thought the former unnecessary and Viatores judged the latter to be unworkable. Brady says that he personally favoured Duff's proposal and 'sensed that Duff was "going out on a limb" from many of his colleagues to find a compromise and, when this was not accepted, felt he had done all he could'.[9]

There would no meeting of minds and the process of disaffiliation of the Viatores from the Legion was completed in under two years, between 1975 and 1976, during a series of five meetings between selected Concilium officers and Viatores praesidia officers. It was a painful business for all involved. At a later stage, a system of *Incolae Mariae*, or 'Marian Residents', was developed in the Legion. *Incolae* are volunteers, generally young people, who take jobs for periods overseas and give time after their day's work to Legion activity. The earliest *Incolae* worked in London, Copenhagen and South Africa. Several went to Iceland with Fr Robert Bradshaw, including a number guided there by the late Tom Smith. Smith was particularly pleased that seven *Incolae* went on to study for the priesthood, two of whom are currently serving in Iceland, one as Vicar General.[10]

In 1948 a Russian woman, Irene Posnoff, visited Duff and proposed to him that the Legion might be started in the Russian Orthodox Church and that it would be relatively easy to do so. Posnoff had joined the Legion of Mary when she was living in Paris. At the time of her Dublin visit she was living in Brussels, where she had founded the Foyer Orientale for the development of relations with the Russian Orthodox Church. Following her meeting with Duff, she proceeded to Rome, where she obtained an interview with relevant Vatican authorities. Duff recounted the 'sensational results' to a friend, Mother Joan, a member of the Irish Sisters of Charity: 'Not only has permission been given for us to start the Legion in the Orthodox Church, but also we are permitted to introduce Orthodox persons into our praesidia and to engage them in the legionary works.' In agreeing to these concessions, Cardinal Tisserant expressed faith in the competence of legionaries.[11] In 1949, the Mother General of the Columbans assigned to one of her nuns the task of translating the Legion *Handbook* into Russian.[12] The nun was a member of the Orthodox Church and had already translated the Legion prayer leaflet into Russian. Ever a student of history, Duff observed, 'Never in the history of Russia has there been a lay apostolic movement. For this reason religion had remarkably little vitality in it and was used as a tool by the state. Therefore the accusation made by Lenin and Stalin that religion was the opium of the people was not absolutely untrue.'[13]

Both the relevant authorities in the Vatican and the Legion were content that praesidia set up by the Orthodox should be under the control of Orthodox authorities and that there would be no question of any Roman or Concilium interference in the affairs of the Orthodox. The Legion agreed that Orthodox praesidia could use an icon of Mary, instead of the usual statue at meetings, and an alternative prayer to the Rosary. This alternative prayer, the Agathistos, which is the Greek equivalent to the Magnificat, is also used by the Uniates in Greece.

In 1958 the Archbishop of Melbourne, Dr Mannix, asked Fr Anthony Cleary, the Spiritual Director of the Senatus of Melbourne, to visit the Greek Orthodox Archbishop for Australia, Archbishop Ezechiel. Cleary asked Ezechiel if he would consider using the Legion of Mary for his own purposes and gave him a copy of the *Handbook*. In light of assurances that the Legion operated by the Orthodox would be under control of the Orthodox, the Archbishop accepted the Legion and agreed that the one organization within the two churches would foster a spirit of unity.[14]

Following the election of Pope John XXIII in 1959, Duff's thoughts began to focus on the Soviet Union. Years earlier a fictional piece had appeared in *Maria Legionis* in which 'Comrade Stalin' was pictured wearing a Miraculous Medal. In 1960 a Legion praesidium in London started a society called the Union of Saint Sergius and Saint John Chrysostom in which Roman Catholics and Orthodox met socially. As a result of a meeting between some members of the group and Bishop Anthony Bloom, the Russian Orthodox Bishop of London, Duff was invited to London. In December 1960 he met Bloom, together with a group of Orthodox priests and lay people. He explained the Legion system and encouraged the Orthodox to take it up.[15]

Two priests, Fr Robert Bradshaw and Fr Seán Moriarty, played an important role in bringing the Legion to the Soviet Union, but the first Irish legionary to visit there, although in an unofficial capacity, was my sister, Deirdre Flanagan (Humphreys), a student in Trinity College where she had taken Russian language classes which were then provided on an 'extra-curricular' basis. In 1959 she went on a holiday to Russia, travelling with a largely American group on what was one of the early tours to the Soviet Union, then just beginning to open to tourists from the West. On her return to Dublin, Duff invited her to give a talk about her visit at the Concilium headquarters to a small group of legionaries in the presence of the Papal Nuncio, Archbishop Riberi. Six years later, in April 1965, Duff wrote to Fr Kevin in Cyprus telling him that two praesidia, one among teachers and the other among shop assistants, had been started by Poles and were functioning in Russia. 'These two praesidia are composed of Orthodox persons but – strangely enough – are utilising our ordinary Rosary.'[16]

From the late 1960s, a small number of legionaries began to travel regularly to Russia on holidays while undertaking a form of holiday apostolate, contacting people they met and speaking to them about the Catholic faith. Fathers Bradshaw, Moriarty and the Carroll sisters were regular travellers. In the words of Duff, 'Since 1969 we have been sending an annual party into Russia on what we call Peregrinatio Pro Christo. This represents volunteers who can afford the money and who give their holidays.'[17] Following initial suspicions, the authorities accepted the visitors. Duff suggested that the authorities, despite the official attitude to religion, were considering allowing the Legion to take root in the Soviet Union. 'Our explanation is that they want the voluntary principle, having nothing of the sort.'[18]

Following the opening of an Irish embassy in Moscow and the appointment of Dr E. J. Brennan as ambassador in 1975, Moriarty and Bradshaw, who had been visiting Russia on a regular basis, made a courtesy call to the Ambassador. They paid a further call in 1976, which resulted in Brennan writing a letter to the Secretary of the Department of Foreign Affairs in Dublin, Paul Keating, enclosing a 'summary record of a courtesy call which three priests connected with the Legion of Mary made on me on 16th July'. Brennan said that the chief point of practical interest was the possibility of an exchange of visits between Metropolitan Nikodim of Leningrad and Frank Duff. Brennan remarked in his letter, 'The account which they gave of their motivations in this matter indicates, to put it mildly, a very practical attitude towards the Orthodox Church and Soviet State power.'[19] Nikodim died in Rome when he visited there in 1978 to attend the installation of Pope John Paul I, who would himself die within weeks.

In the summer of 1978, when Brennan received a similar courtesy call from Fathers Bradshaw, Kennedy and Moriarty, he reported back to the new Secretary of the Department of Foreign Affairs, Bob McDonagh, in terms critical of both the Legion and the Russian Orthodox Church. Referring to his visitors from the Legion, he said:

> Their main selling point, which to me smacks very much of a narrow-minded intolerance calculated to appeal to the traditional xenophobia of the Orthodox Church here, is that the adoption of the Legion system would help the Orthodox to fend off what they uncharitably describe as the 'freak religions' which have arisen in the West and the 'danger' when 'there is growing openness to Western ideas' which could lead to the importation of 'pornography, crime, immorality and drugs'.[20]

Brennan was quoting from the English translation of a Russian memo the legionaries had left with representatives of the Orthodox Church, a copy of which they had given to Brennan. The memo makes two main points in regard to the Legion. It states that the Legion aims to foster the idea of voluntary service, and that it respects civil authority and refrains entirely from politics. With regard to voluntary service, the memo said that the Legion was willing to undertake practically every form of social service and through those works to establish 'contact with every stratum of society, building friendship and community spirit in every way'.[21] The memo emphasized that if the Orthodox Church decided to adopt the Legion system, there would be no attempt to control it from Dublin or to impose Latin practices. 'Therefore if such items as the use of statues are unacceptable, a suitable icon may be used instead.' The memo did indeed refer to 'freak religions', stating that 'Russian and the

Ukraine in particular have a tremendous Christian tradition', and in that context mentioned the 'entry of sects from the West, in particular from the United States'. In the absence of any record of a reply from McDonagh to Brennan, it is open to conjecture what McDonagh thought about the proposed establishment of the Legion of Mary within the Orthodox Church, given that McDonagh's wife, Roisin O'Doherty, had established the Legion in Sweden when she worked in the Irish Legation in Stockholm thirty years earlier, a fact of which Brennan may have been ignorant.

At the September 2009 meeting of the Concilium, reports were presented for the first time in the Russian language by Fr Yury Nachodko, Spiritual Director of Our Lady of Budslav Comitium, Minsk, Belarus, the country most devastated by the Chernobyl catastrophe. Fr Yury was accompanied by Marya Martynenka and Galina Kalevich, respectively President and Secretary of the comitium. Another legionary in the group, Elena Kondratchik, acted as translator. The apostolate undertaken by the Legion in Belarus, where it was established in 1993, includes the visitation of homes, hospitals and orphanages, catechetical instruction and preparation for the reception of the sacraments.[22]

Notes to Chapter 18

1. Duff to Moller, 23 June 1956.
2. Memo from McGuinness to author, 31 October 2008.
3. ibid.
4. Author's interview with Hugh Brady, 14 January 2008.
5. In his appreciation of E. P. McCarron (*The Irish Times*, October 1970), Duff says of McCarron, 'Yet he was supremely accessible, available to all, open to every proposition for good.'
6. The name given to Irish construction workers in London who lived in the Kilburn area of London in the 1950s and the subject of the film *Kings* (2007).
7. Duff, 'The Monks of the West', *The Woman of Genesis*, p. 341.
8. Ivo O'Sullivan later became a lecturer in chemistry in University College, Dublin.
9. Hugh Brady, 'Frank Duff and Viatores Christi': a submission to the Tribunal for the Cause of Frank Duff, 24 March 1999.
10. 'Tribute to Tom Smith', *Concilium Bulletin*, August 2010.
11. Duff to Mother Joan, 22 June, 1949.
12. Duff to Ingoldsby, 29 October 1949.
13. Duff to Fr Tim, 21 May 1954.
14. Duff to Fr Kevin, 10 April 1965.
15. ibid.
16. Ibid.
17. Duff to Leydon, 22 December 1973.
18. ibid.
19. Brennan to Keating, 19 July 1975, DFA/2008/78/11, NAI.
20. Keating to McDonagh, 1 August 1978, DFA/2008/78/11, NAI.
21. Memo to Their Excellencies of the Orthodox Church, DFA/2008/78/11, NAI.
22. Pat O'Hara, 'Belarus Legionaries Visit Legion of Mary Headquarters', *Maria Legionis*, 4, 2009, pp. 13–16.

CHAPTER 19

Building the Nation

'... the Irish people must receive a message. They must have some idea of what peace-time patriotism stands for.'

DUFF, *HIBERNIA*, APRIL 1963

A civil servant by training, Frank Duff was a thinker with the mindset of an entrepreneur, carrying the quality of entrepreneurship into every aspect of life. Because Christianity required 'the duty of love and helpfulness alike to the community and to each individual',[1] Duff sought ways in which to build up communities and encourage national development. As a general principle, he argued that the Irish should move from a traditionally conservative and imitative approach to a more daring one, saying 'We are an ultra-conservative people, not an enterprising one. We are imitative rather than original. We are self-deprecatory in our own ideas and institutions. And to sum up, we will only be found taking a step when it has already been taken elsewhere – especially by England.'[2]

The visionary and entrepreneurial outlook which was the hallmark of his work in the Legion of Mary was clear in his civil service work. The same psychological daring that marked, for example, his approach to the air transport industry, described below, was the same daring which manifested itself when he told a group in the infant Legion of Mary, much to their amusement at the time, that they were 'destined to cover the earth.' Decades after the foundation of the Legion, he wrote to a legionary that he 'saw the whole picture nearly fifty years ago, that is shortly after the start of the Legion. I felt that it was the entry of Our Blessed Lady in a new form into the world.'[3]

Bill Caulfield is one of three people who have read all Duff's 33,000 collected letters – the others are Fr Bede McGregor and Fr Eamonn McCarthy. Caulfield found that the person who emerged from the letters was 'a practical Francis of Assisi' who combined 'poetry with good management'. He remarked that Duff's craving for some recognition from the Archbishop of Dublin for the work of the Legion in its early days reminded him of the prayer of Gerard Manley Hopkins: 'Send my roots rain.' Caulfield believed that Duff's practical side reflected top management ability. His system of records, his deployment of people and his insistence that everyone contribute a share of effort meant that the Legion never became overly dependent either on Duff himself or on any small group within it.[4]

One field where Duff saw opportunity for pioneering development in Ireland was in aviation. In the 1940s, when he was turning his mind to the theme of national development, which he viewed as part of the Legion apostolate, he wrote a memorandum entitled 'Flying'. In the memo, Duff argued that Ireland should aim to be a leader in air transport by seeking opportunities at every stage from the manufacture of aircraft to the training of pilots and ancillary staff. He believed in a network of regional airports, but above all, like Ryanair, he believed in cheap air fares:

> No doubt the services to America, Europe, etc. would be conditioned as to fares and amenities by custom, competition and international agreements. But so far as Ireland is able to assert a separate scale the latter should be away from the present status of flying as a luxury service … . This question of cheapness is cardinal.[5]

In the 1940s a number of allegations of corrupt behaviour were made against persons linked with the government. Tribunals in 1943 and 1947 concerned dealings in stocks of the Great Southern Railways and the disposal of Locke's distillery in Kilbeggan, Co. Westmeath. León Ó Broin was well aware of the broader context when recounting how a small group consisting of himself, Duff, Joe Walshe, Paddy Little and Seán Ryan, editor of the *Irish Catholic*, in whose office they met, would spend time discussing the general betterment of Ireland. Walshe had spent thirteen years studying for the priesthood with the Jesuits before leaving owing to ill health. He subsequently entered the diplomatic service, where in 1946 he moved from being Secretary of the Department of Foreign Affairs to the post of Irish Ambassador to the Vatican. P. J. (Paddy) Little was appointed Minister for Posts and Telegraphs in 1939 and remained so until 1948. Little was the first editor of *An Phoblacht* in 1925 and a founder member of Fianna Fáil in 1926. Close to de Valera, Little mentioned to him that Duff was seeking ways to improve the situation in Ireland. De Valera suggested that Duff be asked to draw up a memorandum for him.

The memo prepared by Duff contained a call for the establishment of a set of 'National Principles', which would generate practical idealism. He was critical of the extant position in Ireland:

> Our present position is that of disillusion, disheartenment, utter perplexity, cynicism, apathy. In such a mood, and with the misgiving creeping into so many hearts that the Nation is no more than a big racket, what chance is there that its children will serve it worthily or sacrifice themselves for it? Elemental instinct in us rebels violently against the notion of mere exploitation in the name of a sacred cause.[6]

Duff explained that the group had been discussing ingredients of and requirements for national life. He said that such requirements begin in the individual and rest primarily on the individual, 'but they unite in the wider effect of making the nation – which in turn helps to shape the individual. The sum-up of those ingredients *is* national life. They form the elements of cohesion.' Dismissing any excuses 'by reference to the sad heritage of the past', he suggested that the use of the term 'idealism' might divert from the grimness of everyday reality where a growing destructiveness, jobbery, perjury and other defects, rather than 'giving value' in a solid sense, suggested a dishonest people. He admitted that the 'grimness' was offset by a host of amiable qualities and talents, but this only rectified matters 'to the same extent that a handsome face offsets cancer'. Certain characteristics which had an air of strength, such as doggedness or defensive capacity, 'exist side by side – or perhaps may be the same thing as – a chameleon-like capacity to yield, to take on the colour of one's surroundings, which so often shows itself when the Irishman goes abroad and which assumes disconcerting guises'.

In drawing up principles and ideals for Ireland, Duff said that terms like 'Democracy', 'Social Justice' or 'A Christian Nation' should not be used 'as mere catch-cries'. Christianity must be authentic, not a mere sham or caricature. Of Christianity in Ireland, he said:

> It is not being practised as a social religion, as concerned with duty in every shape and form and exhibited towards one's fellowmen, individually and corporately. Without the practical living of the full Christian duty the theory is fruitless; without it we are thrown back on the caricature of Christianity.[7]

In his memorandum, Duff offered hope, saying that Ireland had immense possibilities. In order to clarify the meaning of 'Ireland: A Nation' he suggested that the government should select four or five persons of very different types, including at least one Protestant, who would examine the question privately and who would then present a draft set of national principles. The second, later stage would concern the method of implementing these principles.

Little gave Duff's memo to de Valera who retained it for a considerable time before inviting Duff to meet him to discuss the contents. Duff described what happened at the ensuing 'lengthy session':

> He (de Valera) explained that when he read the document first he was rather outraged by it, esteeming it to be sheer pessimism. But he read it again and again, and eventually found himself in the position of having to agree with every word it contained. Actually he made that Memo the basis of his speech to Fianna Fáil on the occasion of the celebration of the 21st birthday of that organisation.[8]

In his speech at the anniversary celebrations on 18 May 1947, de Valera did indeed draw on the memorandum. He explained that:

> When I was thinking of what I might say at this meeting, a memorandum – a rather strange memorandum – was given to me … I might say that I would not have paid

very much attention, I am afraid, to the memorandum did I not know that it had been written by a man who had given much thought to fundamentals, who had already done much 'Do chum glóire Dé agus onora na hEireann,' [to the glory of God and the honour of Ireland], and because of that I read it more than once. I read it twice and thrice – at first it appeared to be unduly pessimistic, but the question was asked: What are our national principles? What do we stand for as a nation? What do we desire to excel in as a nation?[9]

De Valera said that when he read the question posed in the memorandum, he 'naturally thought first of all' of the poet James Clarence Mangan, 'who described Ireland's rightful contribution to the world as the light of moral beauty'. He went on to say that 'We want to stand out for what we have been in the past – a Christian nation.'[10]

Rather than accepting Duff's suggestion to invite a small group to work on national principles, de Valera asked that Duff should himself 'attack that task'. Duff set to work and had completed the task by April 1948, when he wrote to Joe Walshe, then in the Vatican, enclosing a copy. The principles he proposed were based on an overarching Christianity where each cared for his or her fellow man or woman. In turn, the first principle for the State should be the recognition of every person as an individual, not merely part of a herd, just as members of a family are individuals as well as members of the group. The second principle was equality of treatment. All sorts of discrimination – he mentions anti-Semitism – must be eliminated. There must be no favouritism. Here, Duff said, 'the fact must be mentioned that it is generally believed in the country that all positions are filled, and all administrative processes determined, by patronage. That belief is largely erroneous, e. g., the Civil Service system. But sufficient takes place to cause it.'[11] The third principle was that everyone should contribute to the nation according to ability and this included preparedness to undertake some minimum of voluntary work.

Duff duly sent a further communication to de Valera, who within a few weeks was out of office following a general election. When de Valera returned to office in 1951, he did not revert to the matter with Duff, but Duff's concern for the state of the nation continued unabated and he sought practical ways in which his ideas could be implemented. Writing in 1966 to his friend Maurice Moynihan, then Governor of the Central Bank, acknowledging a copy of the bank's report which Moynihan had sent him, Duff discussed the attempts in the report to tackle then current economic difficulties. He said that he was 'nowadays probably less fitted than I one time was to deal with its intricacies', but he thought the report 'represents a courageous pointing to a state of affairs which is intimidating'.[12] He noted that the old rules of government housekeeping had been abandoned and expressed puzzlement at a recent interview given by the Taoiseach, Seán Lemass, in the religious magazine *The Word*, in which Lemass said that the financial rules that applied to a family, i.e., of balancing income and expenditure, did not apply to the nation. Duff remarked to Moynihan, 'In other words, he (Lemass) justified a method of operation on the part of the State which could not be tolerated in the case of the smaller unit. I must say that I cannot assent to that line of thought, and I would very much wish to see it argued.'[13]

In his letter to Moynihan, Duff enclosed a copy of his recently published pamphlet 'True Devotion to the Nation', filling in the background to his first discussion with de Valera in 1947:

> Very many years ago, I used to talk over all these things with my beloved friend, Paddy Little. He was impressed and finally he brought me to de Valera. I had a number of chats with him, and I pleaded that he should set up a government commission which would solemnly set about determining what precisely nationhood meant and obliged. To what extent was it bound by the ordinary rules of thought which would apply to the family or to larger units of society. He did not think the suggestion of that commission was feasible and he requested me to put down on paper what I thought myself on that subject. This I did, and I presented to him the document which forms the first part of the enclosed brochure. He then asked me to expand that into what I would regard as a set of principles. The second and third parts of the brochure are my attempt at that. The fourth part is a recent document which I produced on the subject, and which might be regarded as my own homely effort at attacking the entangled situation which now exists. I would be greatly obliged if you would be able to read through the whole lot.[14]

The earliest example of a practical 'True Devotion to the Nation' project was in Inchigeela, County Cork. It came about as a result of a suggestion to Duff in the late 1950s by Michael McGuinness, then a young doctor, that something might be done about improving the tourist facilities in the locality. In a lengthy reply, Duff congratulated McGuinness on his proposal and suggested that such improvements might be made by using the Legion of Mary. In a letter to Hilde Firtel in 1961, in which he proposed 'venturesome work' for the university students with whom she was dealing in Germany, he described the work of legionaries in Inchigeela:

> I do not know if you have heard of the Inchigeela project in Co. Cork which was run by the Legion. They took that place which is also a beauty spot and they turned it into a tourist resort. It was simply done by stirring up all the people and getting them to work together. They tidied up and beautified it. When this preliminary process was gone through, the place was advertised, and in the first season, 135 visitors were brought in, and subsequently declared that it represented the best holiday they had ever had.[15]

Following the success of the Inchigeela project, attention moved to Tuosist in County Kerry. Twenty-two miles long, running approximately from the Healy Pass to Kenmare, Tuosist is located on the southern side of Kenmare Bay. The population of the parish had fallen from 9,000 in the nineteenth century to 873 in the mid-1950s with no marriages and just two children born over a period of five years. This was the era of the 'Vanishing Irish'. Faced with the extinction of his parish, the priest approached the local Legion of Mary and asked for their help. The Legion mobilized the local community and undertook remedial work of every sort, which included cleaning and painting and persuading a Cork legionary, Marie Caulfield, to provide B&B accommodation.[16] Legionaries were encouraged to holiday in the area and gradually more and better accommodation was provided. Marriages began to take place. In a relatively short time the community had been energized and Tuosist was transformed into a viable tourist attraction, which it remains to the present day. The work in Tuosist was the subject of a documentary in the early 1960s made by a group of priests who formed the television production company Radharc.

In October 1958, a few months before the publication of *Economic Development*,[17] the first True Devotion to the Nation Conference was held. Some legionaries thought that the True Devotion to the Nation programme went beyond the Legion brief, but not Duff, who argued that Christianity in Ireland was being practised in a half-hearted manner in which individualism was uppermost. 'Each man must think in terms of his neighbour, not only of his soul, but of the whole man, his body and environment. This is the centre point of a rightly understood patriotism.' No government, no matter if it had 'the wealth of Croesus and the might of the old Roman Empire', could satisfy all needs.' Rather each individual must be enabled to play his part.[18] According to Duff, Christian responsibility required service of one's fellow man in every shape and form. His point of departure for service to the nation is set out in the *Handbook* in a section on 'True Devotion to the Nation', which says that Jesus and Mary were most perfect Jews, deeply interested in every aspect of their nation and concerned about every person in it.

When Fr (later Bishop) Joseph Duffy, a young priest based in Iniskeen, wrote to Duff enquiring whether work in the Young Farmers' Club and the Irish Countrywomen's Association provided suitable work for legionaries, Duff replied in the affirmative. He remarked that 'a few tabby cats' could create a false impression of the Legion and exhibit it in a false light. Stressing that, with the exception of activities which involved the giving of material relief, 'It is intensely desirable that as many activities as possible would be gathered in under the Legion umbrella. It would mark a very unhappy condition if all these efforts to ameliorate the social conditions were to be abstracted from religious auspices and only undertaken under secular ones.'[19] Duff went on to say that he had for long been advocating 'societizing', by which he meant the creation of societies of different kinds into which would come people who were not prepared to take the step of Legion membership, but who would engage in societies of various sorts that could be run by legionaries and fulfil the work obligation for some legionaries. An early example in Legion history of 'societizing' was the Marian Arts Society. Other examples included choral societies, drama groups and football clubs. The Overseas Club, the Mercier Society, the Pillar of Fire Society and the Common Ground all fell into this category.

An enduring example of a society organized by legionaries is An Réalt, the aim of which is to build up Irish language and culture. The idea for An Réalt originated with Nuala Moran, daughter of D. P. Moran, founder and editor of *The Leader*, an Irish–Ireland journal. Nuala, who also edited *The Leader*, was a member of the Legion of Mary. In a talk to members of An Réalt in 1971, Duff gave an intriguing analysis in which he cast the Irish language in a wider context. He said that the fact that a language was ancient, full of treasures, had shaped history and even religion was no passport to survival. He observed that Mary, the mother of God, has a special name, Muire, while others named Mary are called Máire in Irish. He questioned if that was the case in any other language. He pointed out that the language of Jesus and Mary was Aramaic, a dialect of Hebrew; that Jesus had delivered the Christian message in Aramaic and had said the words of the Eucharist in Aramaic, yet Aramaic was no longer a spoken language.[20]

Travelling on his bike around Ireland, Duff judged many of the towns and villages to be so drab as 'to constitute a deforming mould for the people who lived within them'.[21] Conscious of the environment and opposed to every form of waste, in 1959 he wrote an article in the *Irish Independent* entitled 'The Key to National and Spiritual Welfare: Waste Not, Want Not!'[22] He quoted Frederick Ozanam, a French lawyer and founder of the Society of St Vincent de Paul: 'We are all unprofitable servants, but we serve a Master who is absolutely economic, who lets nothing go to waste.'[23] Duff went so far as to say that there should be no waste, that everything should be put to economic use, to vital purposes. He called this 'the great unrecognised truth of the day'. 'Economy', he said, 'is a first principle of God's action … . Thou shalt not waste. It is really fit to be an Eleventh Commandment.'[24] He argued that violation of this 'commandment' would result in disorder. 'In the nation the disregard of that law will result in maladjustment, inequality, poverty, pain of every sort.' He said that a 'whole school of economists' had promoted the view that 'waste is wealth' – probably a reference to economists who, for example, urged the rapid replacement of durable consumer goods such as cars and washing machines before they were 'worn out' in order to stimulate demand. Then, according to Duff, there is amazement that the national accounts do not balance and that exports are so dear that they cannot find markets. When the 'fallacy of waste' fails, the 'fallacy of debt' is added.[25] When Independent Newspapers sent Duff a cheque for ten guineas for his article, he returned it. When further requested by the *Independent* if the cheque could be paid to the Legion, Duff suggested that the money be divided 50/50 between the Morning Star and Regina Coeli hostels.[26]

In 1972, when the first oil crisis loomed, Duff showed renewed concern about waste in a letter to a businessman regarding the collection of scrap metal. He drew on Legion experience with the collection of waste paper during World War II when a committee of paper merchants built a wooden kiosk into which paper could be deposited in College Green in Dublin. He described how the kiosk was open from about 8am until late at night. The merchants paid the wages of an attendant who covered the portion of the day when Legion members were not in a position to staff the kiosk. 'Our staff was, of course, voluntary and covered the evening period as well as helping to some extent during the daytime.' Duff said that the fact that even the smallest quantity of paper was welcome struck a psychological string: 'people felt they were doing something useful by "posting" even the smallest quantities'.[27] He suggested that, while the kiosk idea might not be feasible, 'perhaps you could arrange with a large number of business premises to station some sort of receptacle just inside their doors'.[28]

Duff's concern for the Irish people extended to emigrants. In the 1950s the Legion began to provide support for the thousands of Irish who were taking the emigrant boats to England. A start was made when a young legionary, Hubert Daly, with the support of Archbishop McQuaid, spent six months assessing the emigrant problem in England. He was joined by Phyllis Dowdall (McGuinness). Legionaries began to meet the emigrants on arrival in England. Fr Aedan McGrath, following his release from jail in China, devoted several years to welcoming immigrants at Euston Station at the end of their tiring journey by boat and train. Legionaries helped the immigrants to find accommodation, which was difficult at a time when many were forced to live in poor conditions. British Rail supported the work by providing a small cabin-type shelter as a meeting place on the platform at Euston Station. Among the legionaries who worked with McGrath was Kathleen Cooney, who retired early from her job in Longford where she managed the Post Office to devote her energies to helping the newly arrived Irish in London.

One of those who recalled being met by legionaries was Frank Dunphy, accountant and manager of the artist Damien Hirst. Dunphy described how he 'was met off the boat by the Legion of Mary and taken to a safe house'.[29] A frequent request was to change Irish money into sterling. One legionary recalled changing two two-shilling pieces, the entire fortune of the emigrant.

Partly in response to work among the emigrants, many of whom were found to have very little knowledge of Catholic beliefs, Duff formalized the Patrician movement in 1955. The aim of the Patricians was to stimulate Catholics to learn more about their faith in order to talk to others about it and 'so that its transforming truths might be operative'[30] in their lives. The germ of the idea for the Patricians began with discussion groups on matters related to faith organized by Tom Doyle for the residents of the Morning Star Hostel.[31] Duff believed that the traditional method of 'learning the Catechism', which he described on one occasion as an 'ordeal',[32] was frequently ineffective and could even act as a deterrent to some persons. At a Patrician meeting, a lay person gives a short introductory talk on a topic related to religion. This is followed by discussion and a break for a cup of tea. After the break, a priest or Spiritual Director gives a short talk, which is followed by further discussion. Patrician meetings last for two hours and vary greatly in their attendance. For example, they may be parish-based, or based in a school or college, or they might meet in a private home. They might be directed towards specific groups of people. Examples of the latter that have operated in Dublin are Patrician groups for diplomats, doctors, taxi drivers and students. They are also held in prisons, hospitals and other institutions. Groups are to be found in various parts of the world: for example, in 1961 Joseph Pilendiram reported: 'I came across a Patrician group right in the heart of Uganda in a place called Mbarara attended by Europeans, Asians and Africans.'[33] A Patrician group for members of the Diplomatic Corps in Dublin in the 1950s and 1960s met in the home of Celia Shaw at Ailesbury Road. Monsignor Benelli, Secretary in the Dublin Nunciature and later a cardinal and close associate of Pope Paul VI, attended several meetings. Another group whose attendance numbered those of different political backgrounds, including W. T. Cosgrave, P. J. Little and General Seán MacEoin, met in a private house in Blackrock, County Dublin during the 1960s, where the chaplains were in turn the former President of University College Cork, Mgr Alfred O'Rahilly, and Dr Michael O'Carroll.

Another initiative which caught Duff's imagination was work for the traveller community. As early as November 1931, when the Legion was ten years old, John C. Joy, SJ, reported on 'the visitation of gipsy encampments by legionaries'.[34] In the 1950s, legionaries in County Meath, in particular Frank Tuite and Kathleen O'Dowd, began to visit travellers in their caravans. O'Dowd described in a letter to Duff how the travellers had been chased 'as one would chase dogs'. On 16 July 1956 a number of legionaries wrote to the *Irish Independent* on behalf of travellers: 'They are hunted from place to place and nobody will face up to the responsibility of treating them as citizens with rights and responsibilities as well as duties.' Soon a praesidium, named 'Our Lady of Flight', was started among the travellers themselves, notably among members of the Hand and Powers families. In 1960 the Sprite Caravan Company provided legionaries with a caravan, fitted inside as a classroom and a club-room which was used for classes and social functions for travellers in

Dublin.[35] In October 1960, *The Irish Times* reported that Duff had accepted a 'mobile school-room' from Mr L. W. Ross of Sprite (Ireland) at Sherrington, Shankill, County Dublin. The school-room, a sixteen-foot caravan, had been designed and built by the staff of Sprite 'as a labour of love' from materials provided by management. The report, which was carried in the Irishman's Diary column of the paper, said that the school-room caravan would be used 'to teach the children of what are known as "itinerants" in the tinkers' camps around Dublin city and county'. The diarist said he was sure that the school-room would be welcomed as 'an instrument of emancipation'.[36]

When the government established a Commission of Inquiry in Itinerancy (1960–63), the Minister for Justice, Charles Haughey, wrote to Duff inviting the Legion of Mary to make a submission. The Legion memorandum identified key issues relating to housing, work and education. The memorandum uses the term 'travellers', remarking 'The term "itinerants" is the official description of persons who always refer to themselves as "travellers"'. A card was received by Duff from K. J. O'Doherty, 'King of the Tinkers', thanking the Legion of Mary for 'wonderful work for my people'.[37] In a recent book on Irish travellers, Aoife Bhreatnach refers to the work of the St Vincent de Paul Society and the Legion of Mary for travellers and observes, 'The relative generosity of the charitable organizations contrasts with the refusal of local and national authorities to extend aid to nomadic and illiterate Travellers.'[38]

Duff was enthused by the arrival of Telefís Éireann (TÉ) in 1961 and wrote a lengthy article for *Hibernia* in 1963 entitled 'Potentialities of Telefís Éireann'. He was positive about the role of television in the provision of entertainment which was, perhaps, its most important function. He said that TÉ could bring an element of much-needed 'brightening' to life in the countryside. However, he felt there was little that was characteristically Irish about TÉ, at least no more than there would be 'in a good-class foreign newspaper containing an Irish inset … I cannot but think that the most effective teacher in Ireland to-day – TE – is only like the "Sunday Times" or the "New York Times" with an Irish inset.'[39] He thought that Telefís Éireann could do more than it was doing in 'moulding the mind of the nation'. He gave examples of the sort of issues which he thought should be dealt with – many of which subsequently were – including emigration, unemployment, clean sport, excessive drinking, the slaughter on the roads and the building up of industry, as well as the proper administration of the law, public spirit and Christian standards generally. He expressed appreciation that the *Broadsheet* programme had examined misbehaviour in sport, which was exercising a corrupting influence on players and spectators. He regarded the 'human holocaust' on the roads as a scandal and quoted a judge who had remarked that if cattle were being mowed down at a similar rate there would be an outcry that would compel action. He argued that the Irish people must receive a message; they must be given some idea of 'peacetime-patriotism'. The 'honour of Ireland must not be a mere sentimental, meaningless phrase, but a motive'. He urged the introduction of good history programmes and gave the example of the BBC *You Were There* series, casting back the TV cameras on past episodes but with a 'hustling reporter' recounting history as it happened.

Duff wished that the question of nationhood be examined in a serious manner – a wish that is pertinent today. He was unconvinced that worthwhile ideals were being placed before the people. In 1973 he asked, 'What exactly is the aim of Ireland today?' He said that when he was growing up, the dream of his generation was that 'when freedom and the control over our own affairs and education had been gained, Ireland would be a light to the world'.[40]

Notes to Chapter 19

1. Duff, *Hibernia*, 1963.
2. Duff, 'Flying', memorandum 33, undated, but its contents suggest the 1940s, LOMA. Carmel Duff says that Duff wrote a memorandum on the development of airlines before the establishment of Aer Lingus in 1936.
3. Duff to Starczewska, 22 August 1969.
4. Author's meeting with Bill Caulfield, 11 March 2009.
5. Duff, 'Flying'.
6. Duff, *True Devotion to the Nation*, p. 4. The memo for de Valera was published as the first section of this booklet many years after it had been written.
7. ibid, p. 8.
8. Duff to Walshe, 27 April 1948.
9. Speech by Éamon de Valera, P 2081/2082, UCD archives.
10. ibid.
11. Duff, *True Devotion to the Nation*, p. 19.
12. Duff to Moynihan, 16 August 1966.
13. ibid.
14. ibid.
15. Duff to Firtel, 20 February 1961.
16. Author's interview with Bill Caulfield, 11 March 2009.
17. Book published by T. K. Whitaker, Department of Finance, which helped to spearhead Irish economic recovery.
18. Duff, *True Devotion to the Nation*, Introductory Note.
19. Duff to Duffy, 26 June, 1954, LOMA.
20. Duff, 'The Faith, the Nation', talk to An Réalt, 1971, tape 91, LOMA.
21. Ó Broin, *Frank Duff*, p. 97.
22. *Irish Independent*, 7 February 1959.
23. Duff, 'Waste not – want not!', *Mary Shall Reign*, p. 91.
24. ibid, pp. 92–93.
25. ibid.
26. 26 January 1961, file in Myra House with Regina Coeli minutes.
27. Duff to McCarron, 25 July 1972.
28. ibid.
29. Frank Dunphy in interview with Eoin Butler, *The Irish Times* Magazine, 20 September 2008, p. 6.
30. Words from the Patrician prayer recited at the start every Patrician meeting.
31. Redmond, *So Great a Cloud*, p. 160.
32. Duff to McGarry, 28 January 1957.

33. Pilendiram to P. Flanagan, 14 January 1961, author's possession.
34. John C. Joy, SJ, 'Catholic Action in Ireland: the Legion of Mary', *The Irish Monthly*, vol. LX, no. 701, November 1931, p. 682.
35. Anon., 'At the Caravan Blessing Ceremony', *Maria Legionis*, no. 2, 1961, p. 34.
36. *The Irish Times*, 10 October 1960.
37. LOMA. The card bears an English postmark.
38. Aoife Bhreatnach, *Becoming Conspicuous: Irish Travellers, Society and State, 1922–70*. Dublin: University College Dublin, 2006, p. 72.
39. *Hibernia Review*, April 1963.
40. Duff to McGuckian, 22 December 1973.

CHAPTER 20

Before the Second Vatican Council

'This is the heart of the whole matter. A heavy brake on true progress in the Church had largely been the unconscious attitude that lay people were there mainly to be disciplined in their wider spheres of activity.'

EDMUND FLOOD, OSB, *VATICAN COUNCIL IN PRACTICE*

A few years before the convening of the Second Vatican Council, Duff expressed the belief that 'The Legion is new, it is *sui generis*. The Legion belongs to a new order of thought amongst the apostolic societies.'[1] By then the Legion had spread from its small beginning in Francis Street in Dublin to about one half of the dioceses of the Catholic Church. According to Duff, the 'active principle of the apostolate' was 'one big idea'; one of the chief marks of the Church was that of apostleship.[2] A layperson who is not apostolic 'falsifies the very first idea of the Christian Church, i.e. that the Christian is the *alter Christus*. But so much has this necessary Christian characteristic become obscured in modern times that the ordinary lay person does not conceive himself to have any duty whatever in that direction.'[3] The apostolate was not something for, at most, an educated category of persons. It was for *all*.

Among numerous examples of Duff's belief in the capacity of those with little education for the apostolate was one drawn from his experience during his visit to Rome in 1952 to meet Pope Pius XII. Following the visit, he wrote to a priest friend about a praesidium composed of 'servant girls' that he had attended there. It was, he said, 'the real article. If the others, which come into being there, are of the same calibre, we need not have the slightest doubt as to the future.'[4]

Like John Henry Newman, Duff understood that knowledge is not the same as virtue, and the imparting of knowledge to the laity is distinct from the creation of an apostolic laity. Writing in 1956 to Fr Mangan, Secretary to Archbishop McQuaid, Duff suggested that Catholic education all over the world had erred into an 'adoration of *mere* knowledge to the detriment of more important things e.g. spirit and action'. He said that the belief that 'knowledge *automatically* radiates itself is a fatal delusion … . We have been pouring knowledge into children in Ireland, and it has only come out as Dead Sea fruit to an alarming extent.'[5] He stressed the distinction between knowledge and virtue many times; for example, he wrote, 'Knowledge and virtue are not the same thing and they can be at opposite ends.'[6] To Fr Conley Bertrand, who was active in the Legion in Louisiana, he said, 'To have virtue in its reality, one must practise it.'[7] Apostles were formed by example and by the actual experience of apostleship. In a key passage in the *Handbook*, Duff set out his plan for the formation of apostolic legionaries. He supported the master and apprentice system of training, with its emphasis on learning through the process of work itself in the company of an experienced co-worker and within the praesidium setting under the guidance of the Spiritual Director. Apostles were not formed by listening to learned lectures – the danger of the lecture system was that it produced theorists who might be disinclined to 'devote themselves to the humble employments and the laborious following up of individual contacts, on which everything really depends.'[8]

Duff questioned the emphasis placed by the Catholic Action Movement on study and attendance at lectures and courses of instruction as a prerequisite to the apostolate. Writing to an Australian legionary in 1939, he said:

> I must say you have hit the nail right on top of the head in your remarks on the subject of study as a preparation for Catholic Action. Imagine giving a duck a course of 100 weekly lectures on the subject of how to swim – and all the time preventing him from swimming! At the end of that time he would positively have forgotten how to swim. Now that is what this absurd preoccupation about study is accomplishing in Catholic Action. It positively gets people out of the way of action. As Thomas à Kempis says: 'What good is it to be able to talk learnedly about the Holy Trinity if we do not serve the Holy Trinity.'[9]

The question of legionary training is intrinsically linked in the Legion system to the Spiritual Director, who is described in the *Handbook* as 'the very mainspring of the praesidium.'[10] It is the Spiritual Director who has the primary duty of developing in the members those qualities which, when brought to bear on Legion work, determine its success or failure. 'Thus building patiently, fitting stone on stone, he can hope to erect in each member a fortress of the spirit which nothing will disintegrate.'[11] The 'allocutio', a brief address given at each Legion meeting by the Spiritual Director, is usually based on some aspect of the *Handbook*. Duff believed that the difference between the praesidium, where the allocutio has been thoroughly done, and the praesidium, where it has been badly done, will be precisely the 'difference between a trained and an untrained army'.[12]

The problem in endeavouring to develop a Legion and Church model built on an intimate cooperation of priest and people in the days before the Second Vatican Council, especially in Dublin, was that the Legion could not find many priests who shared this view of the Church. The Legion experienced difficulty in finding priests who were willing to act as Spiritual Directors to praesidia because the priests often did not see a role for the laity in what they regarded as their own exclusive sphere of activity. Typical of those who appealed to Archbishop McQuaid for help in finding Spiritual Directors was Mrs Eileen Liston, a committed legionary who was also President of the Irish National Teachers' Organisation. Liston's extensive correspondence with McQuaid covered matters relating to the Sancta Maria Hostel and clubs run by the Legion for German girls who came to Dublin after World War II.[13]

In 1957 between one third and one half of praesidia in Dublin had no Spiritual Director, and very few of those who took on the role of Spiritual Director attended the weekly praesidium meeting. In view of this, McQuaid established a committee of three diocesan priests, Fr Gerald Healy (later Canon), Fr Cathal McCarthy (later Canon and Archdeacon of Glendalough), Dean of Clonliffe College and the Archbishop's Secretary, Fr Mangan, to examine the situation. The objective was 'to supply the Legion of Mary in the diocese with an adequate supply of competent spiritual directors'. A survey of Spiritual Directors was carried out, a briefing document or *Praenotanda* was prepared by one of the secretaries in Archbishop's House with the advice of Healy[14] and a meeting was held in Archbishop's House on 15 July 1960. The *Praenotanda* outlined the extant situation in the Dublin Archdiocese and its effects on the Legion. It is an important document because it explains why Dublin priests, in general, took no interest in the Legion. It is a frank document, reflecting the courage and honesty of the authors. At the outset it stated that, since 'very few priests believe that lay folk can and should engage in the group exercises of the spiritual works of mercy', it is not surprising that amongst the senior clergy especially there are some few who refuse to have anything whatsoever to do with the Legion and who 'endeavour when they can to suppress the works of the Legion if not the Legion Praesidia themselves'. These priests, among the ranks of the senior clergy, 'regard the entire movement [the Legion of Mary] as a subtle and very subversive intrusion into their professional work, which work, if they cannot do themselves, they consider should be left undone'. Other priests, the 'large majority … are less inimical and are merely passive in their attitude about these issues, without however abandoning one whit their disapproval of the principle that lay folk could and should engage in the spiritual works of mercy'. As time goes on, however, these priests are inclined 'to recognise that the existence of the Legion of Mary is a fact that cannot be passed over and that it has done and is doing good'. However, this recognition did not imply a willingness on the part of those priests to engage with the Legion.

At best they are inclined to regard the Legion or similar groups as a nuisance indulging in the expensive luxury of the spiritual works of mercy to which they are not entitled by their status. And since these priests see no need for the apostolic formation of lay folk for the group performance of the works of mercy, they, of course, see no need for the spiritual direction of these groups.[15]

Almost two years after the July 1960 meeting, in March 1962, Healy prepared a memorandum on the Legion of Mary in the Archdiocese of Dublin, summarizing the situation with regard to Spiritual Directors and containing extensive statistical material. On 5 March the Archbishop wrote to McCarthy, 'I have today received the report on the position of spiritual directors for the Legion of Mary in Dublin.'[16] The central thrust of Healy's report was that the diocese should take action to improve the supply and quality of Spiritual Directors for the Legion and that it was in the interest of the Archbishop and of the Archdiocese to see that this was done. The report is frank in its criticism of the extant position, quoting a German clerical enquiry of 1960: 'What is the matter with the Dublin clergy?'[17] The report listed the main advantages of supplying the Legion with effective Spiritual Directors. These included the fact that it would 'ensure that the services of this widespread and useful organization would be used to the maximum advantage of the Church; it would improve the value and effectiveness of the Legion of Mary in Dublin and indirectly throughout the world' and 'It would enhance the influence and prestige of the See of Dublin wherever in the world the Legion of Mary operates.'[18] According to Healy, there was no effective follow up to this memorandum or to the work of the three-man Committee.[19] However, on 25 April 1965, a few months before the final session of the Second Vatican Council, a meeting between Spiritual Directors and the Presidents of the Dublin curiae was held in Mount Anville convent and addressed by McQuaid. In McQuaid's memo of the meeting, he said that when a praesidium needed a director, the curia 'should notify him and *suggest* a priest'. He said that some priests seemed indifferent to the Legion, but 'if they were made directors, they would, for the first time, have a chance of studying the system. The call on their priesthood would not always go unanswered.'[20]

In March 1960, Duff, together with the President of the Concilium, John Gavin, and the Spiritual Director of the Legion, Fr Donnchadh Ó Floinn, travelled to Rome to attend the episcopal ordination of Mgr Corrado Bafile. Bafile, a native of Aquila in Abruzzo, Italy, was an attaché of the Vatican Secretariat of State. He had been chaplain to the Abruzzo community in Rome and Spiritual Director to the Legion of Mary in Rome for about twenty years. In February 1960, Bafile, who before becoming a priest had studied chemistry at the University of Munich, was appointed by the Pope as Apostolic Nuncio to Germany. He was consecrated archbishop by Pope John XXIII on 19 March 1960 in the Sistine chapel. When he died 45 years later at the age of 101 in 2005, his funeral Mass was presided over by Cardinal Ratzinger.

On 21 March 1960 Duff, Gavin and Ó Floinn were received by Pope John XXIII. Duff described the meeting: 'Monsignor Bafile came in with the three of us. The Pontiff came forward to meet us and then led us to the middle of the room where all of us remained standing in a little semi-circle. He was most benign, and he talked much in regard to his good-will for the Legion.'[21] At the conclusion of the Papal Audience, Duff described how 'the Holy Father placed his hand upon Bafile's shoulder and remarked "Here is your Cardinal Protector"'. Since there was no question of Bafile becoming a cardinal for many years – he would be made cardinal by Paul VI in 1976 – Duff interpreted the Pope to mean that Bafile represented his voice to the Legion, specifically in relation to a lengthy three-hour meeting between Bafile and the Legion group on the following day.[22] Among the matters discussed at that meeting was the proposition that the Spiritual Director of the Concilium might be appointed directly by the Holy See rather than by the Irish hierarchy, as was, and continues to be, the practice. Mgr Bafile assured the legionaries that there was no question of asking for the relocation of the Legion headquarters from Dublin to Rome because such a move would involve the employment of a paid staff, which would be destructive of the Legion ideal. Bafile realized that 'Only Dublin would provide the great band of competent workers whom he had seen in operation during his visit.'

Gradually Duff began to receive some degree of recognition from both Church and State. The earliest recognition had come from the Holy Ghost Congregation when in 1948 they made their Blackrock College alumnus an honorary member of the Congregation. In 1956 he was awarded the Marianist award from the University of Dayton in Ohio. In 1961, the Archbishop of Dublin offered Duff a Papal Knighthood of St Gregory. In April 1961 the Archbishop wrote to him pointing out that weeks had elapsed since the matter of the knighthood was first raised and asking him for his decision regarding 'the honour that I had requested the Holy See to confer on you'. Duff replied that he had been giving thought to the knighthood and had come to the conclusion 'that in view of the position in the diocese [Dublin] it would represent an incongruity for me to receive it' – presumably a reference to the negative approach of the Dublin authorities to the Mercier and Pillar of Fire Societies together with the censoring of some of his writings. He said that he would eagerly accept the knighthood 'if I could think that it would mean a new era. But I do not think it would.' Nonetheless, he ended by expressing gratitude to the Archbishop 'for this mark of favour, which is the only distinction I have ever been offered in my own country'.[23] On 26 April 1961 the Archbishop conveyed Duff's decision to Mgr Storero[24] in the Dublin nunciature and the matter appeared to rest. However, some months later, in October, Duff called to see the Archbishop and signalled a change of mind on the matter, but he did not give reasons. In a memo written following their meeting, the Archbishop recorded that he asked Duff if he wished 'to enlarge on the situation', to which Duff replied that he wished to say nothing further.

The Archbishop and Duff then proceeded to discuss 'Legion affairs, chiefly among the Orthodox'. According to Fr Bede McGregor, who later discussed the episode with Cardinal Bafile, when Bafile told Duff that his refusal of the knighthood would damage the Legion, Duff immediately agreed to accept the honour.[25]

In 1962 Duff received the Humanitarian Award of Variety International. The award is given to those who have shown unusual understanding and devotion to humankind in the previous year and the granting of the award is the climax of the Variety Clubs International Convention, which that year was held in Dublin. The award was presented to Duff at a ceremony in the Theatre Royal by President de Valera, at which the Taoiseach, Mr Lemass, was present. A couple of years earlier the winner of the award was Jonas Salk, who discovered the polio vaccine. Earlier winners included Winston Churchill, Albert Schweitzer and Helen Keller.[26] In accepting the award, Duff described himself as 'the least worthy recipient of such an honour'.

In 1968 Duff was awarded an Honorary Doctorate of Laws (LLD) by the National University of Ireland. The Chancellor of the university, President de Valera, conferred the degree. According to Ó Broin, de Valera 'warmed' to the Legion over the years and on his return from a visit to the Holy Land in 1950 had given a lengthy talk about his experiences there to the residents of the Morning Star Hostel.[27] On the occasion of the conferral of the LLD degree, Duff remarked that it would have pleased his mother. Today the framed parchment hangs on the wall of what was his mother's bedroom in Morning Star Avenue.

If the 1960s brought some recognition for Duff's work, they also brought health problems, as well as one of the greatest trials of his life – the threat to close the Regina Coeli Hostel. As the 1960s began, Duff's hearing, which had been a problem for years, continued to deteriorate and his brother-in-law, Vincent Monahan, arranged for him to have an operation in the London Clinic. The successful operation took place in London on 17 December 1960. His room was next door to that of film actress Elizabeth Taylor, whom he encountered and described as 'ravishingly beautiful'.

In June 1963, the Dublin Health Authority (DHA) declared that the condition of the Regina Coeli Hostel buildings had deteriorated and that they were no longer suitable to house their residents. The DHA wanted the eastern block, which housed forty elderly women, to be vacated immediately, eventually saying that twenty of the women could be housed in the Mendicity Institute. An order to quit notice was issued. Duff wrote:

> What faced us was the abomination that two hundred and fifty of the most helpless and vulnerable of the population were to be cast to destruction. In one minute the work, which had taken thirty-three years of desperate striving and devotion on the

part of many to build up, was going to be hurled to the winds. So that it was not a question of only the two hundred and fifty but all the multitudes who would in the future be subjected to shipwreck by the taking away of the ark which could have saved them. That prospect was beyond bearing. I cannot think about it, even at the present moment, without quivering with pain. Death seemed a happy way of escaping the torture of it. And you know that it is one of our little recourses in times of weakness to wish that we were dead! But that marks a surrender in us, an escape.[28]

Drawing on St Paul, who said that strength is developed in weakness by fighting the weakness, he sought with Mary 'to stand upright in her at the foot of her Son's Cross and her own – merging my pain in hers'. Doing this 'reduced my own position to proper perspective; my torture lessened; I held control'.[29]

Duff proved his capacity to fight. In an interview with *The Irish Times*, he explained that the DHA planned to demolish the hostel 'but have not told us where we are to accommodate all the helpless, unfortunate and vulnerable people we are looking after'. He claimed that through their work in the hostels, legionaries were engaged in a 'great social experiment'.[30] The DHA also demanded repairs to houses the Legion owned in North Great George's Street, where 44 families were accommodated before their reintegration into the 'normal community housing stream'.

Duff agreed to a television interview about the proposed closure. During the interview he said that if the threat to close the hostel were to be carried into practice, he would chain himself to the railings of the hostels – he was nearly seventy-four at the time – and the ensuing spectacle would represent the biggest eviction scene in Irish history. Seeing the interview, a friend of his approached W. T. Cosgrave, then retired from public life. Cosgrave in turn contacted Seán MacEntee, the Minister for Local Government. This contact was instrumental in leading to a backdown by the DHA. On 2 February 1966 the DHA approved plans and sanctioned financial support for building work at the Regina Coeli Hostel. The following day Mrs Flanagan, wife of the Minister for Health, visited the Hostel. Reconstruction work was carried out, but fear of closure continued to linger over the hostels. In 2007 full ownership of both hostels was conferred on the Legion of Mary, eighty years after the buildings were first granted for use by the Legion. Major reconstruction and renovation of the hostels started in 2008, funded mainly from resources accrued by the Legion through the sale of some other property it owned.

The battle to save the hostels took its toll. In June 1963 Duff embarked on his final six years as president of the Concilium. He served two three-year terms in the 1930s, 1940s, 1950s and 1960s, but from 1969 he would never again hold Concilium officership. By December 1963 he was exhausted. When Hilde Firtel complained about the failure of the Concilium to give sufficient priority to the position of the Legion in Germany, he replied that she could not realize the sort of struggle which he had been waging. He wrote, 'This year has been the worst one in my history so far as failure to cope with things has been concerned.'[31]

On 10 February 1964, shortly after commencing a talk to Social Science students at the Newman House premises of University College Dublin, Duff collapsed. One of those present was Blathnaid Ó Broin, a daughter of his friend, León. He had travelled to St Stephen's Green that day by bus rather than by bicycle and Blathnaid drove him back to his home. Next morning he struggled to Mass in Church Street, but collapsed again on his way home. His sister Geraldine and her husband drove up to Dublin to take care of him. A blood vessel had burst in his brain, possibly brought on by sheer exhaustion following the tremendous battle regarding the hostels. Duff spent five months at the Monahans' home in Navan, interrupted by a period in the Mater hospital in Dublin. One of the visitors he received while in the Mater was President de Valera who, Duff said, spoke to him of concerns which gripped his mind. At one point in Navan he received the sacrament of the sick, or extreme unction as it was then called. He expressed no fear of death; rather, he said that he looked forward to being reunited with members of his family. Although he spent much time resting in bed, he also did a good deal of work, including work on revising the Legion *Handbook*.[32] He took regular walks in his beloved Boyne Valley and returned to Dublin greatly restored. Further triumphs and trials awaited him as he passed his seventy-fifth birthday in June 1964.

From the early 1960s the exchanges between Duff and Archbishop McQuaid became increasingly friendly. With the exception of the exchange in regard to the Conferring of the Knighthood of St Gregory in 1961, the diocesan files in the 1960s and early 1970s are full of cordial exchanges, sometimes between Duff and McQuaid, sometimes between the Spiritual Director of the Concilium, Fr Tom O'Flynn, and McQuaid. When, on 22 March 1963, Archbishop Walsh of Tuam wrote to McQuaid referring to a hearsay complaint about the Legion, McQuaid replied immediately with a robust defence of the Legion: 'In my experience where the Legion makes a mistake, it is due to the apathy of the spiritual director, or perhaps the complete lack of a spiritual director. I find them [legionaries] very amenable to even a suggestion.'[33] Sometimes Duff sought advice from McQuaid, as in regard to the proposals of a group of French legionaries for a meeting with bishops during the Second Vatican Council. In January 1965 the Archbishop, in a letter in which he described Mary as the test of 'ecumenism as well as the apostolate', volunteered to defend the Legion perspective if occasion arose at the Vatican Council. He remarked, 'I do not know what the Cardinal [Suenens] means by "The Legion in the next Session", but, please God, I will be there and if the Legion comes up, I must be reckoned with.'[34] It is not clear what Suenens or McQuaid may have had in mind but they might have been referring to proposals to alter the Legion system in some manner or to transfer its headquarters to Rome.

On two occasions in the 1960s Duff sought the Archbishop's advice regarding alterations to the *Handbook*. In April 1963 Duff proposed a change in the *Handbook* regarding the conditions governing Adjutorian membership.[35] The Archbishop queried Duff's use of the word 'invalidate'.[36] Duff then asked the Archbishop for his own suggestion. In place of the word 'invalidate', the Archbishop proposed 'would not be regarded as a notable failure in the duty of membership.'[37] The Archbishop's formula was incorporated as follows: 'Failure once or twice a week to fulfil the required condition would not be regarded as a notable failure in the duty of membership.'[38] In May 1963 McQuaid wrote of the 'irreplaceable apostolate' of the Legion. In a letter to Duff he said that he would like to confide to the Legion the apostolate of the trade unionists: 'The work of very grave import that I was anxious to confide to the Legion is the apostolate of the Trade Unionists … . I should value your opinion, for I am anxious to utilise what is a proved and irreplaceable apostolate.'[39] The following year McQuaid agreed to the secondment of a priest of the Archdiocese for Legion work on the Scottish island of Islay: 'The Scotch apostolate has an epic character … . I am grateful for the chance of sharing in this apostolate.'[40] In January 1965 the question arose of an alteration in the *Handbook* regarding the judgement of suitability of persons for membership. Once more Duff suggested that McQuaid might draft the amendment. The letter is marked by the Archbishop, 'Very well. I shall at once draft.' Once more the wording suggested by the Archbishop was incorporated into the *Handbook* and Duff wrote to thank McQuaid for his help, saying 'We welcome this as a great improvement, removing the intimidatory stipulations which have tended to exercise a restrictive effect on recruiting.'[41]

Notes to Chapter 20

1. Duff to Audet, 14 January 1957.
2. Duff to Ernestine, 21 January 1957.
3. Duff to Geech, 23 January 1957.
4. Duff to Murphy, 9 January 1953, file 1643, LOMA.
5. Duff to Mangan, 31 January 1956, LOM file, DDA.
6. Duff to Br Oliver, 28 December 1968.
7. Duff to Fr Bertrand, 18 December 1968.
8. *Handbook*, 1993, p. 66.
9. Duff to Eileen, 4 January 1939.
10. *Handbook*, 1993, p. 210.
11. ibid., p. 211.
12. ibid., p. 114.
13. Liston to McQuaid, 30 March 1953, LOM file, DDA.
14. Author's conversation with Healy, 30 September 1999.

15. Memorandum entitled 'Praenotanda', discussed at meeting in Archbishop's House, Dublin, 15 July 1960, LOM file, DDA.
16. McQuaid to McCarthy, 5 March 1962, LOM file, DDA.
17. *The Legion of Mary in the Diocese of Dublin: A Memorandum*, p. 2, LOM file, DDA.
18. ibid., p 3.
19. Author's conversation with Healy, 30 September 1999.
20. Memorandum of Archbishop's talk at Mount Anville, 25 April 1965, LOM file, DDA.
21. Duff to McGrath, 30 March, 1960, LOMA.
22. ibid.
23. Duff to McQuaid, 23 April 1961, LOM file, DDA.
24. Storero was then counsellor at the nunciature. He would later return as Papal Nuncio.
25. Author's conversation with Fr Bede McGregor, OP, 15 October 1999.
26. *The Irish Times*, 19 May 1962.
27. Ó Broin, *Frank Duff*, p. 93.
28. Bradshaw, *Frank Duff*, pp. 188–89.
29. Frank Duff, 'I have suffered with him whom I saw suffer', *Virgo Praedicanda*. Dublin: C. J. Fallon, 1967, p. 122.
30. *The Irish Times*, 3 August 1963.
31. Duff to Firtel, 15 December 1963, LOMA.
32. Bradshaw, *Frank Duff*, p. 193.
33. McQuaid to Walsh, 25 March 1963, LOM file, DDA.
34. McQuaid to Duff, 4 January 1965, LOM file, DDA.
35. See Glossary.
36. McQuaid to Duff, 29 April 1963, LOM file, DDA.
37. McQuaid to Duff, 2 May 1963, LOM file, DDA.
38. *Handbook*, 1993, p. 96.
39. McQuaid to Duff, 25 May 1963, LOM file, DDA.
40. McQuaid to Duff, 21 April 1964, LOM file, DDA.
41. Duff to McQuaid, 26 February 1965, LOM file, DDA.

CHAPTER 21

The Second Vatican Council

'Go into the whole world, and take the Gospel to all people.'
MARK 16:15–20

The fourth and final session of the Second Vatican Council opened on 14 September 1965. Cardinal Suenens described the standing ovation that marked Duff's arrival:

I had the joy of having the Pope invite Frank Duff as an auditor to the Vatican Council. When Cardinal Heenan, Archbishop of Westminster, who held the floor at precisely the moment that Frank took his place, saw him enter, he publicly announced the fact to the assembly. The 2500 bishops rose to give him a warm and moving ovation. It was an unforgettable moment: the thanks of the universal Church to the pioneer of the lay apostolate.[1]

Thirty-five years later, in a homily at Mass in University Church in Dublin marking the centenary of the death of John Henry Newman, Revd Professor Donal Kerr referred to the acclaim given to the Legion and Duff by that standing ovation. He observed that at that point it could be said that Newman's prophetic insight on the role of the laity was fully vindicated.[2] Newman himself had chosen the Oratorians, founded by St Philip Neri, as the group of priests most appropriate for himself and his companions. In the words of Fr Stephen Dessain, 'The Oratory exists for the sake of the Laity,'[3] so it is not surprising that Oratorian priests have frequently acted as Spiritual Directors to the Legion of Mary in different parts of the world. For example, Fr Florian Calice is Spiritual Director to the Senatus of Austria.

When the Council opened in 1962, no lay auditors had been invited. At the start of the second session in 1963, regulations were changed to provide for the admission of 'some distinguished laymen' who might speak with the special permission of the Pope. A few prominent Catholic philosophers and writers, for example Jean Guitton, were invited, as well as leaders of some lay organizations. Recuperating from the serious illness which had befallen him, Duff replied to a friend's query, wondering why he had not been invited to the Council:

Really I have no ideas on the subject. It has been quite impossible to diagnose the reasons which led to the inviting of those who were brought to Rome; some of them

> were really quite small fry indeed, and some of them, though prominent people, were not engaged in the ordinary apostolate. Here I refer to such as Jean Guitton, the French writer. Then, the President of the Central Council of the St Vincent de Paul Society was not, so far as I am aware, invited … . The question however is in the sentimental order only because, if I had been invited, I could not have gone. The health issue settled all that.[4]

The absence of Duff from the first list of lay invitees did not go unnoticed. In the newspaper *The Catholic Standard* a leading article referred to 'The Great Absentee', highlighting Duff's absence.[5] Cardinal Suenens, who by this stage had become a defining figure at the Council, suggested to the Pope that Duff should be invited. The invitation duly arrived and Duff set off for Rome on 11 September 1965. He travelled on the plane that was taking the Irish bishops on the three-hour flight, later contrasting the trip with the two-and-a-half-day journey by train and boat when he first went to the city in 1931. At Rome airport he was met by legionaries from Rome and by the Dominican priests Bishop Crawford and Fr Ronan Cusack, at whose House, San Clemente, he stayed while in Rome. The Prior at San Clemente was well known to Duff: he was Fr Anselm Moynihan, brother of John and Maurice Moynihan, and Vice-Postulator of the Cause of Edel Quinn. On the day following his arrival, Sunday, Duff engaged in some sightseeing, visiting the Colosseum and the Forum. It was the only day's sightseeing of the ninety-seven days he spent in Rome. He was comfortable in San Clemente and wrote to Celia Shaw that he was 'in clover' there.[6]

The daily proceedings of the council began with Mass, always a sung one, frequently a high Mass. On Fridays Mass was celebrated in one of the many Eastern Rites. Duff received Holy Communion at the opening Mass each day, four times from the hands of the Pope. Then the business of the day began, 'for the Council was a Parliament'.[7] The deliberations of the council were carried on in Latin, and although Duff was good at Latin, his impaired hearing combined with the many different accents of bishops from all over the world made understanding difficult and tiring. At 11am there was a break in proceedings and Duff would set out for the famous coffee bar nicknamed 'Bar Jona', a reference to the time when Jesus called Peter 'Simon Bar Jona', but he seldom got there since he was constantly approached by bishops who wished to discuss Legion matters. Duff described the coffee bar as 'a delightful place' where personages from the council drank, smoked and chatted. He remarked, 'Never have I seen so many big pipes all together.'[8] By lunchtime he was generally exhausted. He would usually meet up in the Piazza of St Peter's with the three Dominican bishops who were staying in San Clemente: Archbishop Finbar Ryan of Trinidad, Bishop William Fitzgerald, Ryan's coadjutor, and Bishop Egidius Crawford. Together they would return to San Clemente where, after lunch, he took a rest. Afternoons and evenings were occupied with Legion work.

The intention to call a general council of the Church had been announced by Pope John XXIII on 25 January 1959, less than three months after his election. The key to the Pope's thinking on the programme for the Council was that bishops should see it as an examination of their faithfulness to the commandment of Christ to take the Gospel to all people.[9] As the opening approached, the Pope expressed the belief that the council could restore 'the simple and pure lines that the face of the Church of Jesus had at its birth'.[10]

The council opened on 11 October 1962, which in those days was the feast of the maternity of Our Lady. In *What Happened at Vatican II*, Professor John O'Malley, SJ, provides a comprehensive account of the Council.[11] He explains that a draft schema (text incorporating proposals or plans) on the Church, the *De Ecclesia* schema, containing eleven chapters and an appendix on the Blessed Virgin, which had been prepared by seventy experts under the chairmanship of Cardinal Ottaviani, was presented to the council on 1 December 1962. The essence of the schema was that lay people, although the vast majority of the Church, did not have any role in the apostolate and lived in a material world which had little to do with Christianity. This view of lay people was strongly supported by many bishops and cardinals but came under attack from others, including Döpfner and Frings. Frings said that the schema was not catholic in the sense of taking proper account of the long tradition of the Church, Eastern as well as Western, but rather was based on more recent history. The strongest criticism came from Suenens, whose speech on 4 December 'was the decisive one in the debate and received vigorous and prolonged applause from the bishops'.[12] Suenens emphasized the need to look first at the nature of the church as the Mystical Body of Christ (*ad intra*), then to look at the mission of the church to preach the Gospel to all people (*ad extra*) and for dialogue between the Church and the World.[13] He proposed, as the central theme of the council, 'the Church of Christ, light to the world'. In the words of Dom Edmund Flood, the 'heart of the whole matter' was the understanding that the hope of the world is Christ who would work in the world through *all* His people, a large and varied group, rather than through an exclusively clerical group alone. 'A heavy brake on true progress' had resulted from considering that the laity 'had no positive part to play in the life of the Church'.[14]

The draft *De Ecclesia* schema prepared by Ottaviani's group was rejected by the council. Suenens had sown the seed for a new document 'utterly unforeseen up to this point', and 'the one perhaps most revelatory of the council's meaning, *Gaudium et Spes*, The Church in the Modern World'.[15]

On 6 December 1962 Pope John announced the establishment of a central steering committee or coordinating commission, chaired by Cardinal

Cicognani, the Secretary of State. Of the seven members of the steering committee, only Suenens and Döpfner were members from beginning to end. In the eight months between the Opening Session and the Second Session, the steering committee prepared a new draft of *De Ecclesia*, which contained four chapters on the Mystery of the Church, the hierarchy, the laity and the call to holiness. The committee selected five key texts as a basis for the agenda for the next session of the council. These concerned (i) The Church, (ii) the Virgin Mary, (iii) Bishops, (iv) Lay Apostolate, (v) Ecumenism. In effect the committee had provided the essential shape for the Vatican Council.

Pope John XXIII died on 3 June 1963. Following the election of his successor, Paul VI, the new Pope introduced important organizational changes into the council, which effected a streamlining operation. He chose to retain the steering committee/coordinating commission with Cicognani as chairman, but he replaced the council of presidents, the group of ten cardinals, one of whom had acted in turn as president of the daily meetings of the Council, with a group of four moderators. The moderators, all members of the steering committee, were Cardinals Agagianian, Döpfner, Lecaro and Suenens.

On 29 September 1963, the 'Pauline Council' opened. The new version of *De Ecclesia*, which opened with the words *Lumen Gentium cum sit Christus*, 'Christ light to the nations', was placed before the Council. The document dealt first with the bishops and clergy and then with the laity, which reflected the traditional way of looking at the Church – first the clergy and then the laity. Suenens argued that the document should first consider what it is to be a Christian before considering the two different ways of being a Christian – clergy or lay. The layperson was a full Christian with rights and responsibilities of bringing Christ into the world. Leaders and led form a united body working in 'a common undertaking'. Suenens concluded by recommending an increase in the number of lay auditors, which should also include women, 'who, lest I am mistaken, make up half of the human race'.[16] In due course, his close collaborator, Veronica O'Brien, would spend one week in the Tribune of the Auditors in St Peters.[17]

A majority favoured the new draft, which took on board the changes proposed by Suenens. Bishop Wright of Pittsburgh declared that 'the faithful have been waiting for four hundred years for a positive conciliar statement on the place, dignity and vocation of the layman'.[18] The conservative attitude embodied in the first draft still received support from a number of bishops, and the debate on the section which dealt with the bishops began on 4 October and continued for twenty-three days with no end in sight. Then on 29 October, with Suenens presiding, it was decided to take a vote on whether doctrine on the Virgin Mary should be treated in *De Ecclesia* or in a separate schema. Two members of the Doctrinal Commission were selected to present the arguments. Cardinal Rufino Santos of Manila spoke in favour of a separate schema, while Cardinal Franz König of Vienna spoke for incorporation into the general schema. The Curial party, which supported a separate schema, lost by the slimmest of margins and the tide turned against the conservatives.

At the end of his closing address to the Second Session on 4 December 1963, Pope Paul VI electrified the Council by announcing that he was travelling to the Holy Land as a pilgrim the following January. No Pope had left Italy for one hundred and fifty years and no Pope had left the Vatican since 1870, until Pope John XIII made a pilgrimage to Assisi and Loretto in October 1962 to pray for the success of the Council. When the Third Session of the Council began on 14 September 1964, the third draft of *De Ecclesia*, which became known in English as the Dogmatic Constitution on the Church and in Latin *Lumen Gentium*, was ready. Following further debate and deliberation, votes were taken on chapters, and in some instances on parts of chapters, until the Decree was passed.

On 7 October 1964 the schema on the Apostolate of the Laity was taken up and debated for five days. The schema was criticized by bishop after bishop for not showing the real basis of the lay apostolate, which derived from baptism. Quite a few speakers, following the lead of Cardinal Ritter, criticized the document for its 'clericalism', among them the Polish Jesuit Archbishop Kozlowiecki of Lusaka, Northern Rhodesia, who stated that 'clericalism is the No. 1 enemy of the Church'.[19] Another who shared that view was Archbishop D'Souza of Bhopal, India, who said that it was time 'to start considering the laity as grown-ups'. In an intervention from Suenens on 9 October, he specifically mentioned the Legion of Mary and called for greater clarity of understanding regarding the nature of Catholic Action.

The Third Session of the council ended on 21 November 1964, the feast day of the Presentation of Mary in the Temple, with a public session in St Peter's Basilica during which Pope Paul promulgated three documents: On the Church (*Lumen Gentium*), On the Oriental Churches (*Orientalium Ecclesiarum*) and On Ecumenism (*Unitatis Redintegratio*). The Pope spoke at length on chapter 8 in *Lumen Gentium*, which is devoted to Mary, and ended by conferring on the Blessed Virgin Mary a new title, that of 'Mother of the Church'.

Duff arrived for the fourth and final session of the council at which the Declaration on Religious Liberty was approved, as was the Declaration on non-Christian Religions (*Nostra Aetate*). Documents on the Lay Apostolate (*Apostolicam Actuositatem*), on the Missionary Activity of the Church (*Ad Gentes Divinitus*), on the Ministry and Life of Priests (*Presbyterorum Ordinis*) and on the Church in the Modern World (*Gaudium et Spes*) were all finalized during the fourth session. It was fitting that Duff was present when the document on the Apostolate of the Laity was promulgated on 18 November.

During the ninety-seven days he spent in Rome, Duff gave thirty-two addresses, an average of one every three days, to groups of bishops, heads of religious houses, seminarians and legionaries. On one occasion he addressed the one hundred English-speaking bishops and on another he addressed the French bishops in the French language. Soon after his arrival in Rome he had been invited to the Novitiate of the De Montfort Fathers where, as their first lay member, he was given a 'State Reception'. He delivered a talk of one hour in French, reporting to a friend, 'St Louis Marie unquestionably helped me. I got home at 5.30 [p.m.] in a state bordering collapse. I had to rise at 6.15am.'[20] One month after his arrival in Rome, he wrote to a friend, 'The Council is a thrilling business. … As a spectacle it is brilliant.' He said that he had met innumerable bishops and 'the Legion is known to all'.[21]

Duff was interviewed for Vatican radio by a Redemptorist priest, Fr Million. Million's lead-in referred to some of the highlights of the council during the previous week, saying that it was the week 'when Cardinal Heenan of London had the bishops in St Peter's clapping for an Irishman, for Mr Frank Duff, the president of the Legion of Mary'.[22] Heenan's reference to Duff's presence came during the discussion of the Schema on the Priesthood. Million pointed out 'how much the priesthood today depends upon and makes use of the Legion of Mary'. Duff responded by saying that 'From the very first moment, the Legion has asserted that it aspires to be the handmaid of the priest.' He said that the apostolate of the church is one – it has its leaders and it has its rank and file, and 'the Legion has never contemplated any higher role for itself than that of being the rank and file'. Asked whether he visited Legion groups around the world, Duff replied, 'I am afraid that I am the reverse of a globetrotter. I have travelled very little and that really rather as deliberate policy.'

On 23 November, the Feast of St Clement, Duff wrote again to Celia Shaw saying that a 'mighty luncheon' was due to take place in San Clemente at which the guests would include Cardinals Cicognani and Browne, Archbishops McQuaid and Morris, and the Master General of the Dominicans. He said that it would be his first encounter with the Secretary of State, Cicognani. He said that he did not think there was 'any likelihood of my seeing the Pope. He is taking the hierarchies of several countries at a time. Ireland is coupled with some others.'[23] In a postscript to the letter, he remarked, 'I do not touch on the shattering bomb of Mr Cosgrave's death.' Cosgrave's son, former Taoiseach Liam Cosgrave, said, 'The last letter W. T. [Cosgrave] wrote was to him [Duff] the actual day he got his final attack: 15 November 1965. He died on the 16th.'[24] That final intimate exchange of letters between the two men was testimony to a unique and historic friendship.

When Duff heard of the death, he wrote to Cosgrave's brother-in-law, Frank Flanagan, saying that he was 'quivering under the shock of the news', which had been completely unexpected. In fact, he had written to Cosgrave, having heard that he was 'in his usual good form'. He received the reply after Cosgrave's death. He went on to report a strange occurrence in the early hours of that morning: 'A heavy knock sounded on my door. I knew it could not be anyone [calling me to get up] at that time and eventually decided it was something which only seemed to be on my door. But when I heard the awful news I connected the two events.' He heard the news as he was entering St Peter's that morning. Archbishop McQuaid told him that he had offered Mass for Cosgrave and many other Irish bishops said they would do likewise. Duff said that 'As a Laureate member of the Legion, a novena of Masses will be offered for him by the Concilium. I also will have Masses said for him.' He continued:

> To-day when I returned home from the Council I found waiting for me his reply to the letter which I had written him. It was a lovely letter seeming to indicate that he was in excellent health. I will always retain it as a keepsake of him. When will we get his like again? He was very close to my thoughts while here and I often referred to him in speaking of my first visit to Pius XI in 1931 which he made possible.
>
> It is an additional grief to me that I am unable to attend his funeral. May his great soul rest in peace.[25]

In a subsequent letter in which he described the Requiem Mass in Rome, Duff said simply of Cosgrave, 'He was ripe for Heaven and he has obtained it.'[26] The Requiem, said by Cardinal Conway, had a big attendance with, Duff thought, all the Irish bishops, as well as a number of Irish Missionary Bishops. Charles Haughey represented the Irish government. In his letter Duff added that the Pope had said that he would see him after the council, so that he would not therefore be returning to Ireland on 9 December as had been arranged. He said, 'I will feel very lonely when the special plane [containing the Irish bishops] flies off.'[27] The solemn closing of the council took place in the piazza of St Peter's on the Feast of the Immaculate Conception, 8 December. After Mass the Pope blessed the cornerstone of a new church in Rome, dedicated to Mary, Mother of the Church.

The private audience with Pope Paul VI took place on 11 December. Duff described the meeting: 'He met me standing. He took my hands into his and said: "I am happy to receive your visit. I want to thank you for your services to the Church and also to express appreciation for all that the Legion of Mary has done."' Duff said that he stammered out some words of thanks and that the Pope motioned him to a chair, then sat down himself and waited for Duff to speak. Duff went on to say that he foresaw a period of turbulence with clamour for change of every kind, during which the Legion would find it hard to survive on its own and maintain its essence without support. He feared, for example, that the Rosary, which was intrinsic to the Legion prayers, would be jettisoned. The Pope replied, 'The Legion has served the Church faithfully and the Church will protect the Legion.'[28]

Duff welcomed the *De Ecclesia Decree* wholeheartedly. Before the council started, the Legion had received a request from the Vatican, which Duff deemed 'an immense compliment', to forward a copy of each translation of the *Handbook*, a total of thirty-six at the time, for circulation to the drafting committees. He said that 'personages who participated in the Council have not hesitated to declare that paragraph 8 of the *De Ecclesia Decree* was based on the Legion Handbook to the extent of being a paraphrase of it'.[29] Duff said that by the time of the council, the Legion had proved that 'an apostolate could be turned out by all classes of persons, all races, all classes down to the very simplest elements of the population'.[30] The council represented an endorsement of the role of the laity in the manner envisaged by Duff many decades earlier. Dealing with the foundations of the lay apostolate, the Decree on the Laity says:

> From the fact of their union with Christ the head flows the laymen's right and duty to be apostles. Inserted as they are in the Mystical Body of Christ by baptism and strengthened by the power of the Holy Spirit in confirmation, it is by the Lord himself that they are assigned to the apostolate … .
>
> The perfect model of apostolic spiritual life is the Blessed Virgin Mary, Queen of the Apostles … who co-operated in an entirely unique way in the Saviour's work.

The document on the laity says that 'their activity is so necessary within church communities that without it the apostolate of the pastors is generally unable to achieve its full effectiveness'.[31] At the council the real nature of the church emerged or re-emerged as 'the whole brotherhood of Christ'.[32] In the Decree on the Ministry and Life of Priests (*Presbyterium Ordinis*) it is stated that priests 'should unite their efforts with those of the lay faithful and conduct themselves among them after the example of the Master'.

Duff insisted that the Legion of Mary did not regard itself as a lay organization with 'Lay' spelt in aggressive capital letters because that species of Catholic Action suggested a separateness from, and independence of, priests. Rather, in the Legion priests and people are united as one body.[33] The Pauline analogy of the human body provides a powerful image to depict the unity of the church: the Body of Christ. The role of the priest is analogous to that of the human head and thus to the Mystical Head. In a nutshell, the Council says that the priest and laity must work together in order that the Church, the Body of Christ, may fulfil its mission to preach the Gospel to everyone. Without the priest there can be no fullness of the lay apostolate; without the laity there can be no fullness of the priesthood. Without the priest, the vast potential of the laity remains untapped. A great reservoir remains just that – it does not flow into life-giving circulation. Instead, it stagnates. Priests are asked to endorse the role of the laity, allowing them freedom and room for action, and on suitable occasions inviting them to undertake works on their own initiative. This emphasis on the sacred duty of bishops and priests towards the laity 'runs like a golden thread though the Council documents'.[34] Christ's prayer in John 17 'that they may be one' is frequently used in an ecumenical context, but it may be applied tellingly to the unity of priest and people which the council firmly stresses and which is vital to the life of the Church.

The council stressed the role of Mary in bringing Christ to people:

> Hence the Church in her apostolic work also rightly looks to her who brought forth Christ, conceived by the Holy Spirit and born of the Virgin, so that in the church Christ may be born and grow in the hearts of the faithful.[35]

Cardinal Suenens, in a reference to the position of Mary in the council, noted its relevance to the Legion of Mary when he wrote, 'By uniting Mary with the apostolate, the Legion strives not to separate, in its soul and action, what God has united. The Second Vatican Council at my request willed to emphasise this alliance which is the soul of the Legion of Mary.'[36] Duff believed that the council had 'risen to the heights' in regard to Mary. He said that 'Doctrine cannot be subordinated to devotion. She cannot be exaggerated, but neither can she be minimised.'[37]

The writer Louis McRedmond recalled two meetings with Duff at the Irish College in Rome in the autumn of 1965:

> On the first occasion Frank was clearly happy with the progress of events. He remarked that the Council was simply catching up with what the Legion had stood for all along .... On the second occasion I found him in some distress, being disturbed by the views of people on the extreme wing of progressive opinion. I recall in particular his understandable upset over the man who told him he would not genuflect 'before a basket of bread': a phrase I could not forget.[38]

Those two meetings captured well two aspects of the council – the endorsement of the role of the laity and the upheavals to come.

When Duff returned to Dublin, he wrote to Fr Anselm Moynihan early in 1966 saying, 'It is hard to believe that two months have flown by since I bade farewell to you at the airport. That was a sad evening because it dissolved the fellowship of a wonderful three months. I cannot see how I can express sufficiently my gratitude for having taken me into San Clemente.' He concluded by repeating his thanks 'for the great treat afforded to me by my residence among you for those 97 days'.[39] Duff was approaching seventy-six years of age and entitled to peaceful retirement. In fact, great challenges faced him as he entered his final three-year term as president of the Concilium, a term which would end in 1969 when he was eighty years old. These were turbulent times in the Church in Ireland and elsewhere, reflected in the departure of thousands of priests and religious from their ministries.

Notes to Chapter 21

1. Suenens, *Frank Duff*, p. 79.
2. Homily preached by Revd Prof. Donal Kerr, 5 August 1990, University Church Dublin.
3. Charles Stephen Dessain, *Cardinal Newman, the Oratory and the Laity*. Undated, second impression, p. 3. Published privately by the Birmingham Oratory.
4. Firtel, *A Man for Our Time*, p. 103.
5. Ó Broin, *Frank Duff*, p. 85. The article was written by Dr Michael O'Carroll.
6. Duff to Shaw, 2 October 1965, Ms 31670/2, NLI.
7. Duff, 'Ninety-Seven Days in Rome', *Maria Legionis*, 1/1966, p. 9.
8. ibid.
9. Leon Joseph Suenens, *Memories and Hopes*. Dublin: Veritas, 1992, p. 67.
10. Xavier Rynne, *Letters from Vatican City*. London: Faber & Faber, 1963, p. 67. Xavier Rynne was a pseudonym for Francis Xavier Murphy, an American priest who had written on the Council in the *New Yorker* magazine and who became a *peritus* (expert) at the Council.
11. John W. O'Malley, *What Happened at Vatican II*. Cambridge, Massachusetts: Harvard University Press, 2008.
12. E. Flood, *Vatican Council in Practice*. London: Ealing Abbey, 1966, p. 30.
13. Rynne, *Letters from Vatican City*, pp. 225–26.
14. Flood, *Vatican Council in Practice*, p. 32.
15. ibid., p. 158.
16. O'Malley, *What Happened at Vatican II*, p. 187.
17. Duff to Zacherl, 12 May 1967.
18. Flood, *Vatican Council in Practice*, p. 31.
19. Rynne, *Letters from Vatican City*, p. 73.
20. Duff to Shaw, 2 October 1965, Ms 31670/2, NLI.
21. Duff to Flanagan, 9 October 1965, author's possession.
22. Audiotape 153, LOMA.
23. Duff to Shaw, 23 November 1965, Ms 31670/2, NLI.
24. Liam Cosgrave to author, 8 December 2010.
25. Duff to Flanagan, 19 November 1965, author's possession.
26. Duff to Flanagan, 28 November 1965, author's possession.
27. ibid.
28. Frank Duff, 'Ninety-Seven Days in Rome', *Maria Legionis*, 1/1966, p. 10.
29. Duff to Holland, 6 November 1975.
30. ibid.
31. Quoted by Mgr Basil Loftus, *The Catholic Times*, 10 February 2008.
32. John Horgan, *The Church Among the People*. Dayton, Ohio: Pflaum Press, 1969, p. 17.
33. Duff to Cleary, 16 February 1938.
34. Loftus, *The Catholic Times*, 10 February 2008.
35. *Constitution on the Church*, number 65.
36. Quoted in O'Carroll, *A Priest in Changing Times*, p. 142.
37. Duff, *Virgo Praedicanda*, pp. 231–32, quoted in Ó Broin, *Frank Duff*, p. 84.
38. McRedmond to author, 30 October 2008.
39. Duff to Anselm Moynihan, 25 February 1966.

CHAPTER 22

War and Peace

'No change will worry the tranquillity of your Christian lives.'
ARCHBISHOP MCQUAID, 1965

On his return from the Vatican Council, Archbishop McQuaid sought to reassure the people of his diocese when at an event in the Pro-Cathedral in December 1965 he said, 'You may have been worried by much talk of changes to come. Allow me to reassure you.'[1] In the event the council would be challenged both by the modernizers and the conservatives. The Legion of Mary was not immune from the turbulence. In January 1966 Duff suffered a recurring cold and influenza, which lasted for over two months. Quarrels within the Concilium concerning possible changes to the Legion system were made more trying because of this bout of ill-health. Among the advocates of changing the *Handbook* was Harry O'Carroll, a legionary of long standing. A couple of years later, Duff experienced a further blow to his health. When cycling in the dark in the Wicklow mountains, he had a fall from his bicycle and damaged his knee. But he had a remarkable capacity for recovery and was soon cycling again.

Trouble arose in the Legion in a number of countries, including Holland, France, Germany and Brazil, where changes were sought in its system. For example, the Senatus of Frankfurt wanted all the Latin terminology in the Legion to be excised and for the *Handbook* to be totally rewritten. It was proposed that the 'militarist' aspect, including the Legion title itself, should be abolished.[2] Fr Donnchadh Ó Floinn, who had been Spiritual Director of the Concilium since July 1955, resigned in April 1966 and was succeeded by Tom O'Flynn, CM, who remained until his death in 1984. Ó Broin summarized Duff's position on the post-conciliar situation:

To be progressive was a duty, he conceded, but 'we should ascend, as we climb stairs, one step at a time'. In the Council's Decree on Adaptation and Renewal of the Religious Life he found a phrase to which he reacted warmly. It urged that Institutes should keep before them their founders' spirit and special aims and should hold their sound traditions faithfully in honour … .

He would also insist on the retaining of the Rosary, which had become a victim of the false *aggiornamento* of Vatican II. A campaign to abandon it altogether had to some extent been successful. It was being said that it was a prayer for ignorant people; that there was no room for it in these days of enlightenment.[3]

By contast with those who saw the Rosary as a prayer for the uneducated, Duff, like Newman, who said that the Rosary 'makes the Creed a prayer', realized that it is profoundly scriptural, covering the central episodes of Christian faith from the Incarnation to the Resurrection.

Following the Council, Duff submitted two memoranda to the Vatican. One concerned the varying demands for changes in the Legion system; the other concerned the introduction of a shorter version of the Roman breviary for use by legionaries. On receiving the memoranda, Secretary of State Cicognani sought information from the Archbishop of Dublin regarding the Legion. In his reply to the cardinal, McQuaid said that it was free of 'the spirit of unreasoning, or even bitter, criticism that now marks some groups of lay people'. He said that it was 'very consoling to state that the attitude of the Legion to the bishop's authority and to the Spiritual Director's guidance is uniformly submissive'. He stressed that the zeal or apathy of the Spiritual Directors were important factors in the success or failure of Legion endeavours and attributed the acceptance by the Legion of spiritual authority to 'the marked spirit of prayer in the Legion', concluding by saying that in his experience as a bishop 'the success of the Legion – and it has succeeded where no other form of Catholic organisation has been of avail – depends on accepting the Legion organisation in its totality'.[4] In due course the Vatican, in the form of a reassuring message from Cardinal Dell'Acqua via Archbishop McQuaid, replied to Duff's submission. When McQuaid transmitted the Vatican letter to Duff, he commenced his covering letter 'My dear Frank' for the first time that this writer could find in their correspondence of thirty years.

In 1968 Pope Paul VI published the encyclical *Humanae Vitae*. The reaffirmation of the Church's traditional teaching on birth control triggered a wave of negative reaction, especially in North America and Europe. Much of the criticism took the form of a personalized attack on the Pope. On 7 September 1968 Duff wrote to the presidents of regional and local councils of the Legion of Mary throughout the world without referring to the encyclical but urging loyalty to the Pontiff. In November Cardinal Benelli wrote to Duff expressing on behalf of the Pope 'heartfelt gratitude' and assurance of 'His prayers that God may richly bless you and the Legion of Mary for your unremitting dedication to the cause of the Church.'[5]

Disagreement of another sort occurred when a dispute broke out regarding the Overseas Club. In 1961 it had acquired number 7 Harcourt Terrace and later the adjoining house at number 6 was acquired. The purchase of number 7 was financed by a gift of £6,000, given by Nan Cassidy of the well-known Cassidy's fabrics family, who was a cousin of Duff.[6] The purchase of number 6

Harcourt Terrace and the renovation and adaptation work was financed by a loan from the First National Building Society. Residential accommodation for students, including married couples with children, was provided at reasonable rates in 25 self-catering apartments. There was no discrimination as to race or creed, with Muslims, Buddhists and Hindus frequently a majority of the residents.

In 1970 the Irish Council for Overseas Students (ICOS), later known as the Irish Council for International Students, was established to provide a range of services to support international students and educators in Ireland. It was agreed that the Council would base its activities in the Harcourt Terrace premises of the Overseas Club and a government grant towards the running cost of the premises would be divided between the Legion of Mary and ICOS. ICOS had been established by the universities and churches, in consultation with, and financially supported by, the Department of Education, under whose auspices it initially operated. In 1975 responsibility for the administrative grant for ICOS was switched to the Department of Foreign Affairs.

A finance committee, many of whose members had no connection with the Legion of Mary, had been established in the 1960s to raise funds for the Club. The committee, chaired by Brian D'Arcy Patterson, included Fergal Smithwick, whose firm of Chartered Accountants, Messrs Kean and Co., audited the accounts of the Club. Contributions came from a number of other sources, including, according to Professor Louis Smith, Chairman of ICOS in the 1970s, African bishops. According to Smith, 'The combined organisations [Overseas Club and ICOS] were working smoothly when I was invited to be Chairman, succeeding [Cearbhall] Ó Dalaigh who became President of Ireland.'[7] Ó Dalaigh continued to be President of ICOS and Smith remained in contact with him. But then, according to Smith, the Council was asked by the Legion to quit the premises. Difficulty arose because of an overlap between the Legion of Mary, the Overseas Club, the Finance Committee and ICOS. Writing in February 1977, Seamus Grace, former Vice-Principal of Blackrock College and Legion envoy to South America, stressed the significance of monetary matters.[8]

The Club operated until 1976. According to Enda Dunleavy, when budgetary shortfalls developed, the Club asked the Legion Concilium to underwrite its overdraft, pending receipt of the annual grant. As debt grew, it outstripped the ability of the grant to cover the annual shortfall, and it appeared that the only option was to sell the premises to pay off debt. When the Legion put the premises on the market, the Overseas Council refused to quit. However, it did quit when the premises were entered and occupied by a campaigning Women's Group and their condition deteriorated. They were eventually sold in the 1980s to a firm of architects, one of whom, according to Smith, had earlier prepared a report on the buildings.[9] Smith placed blame for the closure of the premises on Duff's shoulders, although Duff was in his late eighties at the time and had not been an office holder in the Legion for a number of years. Although the Overseas Club closed, ICOS continues its valuable work at premises in Donnybrook in Dublin under the direction of CEO Sheila Power and its board.

If quarrels occurred in the years after the Vatican Council, peace was also made. A high note between McQuaid and Duff was struck at the time of the Golden Jubilee of the Legion in 1971 when the Archbishop accepted an invitation to address the celebrations on 5 September. The Papal Nuncio was also invited, but Fr O'Flynn, the Spiritual Director of the Concilium, said the 'diocesan character of the occasion [is] to be preserved'.[10] On 1 May, O'Flynn wrote to the Archbishop asking whether the Mass for the Jubilee should be that of the Holy Spirit or of the Blessed Virgin. The Archbishop graciously replied that the choice should be left to Duff. In his address at the Jubilee Mass, McQuaid recalled

> … with all due gratitude the grace of holiness that has made the Legion so closely resemble the life and work of the Redeemer Jesus Christ and His Virgin Mother. The favour of an obscure and lowly origin here in Francis Street vividly recalls the cave at Bethlehem. Even the hostility that has so constantly marked the progress of the Legion in the holiness of its apostolate is paralleled by the treatment meted out to God made man, our Saviour (Hebr. xii, 3). Well may we rejoice that, under the inspiration of the Mother of the Divine Redeemer, her Legion has welcomed their trials in the spirit of her Faith. The patience of their charity slowly vanquishes the enmity of those who cannot understand that 'the servants are not greater than their Master' (John xv, 20) … .
>
> In the humility of her Fiat at the Incarnation the Legion has deliberately subjected itself to the guidance of the Church of Christ. In the praise of her Magnificat, it has rejoiced that God has done great things through its lowly agency.

In his Christmas letter to the Archbishop in 1971, the last Christmas of McQuaid's reign in the See of Dublin, Duff wrote, 'May the Lord and His mother whom you have served unflinchingly use this time of bounty to bless you most abundantly.'[11]

On the occasion of the Golden Jubilee of the Legion, the Bishops of Ireland collectively wrote to Duff in terms of unqualified endorsement and appreciation. As McQuaid had done in his address at the Jubilee Mass, the bishops also referred to the difficult beginnings of the Legion and to their belief that only the power of God could explain its constancy. They said that the origins of the Legion of Mary were marked by 'obscurity, poverty and even hostility that are seen at the outset of Our Divine Saviour's Life in Bethlehem and Nazareth'. Yet in the plan of God, the faith and courage of the founding members merited grace not only of survival, but also of extension throughout the countries of the world. They firmly concluded that 'No other power than that of God, no other inspiration than that of the Holy Spirit, no other protection than that of the Mother of God can adequately explain the supernatural constancy of the Legion of Mary.'[12] In his reply to the bishops, Duff wrote, 'It forms a happy retrospect that the Legion has not failed notably in its duty of love and obedience to authority. May that feature ever continue in it as its special mark. Without it, may the Legion perish.'[13] Throughout the difficulties he had experienced, Duff remained loyal and obedient to the Church authorities, so that McQuaid could describe him in a letter to Nuncio Sensi as 'utterly loyal'.[14]

The year following the Legion Jubilee, Dr Dermot Ryan succeeded McQuaid as archbishop. He invited Duff and Concilium officers to a meeting at which he stated his regret about what had happened to the Mercier Society. This stimulated the launch of the Pauline Circle, which continues to operate, though on a smaller scale than the Mercier. When the Mercier Society was reconstituted as the Pauline Circle in 1976, some of the surviving members of the Mercier participated. These included Frank Duff, Canon Proctor, Fr Michael O'Carroll and James P. Cummins, who had been the original chairman. Dr Michael Ferrar did not live to see the revival of the Society, but his sister, Elizabeth Ferrar, who had a distinguished missionary career in India, attended regularly. Dr Simms, then living in Armagh where he was Archbishop, was unable to attend, but when he retired from Armagh he came to deliver an address to the Pauline Circle entitled 'A Decade in Armagh'.

In February 1975 Duff's surviving sibling, Dr Geraldine Monahan, became ill. He was driven down to Navan during the night to be at her bedside when she died in July 1975, concluding a remarkable record of being present at the death of each of his siblings. Duff, who had been the eldest in the family, was now the sole survivor. He soldiered on. In March 1976 he was invited by the President of Maynooth College, Dr Tomás Ó Fiaich (later Cardinal), to address the students. In a letter to Fr Aedan McGrath, he wrote that he had received an invitation from the President of Maynooth to go down and talk there and that a group of legionaries went down to County Kildare with him and they were received with acclamation. Duff was left in no manner of doubt as to Ó Fiaich's positive attitude towards the Legion.[15] Possessed with a keen sense of history as well as a deep faith, Duff remained optimistic about the future of the Church. In the concluding essay in his collection of essays, *The Woman of Genesis*, published four years before he died, he wrote:

> The Church is in what we see as a deep winter, but which very many think to be a dying … . Out of that winter the Church is destined to emerge not only intact but as in the spring of nature, that is to a renewal of life. It will cast off much of its decayed substance and it will be bursting with expansion and efflorescence.[16]

Later in 1976, Duff suffered another bad fall from his bicycle, this time in Kerry on the road from Fenit to Ballybunion. In 1978 there were a couple of break-ins at his house. On both occasions he was resting. On the first occasion, when he heard the intruders, he picked up a stick beside his bed and chased them downstairs, slipping on a mat in the hallway. On the second, he was resting, having returned from the funeral of the Earl of Wicklow. He was attacked and beaten by the intruders and ended up in hospital. *The Irish Times* reported on 11 February 1978, beneath a photograph captioned 'Legion of Mary founder attacked', 'Mr. Frank Duff, the founder of the Legion of Mary, who was under observation in a Dublin hospital last night after being struck on the head with a metal instrument by an intruder at his home.' The report went on to say that he had received a wound over his right eye, but was described as 'fairly satisfactory' by the Richmond Hospital, where he was detained overnight. After being struck, he managed to make his way downstairs and asked a man in the street to bring him to the nearby Richmond. It was thought that one, or possibly two, intruders were involved and part of the house was ransacked. He survived the attack, but in April was admitted to hospital with cardiac congestion.

Neither the attacks nor the cardiac problem deterred him from travelling to Rome the following year to attend the Council for the Laity and to meet the new Pope, John Paul II. No doubt he reflected on his earlier visits of 1931, when he met Pius XI, 1939, when he met Pius XII a few months before the outbreak of war, and 1952, when he met Pius XII once more. There were also the meetings with John XXIII in 1960 and Paul VI in 1965. Now he was back to meet a new Pope, whose motto, *Totus Tuus*, was taken from de Montfort. On the trip to Rome in 1979 Duff was accompanied by Concilium Officers James Cummins, Enda Dunleavy and Lily Lynch. On 10 May they attended the Pope's Mass in his private chapel and had breakfast afterwards with him. The Pope said to the legionaries, 'Victory comes through Mary.' It was a few weeks before Duff's ninetieth birthday. He took seriously the observation the Pope made to him to the effect 'You will be a young man until you are ninety.' On 7 June 1979, his ninetieth birthday, he was in Mount Melleray, where the monks invited him to plant a tree. The following September he was in the Phoenix Park to attend the Pope's Mass there and was one of those who received Communion from him. The next day the Pope travelled to Knock, where his visit coincided with the annual national Legion Pilgrimage to the Shrine. Although not in Knock himself, Duff's thoughts may well have gone back to the time in 1952 when he and Jack Nagle had taken the Knock documents to Rome.

On 1 April 1980 Duff gave his last talk at the Pauline Circle. The title was 'Julian Seeks to Confound Christianity by Rebuilding the Temple'. He delivered the same talk to the Pillar of Fire Society three weeks later. It was an optimistic talk in which he said that a springtime of renewal lay ahead for the Church. He continued to attend the monthly Pauline meetings, including the November meeting, which took place on the Tuesday before his death. In June he went as usual on the 'Whit' trip to Melleray. On the way back he went to Thurles on 7 June, his ninety-first birthday, to attend the ordination of Fr Michael Kennedy, who is currently parish priest in New Inn, Tipperary. Kennedy, who had been an unbeliever for a time, joined the Legion because a girl he knew was a member, regained his faith and went to Maynooth to study for the priesthood. There, he became the mainspring of a Legion revival and of the summer projects for young people, later called *Maria et Patria* (Mary and Nation). Fr Kennedy went to Russia a number of times on *Peregrinatio Pro Christo* projects with Fr Bradshaw and Fr Moriarty.

In October Duff gave his final public talk at the Hallowe'en *Peregrinatio Pro Christo* Conference. This talk merits attention because of its 'last testament' status. It is filled with optimism for the future of the Church. He said that the Church is only attractive to the extent that it is true, and it is only true to the extent that it has all its doctrines, and these in right proportion. He said that the proper role of Mary has a vital part in faith: 'To leave out Mary would be equivalent to altering its appearance and character to the degree that it would not be recognisable.'[17] In a few paragraphs he summarizes Mary's role as Mother of Christ and as co-operator with Him. He speaks of how Mary was brought into a close identity with the Holy Spirit, an identity which stops short of being absolute or of the Spirit becoming incarnate in Mary, because Mary remains completely human. Referring to St Paul's Letter to the Philippians, Duff points out that man is permitted to contribute to the maximum possible extent to the working out of his own salvation. In this arrangement Mary establishes the pattern. She is the New Eve. He then refers back to his discovery of Mary's role through the exposition of de Montfort. In the Legion there is a mechanism whereby ordinary people can work to bring Christ into the world. He refers to Paul VI's remark that what he liked best about the Legion was 'that it knew how to utilise the little people of the world'.[18] 'Pope John said something which is most precious of all, namely that the Legion of Mary presents the true face of the Catholic Church.'[19] It is not difficult to understand why Duff cherished this remark from the Pope, who had wished for the restoration of 'the face of the Church of Jesus Christ' that it had at its birth – the face of the Church being no less than the face of Christ.

Drawing on the observation that victory comes through Mary that John Paul II made to him in 1979, Duff went on to 'dream with Mary' of bringing the whole world to Her Son. But it was a dream firmly rooted in a method. He referred to a cover of *Maria Legionis* years earlier, which showed Mary in the midst of the Apostles at a planning meeting:

It endeavoured to depict something which must really have taken place. Unquestionably the Apostles met for that purpose of allocating districts for evangelisation, and just as certainly they had Our Lady in their midst. Before them lay some sort of map of the known world, the nearer parts probably accurate enough, the farther ones less so, varying from sketchiness into pure fantasy.[20]

He spoke of a meeting held a month earlier by the Peregrinatio committee and the Concilium officers at which they met around a statue of Mary and spent a full day ranging over many maps covering the entire world in deep and accurate detail. The minds of those present were absorbed by the thought of how to bring the Faith 'to three thousand five hundred million people who have not got it; while at the same time stirring up the five hundred million who have the Faith but who should have it better'. While a sceptic might regard this as sheer madness, Duff believed that the Legion provided a way to tackle the task. He told legionaries that 'Dreaming with Mary is the most solid of actions for she adds in the substance.' He urged them to 'think in terms of the apparently impossible' and concluded, 'Mary will make the dream come true.'[21] The Legion of Mary has as its keynote the aim of getting in touch with every man and woman, and doing so with the 'soft eyes' of Mary, never as 'judge or critic'.[22]

Duff appeared to be in good health in the late autumn of 1980 and was planning a short weekend cycle trip to Howth. He had treatment for a rodent ulcer on his forehead, but it did not pose a serious threat. At the start of November he confided to Michael McGuinness that he was concerned about his sight and that he had arranged an appointment for the following week with Dr David Mooney, the Dublin ophthalmologist whose father he had attended. He added that if he were to lose his sight, he did not know how he would manage, as he would be helpless between that and his deafness. It was a potential burden that he would not have to bear.

Duff's final day on earth on 7 November 1980 reveals his priorities in life. Having attended his regular morning Mass in Church Street, he then went to a second Mass at the funeral of Joan Cronin, a former Legion envoy. Fittingly, it was his friend and cycling companion Fr Herman Nolan who celebrated the funeral Mass and gave Holy Communion to Duff. Following the Mass he told Nolan that he felt unwell.[23] He was accompanied home to take a rest. He died in bed later in the afternoon. When Nellie Jessop, an indoor sister in the Regina Coeli Hostel, found him it was clear that he had only just died as his body was still warm. His eyes were directed towards the old-style picture of the Sacred Heart of Jesus that hung on the wall opposite his bed.

Fr Michael Ross, a Salesian priest, was in the Morning Star Hostel where he had just brought a homeless man whom he had encountered earlier at a City church. Ross was called to Duff's bedside and John Mulligan SJ, a former

Blackrock College man whose father had known Duff and who was parish priest in nearby Halston Street, came with oils to give the last rites. Dr John O'Leary, the GP who had treated Duff from time to time, certified his death and signed the death certificate. Fanagans, the Dublin undertakers, removed Duff's body to their funeral home in Aungier Street. In Fanagans, as Fr Herman observed, Duff's remains lay directly opposite the site in Whitefriar Street, where he had encountered Joseph Gabbett all those years before. Following preparation, the remains were returned to the chapel in the Regina Coeli Hostel to lie in an open coffin.

An item at the end of the evening news on Radio Telefís Éireann on Friday 7 November 1980 was the announcement of the death, in Dublin, earlier that day, of Frank Duff. Although the announcement followed that of the death of movie actor Steve McQueen, momentum built over the succeeding days as tributes flowed in from Ireland and around the world. Thousands filed past his coffin, often forming lengthy queues down into neighbouring Brunswick Street. Among those who came to pay their respects was the Taoiseach, Charles Haughey, whose sisters, Ethna and Maureen, were members of the Legion of Mary. Traffic in Dublin came to a halt as Duff's remains were removed to Westland Row on 12 November, five days after his death. The Auxiliary Bishop of Dublin, James Kavanagh, received the remains and was principal celebrant at the Mass which followed that evening. He said 'If ever a man went straight to Heaven, it is Frank Duff.' In the homily, preached by Canon Francis Ripley from Liverpool, he said, 'All who knew Frank Duff well regarded him as a saint.'[24] At the funeral Mass on 13 November the chief concelebrant, with three archbishops, ten bishops and thirty-five priests, was Cardinal Ó Fiaich.

> The President of Ireland was there, the government was there in force, members of the Dáil and Senate, the Lord Mayor of Dublin, dignitaries and celebrities of every sort, Protestant as well as Catholic – a former Anglican Primate among them – and a vast concourse of people … tens of thousands of ordinary 'common-or-garden' Dubliners lining prayerfully the footpaths, he was carried through the centre of the city and out to Glasnevin cemetery where he was buried in the family grave.[25]

The Irish Times reported that the 4,000 people who filled Westland Row Church for Duff's funeral Mass heard Cardinal Ó Fiaich say that he may be recognized by the Roman Catholic Church as 'the Irishman of the Century'. Ó Fiaich said that the Legion of Mary had been promoting the ideals of the Second Vatican Council for decades before the Council assembled; Duff had challenged complacency in the Church; he had been radical in stressing the role of lay people in the work of evangelization; he had given women a prominent role in the Legion. The cardinal described Duff as 'a man of personal charm, self-effacing modesty, absolute integrity and unshakable courage'.[26]

A telegram from Pope John Paul was read by the cardinal. In it the Pope said that the organization founded by Duff had made countless lay Catholics aware of their indispensable role in evangelization and sanctification and he imparted his blessing to all its members. In his 'Irishman's Diary' column in *The Irish Times*, Kevin Myers concluded: 'A final note. Dublin was paralyzed by the huge traffic jam resulting from Frank Duff's funeral. Allow him a small chuckle from the grave. At the age of 91, he spent his last summer on a cycling holiday around Ireland.'[27] Duff had planned a short trip with some friends around the Hill of Howth for 8 and 9 November 1980. When he died, his bicycle was in the hall downstairs and his packed bag was on the carrier ready for the planned departure the following morning.

Duff died intestate, an uncashed cheque for his civil service pension on a table in his house. His surviving relatives included his cousins Carmel Duff and Ivy Freehill. Ivy, a daughter of Eugene Freehill, was a member of the Church of England and headmistress of a school.

Notes to Chapter 22

1. See *John Feeney, Man and the Mask: John Charles McQuaid*. Dublin: Mercier Press, 1974, pp. 54–55 and John Cooney, *John Charles McQuaid*, 1999, p. 371.
2. Ó Broin, *Frank Duff*, p. 106.
3. ibid., p. 107.
4. Memorandum on the Legion of Mary by Archbishop McQuaid, transmitted to Cardinal Cicognani, 24 February 1966, LOM file, DDA.
5. Benelli to Duff, 26 November 1968.
6. Nan Cassidy was related to Bridget Cassidy, a sister of Duff's maternal grandfather, Michael Freehill.
7. Louis Smith, unsigned memo, but with covering letter to 'Mr Rush' dated 14 November 1999, ICOS archives.
8. Statement by Seamus Grace, 23 February 1977, ICOS archives.
9. Author's meeting with Professor Louis Smith, former Chairman of the Council, 18 January 2008.
10. O'Flynn to McQuaid, 21 April 1971, LOM file, DDA.
11. Duff to McQuaid, 22 December 1971, LOM file, DDA.
12. Bishops to Duff, 23 June 1971, LOM file, DDA.
13. Duff to Bishops of Ireland, 4 November 1971, LOM file, DDA.
14. McQuaid to Sensi, 11 October 1963, LOM file, DDA.
15. Duff to McGrath, 25 March, 1976.
16. Duff, *The Woman of Genesis*, pp. 516–18.
17. Frank Duff, 'Dream of Conquest with Mary', *Maria Legionis*, vol. 26, 1/1981, p. 3.
18. ibid., p. 4. Pope Paul's remark was made when, as Mgr Montini, he spoke to Joseph Walshe, Irish Ambassador to Rome. In a letter to Veronica O'Brien, 22 February 1952, Duff described Montini's remark as a 'very acute perception of the Legion'.
19. Pope John XXIII to the legionaries of France, 13 July 1960.
20. Duff, 'Dream of Conquest with Mary', p. 5.
21. Duff, 'Final Testament to the Legion', *Victory through Mary*, p. 519.
22. *Handbook*, p. 299.
23. Author's conversation with Fr Herman, 16 June 2008.
24. 'Final Tribute to Frank Duff', *The Universe*, 21 November 1980.
25. Ó Broin, *Frank Duff*, p. 123.
26. 'Thousands honour Frank Duff', *The Irish Times*, 14 November 1980.
27. ibid.

CHAPTER 23

To Walk the Common Path

'It is better … to walk the common path in an heroic manner.'

DUFF TO MARGARET DINTER, 1 JUNE 1949

At the meeting of the Concilium in November 1980, the first following Duff's death, a number of tributes were paid, including one by Fr Michael O'Carroll, who spoke of Frank Duff and priests. O'Carroll had known Duff since he was a young priest and was aware of his early difficulties with Church authorities in Dublin. He had first-hand experience of the closure of the Mercier and Pillar of Fire Societies. He pointed out that the very seminary system established by the Council of Trent to defend the Church in the post-Reformation period indirectly served to do two things which created roadblocks on the way of the lay apostolate: it tended to make the clergy into a caste and it segregated them in activity from lay people. Duff had provided a way to remove those roadblocks. His greatest insights, the bedrock ideas of the Legion of Mary and of Duff's life, centred on the unity of all baptized – priests and people – in the Church, the Mystical Body of Christ.

Frank Duff was a thinker who considered that 'It is our noblest privilege to think.'[1] He enjoyed applying his mind to problems, whether these concerned the exchange rate of the currency when he was in the Department of Finance or matters of Church teaching. He endeavoured to communicate his thoughts in the clearest possible manner, saying that he was encouraged to do this by some words of Archbishop McQuaid's, given in the *Handbook*: 'There cannot be in the Church's teaching an inner body of doctrine which only a few can grasp.'[2] The accuracy of McQuaid's statement was proved by the fact that countless legionaries, 'ordinary and even simple people, have completely grasped those ideas and made them food and fibre for their lives.'[3]

A believer in committed idealism, Duff maintained that 'Man is small but a man who is in earnest about an idea is not small. He is going to influence others, and nobody knows where that is going to end. Let our dominating idea be the glory of God and the salvation of souls.'[4] Duff's eyes were opened to the idea of Mary's role by his reading of de Montfort while he learned much about the Mystical Body of Christ from two other French writers, de la Taille and Olier. In an article entitled 'Thinking in Christ', he quotes Olier: 'The Christian is properly speaking Jesus Christ living in man.'[5] Duff then remarks, 'There is no more extraordinary idea than this one of the Mystical Body.' When the fullness of the idea of the Mystical Body dawned on him, he says that he was 'overwhelmed':

For long I did not realise that the Mystical Body represented a real union. I only connected it with that text of St. Matthew (25:47–50) where Our Lord declares that what is done to the afflicted ones is done to Him .... I was simply overwhelmed when the fullness of the truth dawned on me.[6]

Duff's earnestness about bringing Christ into people's lives was recognized when, on Wednesday 14 January 1998, the Tribunal for the Cause for his beatification, a necessary stage on the path to canonization or declaration of sainthood by the Church, was inaugurated by Archbishop (Cardinal) Desmond Connell on behalf of the Archdiocese of Dublin in Nazareth Hall at the Legion of Mary headquarters. The following were sworn in as members of the tribunal: Mgr Jerome Curtin as Episcopal delegate; Fr Joseph Moran, OP, Spiritual Director of the Concilium, as promoter of justice; Fr Bede McGregor, OP, vice-postulator of the cause; Ms Anna B O'Connor and Ms Ann McCawley as notaries. In the course of his homily during the Mass which preceded the inauguration of the tribunal, Archbishop Connell said:

We think of Frank Duff this evening; we think of the way in which he lived; we think of his vocation, the call that he received from God and how he responded to that, and we think of the extraordinary influence that he has had on earth, not just here, but throughout the entire world. We think of the way in which his work anticipated in many ways what was to become so central to the life of the Church, particularly since the Second Vatican Council and the great document of the laity *Christifideles Laici*.[7] And so, the example of Frank Duff is of great importance in the life of the Church and will be of importance for the future. In seeking to have him beatified and eventually canonised, we are, of course, anxious to see his work recognised; we are anxious to see his own great person recognised by the Church. But we are anxious also that the Church would give this particularly important endorsement to his creation, the Legion of Mary.[8]

The Catholic Church has its tests for sanctity: miracles are required, or martyrdom. Pending the judgement of the Church, what can be said of the spirit of Frank Duff? Such a question invites speculation, but it can also be approached in a practical way. How did Duff understand spirituality? How did he understand sanctity? What was his inner life? What was the character of the man? The word 'spirit' derives from the Latin '*spirare*' – to breathe – so that in seeking the 'spirit' of a person, one is seeking the essence of a person's life. An expert in Ignatian spirituality, Joseph Veale, SJ, writes:

I do not think St. Ignatius would be comfortable with either word in the phrase 'Ignatian Spirituality'. 'Spirituality', the word, is bloodless, often too self-conscious, artificial, cut off from the noises and smells of God's world. And as for 'Ignatian', well he would say that Christian teachers do not stand on their own. They take their place in the river of tradition and all they do is to try to live the gospel. There is one way – the Way, the Truth and the Life.[9]

At a time of searching, Ignatius spent almost a year (1523) in Manresa, where he lived by begging alms, taking on heavy penances and neglecting his appearance. By the end of his stay he had become absorbed in the desire to 'help souls'. To do that, Veale tells us, Ignatius 'needed to be ordinary, to be unremarkable'. So one of the first things he did was to wash. Then 'he cut his hair and his nails'.[10] That very practical matter of 'cutting' nails – on this occasion the toenails of the residents in the Morning Star Hostel – was recalled by a Jesuit priest, Fr Harry Naylor. Naylor, who had been born in Kenya with an Irish father and Syrian mother and had come to Dublin to study medicine in the Royal College of Surgeons, also recalled Duff's opposition to racial discrimination:

> Coming to Ireland on 17 March 1949, I got involved with the Legion of Mary, in Assumpta Praesidium, meeting in Dominic Street. Joining the College of Surgeons, we started St. Luke's Confraternity, and I was in the Morning Star Hostel on Wednesdays for tea and clipping toe nails until 8 pm. I often met Frank Duff. However, in September 1951 I joined the Jesuits, and came to Hong Kong in 1960 and have been here since … . I remember contacts with Jews and the Pillar of Fire. I started my Christian ecumenism work with the Legion. I was very much with Frank in the struggle against racial discrimination.[11]

That quality of ordinariness was significant to Duff because he insisted that the Legion of Mary was for the ordinary Catholic. He wrote, 'The Legion life is not a unique life, and it is not a heroic life; it is common Catholicity as God intended it and as the Church sees it, nothing more.'[12]

On 7 November 2000, the twentieth anniversary of his death, William Bridcutt, a Church of Ireland Minister and chaplain to Mountjoy Prison, read a paper to the Pauline Circle entitled 'Mr. Frank Duff: A Protestant looks at his writings.' At the outset Bridcutt described himself as someone who 'has been in debate with members of the Legion of Mary on an occasional basis over a period of about forty-five years'. Bridcutt emphasized Duff's desire to communicate with 'ordinary people' and to engage them in the work of the Church:

> Zeal, determination and single-mindedness shine through his writings. He had a firm and clear grasp of the teaching of his church which enabled him to teach ordinary people the essential points of difficult subjects. In a paper into which he obviously put a great deal of work (Mary and the Holy Spirit), he says, 'Have patience with me in this most difficult of tasks. I attempt what I have always tried to do, that is to reduce things to simplicity.' For a teacher to do this he needs to know his subject. 'What', he asks, 'would St. Francis Xavier think of you if he could have cast his vision forward to your time? … You represent something unthought of in his day, that is the entry of the

ordinary people into the direct working for souls.' Mr. Duff had great visions for the Legion using ordinary people.[13]

In his booklet *Can We Be Saints*? Duff focuses on the call of *everyone* to sanctity. He says that most people think of saints as people who do extraordinary penances and work miracles. But he maintains that neither is essential. Citing Newman as conveying the idea correctly, Duff says that a saint is one who, with the object of pleasing God, does his or her ordinary duties extraordinarily well. Such a life may be lived out without a single wonder in it, arouse little notice, be soon forgotten, and yet be the 'life of one of God's dearest friends'. He quotes Newman:

> If you ask me what you are to do in order to be perfect, I say, first do not lie in bed beyond the time of rising; give your first thoughts to God; make a good visit to the Blessed Sacrament; say the Angelus devoutly; eat and drink to God's glory; say the Rosary well; be recollected; keep out bad thoughts; make your evening meditation well; examine yourself daily; go to bed in good time, and you are already perfect.[14]

Duff prayed in a way which emphasized the ordinary daily chores of life:

> Oh, my God, I do not ask for the big things – the life of the missionary or the monk, or those others I see around me so full of accomplishment, I do not ask for any of these; but simply set my face to follow out unswervingly, untiringly, the common life which day to day stretches out before me … . And then to crown the rest, dear Jesus, I beg you to give me this, fidelity to the end, to be at my post when the final call comes, and to take my last, weary breath in your embrace. A valiant life and faithful to the end. A short wish, dearest Jesus, but it covers all.[15]

Duff frequently emphasized the potential heroism which lay in 'common tasks', for example, work in one of the Legion hostels. He noted that 'a glamour can attach to the more spectacular combats, and to martyrdom itself, which can assist us to bear them. But the daily facing of the cross of suffering and frustration, whose shadow stretches out through all the years ahead, can be truly what is called a white martyrdom.'[16] He expressed the same idea in a letter written in 1968 to a Sister of Mercy who had been reading lives of the Legion envoys Edel Quinn and Alfie Lambe. Duff wrote that Quinn and Lambe were 'typical of a very great number of others who have shone with almost equal lustre but of whom the world at large will never hear'.[17] He referred to the recent death of the president of the Regina Coeli Hostel praesidium, Annie Curran, known by her nickname 'Bonzo'. He said that in many ways her life paralleled that of Edel Quinn, 'save that one half-square mile might be said to have represented her sphere of living'.[18] In setting out how to fulfil the ambition to be 'one of God's dearest friends', Duff emphasized the quality of 'ordinariness' and an aversion to the seeking of special 'mystical experiences', saying that it was 'better to be without such things and to walk the common path in an heroic manner'.[19]

Writing on the 'interior life' in the *Handbook*, Duff says that this means that one's thoughts, desires and affections converge on the Lord and that the model for achieving this is Mary. The object of the interior life must be to reach the point where, like St Paul, the Christian can say, 'It is no longer I who live, but it is Christ who lives in me.' To discover the will of God in one's life involves receptive listening and constant prayer. According to Duff there are three interconnected requirements for a Christian life: prayer, mortification and sacraments. Both liturgical prayer and private prayer are ingredients of that life. Mortification may come through fulfilling certain penances, but it also comes from the loving acceptance of the crosses and disappointments of life.[20] He was conscious that strength of character developed from discipline in small ways, remarking 'Though character may be shown in the big moments, it is in the small moments that it is made.' Duff saw suffering as a source of power. To share in the life of Christ and His Mother included sharing in the suffering of their lives. He wrote:

> … if we do not share their lives we do not share their power. If you want to do a big work, you have to get down to the roots of grace. Ultimately this means the carrying of the cross and even the crucifixion. The thinking over and realising of these things is an all-important exercise for us. It is only in the measure that we understand what is taking place that we get full merit from the transaction. In the second place there is a very immense amount of consolation. One would imagine that if we fully realise what is taking place, we could be so consoled that we would hardly feel any pain at all. But that would be another matter, because the pain is intended and is part of the process. No amount of realisation will dispense us from that bearing of pain. But what it will do is to prevent that pain from crushing us. A meaningless affliction is almost beyond bearing.[21]

Duff regarded the Mass as the epicentre of the Christian life, agreeing with Newman that 'Nothing is so consoling, so piercing, so thrilling, so overcoming as the Mass.'[22] He compared presence at Mass with presence at the Last Supper and Calvary, but without its sight and sound, for an essential idea of the Mass is that it be 'an exercise of faith'. Duff was emphatic that it was faith, not emotion, which mattered:

> It is the supreme act of faith to attend Mass, and being a matter of faith, it is separate altogether from the emotions. Some people do feel emotion at Mass but the greater number do not. It is possible to assist at Mass in the most perfect manner and be cold as ice.[23]

As a young man Duff had been influenced by the classic work on prayer written by the French Jesuit Augustin Poulain, *Les Graces d'Oraison*, translated as *The Graces of Interior Prayer* in 1910. Poulain's work has been described as practical, down-to-earth and witty. Duff describes how the effect of reading Poulain was to make him wish to avoid any kind of out-of-the-way spiritual experience:

> When I was young I came across Poulain's book, *The Graces of Interior Prayer*. It was a marvellous study of the lives of those saints who were favoured with mystical experiences. The book showed that there was a very dangerous side to that sort of thing; that according as one penetrated into the supernatural world, one also encountered the evil powers, which reside in it. It required great holiness and expert direction to keep one safe in that territory. The reaction on myself was one of fervent petition that I would never be granted any of those special favours, because I doubted my capacity to deal with the accompanying dangers. That has remained my cast of mind throughout the years.[24]

In line with his wariness of such experiences, Duff wrote to a legionary in 1975 about what he described as a 'real peculiarity': 'The Catholic world at the moment is gone mad on the subject of apparitions. You would think that Catholicism consisted in believing in such and such an apparition and did not go further. A certain amount of that tendency is really leading people astray.'[25] Duff was a believer in the apparitions in Lourdes, yet he described how when he went there in 1928 he 'never felt so matter-of-fact in my life'.[26]

Among Duff's correspondents was an Austrian woman who raised the subject of special revelations. His reply was unequivocal, stressing that the wonderful thing about the Legion of Mary had been its 'freedom from all these visions and revelations of every kind'.[27] On another occasion, when the same woman wrote claiming that she had been in receipt of 'great favours' such as hearing words spoken to her by Our Lady, Duff replied, 'I have never had those sort of favours myself, nor do I desire to have them.'[28] On yet another occasion, in response to mention of 'manifestations of Our Lady', Duff wrote, 'The way of pure faith and darkness is a far better way, and certainly a safer way.'[29] He wrote in a similar vein to Veronica O'Brien, warning her to steer clear of 'voices and visions and wonders'.[30] He said 'The idea of the Legion is normal religion. It is intended for the ordinary man and woman.'

Nuns frequently wrote to Duff for insights into the spiritual life. His advice was to concentrate first and foremost on the Mass, the Office and the Rosary. In the 1960s he wrote to one nun that it was no part of God's policy to give us 'immersion in delights': 'Such would not be the way of faith but the way of emotion. The latter is a very perilous position to be in, because it sways backwards and forwards like a pendulum.'[31] Referring to his reading of the lives of the saints, he said:

> [The accounts of their] lives dwell upon the mountain peaks in their cases, i.e., favours, ecstasies, revelations, etc., which they have received. It should be remembered that these latter things were of rare occurrence. They definitely did not represent the

common tide of their lives. If you read the lives of, for instance, St. Vincent de Paul, St. Teresa of Avila, St. Francis de Sales, St. Rose of Lima, St. John of the Cross, de la Salle, Blessed Henry Suso, and indeed all the others – you will find that the great part of their life was spent in a sort of darkness and their biographers describe this darkness as infinitely worse than death. As a compensation for it and for the faith which they showed in that tunnel, immense things were granted to them.[32]

In reviewing a memorandum written by Sister Marie Celestine, a member of an enclosed Order of Nuns, on the subject of Edel Quinn, Duff remarked that there was 'a certain air of unreality about it all'. He said that it appeared to be written about someone 'who was leading a life apart from the general run of mankind … . But Edel was not living that sort of life, but very much the life of the world, thrown up against all the dire problems and difficulties.' He referred directly to the fact that her father 'continued with his betting tactics after they brought disaster upon the family'.[33] To overexaggerate the idea of penances or mortification 'would remove the pursuit of sanctity from this world altogether and make it the affair of angels!'[34]

The fact that Duff did not plunge headlong into any form of devotion is well illustrated by his initial reaction to de Montfort's *True Devotion*. However, when he eventually absorbed de Montfort, his spiritual landscape changed forever. The *True Devotion* is blended into the *Handbook* in an intimate manner with the Legion Promise to the Holy Spirit mirroring de Montfort's consecration to Mary. The *Legionary Promise*, the prayer recited by a legionary when he or she is enrolled as a member of the Legion of Mary, is addressed not to Mary, as perhaps might be expected, but to the Holy Spirit. Michael O'Carroll has pointed out that Duff's emphasis on the Holy Spirit was innovative at a time when the Holy Spirit was 'The Forgotten Paraclete' or 'Le Divin Méconnu'.[35] The Legionary Promise begins as follows:

Most Holy Spirit, desiring to be enrolled this day as a Legionary of Mary, yet knowing that of myself I cannot render worthy service, do ask of thee to come upon me and fill me with thyself, so that my poor acts may be sustained by thy power, and become an instrument of thy mighty purposes.[36]

If the influence of de Montfort was primary, the influence of Newman was also significant in regard to the role of the laity and as a source of insight into the role of Mary. In a letter written to Fr Nivard Flood in 1976, Duff wrote, 'I have always been profoundly affected throughout my life by the writings of Newman. I have read him extensively.'[37] Duff refers to Newman's judgement that 'In all times the laity have been the measure of the Catholic spirit.'[38] One of the problems confronting Newman on his journey into the Catholic Church was the position of Mary. In regard to certain Marian devotions he wrote, 'Such devotional manifestations in honour of Our Lady had been my great *crux* as regards Catholicism.'[39] Going back to the Early Church Fathers, Newman found that Mary was depicted there as the new Eve – an insight that helped Duff to understand her role.[40] In his *Meditations on Mary*, Newman says 'Mary is the *Virgo Praedicanda*, that is, the Virgin who is to be proclaimed, to be heralded, literally to be preached.' Compare this with the concluding paragraph of Duff's essay 'The New Eve':

> Virgo Praedicanda … is inadequately translated as Virgin most renowned. But Virgo Praedicanda means the Virgin who must be preached, which is a different idea … the full meaning of the expression is that we must announce her: the Virgin most great: this Virgin most essential: this co-operator in salvation both in its roots and in its fruits: the woman through whom our Lord came on earth and without whom He could not have come – the new Eve beside the New Adam.[41]

Duff's references to Newman extend to a range of subjects, including the relation of humour and religion.[42] In a letter written to Rudolf Buchberger in 1953, Duff paid this tribute: 'Newman was one of the very greatest figures who have ever stood on the stage of history. His progress into the Catholic Church was an epic.'[43]

Mary was the dynamic of Duff's life.[44] There is a line in a poem 'The Blessed Virgin as the Air that we Breathe' by the English Jesuit poet Gerard Manley Hopkins which captures the outlook of Duff regarding Mary. The line reads 'And men are meant to share her life as life doth air.'[45] Foremost of her qualities was her faith, which was realized as a service, an action, not a sentiment.

Questioned on one occasion about Edel Quinn, Duff said:

> She had a faith that did not shake. Without that foundation you would not have that special characteristic of devotion to Our Lady, whose own faith is singled out for praise in the Gospel … . Things like fear would naturally assert themselves in her. Why did they not carry her away as they do with most people? I suggest that in her case the ground was so drenched with the Holy Ghost that the sparks of temptation did not start a conflagration.[46]

Could there also be an autobiographical element in this insight about Edel Quinn? The opening article in Duff's first collection of essays, *The Spirit of the Legion of Mary*, published in 1956,[47] is entitled 'Faith'. He wrote that 'real faith does not mean an empty sentiment, but an action'. Real faith requires that one is prepared 'to lay down one's life, or be destroyed or ruined in some way or another, in the search for the interests of God'.[48] However, 'The best of us are trying to work with one foot in each world, by which I mean compromising the supernatural with the natural.'[49] In another essay he maintains that:

> The most serious evil which can menace anyone in life is that of having the natural swamp the supernatural. This is not merely a danger; it is almost inescapable. With the dawn of reason itself, down comes the visible, the sensible – that is the natural – on our soul like a great deluge. It proves too much for most of the children of Adam.[50]

Duff believed that with real faith any obstacle could be overcome. He prefaced his article on 'Faith' with the quotation 'With faith o'ercome the steeps Thy God has set for thee' from a poem by the nineteenth-century New England writer Rose Terry Cooke, who wrote about the lives of ordinary women, their dreams and fears, their triumphs and defeats. Duff believed that everyone possessed some element of faith in God. He told a number of friends of his experience as a young man aged twenty-four praying in a church in Dublin. For a fleeting moment he knew a total absence of faith and said that the void was so unbearable that he thought to end his life would bring relief. This led him to believe that there is some echo of faith in everyone, which helps to sustain us in being. Clinical depression, which in its most acute form can lead to a desire to end life, is a different matter, although he was well aware of depression and once remarked how 'everyone has a breaking point'. In a letter to a nun, he wrote that the greater part of his life had been spent in the condition of fatigue, not exactly of a nervous character, but 'just a complete tiredness caused by the incessant and depressing labours'.[51]

Duff encouraged others to recognize what he called 'the sign-language of faith'. He suggested that God gives indications as to what He wants us to do in our personal lives and in relation to others. Duff sought throughout his life to determine what God's plan was for him and to follow that plan regardless of the cost. Yet his approach was almost matter-of-fact:

> When I talk of guidance … I refer to the circumstances of life. All along these dictated my course in a manner which seemed to me to hardly admit any choice whatever. As to my state of life and the method of fulfilling it, these things always stood stark before me and drove me on. It did not appear even to be a case of coming to a fork in the road and having my course determined by the signpost. It was rather a case of coming to no fork at all, just having the highway to march along.[52]

In the chapter on legionary service in the *Handbook*, members are told that the Roman Legion from which the Legion of Mary takes its name was illustrious for loyalty, courage, discipline, endurance and success, and that for worldly purposes. The words of George Herbert are apt: 'How well her name an army doth present, In whom the Lord of Hosts did pitch his tent.'[53] Duff asks that legionaries 'put on the whole armour of God' (Eph. 6.11). With that foundation further virtues will develop, including generosity. The legionary must be prepared for sacrifice and to provide a counter-culture to secular values (Rom. 12.1–2). The legionary must not turn from toil and hardship (2 Cor. 11.27). The legionary must have courage, 'For courage is the soldierly, the Christian quality. It ranks first in the sense that it is the test of all the others.'[54] An entrepreneur, an administrator, Duff was a fighter. He once gave a Christmas present to a friend of a copy of Rembrandt's *Knight*, saying, 'You know I'm a fighter.'[55] Duff remarked to Fr Michael O'Carroll that if he were called before the Lord and asked to account for his life, he would not mention such facts as his daily prayer; rather that on occasion he had 'risked being blotted out' for the Lord.[56] He believed that legionaries should be prepared to bear persecution:

> Then if the Legionaries as a body show themselves able to stand up to any form of persecuting, they have already won the day. Because persecution cannot keep on persecuting indefinitely. If ever a saying were true it is that one of Terence McSwiney's: 'Not to him who can inflict most, but to him who can suffer most, will victory go.'[57]

Duff introduced a talk to legionaries on 'Fear' with a quotation from Sir Walter Raleigh, 'Fain would I climb, yet fear I to fall,' telling legionaries that 'Courage has become your profession.' He defined sanctity as 'heroic virtue, and heroism means the defying of fear … . Our Blessed Lord … specified the laying down of one's life as the acid-test of quality and love. Are you prepared to lay down your life for duty?'[58] Fear of every sort must be banished because of its 'blighting influence'.

Duff insisted that religion is a virile thing – a tough thing, in fact: 'Religion must be the toughest of things, and the people who are practising religion should be tough, essentially tough … . I cannot but feel that there is an overstressing in religion of the importance of sweetness, and that the impression exists that the strong things must yield to it.'[59] Duff refers to two saints – Paul and Jerome – as 'hot-tempered men, strong of temper and strong of speech'. He maintained that if we do not see the necessity of toughness 'then we are earning for religion the reputation of being a soft thing that only softies practise'. 'But', he asks, 'were you sent into this world to have a sort of sweetmeat existence?' Duff then presents Mary – the woman who stood at the foot of the Cross – as the model of courage, saying that the people are too inclined to think of Mary as just a 'sweet, amiable sort of person, possessing incredible sweetness and beauty and gentleness and love and all such delights'. But of all women, she was the most strong: 'She was the strong Woman. The Mary of the Gospel, the Queen of the Legion was no shrinking miss … . Do not let us misunderstand her.'[60]

Notes to Chapter 23

1. Duff, 'Thinking in Christ', reprinted in *Maria Legionis*, 1/2008.
2. Duff, 'Mary and the Holy Spirit', *The Woman of Genesis*, p. 74.
3. *Handbook*, p. 200.
4. Frank Duff, *Can We Be Saints*? 1958 edition, p.22. First published by the Catholic Truth Society.
5. ibid.
6. Duff, 'The Nun's Vocation', *The Woman of Genesis*, p. 507.
7. See Glossary.

8. Inauguration of the Diocesan Tribunal for the Cause of the Beatification of Frank Duff, *Maria Legionis*, vol. 41, 2/1998, p. 2.
9. Joseph Veale, 'Ignatian Spirituality' in Stephen Costello, (ed.), *The Search for Spirituality: Seven Paths within the Catholic Tradition*. Dublin: Liffey Press, 1982, chapter 7.
10. ibid., p. 7.
11. Henry Naylor, SJ, letter to author, 23 February 2003.
12. Frank Duff, 'Faith', *The Spirit of the Legion of Mary*. Glasgow: John S. Burns & Sons, 1956. First published in *Maria Legionis*, 1939.
13. Willie Bridcutt, 'Mr. Frank Duff: A Protestant Looks at his Writings', manuscript, 2000.
14. Duff, *Can We Be Saints*?, p. 2.
15. ibid.
16. Duff, 'I have suffered with him whom I saw suffer', *Virgo Praedicanda*, p. 114.
17. Duff to Sister Patrick, 13 April 1968.
18. ibid.
19. Duff to Margaret Dinter, 1 June 1949.
20. *Handbook*, p. 205.
21. Duff to Sister Noirin, 22 August 1972.
22. Duff to Dillon, Whitsuntide 1975. This letter was drawn to my attention by Phyllis McGuinness. The quotation is from Newman's novel *Loss and Gain*.
23. Duff to Sheila, 27 November 1975.
24. Duff to Sister Maria Joseph, 23 September 1976.
25. Duff to Bud, 6 November 1975.
26. Duff to Shaw, quoted in Ó Broin, *Frank Duff*, p. 41.
27. Duff to Dinter, 26 April 1949.
28. Duff to Dinter, 25 March 1949.
29. Duff to Dinter, 26 April 1949.
30. Duff to O'Brien, 12 March, 1949.
31. Duff to Sister Magdalena, 10 July 1968.
32. ibid.
33. Duff to Anselm Moynihan, 25 February 1966.
34. ibid.
35. O'Carroll, *A Priest in Changing Times*, p. 144.
36. *Handbook*, 1993, p. 90.
37. Duff to Father Flood, 11 May 1976.
38. ibid., p. 60.
39. John Henry Newman, *Apologia Pro Vita Sua*, p. 195. London: Longman, Green, Reader and Dyer, 1878, p. 195.
40. Duff, *The Woman of Genesis*, pp. 448–49.
41. Duff, 'The New Eve', *Mary Shall Reign*, p. 145.
42. Duff, 'Legion Humour', *The Woman of Genesis*, p. 165.
43. Duff to Rudolf Burchberger, 7 March 1953.
44. *Handbook*, p. 12.
45. Gerard Manley Hopkins, 'The Blessed Virgin as the air that we breathe'.
46. Aherne interview.
47. Glasgow, John Burns. The book was subsequently reprinted, with additional essays and an introduction by Fr Aedan McGrath, under the title *Walking with Mary*.
48. Duff, 'Faith', *The Spirit of the Legion of Mary*, p. 18.
49. ibid., p. 25.
50. Duff, 'Weigh the Thought', *The Spirit of the Legion of Mary*, p. 95.
51. Quoted in Bradshaw, *Frank Duff*, p. 188.
52. Quoted in O'Flynn, *Frank Duff*, pp. 21–22.
53. 'Anagram', *The Temple*, 1633. The title of the poem 'Anagram' signals that the letters of the name 'Mary' can be rearranged as 'army'.
54. Duff, 'Fear', *Victory through Mary*, p. 19.
55. O'Carroll, *A Priest in Changing Times*, p. 136.
56. ibid., p. 147.

57. Duff to McGrath, 3 May 1958.
58. Duff, 'Fear', *Walking With Mary*. Glasgow: J. S. Burns, 1958, pp. 35–36.
59. ibid., p. 36.
60. ibid., pp. 40–41.

CHAPTER 24

'He Crept into your Mind'

'He crept into your mind.'
FR HERMAN NOLAN, CP

In a world in thrall to celebrity and all that accompanies it, it is something of an enigma that a man of Duff's achievement appeared 'ordinary' to many who met him. Yet, given his insistence that the organization he founded represented ordinary Christianity for ordinary people, it is not an enigma at all. 'Authentic' is another word used to describe Duff. Authenticity was the quality that struck Archbishop Diarmuid Martin when Duff visited Clonliffe College in the 1960s when Martin was a student for the priesthood.[1] Martin recalled that there was nothing false about the man who arrived on his bicycle at the College to speak to him and his fellow deacons in the months prior to their ordination in 1969.

In his homily at the Thirtieth Anniversary Mass for Duff in Dublin's Pro-Cathedral in November 2010, Archbishop Martin asked his listeners to remember 'especially the tenacity of this outwardly retiring man: tenacity in reaching out unashamedly to bring the message of Jesus to people in the varied circumstances of their lives'.[2] He said that they had come together that day 'to thank God for the charism of Frank Duff: a charism recognised in a special way by the Second Vatican Council'. Duff's charism, or special gift of the Spirit, was to recognize the capacity of ordinary lay people to spread the Good News of the Gospel, and to create an organization whereby lay people and priests could together realize that apostolic capacity.

Louis McRedmond met Duff in Rome when he was a journalist reporting on the Second Vatican Council. He found in Duff an authenticity which reflected a likeable 'degree of innocence':

> I should add that I liked Frank very much, not least because of a degree of innocence, if that does not seem a strange thing to say. What I mean is that here was a distinguished Catholic layman prepared to trust a stranger, a newspaper reporter, with his reaction to topical happenings, apparently not worrying that he might be quoted and even misrepresented on foot of brief conversational comments. A journalist accustomed to often ill-disguised suspicion on the part of persons in public life values trust when he senses it even in casual conversation.[3]

Fr Herman Nolan summarized the unobtrusive aspect of Duff with the insight that 'The most striking thing was that he was not striking. He crept into your mind.'[4]

In the biography of the Jesuit priest who had been Duff's spiritual guide, Michael Browne, fellow Jesuit Thomas Hurley included an appreciation of Browne by Duff. Firstly, Duff found that Browne was a good listener, something which led Duff to encourage legionaries to become good listeners, and secondly, Browne believed in 'the spoonful of honey' approach rather than 'the barrel of vinegar'.[5] According to Duff, Browne 'struck the happy mean':

> He had the outlook of an ascetic and of a man of prayer, but he was always able to come down to ordinary things whenever it was necessary to do so, and he showed that he understood fully the difficulties which one meets in daily life, and he had a tremendous sense of humour … . Altogether he was a most lovable person. Then, his outlook was peculiarly broad and he showed complete sympathy with me and my difficulties. Sometimes I found it very hard to agree with his judgement, but I did obey him fully during all the time I had him as my spiritual director, and I have never regretted it. Subsequent events proved him to have been right in those doubtful cases.[6]

For many, their first encounter with Duff was when they heard him give a talk on some occasion or other. Sometimes the hearer would be unimpressed by Duff's delivery. The late Fr Martin Tierney thought that 'Frank was plain boring as a speaker. He was a man who usually spoke at length in a low unmodulated tone that demanded complete attention.' However, a sentence of Duff's from the first time Tierney heard him speak remained embedded in his mind for more than forty years. It was Duff's claim that 'We are all called to be saints.' To Tierney, it seemed a preposterous vision for an ordinary person to strive to be a saint, but he heard Duff say the same thing many times and thought 'it had the ring of truth'.[7]

Another who judged Duff's delivery on the dull side is retired civil servant Liam Ó Maolcatha, who joined the Legion as a student in University College Cork in 1939 and has completed over seventy years membership of the Legion. He recalls that his reaction to hearing Duff speak in UCC in the early 1940s was that he was a mediocre speaker.[8] But if Duff's delivery seemed boring to some, the content was the opposite. Historian Dr Margaret MacCurtain, also a member of the Legion of Mary at UCC, can remember sixty years after the event a talk Duff gave in 1949 on the 'The Providence of God'. She recalled a reference to Darwin and the fact that Duff mentioned the interdependence of every species on the planet. She said that 'he had all the time in the world' for the students who wished to speak to him after the lecture.

Duff sometimes expressed fearfulness and stage fright in relation to giving talks, something which echoed back to his Blackrock College days when he cried off taking a role in a school production.[9] On one occasion when the late

Patty Kavanagh congratulated him following what she regarded as 'an inspired talk', he replied that 'Before I give a talk, my knees are knocking.'[10]

In contrast to those impressed by his 'ordinariness', there were those who felt the special impact of his presence from the first encounter. Mary McAndrew, a talented artist and former pupil of George Collie, RHA, joined the Legion as a schoolgirl in Eccles Street in 1940 and has maintained unbroken membership for seventy years. She recalled that the first time she met Duff was on a bus to Mount Melleray in 1962 when Muriel Wailes introduced them. McAndrew said simply that 'he made an impact'; that he had 'great tranquillity and the loveliest expression'. She got to know him well over the succeeding eighteen years, becoming a member of his cycling parties and being one of those who helped with his personal typing.[11] She also came to realize that he was 'a determined character'.

Duff's determination was evident in the schoolboy who made the arduous round trip of just under 16 miles or 26 kilometres from Drumcondra to Blackrock College cycling for about two hours daily in all weathers; it was evident in the 25-year-old who completed a cycle of 155 miles in one day and in the 60-year-old man who cycled from Cork to Dublin in one day against the pleading of a doctor he encountered on a brief stop over 20 miles from Dublin. It was evident in the 75-year-old who attended the Second Vatican Council in the wake of a serious illness and in the 91-year-old who persisted in daily Mass attendance to the day he died. Fr Robert Bradshaw and Celia Shaw were among those who observed his determination in relation to prayer. Shaw said that she could never understand how Duff was able to complete the recitation of the Divine Office at the end of even the most exhausting day. Bradshaw attributed this capacity to 'a fierce determination'.[12]

Duff's determination was accompanied by a belief in the necessity of a planned approach to achieve goals. He regarded planning as 'the determination to succeed, to improve' and the antithesis of 'veiled chaos'. A plan is 'thinking on paper'.[13] Time must be given to the preparation of a plan with provision made for everything required to achieve the objective. 'In order to accomplish that we must sit down for a definite session of thought.' He also recommended that:

> It's good to have a reserve plan, or alternative features, to provide for the possibility of your Number 1 going a little astray. You will realise that the very best effort at planning is guessing, to a large extent .... So our guesses are not going to be infallible. If guessing was infallible, betting would be a very profitable pursuit.[14]

Duff believed that personal contact was paramount. He wrote 'The secret of all success with others lies in the establishment of personal contact, the contact of love and sympathy. This love must be more than an appearance. It must be able to stand up to the tests that real friendship can bear.'[15] His personal influence was observed by many, including Fr O'Carroll, who wrote, 'Again and again I have noted how people of character were mentally moulded and morally motivated by him.'[16] A remarkable example concerns the case of Mary Phelps. Phelps, who grew up in Indiana, joined the Legion at the age of eighteen. She worked as a secretary at Notre Dame University and then for Mgr Fulton Sheen at the Catholic University in Washington. With a group of legionaries, she went on a trip to Dublin, where she met Frank Duff. Expressing a yearning to do more in the Legion, Duff suggested to her to 'Go to Philadelphia. There's a great need there.' And so she did. She married Bill Peffley, also a legionary, and a Legion family was born. The Peffleys, who have run a Catholic bookstore for fifty years, have seen the number of legionaries in Philadelphia grow to 2,500 active members and 18,000 auxiliaries. They have three children, Natia, Fran (Francis), called after Frank Duff, and Edel. The two girls met their husbands through the Legion, while Fran was ordained a priest in the Arlington Diocese in 1990. He serves there as Spiritual Director of the diocesan council of the Legion of Mary.

Just as he had been 'captivated' by Gabbett, Duff 'captivated' others – men and women. His approach was sympathetic rather than stern. He remarked that 'The flower that would have opened under the influence of the gentle warmth of softness and compassion closes tightly in the colder air.'[17] Síle ní Chochláin said that what struck her about Duff 'was the interest and care he took with each individual he met. He was a man of wisdom, he could be forthright in manner; he was kind, practical and had a wonderful sense of humour.'[18]

Any attempt to capture Duff's character would be deficient if it did not include the value he placed on humour. He described humour as a 'wonderful balancer'.[19] He believed that the note of Catholicism should be an 'easy joyousness', in contrast to the note of Puritanism which is one of 'grim repression'. The schoolboy who wrote to the *Freeman's Journal* in 1906 was still in evidence fifty-five years later when he consulted a friend about the regalia associated with the papal knighthood he had been awarded. He said that he had no objection to 'wearing a sword, at least occasionally', but that certain aspects of his case were exceptional:

> I understand that I am the only living specimen of a Grand Officer of the ancient and pious Order of St Gregory the Great who goes around on a bike … . It will be realised that if I allow it [the sword] to dangle in the conventional manner from a sword-belt there is the greatest possible danger that it may entangle itself in the spokes with the result that there would be no longer any existing specimen of a Grand Officer who is going around on a bike. Is it permissible therefore to carry the sword on an ordinary spring carrier?[20]

Duff got up to tricks at times. On one occasion when the Chinese Legion envoy, Teresa Su, sent Christmas cards to the Concilium officers, Duff intercepted the card to Jimmy Cummins, then unmarried and of a certain age. Duff had an inscription in Chinese inserted into the card and a typed note was added 'Dear Brother Cummins, I have learn [*sic*] that you have a girl in every Curia. Please may I be your girl for China?' Jimmy was delighted, wondered what the Chinese inscription signified and sought the aid of a priest who knew Chinese. The priest suggested that Chinese characters could cover a range of meanings, so that, while the characters at face value meant 'Legion of Mary', there could also be a hidden reference, which Duff was quick to propose might be a reference to St Augustine's 'Love, and do what you will,' which Jimmy seemed eager to believe. Some time later there was a party for Jimmy, who had decided to try his vocation at the Beda, the seminary for late vocations in Rome. Duff recounted the episode. Jimmy was reduced to such thoughtful silence that Duff was led to speculate on what might have been his response to the unsuspecting Teresa Su. There was a happy ending for Jimmy when he left the Beda and later married the accomplished London legionary Doreen Schooling.

Another example of Duff's inventiveness in the land of tricks concerned the collection of used postage stamps. Saving stamps for the 'Missions' was a constant practice at the Concilium office. For the purpose Duff obtained a box and cut two holes in it marking one hole 'Large Stamps' and the other 'Small Stamps'. He enjoyed seeing people carefully cut and segregate stamps before putting them into the slots. Then one night on the bus home to Donnybrook, Mary Rowe said to Eileen O'Connor, who was in the know: 'Frank needs to have his head examined. All those stamps go into the one box.'

Frank Duff stressed the need to have respect for others including respect for their customs and culture. He made the following telling observation to a legionary working in the Middle East in 1958:

> That is a very convincing incident which you cite where the Nuns were expelled because they would not grant a holiday to the children in connection with the Arab Republic. They deserve to be expelled in these circumstances. How can people expect to make conversions in a country if all the time they are thwarting and despising the national aspirations of that people! To remain 'foreign' in a country is to fail as Missionaries.[21]

Duff's work in the Mercier and Pillar of Fire Societies provided abundant evidence of his respect for those who did not espouse Roman Catholic beliefs and his desire to build a forum for 'mutual understanding'. In a letter to Fr Aedan McGrath he wrote that one should never allow aggressiveness to develop even when under attack.[22] When a nun wrote to him from Port Harcourt in Nigeria in 1946 expressing anxiety regarding one of her brothers who had left the priesthood, he warned of the danger of trying to force her brother in any way, saying that 'The very essence of successful apostleship lies in this gentle approach to people.'[23] Two years later, he urged 'judicious gentleness'. 'Refrain from forcing, refrain from preaching.'[24] Later in the same year he urged that the nun's parents should give their son sympathy and understanding: 'He is their child .... Even if the whole world turns against a man, his own parents should not.' Twenty years later, Duff was still in correspondence with Sister Jarlath, who was then based in Nigeria. He continued to write to her in positive terms about her brother.[25]

Duff regarded patience as of special importance in dealing with the mentally ill and advised against overdosing them with religion: 'Do not deluge them with religion. But do not leave it out either.'[26] He made the challenging observation, 'An intriguing thought is that one of the charges hurled against Our Lord frequently was that He was mad.' He urged legionaries to think of the words which the Church applies to Mary: 'For the memory of me is sweeter than honey, and the possession of me sweeter than the honeycomb' (Sir: 24.20).

Duff showed great interest in any personal aspects of an individual's life which might be a source of worry to him or her and he frequently proposed a line of action. In correspondence with Michael Ekeng, who suffered from piles, Duff said he was sorry to read that Ekeng's 'old enemy – the piles – have returned' and urged him to seek attention in one of the hospitals and not to 'let the ailment drift too far, least it might become chronic'.[27] In a letter to Alfie Lambe, Duff expresses concern on hearing that Alfie was having a tooth extracted. He urges caution, asking if it were not possible to restore the tooth through filling, saying that he had at that point retained all his own teeth through a regime of care and contrary to his dentist's leaning towards extraction.[28] In 1960, when Fr Aedan McGrath was working in London, Duff asked him if he could get some Rhinitol for Dr O'Connell, the Secretary to the Archbishop, who was suffering from nasal catarrh. He remarked: 'This remedy is not available in Ireland. If you could buy a few bottles of it and have them conveyed over here by the first Columban [priest] who is travelling, I would be grateful. But I make this stipulation that payment must pass in respect of the transaction.'[29]

Dr Michael McGuinness observed that Duff was very interested in medicine and often talked to him about medical matters. But it was not just the medical problems of persons that concerned Duff; he was interested in every aspect of their lives. On one occasion, when writing to a Canadian legionary, he ended his letter by asking, 'How is that wine-coloured dress doing?'[30] And in a letter to Edel Quinn, who had mentioned that her typewriter was being repaired, he asked, 'Is this the one and only Baby Empire? What thoughts of pleasant days that brings back, when we were searching all over the place for that little machine, and doing all that other buying on the eve of the start of your momentous trip.'[31]

When a question was put to Duff or a problem was raised with him, he never simply issued instructions – he gave reasons for his response. A case in point concerned an overseas correspondent who wrote to him regarding the immodesty of certain women's fashions. The correspondent wanted the Legion to take some definite attitude on the matter. Duff declined, saying that no two persons would be found to agree on precisely what constituted immodest dress. Furthermore, he said the Legion was an organization of men and women and both must be considered:

> If the Legion allowed itself to be drawn into a situation where it was prescribing the precise length of a skirt which constituted modesty, and also as to the amount of neck that could be legitimately exposed – the Legion would become an absolute mockery, and the immediate consequence of this would be that all the men would clear out.[32]

When a Limerick woman wrote to him deploring the wearing of trousers by women and quoted the Book of Deuteronomy in support of her complaint, Duff disagreed, saying that the prescriptions of Deuteronomy would not apply today, and that the Church had abolished many of the old observances. Probably to the surprise of his correspondent, he said 'There is no more decent garb than trousers,' arguing that they provided a favourable contrast to 'extra short skirts'![33] On another occasion in the 1950s a nun wrote suggesting that women members of the Legion should wear hats at Legion functions as a mark of respect. Duff took trouble to explain why he disagreed firmly with her proposal, supplying a number of reasons, including the following decisive one:

> Bedrooms are usually provided with an abundance of pictures or statues. Therefore if we want to exhibit proper respect towards those objects, should women not wear their hats in bed? … Do not let us do anything that will win for religion the reputation of being narrow or of interfering with the ordinary course of proper life or of being puritanical in any way.[34]

Sometimes instances would be cited to Duff of 'indiscretions' of legionaries and no doubt such may be the case in any large organization from time to time. A common accusation was that legionaries, contrary to correct Legion practice, were asking people 'if they were saying their prayers'. When a statement of such kind was made, Duff would first seek to establish whether it was from personal experience or some third party. It was frequently found that this particular problem arose in relation to recruiting auxiliary members. Auxiliary Legion members do not undertake active work but rather undertake to say certain prayers daily, including the Rosary. An active legionary might check with potential auxiliary members whether they already recited the daily Rosary, in which case it would not be necessary to recite an additional daily Rosary as 'they were already saying one'.[35] Or a legionary might enquire whether, after a trial period of three months, an auxiliary wished to be placed on the auxiliary roll, clearly signifying commitment to say the required prayers daily.

Duff was a man for whom family and friends were of the greatest importance. Not long before he died, he arranged for the family grave in Glasnevin to be tidied and for the names of all the members of his family to be inscribed on the headstone. It was as though he wished to keep all the members of the family together, although his sister, Geraldine, is not buried in Glasnevin, but in Navan, alongside her husband, Vincent Monahan.[36]

In a handwritten note on a slip of old paper Duff wrote: 'There is no happiness like that of Friendship.'[37] Duff once remarked to Fr Bradshaw how at every time in his life 'I always had some special friend.'[38] At school there was Michael Davitt; in the civil service he was close to Jack O'Callaghan, Ulick McNally, John Leydon, León Ó Broin and Seán Moynihan. In the Vincent de Paul, Joseph Glynn and Matt Lalor were friends and mentors. Joseph Gabbett had a special place in his affections, as did Fathers Browne, Toher and Creedon. Over the years in the Legion there was Celia Shaw and Edel Quinn, Jimmy Cummins, Jack Nagle and Tom Doyle, Fr Herman Nolan and the other members of his cycling group, the 'Sprockets', so called after the wheel with teeth around which the chain rotates in bicycles.

Duff had a special affection for the late Davy Munro, his wife Mary and their family, for Michael and Phyllis McGuinness and Marie and Enda Dunleavy and their families. Such was the reality of Duff's friendships that they have entered the world of fiction. In her Booker Prize-winning novel *The Gathering*, Anne Enright tells of Frank Duff 'with the Milk Tray' (chocolates) calling to visit grandmother Ada Merriman at Christmas time in 1967. In the novel, Enright describes Duff as 'this dotey, clever man' who in 1925 when 'Ada met Charlie … was engaged in the Legion of Mary's first, great work'. He 'was talking girls out of brothels, and buying off their madams'.[39]

Duff had many friends who were not Catholics. To quote an *Irish Times* writer, 'He has many friends outside his own communion, for, though he would like everyone to be of his own faith, he would be horrified at the thought of offending any man's freedom of conscience.'[40] Duff was particularly close to children. In turn, children responded to him with trust. Typical would be the attitude of Susan McGuinness, daughter of Phyllis and Michael McGuinness, when as a young child she reacted to the news of Duff's death by saying 'He was my friend.' Over fifty years ago, in a talk to parents which showed deep insight into the mind of the child, Duff insisted, 'From the start you must treat them [your children] seriously as persons, respect them, even reverence them.'[41] He said that a child must be given 'real proofs' of parental love – sympathy, interest and respect. No child would flower in an atmosphere of fault-finding and criticism.

On a visit to my home in the 1970s Duff noticed that items in a toy carpentry set belonging to my eldest son, as well as a small wooden deer, were damaged. He insisted on taking them with him in order to repair them. Some days later the late Lelia Carroll, a legionary who lived nearby, arrived with a package containing the items and a letter in Duff's handwriting. The letter included the following:

> Here are the mended articles. The hammer and the saw are much stronger than when new. It will be interesting to see how long they last!
>
> One of the ears of the deer is missing. It seems to be a new break, so that you may have the pieces somewhere.
>
> The base is not even so that the deer tends to fall. If you pasted some paper or cloth along the side of the base, it would make things safe.[42]

The Legion has always encouraged a social dimension to its activities – the Legion 'cup of tea' captures the essence of this. Following Legion meetings, legionaries often gather together for a cup of tea and informal chat. The 'tea break' mid-way through a Patrician meeting is an essential and important feature which caters for the aspect of social contact. Duff encouraged Legion holidays and cycling trips, and indeed other forms of entertainment, including operettas. From his first visit to Melleray in 1919 the practice grew of an annual trip there timed to coincide with the Whit Bank Holiday weekend. Mary McAndrew has vivid memories of the Melleray trips. Sometimes on sunny afternoons the group would sit in the sunshine in 'Bradshaw Field', so called after Fr Bradshaw, and they would entertain each other. McAndrew recalled how Duff once held the group spellbound with Brer Rabbit stories. He had a fondness for Afro-American tales of the Old Plantation, perhaps not politically correct today, using the term 'a Brer Rabbit solution' in his correspondence on one occasion to signify 'lying low and saying nothing'.[43]

Duff also enjoyed music and in the course of one particularly wet week in Melleray cooperated with other legionaries to compose a Legion Operetta called *Hanratty* into which the composers introduced many of Duff's favourite airs from Gilbert and Sullivan. His own 'party pieces' were 'My Old Shako' and 'The Little Tin Soldier', sung with varying degrees of gusto and pathos as called for. The former is an old soldier song named after the tall cylindrical military cap which often boasts a plume or a tassel. The chorus lines are:

> We roamed along together, you and I, my old shako!
> And here's a health to all the pretty girls we used to know
> Ten, twenty, thirty, forty, fifty years ago!

Dick Dunne, a legionary, a first-class clarinet player and brother of the conductor Proinsias Ó Duinn, had many exchanges with Duff in regard to music. He said that Duff was ever anxious to align development in the spiritual life with the development of natural talent. Dunne often brought his clarinet to Legion reunions and on one occasion Duff told him that he was anxious to improve the standard of entertainment at these. A number of gatherings were held in the 1970s, sometimes in Duff's house, to discuss how standards might be improved. Dunne had a talent for aligning words with melodies; for example, he took the Concluding Prayer of the Legion and put it to music from Wagner's *Tannhauser*, 'O Star of Eve', and Gounod's *Faust*'s 'Soldier's Chorus'.[44] Dunne also helped Duff and other legionaries in the production of an opera called *Moscow Moments*. The sentimental storyline centred on a medal of Mary falling into the printing press at *Pravda* and appearing in all the newspapers on that day. The idea seems to have come from Duff, whom Dunne described as 'a Romantic, if not a Surrealist'.[45]

Cycling holidays had a regenerative effect on Duff in helping him to return to the grind of his everyday life. In 1957 the first cycling holiday to include women took place. Eileen Sheehy and Una Twomey went, before embarking on envoyships to French West and Equatorial Africa and Bolivia respectively. The other women participants were Muriel Wailes and Eileen O'Connor. Muriel Wailes was known to complain that Duff might bring them on long cycles before breakfast to find a country church with morning Mass. This difficulty was solved in 1968 when Fr Herman Nolan became a regular member of the cycling party.

Nolan recalled an occasion in November1969 when Duff, then aged eighty-one years and five months, said to him, 'Before we go into the dark tunnel of winter, would you be ready for another fling? Any chance you could get off Confessions and I'll meet you at Westland Row?' Nolan remembered that there was heavy rain during their weekend trip, but Duff persisted. They crossed the mountains close to Lugnacoille and despite an injured knee got to Donard, where he discussed the making of the film the *Blue Max*, which had been filmed in the vicinity. Nolan remarked, 'You could not help following Frank.'[46]

A second pastime Duff developed alongside cycling was that of photography employing a Leica camera. His interest in photography went back to his schooldays and even further back to his grandfather, Michael Freehill. He began to take pictures in the course of his summer cycling holidays and in the autumn he would revive memories of the trips by having a 'slide show' for his friends. Duff loved beauty both in its natural and in its material manifestation. His fondness of natural beauty was deep, whether of the Boyne Valley or of Connemara. Surveying some particular scene, a legionary remarked on the appropriateness of the Canticle of Daniel, and Duff replied that it was his 'favourite psalm'.[47]

Duff also appreciated material beauty. There are many examples of the care he took in regard to artistic design. The stained glass panels above the entrance door to the Morning Star and Regina Coeli hostels came from the Harry Clarke studio. The minutes for the Regina Coeli in 1929 record: 'Mr Clarke took a great interest in it when he heard of the objective of the Regina Coeli.'[48] Illustrations by the artist Richard King sometimes appeared in *Maria Legionis*, starting with a picture of St Michael the Archangel in 1935. An illustration by King is used on the cover of the Concilium Bulletin. Onyx was Duff's preferred stone and it forms the base of the Vexillum. He went to trouble with the execution of the Sanctuary Lamp in the Regina Coeli, which was fashioned by the firm of Dingleys in England which had also made the Vexillum.[49] Special drawings were obtained for the design and the lamp was presented by Mr Sullivan of Shrewsbury Road.[50] In the early 1950s, Duff commissioned the woodcarver John Haugh, who had recently exhibited at the Brown Thomas Little Theatre, to make a set of Stations of the Cross for the oratory in the Regina Coeli. Duff helped to procure cherrywood for the purpose from trees grown in Cong, Co. Mayo by the Department of Forestry. When it came to making a tabernacle for the chapel in the Morning Star Hostel, Fr Herman recalled visits to O'Neill's marble works on the Ballyogen Road to acquire the right material. In the course of one visit, Duff remarked: 'You know, Fr Herman, I always had a weakness for the perfect thing.'[51]

If Duff encouraged and welcomed social activities, he was also a man who was happy on his own with a book. He read extensively, ranging beyond the spiritual classics and religious subjects to history and science, with which he had a fascination, to detective stories. His collection of books includes a large number of the last, especially by favourite writers Rex Stout and Erle Stanley Gardner, together with books on scientific and educational themes, including Maria Montessori's *The Child in the Church*, edited by E. M. Standing. Duff regarded *Time* magazine useful for highlighting in a concise way many developments worldwide and he had a regular subscription to *National Geographic*. He had a particular interest in reading about those who travelled to remote areas of the world in pursuit of science, like Wallace and Darwin. Explorers who endured hardships appealed to his sense of adventure and he sometimes drew on their example as an ideal for legion envoys.

Duff believed in the 'Economy of Salvation' – everything had to be paid for, and that extended down to the smallest material items. Fr Herman recalled a number of times when Duff put this belief into practice. Duff had a good racing bicycle, but preferred the old-fashioned style of high handlebars. On a mission to Joe Daly's shop in Dundrum to collect a set of handlebars, Daly did not wish to make a charge, but Duff insisted on paying for them. On another occasion, not many years before his death, Duff was on a cycling trip in Kerry where, close to Tarbert, he collapsed and was taken into a nearby cottage, where the elderly woman of the house put him sitting in a súgan chair. A passing driver with van and trailer was asked to take Duff back to the B&B where he and the cycling group were staying. He spoke to Fr Herman about making a payment to the Good Samaritan and when he heard that Herman had already made a payment insisted on refunding Herman. Gratitude was another feature of his character. His letters are filled with expressions of gratitude to priests, legionaries, friends and anyone who offered support for the Legion, material, spiritual or of any kind, no matter how apparently small.

Like every human being, Duff was not without faults. He had a temper, which he generally managed to keep under firm control.[52] Mary Duffy, the first Legion envoy, is reputed to have said that Duff's saintliness resided in the constant struggle to control his temper. In a letter to Celia Shaw referring to an earlier disagreement, he admitted to ill temper, saying:

> I felt it was I who was the guilty party in giving way to ill temper. I never believed for a moment that you were attacking me. You simply stumbled upon one of my many weak points that I am unable to stand up with equanimity to persistent contradiction … . This is something that you and I should be careful about. We are both very unpleasantly obstinate.'[53]

According to Fr Herman, Duff 'could fight with women'. For example, on bicycle trips he would occasionally have quite strenuous arguments with Muriel Wailes. Mary McAndrew recalled one such row. Arriving late one evening at a B&B, it transpired that Wailes, who had been responsible for making the reservations, had failed to make them. According to McAndrew, Duff was livid – he became taut and was 'grinding his teeth'.[54]

While 'falling-outs' occurred, so too did reconciliations. Fr Herman was particularly pleased that on the occasion of Joan Cronin's funeral, the day of his death, Duff shook hands with Harry O'Carroll, a legionary with whom he had had a long-running difference regarding the *Handbook*. Likewise, Tadhg McMahon, who had disagreed with Duff over Viatores Christi, recalled how Duff walked over to him and shook hands after the same funeral Mass.[55] Duff's general approach was to look for the good in people. In *Can We Be Saints*? he expressed the belief that the secret of all real influence is affection. In seeking to influence others, he suggested a simple rule: 'Look only for good qualities in anyone you meet; you will find them. Never look for faults, for you will find them.' It is significant that the final chapter of the *Handbook* is a reflection on the relevance for the Legion of Mary of St Paul's great letter to the Corinthians on the character of love (1 Cor. 13.1–8). In his opening address to the Priests'

Conference, referred to earlier, Dr Diarmuid Martin remarked that major work in the Church by personages such as Duff is dependent on spiritual roots embedded in that person. Fr Herman observed that Duff was 'assiduous at prayer' and recalled seeing him late at night in the Gallery at Mount Melleray, reading his Office. Fr Nivard Flood, a Cistercian, had similar memories. Speaking of the regular visits by Duff and legionaries to Mount Melleray at Whitsuntide (Pentecost), he said that his clearest memory of Duff's visits was seeing him 'wrapped in prayer for long hours, when from the Guests' section in the Abbey church, he assisted at the Office of Matins and Lauds, followed afterwards by two rounds of private Masses'.[56]

It is fitting to leave the last words on the supernatural to Duff – words from a talk that he gave to deacons in Thurles seminary, County Tipperary:

> Now perhaps you will forgive me for being personal. I absolutely hate it, but if I am not to talk to you to some extent out of my own background, I have really no other claim to address words to you at all. I am not a professor of religion, and I'm certainly no *peritus* in that department. The only thing which I have to point to is considerable experience. Therefore willy-nilly, I have to refer to it ... .
>
> I have believed intensely in the spiritual order and I have never sacrificed it to the other. I have said the Divine Office since 1917 without missing a single day or a single hour, and think I could say, a single line of it. Likewise I have said daily the Rosary and the Seven Dolours. I have never missed daily Mass in that time, except in circumstances of absolute physical inability.
>
> It is my conviction that anything useful which has come along has proceeded from that stressing of the purely supernatural. I think it meant that I was depending on the Lord and his mother, and not on myself. I would say that one important result followed: that I was saved from vulgar pride. When there was development I was not tempted to ascribe it to my own abilities. Of course, one has to pay a price as well, the Christian price of torment and suffering. If unwilling to face up to that, avoid the priesthood.
>
> Next we come to the question of Our Lady. She is completely indispensable.[57]

Notes to Chapter 24

1. Dairmuid Martin, Opening Address, Priests' Conference held at the Emmaus Centre, Swords in County Dublin, May 2007.
2. Diarmuid Martin, 'Through Him the Lord Worked Great Things'. *Irish Catholic*, 25 November 2010.
3. McRedmond to author, 30 October 2008.
4. Author's interview with Nolan, 23 November 2007.
5. Hurley, *Father Michael Browne*, p. 232.
6. ibid. pp. 195–97.
7. Martin Tierney, 'We are all called to be Saints', *The Irish Catholic*, 27 December 2007.
8. Conversation with author, 10 December 2007.
9. See Chapter 2.
10. Meeting with the late Patty Kavanagh, 26 January 2008.
11. Interview with Mary McAndrew, 21 February 2008.

12. Discussion between Bradshaw and Shaw, tape 110, LOMA.
13. Duff, 'Planning' tape 71a, LOMA.
14. Duff, 'Good Planning', tape 14b, LOMA.
15. *Handbook*, p. 15.
16. O'Carroll, *A Priest in Changing Times*, p. 143.
17. *Handbook*, p. 281
18. Special supplement to the *Irish Catholic*, 31 October 2002.
19. Duff, 'Legion Humour', *The Woman of Genesis*, p. 165.
20. Duff to Bernard, 12 December 1961.
21. Duff to Andy, 5 May 1958.
22. Duff to McGrath, 3 May 1958.
23. Duff to Sister Jarlath, 21 November 1946.
24. Duff to Sister Jarlath, 23 January 1948.
25. Duff to Jarlath, 9 September 1967.
26. Duff, 'You came to me affectionately when others called me mad', *Virgo Praedicanda*, p. 41.
27. Duff to Ekeng, 27 November, 1951.
28. Duff to Lambe, 12 June 1954.
29. Duff to McGrath, 30 March 1960.
30. Duff to Ernestine, 26 January 1957.
31. Duff to Quinn, 16 April 1944.
32. Duff to Holzgang, 25 May 1972.
33. Duff to Anne, 11 September 1976.
34. Duff to Nixon, 20 February 1957.
35. Discussion between Bradshaw and Shaw, tape 110, LOMA.
36. Information supplied to author by Carmel Duff, 1 May 1982.
37. Among Duff's unpublished memos, which were assembled and typed by Mary McAndrew.
38. Bradsaw, tape 118, LOMA.
39. Anne Enright, *The Gathering*. London: Jonathan Cape, 2008, p. 92.
40. Portrait Gallery: Frank Duff, *The Irish Times*, 3 October 1959.
41. Duff, 'Thy Children as Olive Plants,' *Walking with Mary*, p. 176.
42. Duff to Finola, 22 May 1974, author's possession.
43. Duff to Sweeney, 14 November 1935.
44. Dunne to Duff, 7 October 1965.
45. Author's interview with Dick Dunne, 3 December 2008.
46. Comments made by Nolan, 14 December 2002 at a meeting at Concilium Offices to discuss making a video on Duff.
47. Bradshaw, *Frank Duff*, p. 173.
48. Minutes of the Regina Coeli, 17 May 1929, Myra House.
49. Information supplied to author by Enda Dunleavy, 31 October 2008.
50. Minutes of Regina Coeli, 2 July 1954.
51. Author's interview with Nolan, 23 November 2007.
52. My late sister Margaret (Peggy) and the late Jimmy Cummins are two people who told me that they had witnessed episodes of anger.
53. Duff to Shaw, 29 March 1929, Ms 31670/2, NLI.
54. Author's interview with Mary McAndrew, 21 February 2008.
55. Author's interview with Tadhg McMahon, 9 June 2008.
56. Nivard Flood OCSO, 'My Memories of Frank Duff', 10 July 1982, ms, LOMA.
57. Duff, Talk to Deacons, Thurles, tape 105, LOMA.

CHAPTER 25

In the Spirit of Faith

'You are destined to cover the globe.'
DUFF TO EARLIEST LEGIONARIES

A long life carries its own peculiar risks. The man who lives long risks that many of his friends and family will predecease him. This happened to Duff, all of whose siblings and many of whose friends died before he did. He lived alone for thirty years from the time of his mother's death in 1950. A long life risks being blotted with the infirmities of age, an eventuality from which Duff was spared, due perhaps to the regular fresh air and exercise he got from riding his bicycle. As he said himself, his life was one of 'the most intense activity'. But that intense activity was necessary for him to reach his goals:

> I do not think it would be possible to live at a higher pitch of physical exertion. I have also been what, externally, looks like successful. I have achieved most of my aims. Possibly that really betokens a degree of failure because so many of our models, the saints, lived and died in the midst of the ruins of their works – as a total desolation.

Duff lived to see the Second Vatican Council promulgate the role of the laity, which had been obscured across the centuries. In the Legion of Mary he gave concrete form to the idea of the laity united with priests in the single apostolate of Christians to bring Christ to the world. He maintained that the Legion of Mary 'pivots upon the priest. It declares that it is an extension of him.'[1] He delighted in the fact that the Legion was the source of a multitude of vocations to the priesthood and religious life, including from the ranks of Legion envoys. He took a special interest in seminary praesidia, the first of which was established by the Society of African Missionaries in Dromantine, Co. Down, in Northern Ireland in 1941. He would have been happy to find several legionaries among Dublin diocesan priests, including Fr Pádraig Ó Cochláin, parish priest in Finglas, Fr Gerard Deegan, administrator in Milltown, and Fr Paddy Gleeson, chaplain in Trinity College.

The Legion method succeeded in capturing the hearts and minds of millions including learned and illiterate, black and white, rich and poor, men and women, working quietly, openly, yet in obscurity. And Duff believed that every man and woman possesses apostolic potential, saying 'if there is one thing which the Legion has proved … it is that the people, even the simplest among them, can be mobilised to an apostolate and enabled to carry it through effectively'.[2]

Duff's life began in modest surroundings in Phibsborough on the north side of Victorian Dublin. He grew up as the cherished eldest child of his parents who sent him to the best day schools – Belvedere and Blackrock College. His twenty-six years in the civil service, where he made a significant contribution both in the Land Commission and the Department of Finance, were formative both for Duff and the organization he would found. A gifted young man, he was intent on applying his talents and pursuing his civil service career – a career which became all the more important to his mother and family owing to his father's illness, enforced early retirement and early death. But Duff was confronted by a different world when in 1913 he joined the Society of St Vincent de Paul. It proved a tipping point. Some time later, and at first a little reluctantly, he joined the Pioneers. This had the special significance that, unlike the position in the St Vincent de Paul Society, which was then open only to men, the Pioneers included women. And it was within the setting of the Pioneer Council in Myra House in Dublin that the Legion came to life.

Duff's discovery of the role of Mary in God's plan through the reading of de Montfort's *True Devotion* was somewhat comparable to Newman's discovery of Mary's role by reading the Early Fathers of the Church. It marked a defining point on his life's journey, as it had done on Newman's. It represented a point of illumination when, owing to the persistence of some friends and his own, he paused and reflected until during a visit to Mount Melleray he realized the truth of de Montfort's proposition. That insight would become the basis for legionary work: 'in the spirit of faith, and in union with Mary, in such fashion that in those worked for and in one's fellow members, the Person of Our Lord is once again seen and served by Mary His Mother'.[3]

A life of Frank Duff necessarily must speak about the Legion of Mary, as the Legion increasingly became his life. But his civil service years were important also. He once remarked that it was in his family 'to be a civil servant' as his mother, father, brother and uncle had all been. On the death of E. P. McCarron, former Secretary of the Department of Local Government and Public Health, in October 1970, Duff wrote an Appreciation in *The Irish Times*. He said that his aim was to cast a true light on 'a largely hidden career which stands the risk of being buried in oblivion'. Most of McCarron's achievement was worked out in the patient details of administration. During his official life he worked every day, 'planning, interviewing and in the general running of a big Department'. Yet according to Duff, McCarron 'was supremely accessible, available to all, open to every proposition for good'. Duff said that McCarron represented his

> … ideal of an administrator; a Christian mind who instinctively reached out towards the solution of problems and the helping of people; one to whom you could have access, who would listen, and whose keen mind saw more clearly than you did, and who had the capacity to get the normally torpid official systems to share his own enthusiasm and to move at his pace.[4]

There is much in this appreciation of McCarron which provides a key to Duff. For Duff, as for McCarron, the civil service was a moulder, a formative influence. The influence is evident in the Legion of Mary system, which is based on clear rules with a clearly defined reporting structure – individual member to praesidium, praesidium to curia, curia to Concilium. The influence is also apparent in the meticulous files Duff kept in relation to Legion matters and of his vast correspondence. In a letter to Seán Ó Faoláin written in 1944, ten years after he left the civil service, he said that his cast of mind was 'mechanical rather than literary. I was a civil servant. Much of my official life was spent in the Department of Finance. There we were encouraged to develop a good style, but never such as in any circumstances to obscure one's meaning or to neglect the facts.'[5]

Although Duff's contribution was substantial, his civil service career, to use his own phrase in relation to McCarron, has been 'buried in oblivion'. Both in the civil service and in the Legion of Mary he was a tireless worker, 'available to all, open to every proposition for good'. His character was entrepreneurial. He could invest an idea with life. Fr Michael O'Carroll says, 'To invest ideas with life, to make them vital – what the French call *idées-forces*, is the problem of the great doers. Nor let us forget an ancient word of the Greek dramatist, Aeschylus, "The doer must suffer."'[6] Wherever or whenever Duff encountered a problem in the civil service, in the Legion or elsewhere, he sought a solution, arguing that the solution to every problem, even the most apparently intractable, could be broken down into a series of steps. He maintained that there was little value in being 'disillusioned or embittered or anything else about the condition of affairs around us'. The important thing was to work constructively for improvement.[7] Encountering prostitutes, he recognized that many needed a refuge if they were to extricate themselves from prostitution and build alternative lives, so he opened the Sancta Maria Hostel. When Duff encountered down and out men, he created a home for them in the Morning Star Hostel. He did likewise for homeless women in the Regina Coeli Hostel. The Dublin hostels became prototypes for hostels elsewhere, including one in Paris established with the aid of a French general who visited the Morning Star in Dublin and actually stayed there. A Morning Star Hostel was opened in Belfast on 25 March 1939, the twelfth anniversary of the opening in Dublin. Belfast also had a Regina Coeli with a *Mater Dei* unit for mothers and children. Cork had a complement of hostels, while Waterford had a Regina Coeli and

Manchester a Morning Star. Glasgow had both a Morning Star and Regina Coeli, the opening of the latter attended by Duff. Some of these hostels have continued as Legion of Mary hostels, while some were unable to continue on a purely voluntary basis and have been integrated with public social services, employing paid personnel.

Young women expressed a desire to visit the cancer wards in the South Dublin Union Hospital and Duff set about arranging for them to do so. In this way the Association of Our Lady of Mercy, which became the Legion of Mary, was started. Duff heard how Irish emigrants to Britain were leaving the Church behind them as soon as they stepped off the boat and he responded by launching the Patricians to enable Catholics to learn about, and to articulate, their beliefs. As he cycled around Ireland in the 1950s, he observed the ravages of emigration and crumbling communities and 'True Devotion to the Nation' was started with impressive results in Inchigeela and Tuosist.

At first the spread of the Legion of Mary was quite slow. It took over nine months from the founding of the first branch, which eventually numbered over seventy members, until the second branch was established. In the first year the Legion gained four branches; in the first five years it counted only nine. It took six years for the Legion to extend to a second diocese; seven to a second country; eight to give the first men's praesidium; and ten for the first branch in the New World, America. From the time of the Eucharistic Congress in Dublin in 1932, the Legion began to spread rapidly across the globe. As Diarmaid Ferriter reminds us, 'The Legion had within three decades established itself on all five continents.'[8] By the end of the 1950s, the Legion was in over half the dioceses of the Church. In 2011 it is to be found in almost every diocese.

In 1957 a correspondent in Australia wrote to Duff expressing the view that the first twenty-five years of any society are the best years. Duff replied that such was generally the case, but that it was something from which the 'Legion of Mary would ambition to emancipate itself'. Because, he continued, 'it means that most Societies are built upon human interest, so that when it evaporates the Society declines. Or else the health of the Society was dependent upon its original founders. When they depart, the Society falls.'[9] The reason for the continued growth of the Legion of Mary must be attributed in no small degree to the emphasis Duff placed on the willingness of each member to play his or her role, rather than on any overriding, and ultimately self-defeating, overreliance on Duff as founder.

If Duff possessed qualities of the fine civil servant – ability, reliability, order and discipline – he also possessed qualities of the successful entrepreneur – vision, courage and the insight to view failure as achievement deferred. He was in essence a fearless risk-taker. In the 'Monto' episode, where he set about providing an alternative life for brothel workers, he risked his reputation as a man of sound judgement. It was a case of a lay 'fool' walking in where clerical 'angels' feared to tread. He tackled a problem when caution dictated the avoidance practised by others. He risked his future livelihood when he resigned from the civil service on a small pension in mid-life to give himself full-time to the Legion before he had been granted recognition, much less even an interview, by the Archbishop of Dublin. At times he risked his physical and mental health by an exhausting workload and a lack of sleep, often working on his correspondence late into the night. Sometimes he set himself challenges, perhaps to test his boundaries, as when he cycled from Cork to Dublin in a single day when he was past 60 years of age.

Duff was a profound thinker who reflected deeply on many different issues and problems, always seeking explanations and solutions. His last public address to legionaries was given at the Annual Peregrinatio Hallowe'en Conference in October 1980, two weeks before his death. His theme was evangelization. He sparked the imagination of his listeners by evoking a picture of the apostles attending a planning meeting with Mary. He urged legionaries to plan in the way he suggested that the apostles had once done in the company of Mary[10] as the objective was the same – how to bring Christ to the whole world. At Hallowe'en 2008, Hugh Brady and a number of the earliest legionary *peregrini* attended the 50th Anniversary Conference in Dublin, where Brady was an invited speaker. He described how the movement had started, and how, when the idea was first debated by Concilium officers, some thought it a 'risky business', but that Duff's intervention had been decisive. Towards the end of 1973, six years before the election of the first Polish Pope – John Paul II – Duff had spoken confidently of 'the first real opening up of the Iron Curtain countries' and of 'those great days just ahead'.[11] At the 2008 Conference, reports were given on a range of projects which had taken place in the previous year, with special accounts given of past Peregrinations to Israel, Poland, and Russia.

In January 2009 the 1,000th meeting of the Concilium of the Legion of Mary took place in Dublin. In the presence of the Papal Nuncio, Archbishop Giuseppe Leanza, the meeting began with the Opening Prayers of the Legion just as at the first Legion meeting, but with the difference that at Concilium meetings the prayers are recited in Latin because the Concilium is an international forum attended by visitors from different parts of the world. A letter was read from the Vatican sending the greetings of Pope Benedict and expressing the appreciation of the Pope 'for the generous service to the church offered throughout the world by so many members of the Legion'.

For purpose of reporting to the Concilium, the world is divided into different zones and reports are taken from different zones in sequence at meetings. On that occasion the zones that reported included areas of Asia and

Africa. For Asia, reports came from Armenia, Bangladesh, India, Pakistan, Nepal, Sri Lanka, Myanmar, Thailand, Vietnam, Mongolia and Kazakhstan. In July 2008 Bernardo de Nardo started a Legion praesidium in Yerevan, the capital of Armenia. De Nardo, from Santa Fé in Argentina, a lawyer by training, is the latest in the long line of Legion envoys. Now a student for the priesthood, in 2007 he had set out as envoy to Central Asia, starting off in Kazakhstan. He had earlier done Legion extension work in Central America and the Caribbean.

The Concilium also heard news from India, which, with a population of 1.1 billion, represents 17 per cent of the world's population. The Christian population comprises three per cent of the total population. In Mumbai, India's largest city, there are twenty-nine senior praesidia with many junior praesidia also. In Pakistan, with a population of 172 million, of which one per cent is Catholic, it was noted that 200 legionaries had attended an annual reunion in Karachi. Nepal was declared a Republic in 2008 and the Legion was introduced there that year by Bernardo de Nardo. Reports also came from Rwanda, Burundi and the Democratic Republic of the Congo, formerly Zaire, in Africa. Following the Rwanda massacres in 1994, the Legion helped to run homes and hostels for homeless and abandoned people, sometimes sharing tasks with the basic Christian communities and working in co-operation with Religious Sisters. It was reported that Legion membership in the Diocese of Kinshasa alone had reached 7,500. The Legion is thriving in Africa. With close to 160 million Catholics in Africa, it is the continent where the Church is strong in terms of numbers, although far from problem-free. At the same time in North America, Catholics amounted to under 70 million. By 2025 one-sixth of the world's Catholics, about 250 million, are expected to come from Africa. In 2009 Pope Benedict selected Africa for his first papal visit. He was following John Paul II, who made sixteen trips to Africa and visited forty-two countries there.

A feature of the 1,000th meeting of the Concilium was a large cake shared by those present, together with the traditional cup of tea, itself part of Duff's legacy. As Duff's influence is reflected across the globe, in Dublin the Regina Coeli and Morning Star Hostels are visible evidence of his legacy to his native city. These quiet havens are homes for the most marginalized where, as Duff insisted all those decades ago, 'an intimate personal acquaintance' must be built with each one. He insisted that the most difficult cases were 'our jewels' because in serving those people 'we can demonstrate what Christian love is and what it demands'.[12] Less visible, but very real, are the thousands of children of lone mothers who grew up in the Regina Coeli and who went on to live ordinary, sometimes extraordinary, lives in the life of the city of Dublin and many other places.

Among those present at the 1,000th meeting of the Concilium was the assistant secretary, Declan Lawlor. Lawlor is not untypical of those who never met Duff and who have been drawn into the Legion since his death. He graduated from Trinity College Dublin with a business degree in 1989 before qualifying as a solicitor. He married and set up in practice. His lifestyle did not then include religious practice, and so he 'lapsed' for a number of years. A chance encounter with a legionary, Alice Creaton, led to the suggestion that he join the Legion. His response was 'not on your life', but nonetheless he agreed to go to a Legion meeting in Phibsborough. In the Legion he discovered a much greater challenge than he had anticipated: he discovered a battle, a battle which began within himself over the priorities in his own life. But he also found a practical system whereby to live his faith. Declan found in the Legion 'the spirit to keep the faith alight', a spirit that is necessary because he believes religion is 'a tough thing'. This echoes a sentiment of Duff, who wrote 'We must remember that Christianity was never supposed to be a tame or humdrum religion. Its Founder plainly regarded it as something which took possession of the whole life and absolutely turned it upside down.'[13] Since joining the Legion, Declan has read all Duff's published writings at least three times. The impression he has developed of Duff is of an 'an understanding man' with great faith who understood people and their problems and explored how faith could help 'to untie the knots' in their lives.

Also present at the 1,000th meeting of Concilium was Fiona Hodge, a young graduate who works in the National College of Art and Design in Dublin. Coming out of mass in nearby John's Lane Church in September 2003, someone asked her if she would like to join the Legion of Mary. Instinctively, she answered 'Yes.' The first meeting she attended was of the praesidium *Regina Pacis* (Queen of Peace) attached to the Regina Coeli Hostel. She remembers her puzzlement when the young women who comprised the group addressed each other as 'sister'. She wondered if they were nuns in some form. While she says that she is 'not a big reader', Hodge described the *Handbook* as 'a genius of a book'. For her, a spirit of encouragement and daring emerges strongly from its pages. Both Lawlor and Hodge are amongst those who organize an annual Youth Conference for the age-group 18–40 at All Hallows College in Dublin, the idea for which emerged at a Patrician meeting and which is going from strength to strength.

The visitation of hospitals and homes and the foundation of the hostels for prostitutes and homeless persons were, and remain, defining works of the Legion. But within the well-tested and well-proven system of the Legion, Duff continually promoted new works and tackled fresh problems, always having an eye for new initiatives for the apostolate. Definite active service must be added to prayer, as he made very clear in a letter to a legionary who proposed to him the quotation from St John of the Cross to the effect that one act of pure love of God, in the sense of a prayer, is greater than all our actions put together. He said that the quotation was universally misinterpreted as seeming to mean that a prayer is worth all possible actions. He said that

> … if love of neighbour is absent explicitly or implicitly, there is no love of God at all. Remember that it is possible to feel a great deal of warmth in prayer, and for that prayer to have very poor roots. I have known people who seemed to be very great prayers and who were certainly very selfish persons. I have no doubt that they thought themselves all the time to be uttering very pure acts of love of God.[14]

Duff firmly held that legionaries should not stagnate by repeating the same simple tasks allotted to them years earlier. He agreed that 'This represents a great demonstration of fidelity on their part but at the same time a certain degree of waste.' He held that legionary service should never be static, constantly urging 'upgrading' of the work, pressing on towards 'heroic work.'[15] 'The heroic and spearheading principle should be always in operation.'

Duff's character was severely tested during the early years of the Legion as he met with an icy response from diocesan authorities. But he worked on, always remaining obedient to these authorities, if at times chaffing at the bit. He took risks, both physical and reputational, as he and his associates tackled the madams and their bullies in the Monto. Inevitably tensions built within him that gained release in his robust sense of humour, by reading detective stories, and in the physical unwinding which came from his continued use of the bicycle throughout this life. But the man who cycled everywhere, read Erle Stanley Gardner and loved practical jokes developed a profound life of prayer, based above all on daily attendance at Mass.

In a tribute to Duff published in the *Belvederian* following his death and which is accompanied by a photograph of a smiling Duff cradling a quail in his hands,[16] Fr Paul Andrews, SJ, described Duff as 'a man of God' saying that 'in the spirit of a pilgrim reaching out towards a holy relic, prizing any contact', Belvedere could record two links with 'this holy and apostolic Dubliner'. Duff came to Belvedere at the age of eight and stayed for two years, 1897–99, and at the very end of his life it was one of the Belvedere community – and an old Blackrock College man – Fr John Mulligan who was called to anoint him. 'We treasure these links with an old Belvederian who was truly a man of God.'[17] Dr Michael O' Carroll, who for much of his life was a member of the Community at Blackrock College, said that 'Frank Duff was courageous to the marrow of his bones.'[18] His fibre was tough and he put that toughness into his organization. But that toughness was more than matched by a gentleness, such as witnessed in his attention to John,[19] the young sufferer from hydrocephalus, which encapsulates my own defining memory of Frank Duff. He combined the man of steel with the maternal.

Notes to Chapter 25

1. Duff, 'The Priest must have members', *Mary Shall Reign*, p. 11.
2. Duff to Suenens, 8 May 1954.
3. *Handbook*, p. 109.
4. *The Irish Times*, 13 October 1970. Duff's tribute to McCarron as 'my ideal of an administrator' was to a man whom many believed was unfairly removed from his post as Secretary by the Executive Council in November 1936 by Seán T. Ó Ceallaigh (Seán T.O'Kelly), Minister for Local Government and Public Health and later President of Ireland. An appointment to the post of Resident Medical Superintendent of Portrane Mental Hospital was at the root of the dismissal of McCarron. See Dáil Debates, vol. 65, 3, February 1937 and Mary Daly, *The Buffer State*. Dublin: Institute of Public Administration, 1997, pp.163–67. According to *The Irish Times*, 1 December 1936, the Portrane appointment was 'a cause of embarrassment to him [Ó Ceallaigh], having regard to political difficulties he had experienced over the filling of a vacancy in the post of resident medical superintendent at Ballinasloe'.
5. Duff to Ó Faoláin, 16 August 1944.
6. Michael O'Carroll, Introduction to Finola Kennedy, *John Henry Newman and Frank Duff*. Dublin: Praedicanda, 1982, p. 4.
7. Duff to Sister Assumpta, 19 January 1957.
8. Diarmaid Ferriter, *The Transformation of Ireland 1900–2000*. London: Profile, 2004, p. 334.
9. Duff to Olsen, 16 January 1957.
10. Duff, 'Final Testament to the Legion', *Victory through Mary*, p. 516.
11. Duff to Molly Corbally, 22 December 1973.
12. Frank Duff, 'Morning Star Ideals,' Audiotape 5, LOMA.
13. Duff to Eileen, 4 January 1939.
14. Duff to Kingston, 13 October 1956.
15. Duff, *The Concilium Correspondents*. Address to the correspondents, 19 January 1975, Published by the Concilium of the Legion of Mary, undated, p. 3.
16. The photograph was taken by Marjorie Quirke.
17. P. A. [Paul Andrews], 'Frank Duff (Belvedere 1897–99)', *The Belvederian*, 1981, p. 118.
18. O'Carroll, *A Priest in Changing Times*, p. 147.
19. See Introduction.

Glossary

Latin Terminology

Acies A Legion function held annually in a church close to the Feast of the Annunciation on 25 March, at which Legion members renew their consecration to Mary.

Adjutorian Higher grade of auxiliary membership where, in addition to the prayers recited daily by auxiliary members, adjutorians undertake to attend daily Mass and receive Holy Communion and to recite daily some Office approved by the Church.

Allocutio A short address by the Spiritual Director or the president given at each Legion meeting.

Auxiliary Auxiliary membership is open to priests, religious and the laity. It consists of those unable to undertake, or who do not wish to undertake, active membership, but who associate with the work of the Legion through the daily recitation of certain prayers. Auxiliary membership is subdivided into two degrees: the basic degree comprising those called simply 'auxiliaries', and the higher degree of auxiliary membership designated *Adjutores Legionis* or *Adjutorians.*

Catena Prayer recited daily by all active and auxiliary members, consisting of the Magnificat with antiphon, versicle and the collect from the Feast of Mary Mediatrix of All Graces.

Christifideles Laici Exhortation of John Paul II on the Vocation and Mission of the Laity in the Church.

Comitium A comitium is a form of higher curia (see below) which supervises one or more curiae.

Concilium The governing or highest council in the Legion of Mary. Its origin was the grouping of the first Dublin Curiae. The Concilium office or international headquarters of the Legion is based in Dublin.

Curia When two or more praesidia have been established in an area, a governing body termed the Curia is established. The Curia is composed of all the officers (Spiritual Directors included) of the praesidia in its area.

Handbook The Handbook sets out the details of Legion organization and explains Legion spirituality.

Imprimatur The Latin form of 'Let it be printed'. It is an official declaration by the Roman Catholic hierarchy that a work is free from errors in matters of faith and morals. Usually an *imprimatur* is granted by a bishop after a ***nihil obstat*** has been granted by a theologian, frequently referred to as 'diocesan censor'. A *nihil obstat* indicates that there is nothing standing in the way of an *imprimatur*.

Incolae Mariae Marian Residents are volunteers, generally young, who work in another country for a short period and give time after work for Legion activity.

Laureate Laureate membership was conferred on a small number of persons whose contribution to the Legion in its early days was considered to be of such significance that the Legion could not have developed without their assistance. These included W. T. Cosgrave, Bartley Oliver and Frank Sweeney. In early editions of the *Handbook*, when the Laureate degree of membership existed, it was noted that Laureate membership was conferred only if the services rendered are 'really notable, such in fact that they place the entire Legion under a lasting debt of gratitude, which can only be acquitted by associating the person in question with the life of the Legion in the capacity of a member, and by the bestowing of a permanent place in its works and prayers'. As the Legion became established, Laureate membership was no longer conferred.

Maria Legionis Official journal of the Legion of Mary, published for the first time in 1937. Published quarterly.

Nihil Obstat The Latin form of 'nothing stands in the way' or blocks publication. It means that a publication has been examined by the Church censor and that it contains nothing offensive to the Church.

Praesidium Basic unit of the Legion, often a parochial branch. It has five officers: Spiritual Director, President, Vice-President, Secretary and Treasurer. Before establishing a praesidium, it is necessary to obtain the permission of the bishop, the parish priest or other responsible priest. This Latin word was used to designate a detachment of the Roman Legion performing special duty, that is, a section of a military line, a fortified post and a garrison. Each praesidium is named after a title of Our Lady, for example, 'Our Lady, Queen of Peace'.

Praetorian Higher grade of active membership where, in addition to the usual duties of members (weekly attendance at a meeting and solid apostolic work), the member undertakes the daily recitation of all the prayers of the Legion, daily Mass and Holy Communion and the daily recitation of some Office approved by the Church.

Quadragesimo Anno *In the Fortieth Year*, encyclical letter issued by Pope Pius XI in 1931, forty years after Rerum Novarum; it deals with social issues.

Regia Lead Council for a specified area.

Rerum Novarum *Of New Things*, encyclical letter issued by Pope Leo XIII in 1891; it deals with Capital and Labour.

Roman Curia The collection of departments and ministries which assist the Pope in governing the Church; the administrative apparatus of the Holy See.

Schema/Schemata Plan/plans based on experience which provides for future responses based on that experience. The term occurred frequently during the Second Vatican Council.

Senatus Lead Council for a country or region based on the original curia with its directly affiliated praesidia, which supervises the curiae and comitiae in its territory.

Tessera The prayer card of the Legion. In Latin, *tessera* had a particular meaning of a tally or token which was divided among friends in order that they or their descendants might always recognize each other. As a military expression, it signified the square tablet upon which the watchword was written and circulated through the Roman Legion.

Vexillum The standard of the Legion which is an adaptation of the standard of the Roman Legion in which the eagle is replaced by a dove, the emblem of the Holy Spirit, and the portrait of the emperor or consul is replaced by Mary.

Viatores Christi Travellers for Christ. They are volunteers who take employment for one or more years overseas and engage in missionary work. The Viatores Christi began in 1960 within the Legion of Mary but subsequently developed into an Irish Catholic lay volunteer missionary association.

Abbreviations

APO	Assistant Principal Officer
CCL	The Central Catholic Library
CM	Congregation of the Missions, known as Vincentians after their founder St Vincent de Paul
CO	Congregation of the Oratory or Oratorians
CP	Congregation of the Passion or Passionists
CSSC	Catholic Social Service Conference
CSSp	Congregation of the Holy Spirit (Congregationis Sancti Spiritus), known as Holy Ghost Fathers
CSWB	Catholic Social Welfare Bureau
CTS	The Catholic Truth Society
CUS	Catholic University School
CYMS	Catholic Young Men's Society
DDA	Dublin Diocesan Archives
DHA	Dublin Health Authority
FDCS	Frank Duff Civil Service
HEO	Higher Executive Officer
ICOS	Irish Council for Overseas Students
JAD	Jesuit Archives Dublin
JAO	Junior Administrative Officer
LLD	Doctor of Laws
LOMA	Legion of Mary Archives
NAI	National Archives of Ireland
NSPCC	National Society for the Prevention of Cruelty to Children
OP	Order of Preachers or Dominicans
OSB	Order of St Benedict or Benedictines
RHA	Royal Hibernian Academy
RTÉ	Radio Telefís Éireann
SVP	St Vincent de Paul Society
TCD	Trinity College Dublin
TE	Telefís Eireann
UCD	University College Dublin

Frank Duff's published work

Frank Duff's published work includes articles in *Maria Legionis*, as well as in some other magazines and newspapers. His books and some pamphlets are listed below.

Can We Be Saints? Catholic Truth Society, 1922 (pamphlet)

The Handbook of the Legion of Mary, first published for private circulation, 1928

The De Montfort Way. New York: Montfort, 1956 (pamphlet).

The Spirit of the Legion of Mary. Glasgow: J. S. Burns, 1956. Reprinted as *Walking with Mary*. Glasgow: J. S. Burns, 1962.

Edel Quinn. Dublin: Catholic Truth Society of Ireland, 1960 (pamphlet).

Mary Shall Reign. Glasgow: J. S. Burns, 1961.

Miracles on Tap. New York: Montfort Publications, Bay Shore, New York, 1961.

True Devotion to the Nation. Dundalk: Dundalgan Press, 1966.

Virgo Praedicanda. Dublin: C. J. Fallon, 1967.

The Woman of Genesis. Dublin: Praedicanda, 1976.

Victory through Mary. Dublin: Praedicanda, 1981 (includes essays published in *Walking with Mary*).

Index